COUNTRY M·U·S·I·C

COUNTRY M·U·S·I·C

70 Years of America's Favorite Music

BOB MILLARD

HarperPerennial

A Division of HarperCollinsPublishers

Title page credits:

Clockwise from bottom left:
Roy Rogers, Minnie Pearl and Gene Autry: In the Southern Folklife Collec-
tion, University of North Carolina, Chapel Hill.
Dwight Yoakam (r.) and Buck Owens: By Alan Mayor.

DESIGNED BY JOEL AVIROM
Design Assistant Jason Snyder

FIRST HARPERPERENNIAL EDITION

Library of Congress Cataloging-in-Publication Data

Millard, Bob, 1951–
    Country music: 70 years of America's favorite music /
Bob Millard. — 1st ed.
        p.   cm.
    ISBN 0-06-273244-7
    1. Country music—Chronology. I. Title.
ML3524.M53 1993
781.642'09—dc20   92-56276

---

93 94 95 96 97 ❖ CW ❖ 10 9 8 7 6 5 4 3 2 1

DEDICATED TO
ROBERT K. OERMANN,
A FIRST-CLASS SCHOLAR
AND A GREAT FRIEND

CONTENTS

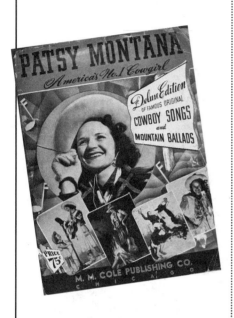

ACKNOWLEDGMENTS

A book of this size and scope necessarily benefits from the labors, guidance, expertise and encouragement of a lot of people. There are many people to thank, but I especially wish to express my gratitude here to the people who helped far beyond reasonable requirements of their jobs, our friendships or relationships.

Thanks, as always, go first to my wife, Lucinda Smith, who has enoucouraged me for years to follow my heart and talents, assuming that we would eventually profit from it. I am in her debt for believing even when I was doubtful. Bob Oermann and Mary Bufwack not only opened their extensive archives and libraries to my research, but Bob often led me through the maze and helped me find things I didn't even know to look for. A scholar and a fan, his knowledge of country music is deep, wide and a marvel to behold. Even when he was smothered in his own television, book, and newspaper work, he always took time to help.

Ronnie Pugh at the Country Music Foundation Library is a reference librarian's reference librarian. For giving me virtual run of his stacks and files, for taking my myriad last-minute fact checking calls, I thank him sincerely. I also gratefully acknowledge Chris Skinker and Alan Stoker at the CMF for their aid and forebearance during my months of research in their facility. Mike Casey, head of the Southern Folklife Collection at the University of North Carolina, Chapel Hill, is another generous librarian with a special appreciation of the researcher's plight.

Finally, thanks are due to my editor at HarperCollins, Robert Wilson. He let me define this project according to my own end-user's vision of pop culture reference books; he readily understood what I wanted to do and was enthusiastic from the beginning. He patiently took my many phone calls, even when they were only the addled outreach of a research-numbed writer just needing to talk in the middle of the afternoon.

All the above share in any credit due me for this finished book. Mistakes, should they be found, are my own.

FOREWORD

The greatest thing about country music is its quality. And even though at times it has been misunderstood, taken for granted, or taken advantage of, the heart of country music endures. Country music's sincerity and honesty have allowed it to withstand time and have made it immortal.

Garth Brooks

PREFACE

When you think strictly in business terms, reflecting on the modest beginnings of commercial country music, the near-fatal blow dealt by rock 'n' roll in the late 1950s, and the post-Urban Cowboy bust, it's a wonder that country music *has* a 70-year history. But it does, and it's a fascinating history of men and women, groups and institutions, the coming and going of record labels, the rise and decline of live radio barn dance programs and the huge growth of full-time record-playing country stations.

The story is found in the annals of television, as well, from Red River Dave McEnrey's appearance on the experimental television broadcasts at the 1939 New York World's Fair to the explosion in popularity of country music videos, the *Country Music Television* cable service and *The Nashville Network*.

And, of course, the main historical record of commercial country music is found in commercial recordings. "Old-time" fiddlers were recorded on Edison's wax cylinders, "hillbilly" string-bands on 10-inch shellac 78s, country radio shows from The Pickard Family and Slim Rinehart on border radio to weekly Grand Ole Opry performances in the '40s were often preserved on enormous transcription disks, some of which survived their momentary utility. Country music of all flavors has been preserved and marketed on every recorded medium developed.

Most of all, the story of country music is the combined story of the people who made it. It is amazing that such deeply influential acts as widely diverse in music and performance style as Appalachian mountainfolk Carter Family and Mississippi's blue yodeling vaudevillian Jimmie Rodgers could have their commercial breaks come at the same time and in the same place, provided by the same man, but they did. As a market for country music grew, new styles emerged and new stylists put their indelible stamps on the loosely defined genre. That genre was ghettoized until very recently as minority music, but has become a favorite of millions of Americans who buy Garth Brooks, Billy Ray Cyrus, Lorrie Morgan, Alabama, and Mary-Chapin Carpenter records and concert tickets in numbers that continue to grow annually.

My purpose in writing this book was, first, to create a truly useful general reference book, containing a lot of the kinds of information I always needed, but could rarely find in existing sources on newspaper deadlines. I also wished to make this book on country music entertaining to the average reader. With that in mind, I organized my writing chronologically—by decade through 1944, when the first country music charts appeared in trade newspapers, and year-by-year thereafter. I also put information in categories such as Most Important Records, Milestones, and Awards when they come into play. Narrative elements, annual essays and Debut Artist entries provide continuity, while sidebars are like miniature encyclopedia entries, hopefully illuminating as well as entertaining.

Because there is so much to tell about country music, its creators and facilitators, its roots and directions, I purposefully decided not to follow the typical "pop culture almanac" formula of throwing in chronologically ordered trivia about society in general, sports, politics, movies, the amount of popcorn consumed by the average American, to provide context for the development of country music. That approach, popular enough in too many quickly assembled almanacs of music, movies, etc., would have filled this volume with irrelevancies. So, journalists, beginning scholars, or even the most casual reader can flip through this book and find something interesting, self-contained and directly related to the history of country music on every page; that and nothing else.

The photographs were chosen from among some of the best archival sources on country music in America. My search and the searches of my friends and helpers focused on older pictures. I thought one of Minnie Pearl's rarely seen first publicity shots, or a picture of Hank Williams in the WSM studios with his band surrounded by the product of his commercial sponsor, would make this book more unique and valuable to the reader. In all cases, attempts were made to assure that the proper copyright owner, if known and where copyrights are claimed, was notified and paid.

METHODOLOGY

The hows and whys of my lists of records, awards and honorifics chronicled in these pages needs some explanation. Let's start with my lists of Most Important Records. Because of commercial country music's minority status in the early decades, much of its early commercial history is anecdotal. Only when a "hillbilly" record was phenomenally successful, crossing into the pop market like Vernon Dalhart's first million-selling country record, "Prisoner's Song," in the mid-1920s, were sales figures revealed. In the first couple of years of "hillbilly" recording, just about every disk or cylinder made by a competent artist was important to some degree because it was another step in finding and building a market. Firsts were important; then, ultimately, success and impact became the measure.

Still, Billboard magazine didn't begin following country records with even the most rudimentary and subjective charts until 1944. Chart compilers would call record distributors, disk jockeys and jukebox operators and ask what was "hot" each week. Methods changed over the years, but there was significant subjectivity in the system until the 1990s, when computerized sampling of actual radio airplay was introduced as an irrefutable standard. The country chart Bible, Joel Whitburn's *Top Country Singles 1944–1988* and succeeding annuals, show what happened in the charts, which could be and generally were manipulated by record labels as much as possible for the benefit of their artists.

This phenomenon becomes particularly obvious in the 1970s and 1980s, when record promotion became a high-dollar, computerized science. You had some artists charting one #1 after another, yet unable to garner a gold record. When as many as 50 different records gained the #1 position each year, it became obvious that reporting sources were in tacit collusion with record promoters, and the numbers had less meaning in sifting out important records and the true hits from "radio fodder." Like hot air balloons, radio fodder looked good going up, but it didn't deliver much cargo. In some cases, records with more long-term popularity were kept out of the higher rungs of these charts because they lacked promotional budgets or the artists were too new for radio programmers to report them high enough, though they played the records incessantly.

For these reasons, I have chosen to list each year's most important records as I see them, rather than pretend to present a completely objective Top 10. While my lists start with Billboard chart data, they are tempered by a feeling that what matters is whether a song actually sold a lot of records, launched or changed a career, had significant impact on the genre over the long run, or if it is still remembered—something that contemporaneous annual charts, however scientifically compiled, cannot know.

As for RIAA's gold and platinum records, which were introduced in the late 1950s, the reader needs to understand something about the apples and oranges of evolving standards. The prime example would be Elvis Presley's first gold record, "Hound Dog"/"Don't Be Cruel," a two-sided hit that occupied the #1 position on country charts for 10 weeks between the two titles. That single earned gold record status by selling more than $1 million worth of product at retail outlets, which was then the standard. In fact, it sold more than five million copies.

The RIAA standards have changed with the growth of the music industry. Unit sales are the measure now, and it takes 500,000 total pieces wholesaled in all configurations to earn a gold record. "Don't Be Cruel" would qualify for quintuple platinum honors today. In my listings throughout this book, such an accomplishment would be designated "5M/S" for 5 million singles sold. Similarly, gold records are identified with "G/S" or "G/A" codes for gold singles or albums.

The record industry got good at manipulating this system, too, though it was potentially financially ruinous to do so. As the standard shifted from retail sales to wholesaled shipments, I'll let you guess for yourself what records may have "shipped platinum," earned the award and yet had truckloads of product returned unsold to the record company. It's rare, but Nashville industry gossip indicates it has happened. Ask any song publisher who is still trying to collect gold or platinum level royalties from a record company for such an RIAA certified gold record plaque on the lobby walls.

Even in reporting gold records, I exercised a certain amount of subjectivity. Some may argue that certain records by Olivia Newton John, Linda Ronstadt, John Denver, etc., do or do not belong on a list of country gold and platinum. I accept that risk.

Grammys, Country Music Association and Association of Country Music awards come along in their respective years and continue today. Especially in their early years, these awards reflected the regions and styles their voting members were associated with. ACM Awards were focused on the West Coast almost exclusively at first, because it essentially was a Hollywood/Bakersfield organization at its founding. Los Angeles and Nashville were competing hubs of the industry, and not likely to promote each other's acts or history with awards in those early years.

CMA Awards were for many years so obviously in orbit around Nashville, WSM and the *Grand Ole Opry* that it was difficult for anyone not of that universe to get inducted into the CMA's Hall of Fame, much less earn recognition for contemporary accomplishments. There were so many more CMA voting members than ACM voters, though, that its awards were thought a little less open to direct label or geographic cabal manipulation.

NARAS, dominated by East and West Coast pop divisions (Nashville still can't get a Grammy Awards Show produced in the more-than-adequate Opryland facilities) opened the Grammys to country with only one category at first. Voters with little knowledge of or taste for rural country music gave that award to northern, urban-based folk singers the first few years. Until the country music industry joined NARAS wholesale, the awards were so dominated by pop industry voters that only pop crossover artists could win a country Grammy. Loretta Lynn was the first real hillbilly to win a Grammy, and that was in the late-'60s. Looking closely at my Grammy lists, the reader will occasionally see the code (NC) next to an entry, signifying a win by country artists in a non-country category.

There is no impartiality in the real world, though, and it would be foolish to expect it in awards balloting. What emerges among these three major awards is a three-way measure that probably recognizes all the best in country music among them. Truth is, country artists are happy to get an award from any of these organizations.

As for the Milestones, they, like the rest of the book, were selected after long and painstaking research that turned up far more facts than would fit into a single volume. I chose for inclusion, first, important births and deaths, then such facts as indicated trends in the country music industry, as well as significant events in individual careers. The most crucial and interesting facts were chosen, though not without much agonizing over others that had to be left out.

Any book of this sort—part history, part encyclopedia, part almanac, and part book-of-lists—is by definition a skimming of the cream. The good news is that this *is* the cream—the best, the most important, the most fascinating details and anecdotes I have found in more than 15 years of covering country music professionally for trade magazines, from *Record World* to *Variety*, for daily newspapers, including the *Nashville Banner* and the *Dallas Times Herald*, and magazines, including *Country Music* and *The Journal of Country Music*.

The bad news is that there is so much more of interest to tell about country music, its sounds, creators and facilitators, than I can include here. If this book has only whetted your appetite for the history of country music, I can heartily recommend the revised edition of Bill Malone's scholarly history, *Country Music U.S.A.*, Bob Oermann and Mary Bufwack's definitive distaff history, *Finding Her Voice: The Saga of Women In Country Music*, Alton Delmore's posthumously published autobiography, *Truth Is Stranger Than Publicity*, Nolan Porterfield's masterfully contextualized biography, *Jimmie Rodgers*, and a subscription to *The Journal of the American Academy for the Preservation of Old-Time Country Music*, just for starters.

The Union Gospel Tabernacle
(later Ryman Auditorium).
credit: Courtesy of the Grand Ole
Opry

THE EARLY YEARS

THE ROOTS OF COMMERCIAL COUNTRY MUSIC

"Country" is the term applied to a wide spectrum of music—from Hank Williams to the New Grass Revival, from Patti Page's smooth version of "Tennessee Waltz" to Bill Monroe's driving bluegrass classic, "Uncle Pen." It ranges from Roy Acuff's ultra-traditional signature "Wabash Cannonball" to the gentle folksy influence of Kathy Mattea singing "Love at the Five & Dime" or the raucous Southern-rock flavor of Travis Tritt's "Put Some Drive In Your Country." In other words, "country music" is a term so stylistically broad that it's almost impossible to define with any categorical precision. It used to be said that country music was simply whatever country folks liked, but the massive popularity of today's top country artists crosses too many demographic boundaries for that old saw to cut wood anymore.

The musical roots of modern country music are equally myriad and complex. There is no more a single modern style that by itself is country than there is a single source from which it sprang. The roots of country music grow from the musical sounds and styles of the various immigrant cultures of America and the assimilation of these sounds and styles over many generations in the slow-changing culture of the Southern farm belt. These diverse roots support a new tree, with continually diverging and reconverging branches.

What we call "the original" traditional country music, the repertoire of The Carter Family and Ernest V. "Pop" Stoneman, for instance, finds its deepest roots in ancient broadside ballads from the British Isles. That tradition of song-stories has been adapted to a variety of beats and melodic families aided by specific musical instruments such as the fiddle, invented in Italy in 1550 and taken to heart in the British Isles. Another important instrumental coloration of country music in America is the frailing plunk of the banjo, an instrument of African origin. Around the 1870s, if not sooner, Southern folk music began to feel the influence of the six-string guitar. The music was further molded by the voices of instruments like the harmonica, upright piano, washtub bass, Jew's harp, dobro, drums, horns, and kazoo, to name a few.

The idea that country music came from the shanty porches of Appalachia is only partly true. The roots of country music were also fed and nurtured in Mississippi Valley cotton fields, on the Old Chisolm Trail, in vaudeville theaters in Richmond and Atlanta, in minstrel tents, and on medicine show flatbed wagons—and in Tin Pan Alley. They came out of the Sacred Harp shape note conventions, from the 1920s Deep Ellum red light district in Dallas, and the Stamps-Baxter gospel singing schools across town, from Baptist and Methodist hymnals, from cross-pollinating rhythms of black field blues and straight-laced white Appalachian nasality as they collided in Drakesboro, Kentucky, or Chattanooga and Memphis, Tennessee. Regional sounds from all of America's grand subsections contributed at one time or another, such as the Gulf States' concoction of dixieland jazz, Cajun, Big Band swing, and old-time fiddle band traditions into Western swing.

Historical and sociological realities alternately preserved the status quo and brought changes in Southern culture that were reflected in country music. The Spanish American War, a brief conflict of enormous impact to the United States just before the turn of the century, brought the Hawaiian steel guitar with its Spanish-Polynesian modal tunings into the American mainstream, and into Southern musical culture. That new influence led to three instruments with distinctive sounds: lap steel, pedal steel, and dobro. By the turn of the century, the spread of the railroads brought African-American construction men into contact with whites in remote pockets of Appalachia. With significant impact, the African-Americans introduced to the dour, rhythmless Appalachian ballad singers the driving rhythms, string bending, finger-picking, and the evocative chord patterns of field blues.

There was no country music, in the sense of a self-conscious commercial genre, until the radio boom in the early 1920s.

Many mavens of high culture—the opera, the symphony and other classical music forms—imagined a lowbrow American public on the verge of being washed beneficially with these highbrow sounds. They had no idea that that gate swung both ways. The music of the common folks—blues, jazz, folk, and country—would find in radio a medium that magnified the individual performer a million-fold. With the radio craze that became full-blown in 1922 and continued for the next several decades, the musical reach of such regional backwaters as the Appalachian Mountains, the Mississippi Valley and delta, Southeast Tennessee and Northeast Georgia, and other hot spots of rural folk and traditional music forms would be vastly extended.

More and more companies had come into the phonograph market as the original patents ran out, causing a general downward pressure on prices. In 1912 there had been only three makers of phonographs; by 1916 there were 46. The lateral cut disk player and two-sided disks became the norm. Census figures told the story of the boom in phonograph sales in America in that period. The value of the nation's phonograph production in 1914 was $27,116,000; by 1919, it had increased to $158,668,000. As the "radio boom" in America slowly got underway in 1919 and 1920, advances and standardizations in radio technologies made the reproduction of the human voice and of music possible, thus promising to make mass media partners of the radio and phonograph. Radio would quickly prove that an audience for rural music existed and record companies would soon follow to serve this new market.

The end of Prohibition, the upheaval of World War II, and the subsequent mobility and urbanization of Southerners in the postwar years jump-started honky-tonk music, colored by the wail of the developing ten-string pedal steel guitar. Legal beer and postwar industrialization were critical factors in molding the society in which modern country music took shape. As country music fans moved from small towns in the South to urban manufacturing jobs in cities like Detroit, Milwaukee, New York, and Los Angeles, they took their music with them.

The genius of country music is indebted to the way individual players of various instruments and myriad root music styles took what they found and redirected it by the strength of their own virtuosity and imagination. They filtered it, ultimately, through the tastes of a rural audience. The impact of black rural Alabama street musician Tee-Tot on Hank Williams' singing style is an historical fact. The finger-picking style of black Kentucky folk guitarist Arnold Schults was passed on to Mose Rager, Bill Monroe, Merle Travis, Ike Everly, and, by extension, Chet Atkins, with each new initiate giving the style his own twist. And where did the man who introduced Earl Scruggs to that revolutionary three-finger roll get it himself? Search the background of every influential country performer and writer, of every creator of a new school or style of country music, and you find that their obsessed imagination perfected and popularized ideas they found floating around their neighborhoods when they were young.

Lyric sources and topics in the 1920s, in the earliest days of commercial country music, could be sacred or pornographic, but usually fell sentimentally somewhere in between. Basically, though, even when Civil War–era pop tunes were cannibalized and adapted to new arrangements and new lyrics, what emerged in the precommercial country music years was music that reflected the hopes, fears, longings, humor, and experience of a people who had hard work, low incomes, rural landscapes, and limited horizons in common, whether they were Montana cowboys, Texas cotton farmers, Mississippi railroaders, or Appalachian scrub farmers. It was a music in many "flavors," each able to get working folks to dance, laugh, or cry.

Thomas Edison and his improved wax cylinder phonograph, 1888.
credit: Bob Millard Collection

Only rich families could afford the early phonographs for home entertainment.
credit: Bob Millard Collection

To this day, country music has kept one thing in common with its progenitor folk forms: At its best it deals in a straightforward manner with real issues of ordinary people, mainly with love and loss, and often with a beat that entices boot-shod feet onto the dance floor. George D. Hay, originator of the "Grand Ole Opry," declared from the very beginning that the Opry would present music that was "down to earth for the 'earthy'." While the country audience has become more urbanized in its views and lifestyles since Hay's day, and country music has become vastly more stylistically varied, the most lasting country music still mirrors that description.

Milestones

- 1848   Uncle Jimmy Thompson born in Smith County, Tennessee.
- 1868   Fiddlin' John Carson born in Fannin County, Georgia, on March 23.
- 1870   Uncle Dave Macon born in Cannon County, Tennessee, on October 7.
- 1883   Vernon Dalhart (Marion Try Slaughter) born in Jefferson, Texas, on April 4.
- 1885   Gid Tanner born in Thomas Bridge, Georgia, on June 6.
- 1885   "Rev." Andrew Jenkins born in Jenkinsburg, Georgia, on November 26.
- 1890   Riley Puckett born in Alpharetta, Georgia, on May 7.
- 1890   Carson Robison born in Oswego, Kansas, on August 4.

1891	Alvin Pleasant Carter born in Maces Spring, Virginia, on December 15.
1892	Reformed riverboat captain Tom Ryman builds the Union Gospel Tabernacle in downtown Nashville. After his death, it is renamed Ryman Auditorium and becomes the long-running home of the "Grand Ole Opry."
1892	Charlie Poole born in Alamance County, North Carolina, on March 22.
1892	Henry Whitter born in Fries, Virginia, on May 6.
1893	Ernest V. "Pop" Stoneman born in Carroll County, Virginia, on May 25.
1894	Sam McGee born in Franklin, Tennessee, on May 1.
1894	Ken Maynard born in Mission, Texas, on July 21.
1895	Carl T. Sprague born in Manvel, Texas, on May 10.
1895	Bradley Kincaid born in Point Leavell, Kentucky, on July 13.
1895	George D. Hay, founder of the "Grand Ole Opry," born in Attica, Indiana, on November 9.
1897	Fred Rose born in St. Louis, Missouri, on August 24.
1897	Jimmie Rodgers born in Meridian, Mississippi, on September 8.
1898	Dock Boggs born in Norton, Virginia, on February 7.
1898	J.E. Mainer born in Weaversville, North Carolina, on July 20.
1899	Sara Carter born in Wise County, Virginia, on July 21.
1899	Kirk McGee born in Franklin, Tennessee, on November 11.
1900	Casey Jones dies in a train wreck in Vaughan, Mississippi, becoming the subject of popular event songs that enter the rural Southern folk music stream.
1900	Clayton McMichen born in Allatoona, Georgia, on January 26.
1901	Benjamin "Whitey" Ford, "The Duke of Paducah," born in De Soto, Missouri, on May 12
1902	Al Dexter (Albert Poindexter) born in Jacksonville, Texas, on May 4.
1902	Jimmie Davis born in Quitman, Louisiana, on November 11.
1903	Wreck of the "Old Southern 97" occurs near Danville, Virginia, later becoming the subject of one of the first records of the commercial country music era.
1903	Charlie Monroe born in Rosine, Kentucky, on June 4.
1903	Milton Brown born in Stephensville, Texas, on September 8.

Capt. Thomas G. Ryman.
credit: Courtesy of the Grand Ole Opry

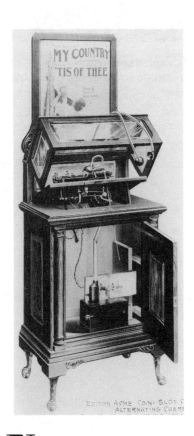

Nickel-in-the-slot phonographs were the forerunners of the modern jukebox.
credit: Bob Millard Collection

1903   Roy Acuff born in Maynardsville, Tennessee, on September 15.

1904   Cliff Carlisle born in Taylorsville, Kentucky, on May 6.

1904   Wilf Carter (Montana Slim) born in Guysboro, Nova Scotia, on December 18.

1905   Bob Wills born in Hall County, Texas, on March 6.

1906   Maurice Woodward "Tex" Ritter born in Panola County, Texas, on January 12.

1907   Gene Autry born in Tioga, Texas, on September 29.

1908   Texas Ruby born in Wise County, Texas, on June 4.

1908   Tim Spencer born in Wise County, Texas, on July 7.

1908   Stuart Hamblen born in Kellyville, Texas, on October 20.

1908   Alton Delmore born in Elkmont, Alabama, on December 25.

1909   Eck Robertson born in Batesville, Texas, on February 27.

1909   Aubrey "Moon" Mullican born in Polk County, Texas, on March 27.

1909   Maybelle Carter born in Nickelsville, Virginia, on May 10.

1910   Clyde Julian "Red" Foley born in Berea, Kentucky, on June 17.

1910   Rabon Delmore born in Elkmont, Alabama, on December 3.

1910   Donald "Spade" Cooley born in Grande, Oklahoma, on December 17.

1911   Smiley Burnette, Gene Autry's movie sidekick "Frog Millhouse," born in Summum, Illinois, on March 18.

1911   Pioneer country recording executive Vaughan Horton born in Broad Gap, Pennsylvania, on June 6.

1911   Zeke Clements born in Dora, Alabama, on September 6.

1911   Bill Monroe born in Rosine, Kentucky, on September 13.

1912   Ted Daffan born in Houston, Texas, on September 21.

1912   Sara Ophelia Colley (Minnie Pearl) born in Centerville, Tennessee, on October 25.

1912   Leonard Slye (Roy Rogers) born in Cincinnati, Ohio, on November 2.

1913   A general dance craze sweeps America in the middle of an economic downturn, leading to a switch in the recording industry to a wide variety of dance tunes.

1913   Louis Marshall "Grandpa" Jones born in Niagra, Kentucky, on October 20.

1913   Lulu Belle (Myrtle Eleanor Cooper Wiseman) born in Boone, North Carolina, on December 24.

- 1914 Floyd Tillman born in Ryan, Oklahoma, on January 8.
- 1914 Frank Kuczynski (Pee Wee King) born in Milwaukee, Wisconsin, on February 14.
- 1914 Ernest Tubb born in Crisp, Texas, on February 9.
- 1914 Jimmy Wakely born in Mineola, Arkansas, on February 16.
- 1914 Hank Snow born in Liverpool, Nova Scotia, on May 9.
- 1914 Patsy Montana (Rubye Blevins) born in Hot Springs, Arkansas, on October 30.
- 1915 Johnny Bond born in Enville, Oklahoma, on June 1.
- 1916 Vernon Dalhart makes his first recording.
- 1917 Leon McAuliff born in Houston, Texas, on January 3.
- 1917 Cliffie Stone born in Burbank, California, on March 1.
- 1917 Leon Payne born in Alba, Texas, on June 15.
- 1917 Elton Britt born in Marshall, Arkansas, on July 7.
- 1917 "Tex" Williams born in Fayette County, Illinois, on August 23.
- 1917 Bill Bollick (Blue Sky Boys) born in Hickory, North Carolina, on October 28.
- 1917 Merle Travis born in Rosewood, Kentucky, on November 29.
- 1919 Earl Bollick (Blue Sky Boys) born in Hickory, North Carolina, on December 16.

Patsy Montana sheet music cover.
credit: Archive of Robert K. Oermann

The Carter Family.
credit: In the Southern Folklife
Collection, University of North
Carolina, Chapel Hill

THE 1920S
THE BIRTH OF COMMERCIAL COUNTRY MUSIC

Despite the 30-year existence of a commercial recording industry, there was no commercial genre called "country music" until broadcast radio appeared in 1922. Rural performers of white Southern folk music went on the air at selected stations within two years after the November 1920 debut of America's first commercial radio station, WDKA in Pittsburgh. A handful of country musicians audaciously made their own way to the Northeastern headquarters of labels such as Columbia Records and Victor Talking Machine Company and managed to record. The labels didn't go after the newly discovered market for "old-time music" and "songs of the hills and plains" until local talent scouts convinced them to send out field recording teams to record hillbilly musicians from the early old-time music radio shows.

WSB in Atlanta was most likely the first radio station to broadcast "country" music, though the term "country music" would not gain prominence in describing the multiplicity of Southeastern and Southwestern musical styles enjoyed by rural American audiences for another couple of decades. WSB found regionally popular semi-professional acts such as old-time fiddlers Uncle Jimmy Thompson and Fiddlin' John Carson, string band leaders Clayton McMichen and Gid Tanner, and blind news vendor and composer of sentimental event songs "Rev." Andrew Jenkins to be immensely popular with Atlanta listeners in early 1923. Atlanta furniture store executive Polk Brockman spent months convincing recordist Ralph Peer of Okeh Records to bring his field recording equipment to Georgia to record both black and white folk musicians. Those Okeh sessions represented the true beginnings of the commercial country music industry.

BLIND RADIO POET

"**R**ev." Andrew Jenkins.
credit: In the Southern Folklife
Collection, University of North
Carolina, Chapel Hill

Jimmie Rodgers is called "the Singing Brakeman," "America's Blue Yodeler," but most critically, "the Father of Country Music." No other entertainer in country music history has been more widely imitated.

Rodgers was raised in Pine Springs and Meridian, Mississippi, partly by his father after his mother died in 1903, but mostly by relatives he and his two brothers were shuttled back and forth between. His father was a railroad section foreman, and Jimmie was so loosely supervised that he often played hookey from school. Sometimes he would ride the rails with his father; other times he would hang out at his uncle's barber shop, learning bawdy songs and stories, and running errands for nickels. He was tough and streetwise long before he reached adulthood.

He was also a musical entertainer long before he developed tuberculosis, quit an unpromising railroad career, and went into music full time. His musical style merged blues, bohemian yodeling, and rural white folk sounds. He won his first talent contest at Meridian's Elite vaudeville theater at age 12. He more than once ran away from home for the carnival life of medicine shows.

Rodgers began touring in earnest with a black-face minstrel show in 1925, ignoring doctor's orders. In 1927, he dragged his second wife, Carrie, to Asheville, North Carolina, where she (a preacher's daughter) worked as a waitress while he imposed himself on a small string band known as the Tenneva Ramblers. The repertoire was broad, including popular tunes of the day, as well as Rodgers' own sentimental paeans to mother, train, and hobo songs. Rodgers' unbeatable charisma topped off the performance, but the act played little and was paid less.

The act had worked part-time on WWNC, but was simply scraping by on hinterlands engagements when Rodgers read of Ralph Peer's Bristol recording dates. He took the band 100 miles north to Bristol, but the night before their session the band disassociated themselves from him and convinced Peer to record them as the Tenneva Ramblers. Rodgers had to practically beg Peer to give him a chance to record as a solo act on August 4, 1927. He gave Peer a hit, an 1860s lullaby, "Sleep, Baby, Sleep." By the end of that year, Victor invited him to Camden, New Jersey, to their main studios, to record again. This time Rodgers introduced his Blue Yodel style, recording the classic "Blue Yodel #1 (T For Texas)." It became his first million-seller.

Though tuberculosis cut his life and career dreadfully short, Rodgers' unique stylings made his name a household word in the South. Even when the stock market crash of 1929 deflated record sales across all genre boundaries, rural folk continued to buy their week's groceries and the latest Jimmie Rodgers record as though the two were equally important to their well-being. In 1929, Rodgers went to Hollywood to make his only film appearance in a 15-minute short entitled "The Singing Brakeman." Short as the film was, it wasn't much shorter than his usual vaudeville circuit performance. Tuberculosis circumscribed his time on stage, and eventually his concert radius, but he stayed active until the week he died.

Jimmie Rodgers—America's Blue Yodeler.
credit: In the Southern Folklife Collection, University of North Carolina, Chapel Hill

An early WLS Barn Dance cast. credit: In the Southern Folklife Collection, University of North Carolina, Chapel Hill

Ft. Worth, Texas, station WBAP was probably the first radio station in the West to air country music. Reaction to WBAP's first evening of old-time fiddling and Hawaiian guitar band music drew an avalanche of supportive telegrams, phone calls, and letters, leading to a series of "barn dance" programs that influenced the format of hillbilly radio shows all over the South and East. The most prominent and influential of these early barn dance shows was the WLS "Barn Dance" originating in Chicago. Even the WSM "Barn Dance" in Nashville, the forerunner of the "Grand Ole Opry," was developed along these lines.

A huge number of amateur or semi-professional string bands and old-time fiddlers were making records in these helter-skelter early days of country recordings, but only a few artists achieved more than moderate sales. They included Uncle Dave Macon, Tanner and McMichen, Riley Puckett, Fiddlin' John Carson, Eck Robertson, and Ernest "Pop" Stoneman; at first, they were content to adapt folk songs whose origins were lost in the folk tradition of the rural South. At the close of the 1920s, the preeminent mountain folk song act, the Carter Family, had begun to leave a mark on the repertoire of country music as few had before and even fewer have since.

George D. Hay, nicknamed "The Solemn Old Judge," was a newspaperman in Memphis when radio first arrived there. He began working on WMC as a "personality" announcer, complete with a steamboat whistle he blew to punctuate his commentary. He loved the South and had little interest in moving to Chicago to work for the nascent Sears, Roebuck station, WLS (call letters standing for "World's Largest Store"), when they offered to hire him as their chief announcer in the spring of 1924. Thinking to dissuade them, Hay demanded $75 per week. He was surprised when they agreed.

Hay borrowed ideas from an Arkansas hoedown he had attended in creating the WLS "Barn Dance" (now defunct), which soon became the most influential country music radio show in America. He brought in Irish tenors, crooners of sentimental songs, and genuine rural string band musicians to program the show. His favorites were the hillbillies.

Before many months had passed, WLS was voted one of the nation's top radio stations and Hay the nation's best-recognized announcer. It was only natural that WSM in Nashville, knowing of Hay's nostalgia for the South, would steal him away when they went on the air in late autumn 1925.

George D. Hay and Uncle Jimmy Thompson in WSM Barn Dance studio.
credit: Courtesy of the Grand Ole Opry

Only two artists recording in the 1920s enjoyed truly phenomenal record sales, running into the millions. These were the versatile Texas light opera singer Vernon Dalhart and the Mississippi-born vaudevillian Jimmie Rodgers. Dalhart's niche was powerful sentimental numbers such as "The Prisoner's Song" and hugely popular event songs, including "Wreck of the Old 97" and "The Death of Floyd Collins." Though borrowing heavily from folk and blues traditions and even Tin Pan Alley sources, Rodgers and Dalhart were essentially singers of newly composed material, rather than interpreters of Southern folk music.

The Nashville country music establishment felt threatened and outraged in the 1970s when pop crossover artists John Denver and Olivia Newton-John had major hit records and won top awards as country artists. What would the Nashville elite have thought of Vernon Dalhart, a Manhattan-based light opera tenor who became the first superstar of hillbilly music?

Born Marion Try Slaughter in Jefferson, Texas, Dalhart, like Conway Twitty, took his stage name from two towns. "Dalhart" was the most widely recognized among more than 100 stage names he used, often recording the same tunes for several labels beginning with his first session for Edison Diamond Disc in 1915. In 1924 the record boom was at its peak, but Dalhart's career as a light tenor was fading. Attempting to find a new niche, the conservatory-trained vocalist recorded Henry Whitter's event tune "Wreck of the Old (Southern) '97" and backed it with a sentimental ballad, "The Prisoner's Song," a composition pieced together from two nineteenth century Tin Pan Alley melodies, with new words penned by Dalhart's brother-in-law.

"The Prisoner's Song" turned out to be the more popular of the two and, in typical Dalhart mode, he recorded it first for Edison and then for Victor. Enormous record and sheet music sales were racked up within two years to make Dalhart country music's first million-seller artist. Dalhart had found a niche.

He followed "The Prisoner's Song" with hillbilly event songs and sentimental ballads almost exclusively. Though one of his stage names appeared on the copyright for "The Prisoner's Song," Dalhart was not a writer. To continue his success, it was critical to Dalhart to establish the first professional hillbilly song sources, particularly Bob Miller, "Rev." Andrew Jenkins, and Carson Robison. Jenkins' "The Death of Floyd Collins" was a tremendous hit for Dalhart in 1926, starting a virtual tidal wave of contemporary and historical event songs as one of the earliest commercial country music subgenres.

Popular records from the first decades of commercial country music continued to be available for several years, and Dalhart himself recorded for twelve or more labels. Dalhart's New York's *Daily News* obituary claimed that in the singer's lifetime "The Prisoner's Song" had sold more than 25 million copies, which, if true, would make it the biggest-selling country record of all-time, Garth Brooks and Billy Ray Cyrus notwithstanding. It was Dalhart's successes in the mid-1920s that convinced Victor to send Ralph Peer into the field looking for "real" hillbilly music and artists.

Though he may have received $1 million in royalties for "The Prisoner's Song" alone, Dalhart faded as a recording artist in the 1930s, becoming the popular, but again pseudonymous, radio voice for "Sam, The Barbasol Man." Dalhart ended his life as a small-town vocal coach in Connecticut, working part time as a night watchman and hotel clerk.

Vernon Dalhart.
credit: In the Southern Folklife Collection, University of North Carolina, Chapel Hill

Improvements in recording technology, microphones, and radio transmission allowed for a greater subtlety and nuance in country music and created demands for better musicianship and more precise harmonies. Country music ended its first decade on a high note and on the verge of becoming a popular style practiced by a new generation of professionals. To come were innovation, change, and survival. The music of poor, working Southern folk on radio and records was spreading across the nation, distilling its regional flavors into more sophisticated and homogenous sounds.

Early Opry stars Uncle Dave Macon and his son Dorris in the foreground; Dr. Humphrey Bate (top, far right) and his Possum Hunters band.
credit: Courtesy of the Grand Ole Opry

1920

Milestones

- Kenneth C. "Jethro" Burns born in Knoxville, Tennessee, on March 10.
- Ralph Peer joins General Phonograph Company, becoming head of the Okeh Records division.
- Already showing signs of tuberculosis infection, Jimmie Rodgers marries a Merridian, Mississippi, preacher's pretty daughter, Carrie Williamson, on April 7.
- WDKA Pittsburgh goes on the air November 2 to broadcast the results of the presidential election. Warren Harding wins; radio is launched as a mass medium.
- James Cecil "Little Jimmy" Dickens born in Bolt, West Virginia, on December 19.
- Rex Allen (Sr.) born in Wilcox, Arizona, on December 31.

Milestones

- Wilma Lee Cooper born in Valley Head, West Virginia, on February 7.
- Arthur "Guitar Boogie" Smith born in Clinton, South Carolina, on April 1.
- Having spent more than 35 years learning his banjo and singing as a private hobby, and three years performing semi-professionally at private functions and in a hotel, Uncle Dave Macon performs at the Morrison, Tennessee school house, passing the hat to raise $17 to buy a door for the local Methodist Church. Later, Macon recalled the event as "the first time I ever played and sang in public."
- Sheb Wooley born in Erick, Oklahoma, on April 10.
- Martha Carson born on May 19.
- Harold Frank (Hawkshaw) Hawkins born in Huntington, West Virginia, on December 12.

Milestones

- WSB, the South's first "high power" radio station, goes on the air with a 100 watt broadcast signal on March 16. Transmitting power is increased to 500 watts on June 13.
- After performing at the Confederate Veteran's convention in Virginia in June, on a lark, Eck Robertson and Henry Gilliland travel to New York City. They appear unannounced in the lobby of Victor Records wearing a rebel uniform and a cowboy outfit. Amused at the novelty and audacity of this pair of old-time fiddlers, Victor records them. Though their release is held up for several months, it marks the first "hillbilly" session of the commercial country music era.

WSB and Fiddlin' John Carson

Owned by the *Atlanta Journal* newspaper, WSB, Atlanta, was the first radio station on the air in the South when it broadcast its originating signals in March 1922. Six months after its debut, old-time fiddle champion Fiddlin' John Carson of Fannin County, Georgia, became the first "hillbilly" musician to perform on radio. Carson performed with a four-piece band. He was a favorite at old-time fiddler's competitions, with his signature selections "The Little Log Cabin in the Lane," "Turkey in the Straw," "Old Joe Clark," and "The Old Hen Cackled (And The Rooster's Going to Crow)." By the time he appeared on WSB, Carson had already won the Georgia state fiddler's competition seven times.

Not all "folk music" found in Carson's repertoire was of true folk—that is, unidentifiable—origins. "The Old Hen...", for instance, was a best-selling pop tune written by Will Hays and first published in 1871. Carson's luck in 1923 in becoming Ralph Peer's first hillbilly artist to record for Okeh started an 11-year career recording folk ballads, minstrel tunes, humorous and sentimental tunes, gospel numbers, and square dance music. The scope of his repertoire was consistent with most regional artists of his day.

Carson never earned much money from his recordings, but the friends he made as a popular political rally entertainer in Georgia gave him a cushion in his declining years. Governor Herman Talmadge awarded him a sit-down job as an elevator operator at the state capitol in his later years.

Old-time music artists make their debut on WSB in September. Fiddlin' John Carson appears first, on September 9, and Clayton McMichen's Hometown Boys string band performs September 18.

Gid Tanner and Fiddlin' John Carson.
credit: In the Southern Folklife Collection, University of North Carolina, Chapel Hill

1923

Most Important Records

"Sally Goodin"/"Ragtime Annie" Eck Robertson / Victor
"Little Log Cabin in the Lane" Fiddlin' John Carson / Okeh
"Arkansas Traveler"/"Turkey in the Straw" Eck Robertson and Henry Gilliland / Victor
"Wreck of the Southern Old 97" Henry Whitter / Okeh

Milestones

WBAP, Ft. Worth, Texas, airs the first country music in the West, an old-time fiddler and Civil War veteran, Captain M.J. Bonner, accompanied by Fred Wagner's Hilo Five Hawaiian Orchestra on January 4. Wagner's ensemble was actually the featured act, but audience response was overwhelmingly enthusiastic for the fiddle music. WBAP scrambles to find more old-time talent, establishing an irregular series of hoedown-style dance music programs in the barn dance format.

David Harrison "Uncle Dave" Macon was a bodacious entertainer whom country music's foremost popular critic, Robert K. Oermann, called a "wise-cracking, story telling, song-singing ol' geezer." Calling himself simply a "banjoist and songster," Macon was a vital link between the nineteenth century and the modern era.

He was born on the Cumberland Plateau in central Tennessee. His father was a Confederate veteran and a well-to-do farmer who moved the family to Nashville when Macon was 13 years old to run the Broadway Hotel. Though he only stayed there three years, young Macon hobnobbed with medicine show, vaudeville, and circus entertainers passing through the hotel. He was a keen student of old songs and stories, carrying them with him well into the twentieth century.

Though he took up banjo when he was 15, Macon didn't turn to public performing for his livelihood until he was 56 years old. He had run a farm and a mule-drawn freight company until the automobile put him out of business in the early 1920s. He simply preferred not to haul his freight in trucks, and he often let his mules lead themselves on their established route while their driver sat back and played his banjo. He was "accidentally" discovered at a private party by a vaudeville theater manager in 1923. He became one of the first "stars" of the WSM "Barn Dance"/ "Grand Ole Opry" and was a key figure of the "Opry" package tent show tours and early "hillbilly music" movies featuring "Opry" cast members. His first Vocalion session, in New York in 1924, featured the tune "Hill Billy Blues," which scholars say is the first use of the term in a record.

Macon's songs, including such colorful titles as "Carve That Possum," "Hold The Wood Pile Down," "Bake That Chicken Pie," "Keep My Skillet Good and Greasy," and "Go Long Mule," were not as important as his presentation. Wearing overalls or, more likely, expensive three-piece suits, he sat with his coat folded away and his hat cocked back on his head, stomping his feet and wailing with great energy and humor in a deep rural Tennessee patois so thick that his records are often incomprehensible today. He had tremendous rapport with his audiences and showed a later generation of country entertainers how to captivate a crowd. The fun of his reissued records remains infectious and personal.

Macon remained a farmer and a popular feature on the "Grand Ole Opry" for the rest of his life, performing regularly until just a few weeks before his death in 1952.

Uncle Dave Macon—original Opry star.
credit: Courtesy of the Grand Ole Opry

Henry Whitter.
credit: In the Southern Folklife
Collection, University of North
Carolina, Chapel Hill

1924

- Audrey Williams (Audrey Mae Sheppard) born in Pike County, Alabama, on February 28.
- Doc Watson born in Deep Gap, North Carolina, on March 2.
- In late March, Henry Whitter, a part-time fiddler from Virginia, travels to New York at his own expense and convinces Victor to let him record his composition, "Wreck of the Southern Old 97." Though the record is not released until December, it is to become one of the most famous of the early hillbilly records, selling even more copies when it is covered by Vernon Dalhart.
- Uncle Dave Macon is egged into performing for the Nashville Shriners, for what he later termed his first fully public professional performance. A local farmer with high lodge standing had repeatedly asked Mason to play the event. Intending to shut the man up, Macon demanded $15. The demand was immediately met, trapping Macon into playing, where he was "discovered" by the manager of a Loew's circuit vaudeville theater and offered a $300 per week tour of the South. Fiddler Syd Harkreader began touring with Macon.
- During the summer, Ralph Peer, having already made a small name for himself recording blues, makes his first foray into the South to record for Okeh. When no black performers are found, Atlanta retailer Polk Brockman quickly rounds up white old-time musicians he knows from WSB. Peer records Fiddlin' John Carson, a WSB favorite, in an empty loft on Atlanta's Nassau Street on June 14.
- Molly O'Day (Lavergne Davis) born in Pike County, Kentucky, on July 9.
- Hiram King "Hank" Williams born in Mount Olive, Alabama, on September 17.
- Dorothy Shay ("The Park Avenue Hillbilly," singer/actress/ radio comedienne) born in Jacksonville, Florida.

Most Important Records

"The Prisoner's Song" Vernon Dalhart / Victor
"The Wreck of the Old 97" Vernon Dalhart / Victor
"Little Rosewood Casket" Ernest Thompson / Columbia
"Old Joe Clark" Fiddlin' Powers and Family / Victor
"Rock All Our Babies to Sleep" Riley Puckett / Columbia

The years 1923 and 1924 were a formative time in the development of hillbilly radio programs and talents. These years also gave rise to numerous careers that, while profitable in their time, soon evaporated from memory like morning dew. The career of prison inmate/hillbilly singer Harry Snodgrass is one of those lost jewels of country music history.

Snodgrass, a convicted murderer, was the singer and piano player for a prison band that in 1923 appeared regularly on WOR. Trade newspaper *Variety* took note of Snodgrass, calling him a "moron." Still, his radio popularity got him a pardon, followed by a recording deal with Brunswick Records.

After his release, Snodgrass parlayed his WOR popularity and public notoriety as the man who sang his way out of prison into a vaudeville stage tour that started in January 1924 in Evansville, Indiana, and broke house records for ticket sales nearly everywhere he went. Vaudeville theaters paid him top dollar for appearances wherever he went. He kept busy on that circuit for the next several years, after which the novelty of the singing convict wore off, and his popularity rapidly declined.

Harry Snodgrass was not a lasting influence on country music, but he certainly was the first ex-con to capitalize on his shady past to formulate an image that would become the genre. Generations later, Merle Haggard, Johnny Rodriguez, and David Allan Coe would perpetuate the image. By singing his way out of prison, Snodgrass also foreshadowed the career of folk music legend Huddie "Leadbelly" Ledbetter, who accomplished the same feat in two different states.

Milestones

- Vocalion launches a "hillbilly" record series they call "Special Records For Southern States," starting with recordings by Uncle Dave Macon ("I'm Gonna Leave You 'Lone"/ "Chewing Gum"), Uncle Am Stuart, and Blind George Reneau.
- Earl Scruggs born in Flintville, North Carolina, on January 6.
- Otis Dewey "Slim" Whitman born in Tampa, Florida, on January 20.
- Georgia chicken farmer and old-time fiddler Gid Tanner meets blind guitar player Riley Puckett at Columbia Phonograph Company's first "hillbilly" recording session on March 7.
- Bonnie Guitar born in Seattle, Washington, on March 25.
- WLS goes on the air on April 12. WLS's first barn dance program is broadcast from the lobby of the Sherman Hotel, Chicago, on April 19.
- Vernon Dalhart (the man of a hundred stage names), his career as a light opera tenor waning, records "The Prisoner's Song"/"The Wreck of the Southern Old 97" for Victor.
- Ira Louvin born in Rainesville, Alabama, on April 21.
- Chester Burton (Chet) Atkins born in Luttrell, Tennessee, on June 20.
- Ernest V. "Pop" Stoneman first records for Okeh's "Old Time Tunes" series ("The Ship That Never Returned"/"The Titanic").
- Jim Reeves born in Panola County, Texas, on August 20.

Most Important Records

"The Death of Floyd Collins" Vernon Dalhart / Victor
"When The Work's All Done This Fall" Carl T. Sprague / Victor
"Rovin' Gambler" Kelly Harrell / Victor
"Letter Edged In Black" Vernon Dalhart / Victor
"Don't Let Your Deal Go Down Blues" Charlie Poole / Columbia

Milestones

↤ Johnny Horton born in Los Angeles, California, on April 3.

↤ Danny Davis (of the Nashville Brass) born in Randolph, Massachusetts, on April 29.

↤ The term "hillbilly" first used in commercial country music.

↤ George Morgan born in Waverly, Tennessee, on June 28.

↤ Vocalist/five-string banjoist Charlie Poole and his North Carolina Ramblers record their most popular number, "Don't Let Your Deal Go Down Blues," on July 27 for Columbia in New York City.

↤ In August, Texas schoolteacher, athletic coach, and part-time singer Carl T. Sprague records his first session for Victor at Camden, New Jersey, pioneering the "singing cowboy" mold in country music with tunes like "When The Work's All Done This Fall."

↤ Billy Grammer born in Benton, Illinois, on August 28.

↤ Guitarist Sam McGee begins touring with Uncle Dave Macon, alternating with Syd Harkreader; Macon also adds a buckdancer to his show, billing the two men as his sons.

↤ Hank Thompson born in Waco, Texas, on September 3.

↤ Marty Robbins (Martin David Robinson) born in Glendale, Arizona, on September 26.

↤ WSM radio in Nashville goes on the air on October 5; owners hire George D. Hay away from WLS.

↤ Dr. Humphrey Bate and a band of neighbors are the first "hillbilly" string ensemble to perform on WSM in Nashville on October 24. Establishing a policy that would hold for the next five years, the station pays them nothing.

↤ The "official" birth of the "Grand Ole Opry" is dated to an appearance by Uncle Jimmy Thompson on WSM on November 28. In short order, the cast is enlarged to include local string bands The Gully Jumpers, the Crook Brothers, and the Fruit Jar Drinkers, in addition to Dr. Bates' Possum Hunters, whose debut on WSM predates the establishment of the WSM "Barn Dance," the progenitor of the "Grand Ole Opry."

↤ Kirk and Sam McGee become regulars on the WSM "Barn Dance," and join Dr. Bate and his Possum Hunters on a

Carl T. Sprague.
credit: In the Southern Folklife Collection, University of North Carolina, Chapel Hill

tour of RKO vaudeville theaters in the Midwest and upper South.

↠ Bradley Kincaid joins the WLS "Barn Dance."

↠ Ferlin Husky born in Flat River, Missouri, on December 3.

How Hillbilly Music Got Its Name

Southern folk music was a loose, nameless aggregation of styles when, on January 15, 1925, it found its first appellation. A no-name string band (Al and Joe Hopkins, Tony Alderman, and John Rector) recorded for Ralph Peer at Okeh studios in New York City on that date. When asked, for accounting purposes, what the act called itself, Al Hopkins replied, "Call the band anything you want. We are nothing but a bunch of hillbillies from North Carolina and Virginia anyway." Almost as a joke, Peer dubbed the act "Hillbillies," unwittingly labeling an entire genre of Southern folk music. Hopkins was uncomfortable with the name at first; it was already in colloquial use as the equivalent of a racial epithet aimed at rural Southerners. Hopkins didn't wholeheartedly embrace the Hillbillies title, despite the band's recording success, until fellow traditionalist string band entertainer Ernest V. "Pop" Stoneman gave his stamp of approval.

The Hillbillies, l–r Tony Alderman, John Hopkins, Charlie Bowman, and Al Hopkins.
credit: In the Southern Folklife Collection, University of North Carolina, Chapel Hill

Most Important Records[1]

"The Dying Cowboy" Carl T. Sprague / Victor
"Ida Red" Riley Puckett / Columbia
"Hand Me Down My Walking Cane" Kelly Harrell / Victor
"Old Joe Clark" Gid Tanner and the Skillet Lickers / Columbia
"Little Log Cabin in the Lane" Ernest "Pop" Stoneman / Victor

1. Unlike today, many artists in the early days of commercial country music recorded the same songs at the same time and had respectable hits from them, based in many cases on regional popularity. In 1926, for instance, "Little Log Cabin in the Lane" was recorded simultaneously by "Pop" Stoneman, Fiddlin' John Carson, Uncle Dave Macon, Fiddlin' Powers and Family, and Riley Puckett. Gid Tanner's hit, "Old Joe Clark," was similarly covered by Stoneman, Puckett, and Powers.

1926

"These recordings in Bristol in 1927 are the single most important event in the history of country music," claims Johnny Cash, and most scholars agree.

In the summer of 1927, hillbilly music had a handful of noteworthy recording artists, including Riley Puckett, Uncle Dave Macon, Charlie Poole, Fiddlin' John Carson, and the pseudo-hillbilly million-selling Vernon Dalhart. What it didn't yet have—artists whose music and musical directions held the potential to shape an emerging industry—it was about to get.

Peer left Okeh to set up his own publishing firm, then made a deal to record Southern folk performers for RCA Victor in exchange for the right to publish all the songs he found. Victor, having tasted the potential of the hillbilly market with Vernon Dalhart, gave Peer a small crew and the latest field recording equipment. That summer, he went into the field and ran ads in area newspapers offering a standard $50 fee

per song and up to 2½ percent royalties. Performers literally came out of the woods and hills to audition.

When Peer set up in the upper floors of a former furniture store in Bristol, Tennessee, on the Virginia border, fruit tree salesman and song collector A.P. Carter came from the mountains with his wife Sara and sister-in-law Maybelle, driving a rattling old truck. They literally needed the recording fee to get back home.

"They wander in," Peer recalled in 1959. "He's dressed in overalls and the women are country women from way back there. They look like hillbillies. But as soon as I heard Sara's voice, that was it. I knew it was going to be wonderful."

Sara and Maybelle were the essence of the act—A.P. didn't even show up for the second day of recordings. The women, and A.P. when he did join in, were as pure an example of mountain folk style as Peer was to find. A.P.'s song collection proved to be a

treasure trove of copyrightable public domain numbers. Known acts such as The Johnson Brothers, Ernest V. Stoneman, and Henry Whitter were recorded in these sessions, but Peer's other significant discovery was Jimmie Rodgers. Quarreling with his band at the last minute, Rodgers accompanied himself but was slow to catch on to what Peer wanted to hear: original songs or old songs that could be updated and copyrighted as though new. Reworking an old vaudeville lullaby from the Civil War era, Rodgers delivered the first of a six-year string of hit records for Peer and Victor in "Sleep, Baby, Sleep."

The Carter's adherence to Appalachian traditions and Rodgers' remarkable charisma and synthesis were to have greater impact on the course of country music than any other acts recording in country's first decade. Their influences, and some of their tunes, are still found in the genre today.

Ralph Peer.
credit: Peermusic

Milestones

- Ray Price born in Perryville, Texas, on January 11.
- Fiddle player Clayton McMichen and banjoist Fate Norris, the core of the Lick The Skillet Band, first meet Gid Tanner and Riley Puckett at a Columbia session. The quartet becomes the seminal string band known as Gid Tanner and The Skillet Lickers.
- Webb Pierce born in West Monroe, Louisiana, August 8.
- Maybelle Addington marries Ezra Carter, brother of A.P. Carter.
- Charlie Walker born in Copeville, Texas, on November 11.
- Rose Maddox born in Boaz, Alabama.
- Freddie Hart born in Lochapoka, Alabama, on December 21.

Most Important Records

"Sleep, Baby, Sleep" Jimmie Rodgers / Victor
"Wednesday Night Waltz"/"Goodnight Waltz" Leake County Revelers / Columbia
"Golden Slippers"/ My Blue Ridge Mountain Home" Vernon Dalhart / Victor
"Lindbergh (The Eagle of the U.S.A.)" Vernon Dalhart / Victor
"John Henry" Gid Tanner and the Skillet Lickers / Columbia

Milestones

- Carl Smith born in Maynardsville, Tennessee, on March 15.
- Charlie Louvin born in Rainesville, Alabama, on July 7.
- During the first week of August, Ralph Peer makes his historic "Bristol Sessions" recordings in Bristol, Tennessee, that feature the first Carter Family, Jimmie Rodgers, and "Pop" Stoneman recordings for Victor.
- Porter Wagoner born in West Plain, Missouri, on August 12.
- Jimmy C. Newman born in Big Mamou, Louisiana, on August 27.
- Leon Rausch born in Springfield, Missouri, on October 2.

Most Important Records

"Blue Yodel #1 (T For Texas)" Jimmie Rodgers / Victor
"Daddy and Home"/"My Old Pal" Jimmie Rodgers / Victor
"Waiting For A Train" Jimmie Rodgers / Victor
"Birmingham Jail"/"Columbus Stockade Blues" Darby and Tarleton / Columbia
"Bury Me Under The Weeping Willow" Carter Family / Victor

1927

1928

WSM was Nashville's second radio station, but it would be the most influential in country music history. WSM (call letters standing for "We Shield Millions") was built by the National Life and Accident Insurance Company as a medium to advertise its products to the Mid-South. Though hillbilly music was not popular in Nashville, it had many fans in the hills and hollows outside town. It was with an eye to a market for inexpensive "industrial life" insurance policies that WSM hired popular announcer and program developer George D. Hay away from WLS in Chicago on the very first day WSM went on the air.

Hay had developed WLS' already-popular "Barn Dance" program and started within weeks to sow the seeds of hillbilly entertainment at WSM in the autumn of 1925. Hay turned to popular regional part-time entertainers Dr. Humphrey Bate and his band (whom Hay would insist on renaming The Possum Hunters to maximize his own "hillbilly" vision of the show) to debut rural string band music on WSM. In rapid succession he added special appearances by old-time fiddler Uncle Jimmy Thompson, then vaudeville circuit banjo player/singer/raconteur Uncle Dave Macon.

By the end of 1925 Hay had the nucleus of the WSM "Barn Dance" program, adding black harmonica virtuoso DeFord Bailey and the duo of Sam and Kirk McGee to the roster in early 1926. The show was instantly popular, and Hay soon enlarged the tiny WSM studio with a glass enclosure. He added several hundred seats to an adjoining room to accommodate the onlookers who came in from surrounding counties each Saturday night to see the entertainers. As the WSM "Barn Dance" took shape in 1926, old-time fiddling, raucous singing and banjo playing, sentimental ballads, event songs, hoedown music, and rural humor became the foundation of what would become the "Grand Ole Opry" in December 1928. The WLS show was a mix of styles, but Hay kept the WSM "Barn Dance" as rural and unpolished as possible.

By late 1928 WSM was receiving NBC network feeds, including a classical music program from New York hosted by Walter Damrosch. In what Hay always maintained was an inadvertent christening, he gave name to the Opry on December 8. Damrosch had programmed a symphonic composition approximating the sounds of a train as his final selection for the evening. Hay began announcing his own local show, brought on DeFord Bailey to play his exhilarating harmonica train number, "Pan American Blues," and said "For the past hour we have been listening to music taken largely from Grand Opera. From now on we will present *The Grand Ole Opry* . . . It will be down to earth for the earthy." The name stuck.

Milestones

- Jimmie Rodgers' popularity grows rapidly and he enjoys a $1,000-per-week vaudeville theater tour on the RKO and Loews' circuits throughout the South and Southwest.
- William Orville "Lefty" Frizzell born in Corsicana, Texas, on March 31.
- Don Gibson born in Shelby, North Carolina, on April 3.
- Vassar Clements born in Kinard, South Carolina, on April 25.
- Dave Dudley born in Spencer, Wisconsin, on May 3.
- "Rabbit" Roy Acuff, 25, is spotted by a scout for the New York Yankees while playing semi-pro baseball for L&N Railroad in East Tennessee.
- Jimmy Dean born in Plainview, Texas, on August 10.
- WLS Chicago is sold in September by Sears, Roebuck to the *Prairie Farmer* newspaper.
- Jerry Wallace born in Guilford, Missouri, on December 15.
- On the second Saturday night in December, at the beginning of what had been the WSM "Barn Dance," the name "Grand Ole Opry" is introduced.

Because black harmonica wizard DeFord Bailey led off the program the night that George D. Hay renamed the WSM "Barn Dance" show, Bailey is credited with being the first person to perform on the "Grand Ole Opry." Among "Opry" artists recording in an ad hoc setting in 1928 for Victor, Bailey was one of the artists at Nashville's first recording session.

Born in Carthage, Tennessee, he was "discovered" by Dr. Humphrey Bate. A small man with a bad limp, Bailey became one of the most popular performers of the "Opry" in its early years,

touring with numerous "Opry" acts, especially Uncle Dave Macon, Roy Acuff, and Bill Monroe, but nearly always being paid less for his appearances than the white acts. Only Uncle Dave Macon stood up for Bailey on tours, often refusing to stay in hotels that wouldn't accept Bailey, though he generally had to vouch to the hotel manager that Bailey was his valet.

Bailey's repertoire was limited. Through the 1930s, his appearances on the "Opry" became gradually fewer, until he devolved into something of a mascot for the show. Unwilling or unable to write

new tunes that could be cleared through Broadcast Music Inc. (BMI) at the time of the broadcast industry's ban on American Society of Composers, Authors, and Publishers (ASCAP) compositions, he was dropped from the "Opry" cast in the early 1940s. Embittered, he opened a shoeshine parlor in Nashville, and for the rest of his life generally refused to perform publicly, record, or talk much about his experiences in country music. Nevertheless, until the advent of Charley Pride in the 1970s, Bailey was country music's lone African-American star.

DeFord Bailey—One of the very first Grand Ole Opry stars. credit: Courtesy of the Grand Ole Opry

All but forgotten by the country music establishment today, Bradley Kincaid was "the voice" of true mountain folk music in the genre's early decades. As a radio and recording artist he was very popular, and his music represented a seed that spawned the folk revival in the 1950s and 1960s.

Kincaid went to Chicago in 1924, singing songs of his Cumberland Mountains home for parties in order to support his college courses in night school. He was "discovered" performing with the Chicago YMCA College Quartet on WLS in 1927.

First on WLS and then through the 1930s and early 1940s at a series of Midwest and Northeastern stations (KDKA, WGY, WBZ, WTIC, WHAM and WLW), Kincaid's unadorned tenor voice and simple guitar accompaniment popularized the pure mountain music of his East Kentucky childhood, songs such as "Barbara Allen" and "Sweet Kitty Wells." He recorded for a variety of labels, but his big-money sideline was selling songbooks. This fact cannot have escaped folk song collector John Avery Lomax when he decided to help free folk singer Leadbelly from a Louisiana prison and take him to New York to popularize him in the late 1930s.

Though Kincaid was a true son of Appalachian culture, he was academically accomplished as well as being a radio performer and songbook compiler. He deeply resented having his music called "hillbilly." Kincaid was a franchise player at any station on which he appeared until a stretch from 1944–1949, when he was overwhelmed by modern country performers such as Roy Acuff and Ernest Tubb on the "Grand Ole Opry." Soon after that he tried radio station ownership and retired in the early 1950s to run a music store in Springfield, Ohio. His most interesting tangential contribution to commercial country music was having given Marshal "Grandpa" Jones his stage name while Jones worked with Kincaid between 1935 and 1938.

WLS Barn Dance star Bradley Kincaid (with guitar) on one of his regular folk song collecting expeditions. (ca. 1926–1929) credit: Bob Millard Collection

Most Important Records

"I'm Thinking Tonight Of My Blue Eyes" Carter Family / Victor
"My Clinch Mountain Home" Carter Family / Victor
"My Carolina Sunshine Girl" Jimmie Rodgers / Victor
"Foggy Mountain Top" Carter Family / Victor
"Desert Blues" Jimmie Rodgers / Victor

Milestones

- Billy Walker born in Ralls, Texas, on January 14.
- Bradley Kincaid makes his first recordings in a fully equipped studio, for Brunswick.
- Sonny James (James Loden) born in Hackleburg, Arkansas, on May 1.
- Jimmie Rodgers purchases a $50,000 mansion near a tuberculosis sanitarium in Kerrville, Texas that he names "Blue Yodeler's Paradise." He will live there only one year.
- Buck Owens born in Sherman, Texas, on August 12.
- Leroy Van Dyke born in Spring Fork, Missouri, on October 4.
- Stoney Edwards born in Seminole, Oklahoma, on December 24.

1929

The Delmore Brothers, Alton
and Rabon.
credit: In the Southern Folklife
Collection, University of North
Carolina, Chapel Hill

THE 1930S
TRANSITION

The 1930s was a period of change and creative growth in hillbilly music. Many "stars" of the genre from the previous decade were already middle-aged-and-older men when they began recording and appearing on radio and vaudeville stages. Young men and a handful of young women rushed into the spotlight as the 1930s dawned. The sheer number of artists recording and performing old-time fiddle, traditional string band, and minstrel music since 1923 virtually guaranteed that mass media exposure would wear out the existing body of folk music and nineteenth century Tin Pan Alley songs enjoyed in Southern rural circles. Traditional folk music became a minority genre under the "hillbilly" umbrella. New music was needed if new artists were to make their marks. Persistent strains of the old music served as the core for stylistic experimentation.

By 1930 a legitimate professional country music industry was developing, decentralized as yet, but with a new generation of musicians and songwriters who intended to make a living from performing music. Their commercial models included the musical synthesis and charisma of Jimmie Rodgers, Bradley Kincaid's profitable mail order songbook sales, and Uncle Dave Macon's barnstorming concert business. The dominant musical influence was Rodgers. Among the artists copying Rodgers' style, and often recording his works or derivative compositions, were Gene Autry, Jimmie Davis, Hank Snow, and Ernest Tubb. Of these, Autry and Davis were so good that their early recordings are virtually indistinguishable from Rodgers'.

A whole category of artists from the 1930s are grouped by scholars as "transitional artists." Their accomplishments represented a step in the evolution of country music, though their styles in this decade (or the acts themselves) did not survive as emulated influences. Included in this category were the Monroe Brothers (Charlie and Bill) whose pre-bluegrass experiments with driving high-tempo rhythms, high-lonesome harmonies, and mandolin replacing fiddle as lead instrument launched them on paths that led directly to what we now know as bluegrass music.

The soft-voiced, precision harmonies, and instrumental perfection of the Delmore Brothers' (Alton and Rabon), as well as their blend of blues and traditional Southern folk music (their boogie synthesis came in the 1940s), advanced the professional standards set by the Skillet Lickers and the musical synthesis begun by Jimmie Rodgers. The Blue Sky Boys, another brother act (Bill and Earl Bollick), took traditional string band music as far as it could go with professionalism but ultimately could not change with the times. They represented a living connection with the urban folk music boom that began in the late 1940s in New York with Leadbelly, Pete Seeger, and Woody Guthrie.

The Callahan Brothers (Bill and Joe), on the other hand, proved that traditional sounds were adaptable, as they migrated across the country from one radio region to the next over the decade. They pioneered the Western swing sound by letting their fiddle band music be effected by Southwestern styles. The Carlisle Brothers were noted for novelty, blues, and risque numbers through the 1930s, and Cliff Carlisle's blues dobro on a Jimmie Rodgers' session put the Hawaiian steel guitar on the road to its ultimate honky-tonk sound. Other brother acts, the Mainers (Wade and J.E.) and the Dixon Brothers, made contributions (Dorsey Dixon of the Dixon Brothers wrote one of Roy Acuff's early hits, "Wreck On The Highway"). Their successes were notable in their regions, but basically they were products of and for their times.

The national economy hit the skids in the 1930s, impacting the record business dramatically. From 1927 to 1932, record sales in America plummeted from sales of 104 million units per year to an anemic six million. Mainstream pop records were now priced around 75 cents to $1.25, a steep price for a farmer, coal miner, or railroad worker to pay. Before the Depression, records had cost as little as 25 cents. Until the arrival of Decca Records in 1934 as a budget label with top-

The Callahan Brothers, Bill and Joe.
credit: In the Southern Folklife Collection, University of North Carolina, Chapel Hill

name talent, hillbilly music became a form best exploited on radio and via the grind of personal appearances.

Country music radio shows proliferated and were not limited to the Southeast. WSM executive David Stone left Nashville for KSTP in Minneapolis/St. Paul and created the "Sunset Valley Barn Dance" program. The "Iowa Barn Dance Frolic" was established on WHO (Des Moines) in 1932. The following year, at WWVA in Wheeling, West Virginia, the Capitol Theater became the original home of the "Wheeling Jamboree," an important early forum for such artists as "Little" Jimmy Dickens, Wilma Lee and Stoney Cooper, Hank Snow, and Hawkshaw Hawkins. John Lair left WLS and established his "Renfro Valley Barn Dance" in 1937. The "Louisiana Hayride" and the "Old Dominion Barn Dance," of Shreveport and Richmond, respectively, are examples of programs that have been revived in the 1990s, though greatly reduced in scope and importance.

The WLS "Barn Dance" grew by leaps and bounds during this decade, starting in 1930 with the addition of Gene Autry to the cast, on the heels of his first hit record, "That Silver-Haired Daddy of Mine." The show moved to the Eighth Street Theater in 1932 to satisfy demand for tickets. An hour's worth of the program was picked up by the Blue Network of NBC Radio in 1933, becoming "The National Barn Dance," and spreading the barn dance format further. Not even New York City was immune. In the early 1930s, WMCA broadcast a regular program sponsored by Crazy Water Crystals, starring Zeke Manners and Elton Britt. That show became the WHN "Barn Dance" in 1935, adding Tex Ritter and Ray Whitley to the cast. Manners created another show in the Big Apple called the "Village Barn Dance," originating from Greenwich Village in 1938. These were far from the most popular shows in New York, but their sheer existence illustrates how country music was beginning to permeate the entire nation.

When Louisville, Kentucky, station WHAS aired John Lair's "Renfro Valley Barn Dance" in 1937, starring Red Foley, Foley proved so popular that he was lured away by Cincinnati's WLW to host the newly created "Boone County Jamboree." In the Southwest, 50,000-watt KVOO in Tulsa, Oklahoma, developed the "Saddle Mountain Roundup" in 1938. Dust Bowl Okies migrating to California brought their appetite for country music with them, facilitating the creation of "The Hollywood Barn Dance" in southern California. Plenty of hillbilly artists of the 1930s who recorded little, if at all, owed their fame almost entirely to radio appearances; these included Grandpa Jones, Buddy Starcher, the father and son team of Asher and Little Jimmie Sizemore, and Lew Childre. In the 1930s, hillbilly artists, whether or not they recorded, were mostly a peripatetic bunch who moved from one station to another every time they exhausted the local market for concerts.

Rockola's popular 1935 model Multi-Selector jukebox.
credit: Courtesy of Country Music Magazine

Asher and "Little Jimmie" Sizemore.
credit: In the Southern Folklife Collection, University of North Carolina, Chapel Hill

Wheeling is nestled in the western corner of West Virginia. When WWVA inaugurated the "Wheeling Jamboree" program in the first week of 1933, it opened an air corridor to the Northeast for hillbilly performers, including many who would become stars in coming decades, such as Little Jimmy Dickens, Hank Snow, Wilma Lee and Stoney Cooper, and Hawkshaw Hawkins.

The station purposely beamed its signal north and east, blanketing Pennsylvania, New York, the New England states, and parts of Canada. Many Northeasterners got their first taste of hillbilly music from the "Wheeling Jamboree." "Jamboree" stars weren't all country music legends in the making, however. One of the show's longest running popular regulars was Pennsylvania ex-coal miner Andrew J. Smik, a balladeer who went by the stage name Doc Williams. Doc joined the "Jamboree" in 1937 as an emcee and singer. He didn't record until 1947 and had little impact on the record market, but he remained a regional favorite well into the 1970s.

Another long-time WWVA regular was Big Slim, the Lone Cowboy (Harry Auliffe). Big Slim had his shot at making records in the late 1930s, and one of his compositions, "Sunny Side of the Mountain," gradually found its way into the repertoire of classic country music. Auliffe and Williams were just two of the dozens of "hillbilly stars" of the 1930s whose fame was as wide as the broadcast beam of their radio home, and no wider.

The "Wheeling Jamboree" is still on the air.

WWVA Wheeling Jamboree cast.
credit: In the Southern Folklife Collection, University of North Carolina, Chapel Hill

Among the sea of stations programming hillbilly acts during "farmers hours" were a handful of big, nationally influential stations. As the ties between advertisers and hillbilly artists strengthened during the decade, radio stations picked their performers based on their understanding of the audience. While WLS and its NBC network "National Barn Dance" exposed a wide variety of sentimental, traditional, popular, and western styles in the 1930s, a series of monster stations that favored simpler styles began to spring up on the Texas-Mexico border as early as 1931. Beginning with Dr. J.R. Brinkley's powerful XER (later XERA)—with studios in Del Rio, Texas, and

Lulu Belle and Scotty Wiseman

The 1930s' best-known hillbilly duet was the husband and wife team of Lulu Belle and Scotty Wiseman, stars of WLS "National Barn Dance" and of a number of movies. They were household names. Scotty was a writer and song collector. Lulu Belle (Myrtle Cooper) was an excellent singer of comedic or sentimental tunes in duets (originally with Red Foley). They both perpetuated the mountain music influence of their North Carolina homes.

Lulu Belle was already a singer and comedy star, dressed in hillbilly gal getup of calico and high-top shoes, when she met Scotty at WLS in 1933. Scotty had sung his way through college in the Bradley Kincaid mode. He moved to Chicago and made his first recordings for the Bluebird label in 1933. His mountain stories and songs made him an instant hit on WLS, and he was invited to tour with the "Barn Dance" package shows almost immediately. He became good friends with Lulu Belle on the road, and when Red Foley's jealous wife ended their duets, Scotty stepped in. They were tagged "The Hayloft Sweethearts." Their signature tune was "Have I Told You Lately That I Love You."

They married in secret two weeks before Lulu Belle's 21st birthday, reputedly on a dare. She tickled their fans by revealing the nuptials two weeks later on the radio. Except for a brief period in the 1940s, they were WLS stars for 25 years, touring with Gene Autry, Fibber McGee and Molly, George Gobel, Red Foley, and Rex Allen and making seven full-length Hollywood movies before retiring to North Carolina in 1958. Rather than open a tourist museum or country music park in retirement, they each had post-music careers. Scotty went back to college to earn a Masters degree and Lulu Belle got herself elected to the North Carolina state legislature in the 1970s.

Lulu Belle and Scotty Wiseman.
credit: Archives of Robert K. Oermann

transmitter towers just across the border—a class of renegade stations called "border blasters" began to be a huge avenue for spreading traditional southern country music.

The real heyday of country broadcasting from the Mexican stations began in 1937 when the Pickard Family went to the border stations with the sponsorship of Peruna tonic. The original Carter Family spent their final years as a working act at XERA, from 1938 to 1941. Numerous country performers, including J.E. Mainer's Mountaineers and the Callahan Brothers, offering primarily traditional repertoires, appeared on these stations, sometimes via transcription disks.

The 1930s was also the decade of singing cowboy movies. Cowboy folksong purist Carl T. Sprague had been the pioneer in cowboy image-making and lyric themes in the 1920s, but it was Gene Autry's rise at Republic Pictures in the early 1930s as "America's Number One Singing Cowboy" that led to a large and successful film genre which created such stars as Roy Rogers, Jimmy Wakely, Tex Ritter, Johnny Bond, Sons of the Pioneers, and others. Autry's compositions in this period ranged from Southeastern to pop-Hollywood cowboy, but all were essentially "country." The songs he wrote for his films widened America's appreciation for "country music," even if his urban fans didn't realize it.

The impact of Autry's cowboy garb (more rodeo costume than trail riding gear, to be sure) gave country music a new image, one that all but replaced the bib overall, slouch hat look promoted so heavily by George D. Hay in the 1920s. Whether or not the act sang Southwestern style music, as did Bob Wills, Milton Brown, and other seminal originators of Western swing, or cowboy lyrics, the cowboy fit a positive "hero" image that America liked, as opposed to the mixed reaction image of the mountain string bands plowboy. So powerful was the cowboy image in country music that 30 years later Hawkshaw Hawkins and Ernest Tubb were still Nudie suit cowboys of the first order.

Roy Acuff, who came from gospel and string band roots and was proud of the sobriquet "hillbilly," was one of the few top country entertainers of the late 1930s who resisted the cowboy image. He threatened to walk off the set of the 1939 Hollywood film *The Grand Ole Opry* if the prop master insisted on trying to dress his band in Texas Ranger costumes. Acuff was something special, and he knew it. While Pee Wee King and a handful of others became star frontmen in the 1930s, it remained for Acuff to add the requisite charisma and emotional power to his singing to separate himself from the "singer in the band" status of most of his contemporaries. Thus, Acuff became the first real "singing star" of country music in the 1930s. After Acuff, singers stepped out in front of their faceless bands, where they remained until the 1980s, when the band Alabama brought ensembles back into vogue.

Gene Autry before he became "America's Favorite Singing Cowboy."
credit: In the Southern Folklife Collection, University of North Carolina, Chapel Hill

John R. Brinkley, born in 1885, was a fascinating, if none-too-savory, American character. Claiming to be an M.D., he had a station and a quack medical clinic in Kansas in the late 1920s, offering "goat gland transplants" that he claimed would rejuvenate the sexual energies of older men. He used country musicians of the traditional, string band vein to attract gullible rural listeners and even toured with hillbilly acts in an unsuccessful 1930 run for governor of the state. His political demise was roughly concurrent with the loss of his U.S. broadcast license, after which he set up XER (later XERA) just across the Mexican border from Del Rio, Texas.

From XERA, Brinkley expanded his ownership of border blaster stations to include XEPN and XEAW. These, as well as XEG, XERF and XENT, emitted signals ranging from twice to ten times the power of the biggest clear channel American stations. His exploits led a number of other renegade radio operators to the protection of the Texas-Mexico border, extending to the early career of Wolfman Jack, whose early 1960s border blasters programs figured prominently in the movie *American Graffiti*.

Before the 1930s were out, stations such as XERA made stars of homespun solo acts like Cowboy Slim Rinehart. Though he never had a record deal, Cowboy Slim Rinehart sold mind boggling numbers of songbooks (often featuring songs whose copyrights he did not own, whose owners he did not pay) and loads of other mail order products, from laxatives to baby chicks. Religious broadcasters who bought time slots on the X-stations tended to be less than scrupulous, occasionally offering the promise of miracles accompanied by "a genuine autographed picture of Jesus" for a suitable "love offering."

Wild-hair right-wing political speakers, no-holds-barred religious shows, and incredible claims for cancer cures gave the X-stations a bad name. In between the con men's pitches, though, traditional southern country music reached a market across rural America and parts of Canada that longed for those sounds of days gone by; nostalgic comfort in the uncertain days of Depression and social flux. "If one could endure the seemingly never-ending advertising, he could occasionally hear a hillbilly song of the best quality (over the X-stations in this period)," observed country music historian Bill Malone.

Border Radio favorites, The Pickard Family.
credit: In the Southern Folklife Collection, University of North Carolina, Chapel Hill

The story of Roy Claxton Acuff is a classic rags to riches tale. Acuff was born in a three-room shack in Maynardsville, Tennessee, in the mountains outside Knoxville, one of six children of part-time Missionary Baptist minister Neill Acuff. From his father's churches, Roy learned to sing loudly, with emotion, and to live by the Golden Rule. He seemed never to have forgotten any of those early lessons in his country music career.

In his younger days, however, he was a wild card, skipping school, shirking work, fighting and spending idle hours teaching himself to balance large objects on the tip of his nose—everything from a broom to a plowshare. He made music as a child, using cheap or homemade instruments, and his father taught him hymns and traditional British ballads. He listened to his father play fiddle on cold winter mornings before the rest of the family was up, but

he cared more about baseball than music as he grew to manhood.

Acuff was a star athlete in Knoxville high schools, earning 13 letters and the nickname "Rabbit." In 1929, Acuff landed a featherbedding job on the L&N Railroad in exchange for playing semi-pro ball for the line's East Tennessee baseball team. He was invited to a tryout for the New York Yankees, but before the tryout he suffered a sunstroke. At 25, his baseball career was over. He had a series of relapses through the next several months and wound up bedfast throughout 1930. He was housebound all through 1931, as well.

While bedridden, Acuff began playing his father's old fiddle, learning by listening to Gid Tanner and Fiddlin' John Carson records. His sister, a semi-professional singer, gave him some singing lessons. In 1932, a neighbor who ran a traveling medicine show heard Roy play fiddle

on the front porch and invited him to join his show. Because it was night work, Acuff agreed. Singing, fiddling, acting in skits in drag or blackface, Acuff learned to sell Mocatan Tonic and to entertain rural people. His success at both brought him out of a long depression and started him on the road to legend.

By 1933, Acuff was leading his own band, the Tennessee Crackerjacks, later the Crazy Tennesseans. They worked on Knoxville radio and played area dances, getting their first chance to record in 1936 for ARC, the company that produced records for a variety of mail order catalog labels. They recorded one of Acuff's signature songs, "Great Speckled Bird," for the first time during these sessions.

Oddly, Acuff blew his first audition for the "Grand Ole Opry" in 1938. Most acts on the show in that year were instrumental, and Acuff's vocals were poor on that occasion. When he became a star on the show later that year, it was because of his singing. He became the first major hillbilly singing star and catapulted the "Opry" into the national spotlight.

Acuff was a serious creative force in country music through the 1940s. His partnership with Fred Rose in Acuff-Rose Publications in the early 1940s established country song publishing in Nashville for the first time. He was a generous sponsor of other talents, particularly Minnie Pearl, and became an elder statesman/ spokesman for country music beginning in the 1950s, when rock 'n' roll threatened it. He never relinquished his position as "King of Country Music" and chief figurehead of the "Grand Ole Opry," living out his final years in a home built next to the back door of the Opryhouse in the middle of Opryland theme park.

Roy Acuff.
credit: Bob Millard Collection

Emerging as the star of the "Grand Ole Opry" almost as soon as he became a regular member at the beginning of 1938, Acuff was at once a modern star and an old-time throwback. A product of the old-time gospel, mountain music, and the Southeastern medicine show, as well as a proponent of fiddle breakdowns, Acuff was most of all a sincerely emotional singer who wore his religious feelings and old-time values on his sleeve. His popularity helped push the "Opry" from the old East Nashville Dixie Tabernacle to the imposing 2,000-seat War Memorial Auditorium, which was attached to the State Capitol. Even the advent of a 25-cent ticket fee did not deter people from packing the house for each performance of the "Opry."

Aside from Jimmie Rodgers, who was primarily a recording star, radio was the main avenue to fame for the majority of hillbilly entertainers in the 1930s, as it was for most other musicians in the medium's so-called golden years. Though WLS' "National Barn Dance" program was by far the dominating country music program of this decade, Acuff put WSM on the road to eventual succession. Acuff's popularity led to the "Opry's" invitation in October 1939 to feed a 30-minute segment into the 26-station NBC Red Network's "The Prince Albert Show," named after its tobacco company sponsor. Acuff was the hands-down choice of the network to host that important segment of the Saturday night "Opry," causing hard feelings among some longer-established stars of the show. Acuff took it all in stride. He was humble when it came to his stardom; he'd work until he dropped, do anything he had to do to promote the "Opry" and country music. Yet he was proud of himself, his Tennessee mountain background, and his music, and, in his salad days, he'd just as soon punch a heckler in the nose as not.

A noteworthy development on that venerable WSM show in October 1939 was the successful audition of Bill Monroe and his Blue Grass Boys. Of all the artists of his period, Acuff was the hardest working entertainer, while Monroe was the greatest innovator and stylist. As bandleaders and musicians, both men would have enormous impact on country instrumentation in the decades to follow. Fiddle was still the chief lead instrument in hillbilly bands in 1939, but it was being challenged by new sounds and instruments with entirely different emotional and dynamic possibilities. Bill Monroe made his mandolin a driving lead instrument to challenge the fiddle. Acuff, though a fiddler himself, soon decided that Clell Summey's blues-laced dobro, that pining lonesome coloration of gospel, hobo, and train songs, should be the key element to his sound. Acuff's focus on the dobro to set his ensemble sound apart from the pack led directly to the bluegrass adoption of the acoustic dobro and the honky-tonkers' development of the pedal steel in later years.

The legends of Monroe and Acuff would grow larger after their most influential years as radio and recording stars.

Johnny Wright and the Harmony Girls, on WSIX, Nashville, in 1936, (l–r) Louise Wright (Johnny's sister), Wright, and Muriel Deason (Kitty Wells). Louise soon quit singing and married Wright's next partner, Jack Anglin.
credit: Bob Millard Collection

Monroe Brothers, Charlie and Bill.
credit: In the Southern Folklife Collection, University of North Carolina, Chapel Hill

Monroe would be known as the "Father of Bluegrass," but Acuff, champion of the hillbilly and string band traditions to the end, would keep the nickname given to him by baseball great Dizzy Dean, who introduced him at a big hillbilly show at the old downtown Dallas Sportitorium during World War II as "King of The Hillbillies," soon modified to "King of Country Music."

1930

Most Important Records[1]

"Lulu Wall"/"Fern Valley" Carter Family / Victor
"Frankie and Johnny" Jimmie Rodgers / Victor
"I Left My Gal In The Mountains" Gene Autry / ARC
"Worried Man Blues"/"The Cannonball" Carter Family / Victor
"Naw, I Don't Wanta Be Rich" Carson Robison / Victor

Milestones

↤ The Dixieliners (Kirk and Sam McGee with fiddler Arthur Smith), one of the all-time best "Opry" string bands, join the "Grand Ole Opry."

↤ John Lair forms The Cumberland Ridge Runners, which featured Lost John Miller and Red Foley. They become WLS "Barn Dance" favorites.

John Lair and his Cumberland Ridge Runners.
credit: In the Southern Folklife Collection, University of North Carolina, Chapel Hill

1. In the early 1930s, Gene Autry's recordings for the American Record Company (ARC) came out on a number of ARC sublabels or master lease arrangements through various mail order catalogs and department stores, including Melotone, Conqueror, Clarion, and Perfect Records labels—sometimes all at the same time. Autry also recorded under various pseudonyms, including Johnny Dodds, John Hardy, Overton Hatfield, Gene Johnson, and others, though his important disks were done under his own name.

Bob Wills' recordings for Okeh and Vocalion represent simultaneous releases for both Columbia sublabels. Roy Acuff's recordings for Columbia might come out as Columbia or Okeh, for reasons best known to that company. Bluebird, for whom many country acts recorded in this period, was a sublabel of RCA Victor Records, on which Victor marketed music to rural audiences.

Women had a rough go of it as country entertainers in the early days. Three who overcame biases and roadblocks to become stars in the 1930s were Patsy Montana and sisters Millie and Dolly Good, the latter two known as the Girls of the Golden West. They were all-around entertainers, writing many of their own tunes, playing instruments, and developing vocal styles that made them instantly recognizable to their many radio fans.

Patsy Montana was a WLS "Barn Dance" star, noted for her intricate Swiss-style yodelling abilities. College-educated, she started out professionally with an all-girl trio, the Montana Cowgirls. Stuart Hamblen nicknamed her Patsy, and Montana became her stage name when, after a few small movie roles, she left California and went to work on WLS with the Prairie Ramblers.

In 1935, she wrote and recorded what was to become the first million-selling country record for a female, "I Want To Be A Cowboy's Sweetheart." Upbeat and packed with tricky yodelling, it remains the test of a true cowgirl singer. Modern acts, such as the winsome Texas ensemble The Dixie Chicks, make it a signature tune.

Girls of the Golden West claimed to have been born in remote Muleshoe, Texas, but were actually from Mt. Carmel, Illinois. Garbed in fringed cowgirl costumes, they became big WLS "National Barn Dance" hits in 1933. They took their stage name from the Bret Harte story and Puccini opera of that title. Their first big radio job was on XER in Del Rio, Texas, but they quit when they found out they were being paid only dime-on-the-dollar compared to male singers. When they became popular at WLS, they began writing much of their own material, songs like "Lonely Cowgirl" and "Give Me a Straight Shootin' Cowboy" that captured the flavor of the romantic West from a female viewpoint.

The Good sisters (original family name being Goad) married in the mid-1930s and moved to star slots at WLW to work the "Renfro Valley Barn Dance" and the "Boone County Jamboree" through the 1940s. They were famous for exquisitely pure close harmonies, harmony yodelling, and wordless high falsetto voicings. They became the first really popular female country duet, blazing the trail for the Davis Sisters and, much later, The Judds. They quit working in 1949.

Patsy Montana.
credit: In the Southern Folklife Collection, University of North Carolina, Chapel Hill

- Roy Drusky born in Atlanta, Georgia, on June 22.
- Doyle Wilburn born in Hardy, Mississippi, on July 7.
- Personally influenced by John Avery Lomax and other Texas folksong collectors of the time, Woodward Maurice "Tex" Ritter leaves law school to sing in New York City. He gets the lead in *Green Grow The Lilacs* on Broadway (which later became *Oklahoma.*)
- Ken Maynard becomes Hollywood's first singing cowboy, appearing in the film *Song of the Saddle.*
- Singer/songwriter Tommy Collins born in Oklahoma City, Oklahoma, on September 28.
- Mexican "border blaster" station XER goes on the air on October 21 with studios in Del Rio, Texas.

1931

Most Important Records

"Blue Yodel #8 (Muleskinner Blues)" Jimmie Rodgers / Victor
"Moonlight and Skies" Jimmie Rodgers / Victor
"New Salty Dog" Allen Brothers / Victor
"Lonesome Valley" Carter Family / Victor
"Strawberry Roan" Beverly Hillbillies / Brunswick

Milestones

- Charlie Poole, hillbilly banjo player, one of the originators of the three-finger picking style, dies on May 21 of a heart attack. His most popular recording was "Don't Let Your Deal Go Down Blues."
- Bob Wills, Milton Brown, and Herman Arnspiger form a band called the Alladin's Laddies. The act later becomes the Fort Worth Doughboys, then the Light Crust Doughboys.
- Leonard Slye (Roy Rogers) and his father leave their southern Ohio farm for Tulare, California, in search of work as migrant farm workers. There, during the following five years, Slye works as a singer and musician. His first act is The Slye Brothers, which he forms with a cousin.
- Boxcar Willie (Lecil Travis Martin) born in Sterratt, Texas, on September 1.
- Harry Stone (who had become "Grand Old Opry" manager in 1930) makes his first move to update the program, hiring its first truly professional act, the smooth-harmonied vocal trio, The Vagabonds (Herald Goodman, Dean Upson, and Curt Poulton).
- Teddy Wilburn born in Hardy, Mississippi, on November 30.
- Bobby Van Osborne, of the bluegrass duo the Osborne Brothers, born in Hyden, Kentucky, on December 7.
- Skeeter Davis (Mary Frances Penick) born in Dry Ridge, Kentucky, on December 30.

Two Texas musicians, Bob Wills and Milton Brown, pushed the fiddle far beyond the string band repertoire in the 1930s in their partnership in the seminal Texas swing ensemble, the Light Crust Doughboys. Wills came from a poor but musical family, soaking up influences from Southern folk, blues, Cajun, jazz, and Mexican dance traditions that surrounded him in childhood. Brown was a church singer who, with his brother Durwood, joined Wills and Herman Arnspiger in the Wills Fiddle Band in 1930.

This quartet played as the Alladin's Laddies on several early Fort Worth, Texas, radio stations, merging swing and jazz with country dance styles, as did the people around that cowboy town

in those days. *Time* magazine later observed of Wills that "His trick was to bring ranch-house music nearer to the city."

Wills' band was sponsored in January 1931 by the Burrus Mill and Elevator Company, and renamed after one of its products, Light Crust Flour. Burrus President W. Lee O'Daniel attached himself to the band as emcee and manager. He used them on radio and in public performances to multiply flour sales. Brown also became a salesman for Light Crust Flour, while Arnspiger and Wills worked as dock loaders and truck drivers when they weren't playing music for the company.

O'Daniel put his commercial purposes ahead of the band's interests, however. Arnspiger left the

group in 1932 and by August 1934 both Wills and Brown were gone from the Light Crust Doughboys to form their own influential bands— Bob Wills' Texas Playboys and Milton Brown and his Musical Brownies. These acts became the two most potent popularizers of the hopped-up Western swing style.

O'Daniel reorganized the Doughboys (most of the originals eventually went to work for Wills) and continued to advertise flour through radio shows and performances. He eventually used his notoriety built through flour sales and Western swing to make successful runs for Texas governor and the U.S. Senate, taking the latter race from Lyndon Johnson in 1941.

The Original Light Crust Doughboys.
credit: In the Southern Folklife Collection, University of North Carolina, Chapel Hill

1932

Most Important Records

"That Silver-Haired Daddy of Mine" Gene Autry & Jimmie Long / ARC
"My Mary" Stuart Hamblen / Victor
"Mother the Queen of My Heart"/"Rock All Our Babies To Sleep" Jimmie Rodgers / Victor
"Twenty-One Years" Bob Miller / Victor
"Moonlight and Skies" Gene Autry / ARC

Milestones

- Faron Young born in Shreveport, Louisiana, on February 25.
- Johnny Cash born in Kingsland, Arkansas, on February 26.
- Dick Curless born in Fort Fairfield, Maine, on March 17.
- WLS "Barn Dance" program moves to the Eighth Street Theater, where it will remain for the next 25 years.
- Carl Perkins born in Tiptonville, Tennessee, on April 9.
- George Gobel becomes a cast member on the WLS "Barn Dance," using the stage name "The Little Cowboy."
- Homer and Jethro begin working together.
- J.E. Mainer, a North Carolina champion regional old-time fiddling competition winner, becomes a full-time musician, getting work on WBT radio in Charlotte. His band consists of J.E. and Wade Mainer, Daddy John Love, and Zeke Morris. In honor of their sponsor, Crazy Water Crystals laxative, they name the group the Crazy Mountaineers.
- Milton Brown quits the Light Crust Doughboys to organize his own band, the Musical Brownies. He is replaced by Tommy Duncan.
- RCA Victor Records signs Wilf Carter (Montana Slim), who becomes the first major country star from Canada.
- Patsy Cline (Virginia Hensley) born in Winchester, Virginia, on September 8.
- Bonnie Owens born in Blanchard, Oklahoma, on October 1.
- Dottie West born in McMinnville, Tennessee, on October 11.

J.E. Mainer and the Crazy Mountaineers.
credit: In the Southern Folklife Collection, University of North Carolina, Chapel Hill

Milton Brown and his Musical Brownies.
credit: In the Southern Folklife Collection, University of North Carolina, Chapel Hill

Most Important Records

"Yellow Rose of Texas" Gene Autry & Jimmie Long / ARC
"Peach Pickin' Time In Georgia" Jimmie Rodgers / Victor
"The Death of Jimmie Rodgers" Gene Autry / ARC
"There's an Empty Cot in the Bunkhouse Tonight" Gene Autry / ARC
"Seven Years with the Wrong Woman" Bob Miller / Victor

The Death of Jimmie Rodgers

Jimmie Rodgers was barely able to get a job singing in restaurants before he recorded for Victor Records in Bristol, Tennessee, in August 1927. He toured hard in his heyday, though he was already in poor health when he got his big break via Victor talent scout and song publisher Ralph Peer. He spent $50,000 (a massive amount in those days) on a mansion in Kerrville, Texas, in part because it was near a tuberculosis sanitarium. He rested for a time there at "Blue Yodeler's Paradise," but by 1930 he moved to San Antonio, Texas, to do a radio show on KMAC.

Rodgers' talent, pluck, and outgoing friendliness in the face of tuberculosis made him a true hero to his fans, an idol in a day when people desperately needed one. His style prompted many imitators in the late 1920s through the mid-1930s, such as budding artists Gene Autry, Jimmie Davis, Frankie Marvin, Bill Boyd, Cliff Carlisle, and Elton Britt, among others. Between 1930 and 1933, his fame and prosperity continued to grow, unaffected by the Depression. But his relentless touring and recording schedule—he wrote, co-wrote, or otherwise got his

Jimmie Rodgers in Kerrville, Texas.
credit: In the Southern Folklife Collection, University of North Carolina, Chapel Hill

name added to the equivalent of two modern record albums per year—doomed him to the ravages of tuberculosis.

Mocking his disease with "T.B. Blues" and "Whippin' That Old T.B.," he was never morbid. He made and spent money like it was going out of style. As his health began to fail seriously in 1932, he simply worked and played harder and faster, and ended up creating a country music legend in the way he died.

Jimmie Rodgers had been in the hospital or convalescing at home for four months before going to New York City in May 1933 to record one last time for RCA Victor. A cot was set up in the studio so he could lay down between takes. He knew he was dying and felt that these last recordings were all he would leave his wife Carrie and daughter

Anita. "I'm not going to lay around one of those hospital rooms and count the fly specks on the wall," he had said about sanitarium life.

After 12 songs were cut, the last being "Fifteen Years Ago," Rodgers went sightseeing on Coney Island, where he began hemorrhaging. He went back to his room at the Taft Hotel, where he lapsed into a coma and died on May 26, at the age of 35. The outpouring of grief in rural America at his death was amazing. An unheard of number of tribute records followed his death, including the Gene Autry hits composed by Bob Miller, "The Life of Jimmie Rodgers" and "The Death of Jimmie Rodgers." "Live fast, die young" is thought of as Hank Williams' legend, but Jimmie Rodgers set that standard first.

Milestones

- Stu Phillips born in Montreal, Canada, on January 19.
- WLS "Barn Dance" goes on NBC Blue Network as the "National Barn Dance."
- Pee Wee King joins the cast of the WRJN "Badger State Barn Dance."
- Roy Clark born in Meherrin, Virginia, on April 15.
- Willie Nelson born in Fort Worth, Texas, on April 30.
- Jimmie Rodgers dies of tuberculosis in the Taft Hotel in New York City on May 6, two days after completing his last recording session for RCA Victor.
- Conway Twitty (Harold Jenkins) born at Friars Point, Mississippi, on September 1.
- Lulu Bell teams up with Scotty Wiseman; they soon become one of the best-loved acts in the long history of the WLS "Barn Dance/National Barn Dance."
- Leon McAuliffe, 16, becomes the youngest member of the Light Crust Doughboys.
- Ken Maynard stars in *The Strawberry Roan*, thought to be the first Western picture titled for a Western song. The trade newspaper, *Variety*, calls these pictures "oaters," after the grain fed to horses.
- Tompall Glaser, of the Glaser Brothers, born in Spaulding, Nebraska, on September 3.
- Songwriter Fred Rose works for WSM radio for a brief time.
- Floyd Cramer born in Samti, Louisiana, on October 27.

Most Important Records

"The Last Roundup" Gene Autry / ARC
"Brown's Ferry Blues" Delmore Brothers / Bluebird
"Down Yonder"/"Back Up and Push" Gid Tanner and the Skillet Lickers / Bluebird
"Beautiful Texas" Light Crust Doughboys / Victor
"Beautiful Texas" Jimmie Davis / Bluebird
"I'm Here To Get My Baby Out of Jail" Karl and Harty / Oriole

Milestones

- Tex Ritter signs to record for American Record Company and is host of "Cowboy Tom's Roundup" radio program on New York City's WHN.
- Jim Ed Brown born in Sparkman, Arkansas, on April 1.
- Gene Autry, already a radio and recording star, gets his big break in Hollywood in a cameo singing appearance in the Ken Maynard film *In Old Santa Fe*.
- Bob Wills and his Playboys move their home base from Waco, Texas, to Tulsa, where they become regulars on KVOO radio and change the name of the band to the Texas Playboys.

Gov. Jimmie Davis.
credit: In the Southern Folklife Collection, University of North Carolina, Chapel Hill

By 1934, the Great Depression had killed off many small independent labels created to record hillbilly music, including Paramount, Black Swan, and Herwin. Okeh, the first label to address black and white folk music in the 1920s, was on the verge of folding. With record prices running from 75 cents to $1.50, hillbilly records other than Jimmie Rodgers' were a hard sell. The whole record industry seemed on the brink of collapse. Then came Jack Kapp and American Decca.

Kapp had been a talent scout for Brunswick Records but saw in adversity a tremendous opportunity to lower prices and sell more records. He arranged to bring to America a branch of the British label, Decca Record Company, Ltd., in business since 1927. American Decca literally redefined the record business in the autumn of 1934. During a recording lull due to a strike by union musicians, Kapp raided other major labels for top-name talent, including Bing Crosby, the Mills Brothers, and Guy Lombardo. Kapp came to terms with the union, then priced Decca platters at 35 cents and forced the entire industry to follow suit.

Jack Kapp was rare among record company executives—he actually liked hillbilly music. Though Decca established studios in New York and Chicago, he let his younger brother David record a wide assortment of up and comers in their own backyards, in places such as Dallas, Houston, San Antonio, New Orleans, Charlotte, and Hollywood. David Kapp found that many hillbilly and Western artists made better records while recording in familiar surroundings. Decca's first country sessions were in Hollywood via field recording equipment in temporary quarters, featuring Stuart Hamblen and, a few days later, Sons of the Pioneers. Jimmie Davis became Decca's first country star, initially with near-perfect imitations of the late Jimmie Rodgers' style. Davis remained with the label for the next 40 years.

Decca was one of the first conscious cross-marketers of country songs, bringing out a pop hit Bing Crosby version of Al Dexter's "Pistol Packin' Mama" in 1934, just months after Dexter's original had become a hillbilly market jukebox smash.

Priced to sell and gunning for quality, Decca's country roster was formidable, including at one time or another such "name" artists as Hamblen, Davis, Gene Autry, Ernest Tubb, the Carter Family, the Carlisle Brothers, Roy Rogers, Sons of the Pioneers, Vernon Dalhart, Bradley Kincaid, Al Dexter, Cindy Walker, Jimmy Wakely, Eddie Dean, Floyd Tillman, Arky the Arkansas Woodchopper, the Delmore Brothers, the Callahan Brothers, Red Foley, Clayton McMichen's Georgia Wildcats, Tex Ritter, Curly Fox, Tex Owens, Texas Ruby and Zeke, Uncle Dave Macon with Sam and Kirk McGee, and Milton Brown & His Musical Brownies.

Not all Decca artists of the 1930s and early 1940s were names we remember, though if only for their unique names some are worth recounting: The Red Headed Briar Hopper (LeRoy Anderson), Pie Plant Pete, the Virginia Possum Tamers, the Jackson County Barn Owls, the Corn Cob Crushers, and the Viking Accordion Band.

Stuart Hamblen.
credit: In the Southern Folklife Collection, University of North Carolina, Chapel Hill

1935

- Pee Wee King moves to Louisville with Frankie More's Log Cabin Boys band to play on the "Gene Autry Show" (they first appear on "Opry" in 1936 and are regulars from 1937 through the late 1940s).
- American Decca Records forms as a budget label, selling records for 35 cents. Stuart Hamblen and Jimmie Davis are their first country artists.
- Bob Nolan, Tim Spencer, and Leonard Slye form the Pioneer Trio, soon adding additional members and renaming themselves Sons of the Pioneers.

Most Important Records

"Tumbling Tumbleweeds" Gene Autry / ARC
"I Want To Be A Cowboy's Sweetheart" Patsy Montana / Vocalion
"Nobody's Darlin' But Mine" Gene Autry / ARC
"Nobody's Darlin' But Mine" Jimmie Davis / Decca
"Under The Double Eagle" Bill Boyd's Cowboy Ramblers / Bluebird
"Cattle Call" Tex Owens / Decca

Milestones

- Elvis Aron Presley born in Tupelo, Mississippi, on January 8; his twin brother dies at birth, a fact that will haunt Presley the rest of his life.
- Long-time Oak Ridge Boy baritone William Lee Golden born on January 12.
- Fred Rose comes back to Nashville and first attempts to write a country song.
- Canadian country pioneer "Montana Slim" Wilf Carter does his first recording sessions for Bluebird.
- Bobby Bare born in Ironton, Ohio, on April 7.
- Loretta Lynn born in Butcher's Hollow, Kentucky, on April 14.
- Cowboy singer Stanley Lealand Weed joins the WLS "Barn Dance" as the character "Tumbleweed."
- Linda Parker, tremendously popular with WLS audiences as "The Sunbonnet Girl" of John Lair's Cumberland Ridge Runners, dies August 12, at the age of 23, of peritonitis after her appendix ruptures while the band is on tour in Indiana.
- The Carter Family signs to record with American Record Company under Art Satherly.
- Hank Cochran (Garland Perry) born in Isola, Mississippi, on September 2.

Louis Marshal "Grandpa" Jones.
credit: In the Southern Folklife Collection, University of North Carolina, Chapel Hill

Most Important Records

"Mexicali Rose" Gene Autry / Vocalion
"Maple on the Hill" Mainer's Mountaineers / Bluebird
"What Would You Give In Exchange for Your Soul?" Monroe Brothers / Bluebird
"Spanish Two-Step" Bob Wills / Okeh-Vocalion

Milestones

- Roger Miller born in Fort Worth, Texas, on January 2.
- Chuck Glaser, of The Glaser Brothers, born in Spaulding, Nebraska, on February 27.
- The Carter Family moves to Decca Records.
- Mickey Gilley born in Ferriday, Louisiana, on March 9.
- Roy Acuff records for the first time, for American Records Company. He cuts 20 songs in a Chicago studio.
- The "Grand Ole Opry" moves from the Hillsboro Theater to the Dixie Tabernacle; Uncle Dave Macon is the acknowledged "star" of the show.
- Glen Campbell born in Billstown, Arkansas, on April 22.
- Roy Orbison born in Vernon, Texas, on April 23.
- The Blue Sky Boys (Bill and Earl Bollick), having been together for about a year, singing mainly traditional sad songs and gospel with incredibly tight harmonies as a duo, sign with RCA Victor Records.
- Patsy Montana becomes the first female country and western singer to sell one million copies—"I Want To Be A Cowboy's Sweetheart."
- Hank Snow signs a contract to record in Canada for RCA Victor Records.
- Tex Ritter leaves New York for Hollywood to make *Song of the Gringo*, the first of 60 singing cowboy movies he will make in his career.
- Charlie Daniels born in Wilmington, North Carolina, on October 28.

Most Important Records

"Steel Guitar Rag" Bob Wills / Okeh-Vocalion
"The Great Speckled Bird" Roy Acuff / Vocalion
"Trouble In Mind" Bob Wills / Okeh-Vocalion
"Right or Wrong" / "Get Along Home Cindy" Bob Wills / Okeh-Vocalion
"Steel Guitar Blues"/"Steel Guitar Chimes" Roy Acuff / Columbia

Milestones

- Don Everly born in Brownie, Kentucky, on February 1.

1936

The Carter Family in their final years together, a nationally popular act on border radio out of Del Rio, Texas.
credit: In the Southern Folklife Collection, University of North Carolina, Chapel Hill

1937

Pee Wee King and his Golden West Cowboys.
credit: In the Southern Folklife Collection, University of North Carolina, Chapel Hill

↦ Freddy Fender (Baldemar Huerta) born in San Benito, Texas, on June 4.
↦ Ray Pillow born in Lynchburg, Virginia, on July 4.
↦ Pee Wee King and the Golden West Cowboys appear in *Gold*

Mine In The Sky, a Gene Autry film, then join the "Grand Ole Opry," becoming the first modern big band to join that program.
↦ Tennessee Ernie Ford gets his first job on radio, as disc jockey on WOAI in Bristol, Virginia.
↦ Top box office cowboy star Buck Jones leaves Universal, which decides to replace him with a singing cowboy. Stanley Lealand "Tumbleweed" Weed, whom they give the stage name "Bob Barker," beats out Leonard Slye (Roy Rogers) for the studio contract because Slye looks too young.
↦ Leonard Slye leaves the Sons of the Pioneers to seek a film acting career, first as Dick Weston, then as Roy Rogers. Roy Rogers gets a contract with Republic Pictures a few months later.
↦ Tommy Overstreet born in Oklahoma City, Oklahoma, on September 10.

- Bluegrass great Sonny Osborne, of the Osborne Brothers, born in Hyden, Kentucky, on October 29.
- "Whisperin'" Bill Anderson born in Columbia, South Carolina, on November 1.
- Merle Travis joins Clayton McMichen's Georgia Wildcats band on WLW's "Boone County Jamboree."
- Jim Glaser, of The Glaser Brothers, born in Spaulding, Nebraska, on December 16.

Roy Rogers and Sons of the Pioneers

Ironically, the core vocalists of America's quintessential cowboy vocal group, Sons of the Pioneers, were all born outside the West. Leonard Slye was born in Ohio, Tim Spencer in Missouri, and Bob Nolan in New Brunswick, Canada. Nolan spent his teen years in Arizona, where he gained a love for the desert that would mark his songwriting career with such exquisite harmonized pictures of the West as "Cool Water" and "Tumbling Tumbleweeds."

Slye was the instigator of the original group, the Pioneer Trio. The addition of musicians Karl and Hugh Farr (who added bass vocals to the harmony mix) to Slye, Spencer, and Nolan rounded out the original Sons of the Pioneers lineup. The hot fiddle and jazz-influenced country guitar work of the Farr brothers was a crucial part of the group's overall sound.

The group was formed in California in 1933. Stoked by the relative sophistication of the L.A. audience and the success of Gene Autry as Hollywood's top singing cowboy, the group found L.A. to be a hotbed of country and western jazz innovation. Sons of the Pioneers joined the early morning show on KFWB in Hollywood, and became the third West coast band signed by Decca in 1935. They performed in the Texas Centennial with Will Rogers in 1936 because of fame accumulated via radio transcriptions, the forerunner of radio syndication.

The act worked in Charles Starrett's cowboy pictures in 1935, but Slye became ambitious to follow Autry as a screen star and left the group in 1937. Using the stage name Roy Rogers, he embarked on a screen career that would overtake Autry's own in the 1940s and translate into a popular television series in the 1950s.

People tend to remember the Sons of the Pioneers as the band that backed Roy Rogers, but it is really the addition of his replacement, Lloyd Perryman, that rounded out the group's vocal legend. Nolan and Spencer also need to be acclaimed for the music they created. Songs like "Over the Sante Fe Trail," "Happy Rovin' Cowboy," "Tumbleweed Trail," "Way Out There," and "He's Gone Up the Trail" were vastly more sophisticated than any hillbilly music at that time. The close, precise harmonies and three-part yodelling gave this unique cowboy act a wide audience through film and radio exposure, though their record sales never approached the more commercial hillbilly-in-cowboy-garb records of Autry.

It is interesting to note that when both Nolan and Spencer quit in 1949, tired of touring, Spencer's replacement was big band singer Ken Curtis, who later became famous as Deputy Festus on television's long-running show, "Gunsmoke." The lineup has changed entirely several times since, but the group's name and repertoire remain active today.

Sons of the Pioneers.
credit: In the Southern Folklife Collection, University of North Carolina, Chapel Hill

1938

Most Important Records

"Wabash Cannonball" Roy Acuff / Vocalion
"There's A Gold Mine in the Sky" Gene Autry / Okeh
"Maiden's Prayer" Bob Wills / Okeh-Vocalion
"Take Me Back to My Boots and Saddle" Gene Autry / Okeh
"When It's Springtime in the Rockies" Gene Autry / Okeh

Milestones

- Norma Jean (born Norma Jean Beasler) born in Wellston, Oklahoma, on January 30.
- Weaver Brothers and Elviry, tremendously popular touring act of the 1920s and 1930s, make the first of 17 movies they will appear in through the late 1940s for Republic Pictures.
- The Carter Family moves to Del Rio, Texas, to appear on XERA radio, where they will stay until the act breaks up in 1941.
- Original Statler Brother Lew DeWitt (writer of "Flowers On The Wall") born in Roanoke, Virginia, on March 12.
- Hoyt Axton born in Comanche, Oklahoma, on March 25.
- Warner Mack born in Nashville, Tennessee, on April 2.
- CBS buys out the ARC Records line, with Columbia becoming the main label and Okeh handling the rest of the country acts thereafter. Art Satherly, at Columbia, continues to be a smart record man in the 1930s, recording Gene Autry, Ted Daffan, Bob Wills, and Roy Acuff.
- Johnny Duncan born in Dublin, Texas, on October 5.
- Melba Moore born in Iron City, Tennessee, on October 14.
- Narvel Felts born near Bernie, Missouri, on November 1.

1939

Most Important Records

"San Antonio Rose" Bob Wills / Okeh-Vocalion
"New Spanish Two-Step"/"Spanish Fandango" Bill Boyd / Bluebird
"It Makes No Difference Now" Jimmie Davis / Decca
"Sparkling Blue Eyes" Wade Mainer / Bluebird
"Back In The Saddle Again" Gene Autry / Okeh

Milestones

- Phil Everly born in Chicago, Illinois, on January 19.
- Razzy Bailey born in Five Points, Alabama, on February 14.
- Don Williams born in Floydada, Texas, on May 27.
- Anticipating a stalemate with ASCAP over a new performance royalties contract, broadcasters organize Broadcast Music Incorporated (BMI).

- Zeke Clements and his Bronco Busters band join the "Grand Ole Opry."
- Sara and A.P. Carter are divorced.
- Red Foley becomes the first country star to have his own national radio network program, co-starring with Red Skelton on "Avalon Time."
- Gene Autry's "Melody Ranch" program is picked up by the CBS radio network, beginning an 18-year run as one of the nation's most popular Sunday afternoon programs.
- David Allan Coe born in Akron, Ohio, on September 6.
- "The Prince Albert Show," a 30-minute segment of the "Grand Ole Opry" hosted by Roy Acuff, is introduced on October 14 on the NBC Red Network.
- Bill Monroe and his Blue Grass Boys successfully audition in October to become regulars on the "Grand Ole Opry."
- Singer/songwriter Dallas Frazier born in Spiro, Oklahoma, on October 27.

Bing Crosby: "Thank God I'm A Country Boy!"

Country and western music, as the multiplicity of country styles became known in the entertainment industry in the 1930s, had broad appeal outside the rural audience, though rarely was a "country" artist marketed beyond that niche. The so-called "sophisticated" tastes of the urban audience could be tickled by country and western songs if they were sung by pop stars, such as Bing Crosby.

Crosby was a remarkably adaptable singer throughout his career, and he proved it in the 1930s and 1940s by including country and western tunes in his repertoire on a regular basis. Many of the songs were pop covers of country hit singles, while others were original western flavored numbers. The first of Crosby's western hits of this period came in 1933 when the crooner was appearing in the *Ziegfield Follies*. He recorded the Billy Hill–penned Gene Autry hit "The Last Roundup" from the show and reached the #2 position in the pop charts. There were no country charts in the 1930s, so Crosby's success might be taken as a token of how broadly popular the Western image was in America and how much appeal country music could have when allowed to reach beyond the audience it was typically limited to. Gene Autry and Roy Acuff also periodically showed up in the pop charts in the 1930s and 1940s as well, but few other country artists made the charts, regardless of sales.

Crosby's country and western hits of the 1930s and 1940s, ranging from #2 in the charts to the Top 25, included:

- "The Last Roundup" 1933
- "Home On The Range" 1933
- "I'm An Old Cowhand" 1936
- "Empty Saddles" 1936
- "My Little Buckaroo" 1937
- "There's A Gold Mine In The Sky" 1938
- "Mexicali Rose" 1938
- "Tumbling Tumbleweeds" 1940
- "Along The Sante Fe Trail" 1941
- "New San Antonio Rose" 1941
- "You Are My Sunshine" 1941
- "Deep In The Heart of Texas" 1942
- "Pistol Packin' Mama" 1943
- "Riders In The Sky" 1949

Dale

Margarete

Uncle Mose

Lew

"Mickey Pooch"

Floyd

In his early days, Floyd Tillman (r.), was featured in this WWVA Wheeling, W, Va. troupe known simply as "Lew Childre and his Act."
credit: In the Southern Folklife Collection, University of North Carolina, Chapel Hill

THE 1940S
WAR, COWBOYS, HONKY-TONK, AND BLUEGRASS

Anticipating its inevitable entry into World War II, the United States had been gearing up for war when Pearl Harbor was bombed on December 7, 1941. When draftees and enlistees left the South and Midwest, where "hillbilly" music had been most popular in the 1920s and 1930s, they took their music with them. Others relocated to labor in industries to support the war effort, taking hillbilly music to places such as Los Angeles, Detroit, Cincinnati, Chicago, and Baltimore. But with relocation came dislocation, and the lives of immigrant Southerners were changed by their new environment. Country music changed, too.

The spread of country music among the urban industrial population is reflected in a survey of Detroit's jukebox operators in 1943, which found country and western records to be the most popular. As legendary country songwriter Harlan Howard put it, "I think there were more Southerners in Detroit than there were in Alabama." More and more country musicians were electronically amplifying their six-string and Hawaiian lap steel guitars to compete with honky-tonk crowd noise. Ernest Tubb, Floyd Tillman, Al Dexter, Merle Travis, Red Foley, Pee Wee King, Roy Acuff, Eddy Arnold, and others were successful in adapting to the demands of jukebox operators, radio stations, and the expanding touring market. Less flexible acts were essentially eliminated because the rural culture that had sustained traditional string bands, brother duos, pre-bluegrass ensembles, and other transition acts had been blown away by urbanization. Mustering out of the military in peacetime, pure traditionalists such as the Blue Sky Boys were never again able to find a significant mainstream country audience.

Mass urban migration and the concentration of men in military installations created a new market for country music concerts. Between 1939 and 1942, successful major package tours were mounted by a WLS "National Barn Dance" cast that included Red Foley, Lulu Belle and Scotty, and others. The WLW "Boone County Jamboree" and the "Renfro Valley Barn Dance" kicked off traveling package tours that frequently played before crowds ranging from 5,000 to 10,000 people. Roy Acuff began a string of musical appearances in Hollywood B-movies that

Tall, craggy-featured Texas Troubadour, Ernest Tubb, had started in the 1930s, imitating Jimmie Rodgers with the encouragement and sponsorship of his widow, Carrie Rodgers. By 1941, when Tubb had his trademark hit, "Walking The Floor Over You," his voice had roughened up and dropped a notch or two from singing night after night in smokey roadhouses and dance halls. With electric guitars and his own song-writing in full bloom, he had come into his own.

The honky-tonk itself had arrived on the American scene by 1941. These county line jukebox beer halls drew rural Southerners, whether they worked in Ft. Worth meat packing plants, Birmingham steel yards, the Baltimore or Los Angeles shipyards, or the Detroit auto and airplane factories. Life in the honky-tonk was primal, sustained by the need for escape. Infidelity, hard drinking, and occasional violence mixed with amplified dance music and sad

songs of love lost set to the wailing cry of the steel guitar. Somehow, Ernest Tubb's music embodied that world better than any other.

Tubb was born on February 14, 1914 in Crisp, Texas, in the prairie land between Waco and Dallas. Self-educated and the product of a broken home, he understood the temptations, pleasures, and pains of his rural audience, though it took a while for this to come out in his music. Tubb worked on San Antonio and Ft. Worth radio stations in the mid-1930s. He signed with RCA Victor's Bluebird label in 1936 to record four songs in tribute to Jimmie Rodgers, but his real popularity came after he joined the Decca roster in 1940, when his own style emerged.

The success of "Walking The Floor Over You" led to a spate of Hollywood film work, including *Fighting Buckaroos* and *Ridin' West* with Charles Starrett. In 1943, Tubb moved to Nashville and joined the cast of the "Grand

Ole Opry," by then an NBC network program. It was in large part due to Tubb's bluesy, slipped, and bent notes, and the other vocal histrionics identified with honky-tonk, that trade publications began to search for a term to replace "hillbilly," finally settling on "country" in 1949. Tubb and fellow-Decca artist Red Foley were responsible for the first fixed studio recording sessions in Nashville, recording in 1945 in WSM's Studio B.

Tubb's legacy includes such memorable 1940s recordings as "Slippin' Around," "Blue Christmas," "Filipino Baby," and the definitive country cover of Leadbelly's "Goodnight, Irene." Though his last single was released in 1979 (a re-recording of "Walkin' The Floor . . .") and he died of emphysema in 1984, one need only listen to certain John Prine records to realize that Tubb's rugged style and phrasing continue to influence contemporary folk and country music.

Ernest Tubb.
credit: In the Southern Folklife Collection, University of North Carolina, Chapel Hill

rivaled the singing cowboy films in box office numbers and, unfortunately, acting standards.

With low production costs, profit margins on radio-linked package shows were enormous. Lulu Belle and Scotty commanded $500 and expenses for each performance, and a Midwest hillbilly ensemble playing homemade instruments (The Hoosier Hotshots) reported incomes as high as $5,000 for a single day's four-show stand. Gates like these brought country music to major theater engagements in big cities such as New York and Washington, D.C. No longer was country music relegated primarily to vaudeville stages, tent shows, medicine shows, and little schoolhouses in rural backwaters.

The influx of big money brought forward a new group of independent promoters and booking agents to the burgeoning country music scene. Joe Frank, who was the pioneer among independent country music agent/promoters, was soon joined by Col. Tom Parker, Dick Bergen, Oscar Davis, and others in representing individual artists, thus filling a niche left by the proprietary package tour operators like WLS, WLW, and WSM. Seeing the success Acuff had as a "star" singer, agents helped country convert from a string band system to a "star vocalist" system, bringing talented vocalists out to front faceless bands.

Roy Acuff and his Smokey Mountain Boys.
credit: Courtesy of the Grand Ole Opry

The whole nation seemed to open up to country music in the early 1940s. California became a hot spot for both hillbilly and Western swing, with Bob Wills and Roy Acuff breaking attendance records in the "Los Angeles County Barn Dance" venue at Venice Pier. Thanks to the "Wheeling Jamboree," Eastern Pennsylvania became one of the nation's hottest spots for country music anywhere as "country music parks" became popular. These outdoor resort venues joined a boom in country music triggered by the move of a 30-minute "Grand Ole Opry" segment called "The Prince Albert Show," hosted by Roy Acuff, to NBC's Blue Network in 1942. Commercial sponsors from Purina to Martha White flocked to identify with country music on radio. Results were positive. Alka-Seltzer, for instance, was a relatively unknown product before sponsoring the WLS "National Barn Dance."

By 1944, more than 600 country music radio shows were on the air coast to coast. WSM jumped to 50,000 watts and enjoyed a clear channel frequency that could be heard from the gulf coast of Texas to Canada, and as far west as the Rockies. NBC carried the "Opry" for a half-hour each Saturday night. The reach of WSM made the "Opry" the most coveted appearance slot in country music. It could virtually "make" national stars. But the strict Saturday night rule at WSM was a problem for performers. No matter how far away an act was performing on a Friday night, they had to be back in Nashville in time to perform on the "Opry" the following night or be kicked off the show. It severely limited performers' earning powers and caused a number of acts who could afford to do so to disassociate from the show.

The military experience was instrumental in exposing country music to a new generation of fans who previously might have poked fun at a genre of music that produced a hit like the maudlin 1936 Karl and Hardy tune "I'm Here To Get My Baby Out Of Jail." It introduced them to Acuff, Tubb, Al Dexter, and others of the new country and western style. Acuff went from a grinding tour schedule that, on a good night, would take in about $100 at the gate in 1940 to playing before crowds exceeding 16,000 in 1943. By the final months of the war, country music was so universally understood as American music that when the Japanese put up loudspeakers over Pacific theater battlefields at night, the insults would include "to hell with Franklin D. Roosevelt, to hell with Babe Ruth, to hell with Roy Acuff."

One of the most popular vehicles for expanding country music's audience in wartime was the Camel Caravan tours, hosted by Bob Hope and featuring top "Grand Ole Opry" cast members. R.J. Reynolds tobacco company organized and sponsored the first of these tours in October 1941, hiring 20 "Opry" acts, including Pee Wee King and his Golden West Cowboys, Eddy Arnold, and Minnie Pearl. By the end of 1942, the car-

Country artists had more than honky-tonk themes, Western swing, and cowboy film scores on their minds during the war. A number of top talents actually contributed patriotic ditties. Roy Acuff penned "Cowards Over Pearl Harbor," surely one of the lesser remembered tunes of the period, but popular in its day. Acuff had another, more philosophical, patriotic single toward the end of the war in "Searching for a Soldier's Grave."

Bob Wills commemorated battles with "White Cross on Okinawa" and "Stars and Stripes on Iwo Jima." Red Foley's "Smoke On The Water" was a big hit, but suffered from the popular perception that German spies with commercial radio connections were using the tune to signal Nazi submarines about U.S. merchant marines

sailing out of New York. Tex Ritter's "Gold Star In The Window" told the story of the all-too-common decoration given to a mother whose son died in the conflict. Ernest Tubb's record, "The Soldier's Last Letter," dealt similarly with the tragedy of war.

Prolific event song writer Bob Miller, whose composing career dated from the 1920s and Vernon Dalhart's recording career, wrote the biggest country-goes-to-war hit of the period. "There's A Star Spangled Banner Waving Somewhere" became a huge hit for Elton Britt in 1942–1943, achieving pop market acceptability and selling more than 1.5 million copies. Carson Robison also made the Top 10 charts in late 1945 with his doggerel "Hitler's Last Letter To Hirohito."

Elton Britt.
credit: In the Southern Folklife Collection, University of North Carolina, Chapel Hill

avan had traveled 50,000 miles, staging 175 shows at 68 army camps, hospitals, air fields, and naval installations. They helped introduce live country music to people who had never before seen it (except in Jimmy Wakely or Judy Canova movies) and handed out free packs of Camel cigarettes, hooking a generation on both. Country music was further internationalized when about 25 country bands were hired by U.S. Army Special Services Division to entertain troops in Europe in 1943.

But the war that raised the genre and a number of individual careers also took its toll. Gene Autry was riding high as the nation's top singing cowboy, more popular in the North than any other country singer, until 1942, the year Autry was drafted. Out of the limelight for the duration, Autry was soon overtaken by Roy Rogers as America's favorite singing cowboy. After his release from the service, Autry went right back to work in movies and radio but was never able to regain the levels of popularity and record sales he previously enjoyed. Though we tend to identify 1940s country music with icons such as Acuff, Autry, and Hank Williams, Eddy Arnold actually came out on top of the country music ranks for the decade, largely because of his late-decade radio and record sales successes. Emerging from the Pee Wee King band with the rustic nickname "The Tennessee Plowboy," the smooth crooner dominated the late 1940s *Billboard* country charts, edging out

Jimmy Wakely and Margaret
Whiting.
credit: Bob Millard Collection

Ernest Tubb and easily outdistancing the next nearest competitors—Red Foley, Bob Wills, and Gene Autry.

Stylistically, the cowboy song lost its punch in the country music market during the early 1940s, perhaps too innocent for a time of such great upheaval and violence, although singing cowboys remained potent movie fare. Yet the Western wear trend continued to hold sway among country performers, making it only natural that an Alabama lumber camp kid, Hank Williams, would adopt it in Shreveport in 1948, when he began making his mark on the newly established KWKH "Louisiana Hayride" radio show. Williams would come to embody in his life and music all the wild side excesses and broken heartedness that came to a generation that felt adrift after the war's end. His best music provided such a powerful window into the post-war working class psyche that his tunes would become pop hits and country standards that have yet to go out of fashion.

Bluegrass music enjoyed its most productive formative period from 1945 to 1948, evolving in ensembles led by Bill Monroe, his brother Charlie, and innumerable others adapting string bands playing in East Tennessee, Virginia, and North Carolina. The music takes its name from Bill Monroe's band, The Blue Grass Boys. Although Monroe is called "The Father of

Roy Rogers.
credit: Bob Millard Collection

Bill Monroe is universally honored as the "Father of Bluegrass." And though he was hardly alone in developing the sound, he was certainly central to its creation, both by his own imaginative efforts and by the Blue Grass Boys bands he assembled with musicians who contributed substantively to the form. Monroe owes much, stylistically, to his bachelor uncle, fiddler Pen Vandiver; his guitarist brother, Charlie; and to black guitarist Arnold Shultz. Chief among the professionals who shaped Monroe's sound are Lester Flatt and Earl Scruggs.

Bill first honed his skills with older brothers Birch and Charlie. The trio worked on the WLS "Barn Dance," teamed with square-dance outfits, then Bill and Charlie went on to become the most successful of the brother duets of the 1930s. They had personality clashes—not to mention occasional fistfights—and broke up in 1938 with Charlie starting his Kentucky Partners and Bill starting his Blue Grass Boys.

Exactly when bluegrass arrived as a style is arguable. Some say it was 1940, when Monroe merged the drive of the old-time string band guitar with Arnold Shults' bluesy timing and swing. Others say that came later—1945 to be precise—when Flatt and Scruggs joined the band. Flatt added a bass string guitar run, off the key of G, that is the best recognized lick of the genre, while Scruggs perfected a syncopated three-finger roll on banjo that revolutionized both the instrument and Monroe's sound. Still others maintain bluegrass didn't firm up as a "school of music," as Monroe calls it, until the arrival in 1948 of The Stanley Brothers—the first Blue Grass Boys imitators. Nonetheless, it is obvious that the tenure of Flatt and Scruggs with the Blue Grass Boys (1945–1948) marks the period when bluegrass music came of age.

Bluegrass is seen by some as a throwback, a nostalgic old-time music that survived the changes of the 1930s and 1940s, when country music became an industry. Nothing could be further from the truth. Bluegrass was conceived as a driving, intricate, complex, and complicated musical show-off for Monroe. He and Charlie used to dare local musicians to come on stage and keep up, much less top them. Though the keening, "high lonesome" sound of the ballad and gospel harmonies are often invoked in descriptions of the music, it would have been long forgotten had it not continued to draw red-hot players to surround a few great, rafter-rattling vocalists such as Monroe, Flatt, the Stanleys, and others.

Nearly lost in the first wave of rock 'n' roll, bluegrass survived in large degree because Flatt and Scruggs were discovered by the urban folk revalists of the late 1950s. Today, there are a few great vocalists and a world of fiery, if mechanical, pickers dominating the field. But the challenge of bluegrass instrumentals—banjo, mandolin, guitar, standup bass, and fiddle—keeps it alive as a traditional form, which it never was in its beginning nor in its heyday.

Bluegrass Music," the style is the creation of a number of stylists. Lester Flatt perfected a flat-picked guitar run in the key of G that had started with Riley Puckett of the Skillet Lickers in the 1920s. Earl Scruggs, then a very young man, polished a three-finger roll picking style on a five-string banjo without which some critics maintain no song can properly be termed "bluegrass." Both men joined Bill Monroe's Blue Grass Boys in 1945 and stayed with him through 1948. Along with Chubby Wise, Howard Watts (who used the stage name Cedric Rainwater and would later play regularly with Hank Williams' Drifting Cowboys band), and, of course, Monroe, they improvised, honed their precision and speed, and generally "invented" bluegrass instrumentalism music as we know it today. Flatt's nasal lead vocals, combined with Monroe's sailing tenor harmonies, defined the emotional singing style of the genre. Overworked and underpaid by Monroe, Flatt and Scruggs left together early in 1949. Their departure so angered Monroe that he blackballed them from the "Grand Ole Opry" until 1956.

Another significant event—portending the end of the Golden Age of Hillbilly Music and the beginning of a new era of country music—was the breakup in 1941 of the quintessential traditionalist hillbilly group, the Carter Family. Having moved to Del Rio, Texas, in 1938 to appear on XERA, the Carter clan was beset by family problems. Maybelle argued repeatedly with her cousin Sara, and Sara divorced A.P. in 1939. Never a major touring act, the Carter Family left behind a treasure trove of gospel and mountain folk music collected and adapted by A.P. through the years, plus a driving style of flat-picking guitar that would remain Maybelle's signature when she later organized her daughters into a latter day Carter Family touring group.

The Carter Family in their final years together, a nationally popular act on border radio out of Del Rio, Texas.
credit: In the Southern Folklife Collection, University of North Carolina, Chapel Hill

A trio of plagues besetting the American music industry in general during the early 1940s actually benefited country music. First, the performance rights organization ASCAP banned airplay of all music licensed by them over a fee dispute with the broadcast industry in 1940. Since ASCAP had generally refused to collect for country and other minority music forms, country composers were rewarded twice in this situation. Broadcasters organized a competing performance rights organization, Broadcast Music, Inc. (BMI), in 1941, then encouraged anyone who wanted to perform over their airwaves to compose new music that could be cleared through BMI.

Since most country music wasn't cleared through ASCAP to begin with, even older songs were able to get increased airplay during this period. Some publishers affiliated with ASCAP quit and joined BMI for their own reasons, including Chicago-based writer-publisher Fred Rose, who in 1942 formed Nashville's first country music publishing company, Acuff-Rose Publications,

Prior to 1942, there were few places to get a hillbilly song published. Ralph Peer's New York–based catalog held classic 1920s music from The Carters, Jimmie Rodgers, Rev. Andrew Jenkins, and others, and the M.M. Cole Company of Chicago published an occasional country standard, including "I'm Here To Get My Baby Out Of Jail," but Nashville, where a significant concentration of commercial country music artists lived and appeared on the "Grand Ole Opry," had no publishers for the country composer.

Fred Rose, a Chicago writer who had had his first country music success writing tunes for Gene Autry movies, withdrew from ASCAP at the height of the broadcaster's ban in 1942 and joined the newborn BMI performing rights organization. He had no Southern or rustic background, but came to understand the appeal and strength of country music watching Roy Acuff cry on the "Grand Ole Opry" while singing a sentimental ballad. At Mildred Acuff's urging, her husband joined forces in 1942 with Rose to set up a publishing company to give honest service and protection of copyrights to "Opry" artists, Acuff not being the least among them. Acuff had no interest in the business, other than financial, and it was Fred and his son Wesley Rose who built the company with many songs initially from Fred and Roy.

Acuff-Rose's Nashville office attracted others, including the Hill & Range catalog, which for a time even eclipsed Acuff-Rose's country success. The song that put Acuff-Rose into the big-time was "Tennessee Waltz," with lyrics penned by Pee Wee King and his guitarist Redd Stewart to the melody of their instrumental theme song, "No-Name Waltz." The tune became a hit in 1948 for King as well as Cowboy Copas, and seemingly was forgotten. In the blush of Tony Bennett's success in the early 1950s with Hank Williams' tunes, pop singer Patti Page remade "Tennessee Waltz" into an enormous pop and country hit in 1952.

With important songs by Acuff, Rose (under his own and a handful of pen names), Williams, King and Stewart, the Everly Brothers, Felice and Boudleaux Bryant, and Roy Orbison, Acuff-Rose Publications served as a model for Opry-connected publishing companies such as Tree International and Cedarwood Music that were established in the early 1950s. More importantly, Acuff-Rose strengthened BMI and created a way for country songwriters to actually collect money owed them for record sales and airplay. Their success and commitment to Nashville as an operating base started the tide that would eventually lead to Nashville's becoming the largest creative and business center for country music.

Fred Rose died in 1954. Acuff-Rose Publications was sold in 1985 to Opryland USA, then a subsidiary of American General Insurance Company.

Patti Page foreshadowed the Nashville Sound country trend. credit: Archives of Robert K. Oermann

and affiliated it with BMI. Creation of Acuff-Rose gave country music composers in Nashville an honest, local organization to protect their copyrights and collect royalties for record sales, just as BMI was collecting airplay royalties for the first time. Moreover, it laid the financial basis for Nashville's Music Row by encouraging other publishers to follow suit.

Compounding a general wartime shortage of raw materials with which records were made, the recording industry was plagued by another problem—a strike against recording companies by the American Federation of Musicians beginning in mid-1942. This strike, known as the Petrillo ban, lasted just over a year before Decca, facing bankruptcy, accepted the union's terms and opened the gates of industrywide compliance in the autumn of 1944. Many country artists recorded for small independent labels in this period, and these labels signed the AFM agreement without hesitation, allowing new country records to be issued throughout the strike. Jukebox operators stocked their machines even more heavily with these new records to make up for slack in the pop field. The impact of country music in this era might be measured by the fact that the first record Decca released after coming to terms with the AFM was a Bing Crosby/Andrews Sisters cover of Al Dexter's "Pistol Packin' Mama." Being able to record during the strike helped build the country music industry's service infrastructure, too. Decca recorded Ray Foley and Ernest Tubb in sessions in Nashville in 1945 in The Castle studio, marking the first country recordings in a permanent studio in a city that would become "Music City U.S.A." At this juncture, Dallas, Atlanta, Hollywood, Louisville, and a few others were just as much in the running to become the recording hub for country artists.

The viability of minority music forms, including black styles and country, was finally recognized by the music press when *Billboard* established its first, abbreviated listing of most popular country recordings, as reported by jukebox operators, in the January 8, 1944 issue. Actually, the magazine called the new chart "Most Played Juke Box Folk Records" and it was something of a catch-all, including pop artists such as Bing Crosby covering "country" records, and jazz artists such as Louis Jordan and the Nat King Cole Trio. *Billboard* added a Best Selling Retail chart for country records in 1948, followed by the first disc jockey survey measuring country record popularity in 1949. Subjective and loosely organized as they were, the survey represented the first system of quantifiable reports of the country music record industry.

Billboard had a problem figuring out what to call this music, first lumping it with jazz and blues in a "Western and Race" news column. Later in the decade, regular charts or columns covering country called the music "folk," then finally

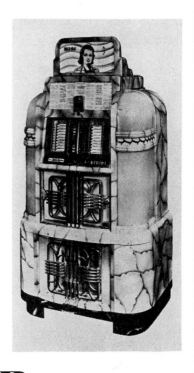

Rockola's popular 1940 model Mystic Music jukebox. credit: Courtesy of Country Music Magazine

"country and western." The latter appellation remains in use, generally out of ignorance. The country music industry resented the lumping of subgenres into an overall categorical name, especially after Western swing lost market share and singing cowboy movies disappeared. (The industry lobbied successfully in the late 1950s to get *Billboard* to drop it in favor of simply "country music.")

The country charts for 1944–1949 were principally dominated by Eddy Arnold, who left Pee Wee King's Golden West Cowboys in 1943 to eventually be promoted by Col. Tom Parker. In the rankings, Arnold was followed closely by Ernest Tubb. Bob Wills, Red Foley, and Gene Autry rounded out the top five. Al Dexter, Tex Ritter, Jimmy Wakely, Tex Williams, and Merle Travis also frequented the charts. Leading radio artists of the decade were Roy Acuff, Pee Wee King, Lulu Belle and Scotty Wiseman, and Bradley Kincaid.

Surprisingly, for all his popularity and lasting influence on country music songwriters, Hank Williams, who first recorded for Sterling Records and signed a songwriting contract with Acuff-Rose Publications in 1946, did not crack the decade's Top 10, as measured by *Billboard*. If stylistic impact is the measure, though, Williams' and Tubb's gritty honky-tonk hits would seem by far the most significant contributions to the genre, particularly at the end of the decade. However, it was Eddy Arnold who charted and sold best in the 1940s, and he alone among his peers is still alive and performing.

1940

Most Important Records

"New San Antonio Rose" Bob Wills / Okeh-Vocalion
"You Are My Sunshine" Jimmy Davis / Decca
"South Of The Border" Gene Autry / Okeh-Vocalion
"Worried Mind" Ted Daffan / Okeh
"Too Late" Jimmy Wakely & Jimmie Davis / Decca

Milestones

→ Johnny Russell born in Sunflower County, Mississippi, on January 23.
→ O.B. McClinton born in Senatobia, Mississippi, on April 25.
→ Rick Nelson born in Teaneck, New Jersey, on May 8.
→ The Wilburn Family, featuring youngsters Doyle and Teddy, join the "Grand Ole Opry." Child labor laws force them off the show six months later.
→ The first "Grand Ole Opry" tent show package tours begin across the South, headed by popular black-face comedy team Jamup and Honey, featuring Roy Acuff and Uncle Dave Macon.

Hiram "Hank" Williams has been a legend for so long, it's hard to remember that had whiskey, pills, and women not killed him at 29, he would probably still be around today. Born in 1923 with a form of spina bifida that gave him a weak constitution, Hank was a small boy raised in rough and ready fashion by a variety of relatives in and around small Alabama farms, towns, and loggers' camps. His mother, Lilly, was the strongest force in his life. His father was institutionalized when Hank was 7 with what would now be called "post-traumatic stress syndrome" from World War I.

He learned to play guitar early from a black Greenville, Alabama, street musician named Tee-Tot. By the time he was 19, Hank was a noteworthy regional bar bandleader, with Lilly booking engagements and collecting money at the door. He wrote, bought, and sold songs for a pittance. Having begun drinking at 11, he already

had a reputation as an undependable binge drinker. He was a "star" on Montgomery station WSFA, but lacked the connections to go further.

Hank married pretty, ambitious blonde Audrey Sheppard in December 1944. Theirs was a tempestuous marriage, as the money that accompanied Hank's success changed Audrey, but not Hank. In the beginning, though, she was the force that made him go to Nashville and seek Fred and Wesley Rose of Acuff-Rose Publications. The Roses got him a few hundred dollars recording his tunes for independent Sterling Records. The Sterling sessions led to a deal with a new major label, MGM Records, and Hank's first hit in 1947, "Move It On Over." Charismatic, sincere, and attuned to the lives and emotions of the rural post-war Southerner like no other artist of his time, Hank had his first chart-topping record with "Lovesick Blues," ironically a

Broadway-style pop song written by Cliff Friend around 1920.

Hank's fame rose from the South like a wind-driven grass fire. He became a regular on the "Louisiana Hayride" radio program in 1948. By the end of 1949, "Lovesick Blues" was named *Billboard's* "Best Hillbilly Record." When he finally made his debut on the "Grand Ole Opry," Red Foley had to calm the crowd down after Hank had been called back for an unprecedented six encores. Then sober for a year, Hank was made an "Opry" regular, which gave him the network platform he needed to become a truly national star. "I'm A Long Gone Daddy," "Wedding Bells," "My Bucket's Got A Hole In It," and "Mind Your Own Business" were his late 1940s hits, but the most prophetic in light of his temporary sobriety was the next to last Hank William's record of 1949: "You're Gonna Change."

Hank Williams and his Drifting Cowboys band.
credit: In the Southern Folklife Collection, University of North Carolina, Chapel Hill

Jimmy Wakely.
**credit: In the Southern Folklife
Collection, University of North
Carolina, Chapel Hill**

→ Jeannie Seely born in Titusville, Pennsylvania, on July 6.

→ Finishing school graduate Sarah Ophelia Colley auditions in her Minnie Pearl character at the War Memorial Auditorium on a late segment of the "Grand Ole Opry" in November. She becomes an "Opry" regular.

→ In December, Roy Acuff hires Minnie Pearl to perform on his tours, paying her $50 per week.

→ Ed Bruce born in Keiser, Arkansas, on December 29.

→ The five-year contract between broadcasters and ASCAP expires on December 31. ASCAP demands a greatly increased licensing fee to allow radio to play music it licenses, which is nearly all popular music written since 1884, excluding most hillbilly music and folk songs. This opens the gates for hillbilly music through the newly-formed BMI licensing agency.

From the earliest days of medicine shows and minstrels, comics have been an integral part of rural entertainment. In the 1920s, Gid Tanner doubled as fiddler and funny man in the Skillet Lickers, and most bands had a designated comedian or two. From the beginning of hillbilly radio, comedy teams such as Sarie and Sallie, Lasses and Honey, then Jamup and Honey were WSM and "Grand Ole Opry" mainstays. At WLS, Lulu Belle and Scotty spiced up their act with humor. "Opry" comedic favorites included David "Stringbean" Akeman, Rod Brasfield, and Whitey Ford, but none came to personify country comedy like Minnie Pearl.

Minnie Pearl is the character created and played by native Tennessean Sarah Ophelia Colley (Cannon). Schooled in Centerville, Tennessee, Sarah was the only country girl at the Nashville finishing school, Ward-Belmont College, in the late 1920s. As a way of gaining acceptance, she used her skills at the piano and her comic voice to entertain her classmates.

Though show business was not a very respectable career for a young lady in that day—especially for a finishing school girl—Sarah landed a job in 1934 with the Wayne P. Sewell Producing Company in Atlanta, traveling around to direct and promote local "entertainments" that raised money for local schools. Sarah drew the Minnie Pearl character from an older woman with whom she stayed during one such hill country production, changing the age and expanding on the character based on memories of lumber mill families from the Grinder's Switch railhead in Centerville. Her cheap straw hat, a $1.98 price tag still dangling from it, became the visual signature of Minnie Pearl, as surely as her squalling greeting—"How-dee! I'm just so proud to be here!"—led off her every performance.

She joined the "Opry" and began touring with Acuff in 1940. The Minnie Pearl character eventually grew from a timid young malapropist to a lusty, squawk-voiced middle-aged country spinster teamed with a bashful rube character created by Rod Brasfield. After Brasfield's death in 1958, Minnie usually worked alone or played off Acuff, her long-time friend. She and Acuff became the two most visible icons of the "Opry." Minnie sang on occasion, but to comic effect; standup comedy was her stock and trade. Through the years, she penned a cookbook, her autobiography, and a collection of country Christmas stories. Surviving breast cancer, Minnie raised money for a women's cancer care center in Nashville that bears her real name.

Sidelined by a stroke in the early 1990s, Sarah Cannon retired and continues to reside in Nashville, but Minnie Pearl remains the heart and soul of country comedy.

Minnie Pearl.
credit: In the Southern Folklife Collection, University of North Carolina, Chapel Hill

1941

The "Grand Ole Opry" Goes Big-Time

By 1941, the "Grand Ole Opry" had already had six homes: three inside WSM studios, the Dixie Tabernacle, the Hillsboro Theatre, and the War Memorial Auditorium. Roy Acuff was the single biggest force in the growing popularity of the Saturday "Opry" and its sister show, the "Friday Night Frolics." In 1941 the "Opry" settled down in a permanent home—The Ryman Auditorium, half a block off the heart of Nashville's Broadway, downtown.

WSM had become a powerful radio station with 50,000 watts and a clear channel frequency, but it was Acuff, again, who finally made the "Grand Ole Opry" a national program. In 1943, R.J. Reynolds asked for him by name

to host a 30-minute "Opry" segment to be called "The Prince Albert Show." In the 1940s, the cast of regulars that most country music fans still identify as "The Opry" was solidified. It included Acuff, Red Foley, Bill Monroe and his classic Flatt & Scruggs version of the Blue Grass Boys, Ernest Tubb, Wilma Lee and Stoney Cooper, Pee Wee King's Golden West Cowboys, Minnie Pearl and Rod Brasfield, Whitey Ford ("The Duke of Paducah"), and others. Uncle Dave Macon remained a crucial link with true nineteenth-century rural music, but by the end of the decade the "Opry" would include Hank Williams and the astoundingly popular country crooner Eddy Arnold.

The program was helped by the increasing visibility of its stars, such as King, Tubb, and Foley, in Hollywood movies, including the first "Opry" cast film, *Grand Ole Opry* and Acuff's Republic Pictures vehicles, *Hi Neighbor* and *O My Darling, Clementine.* As the "Prince Albert Show" was picked up by more and more NBC affiliates, its relatively Southern-style rural purity overtook the WLS "National Barn Dance" as the most important country music program in America. Second-fiddle no longer, the "Opry" management kept careful watch on regional rivals such as the "Louisiana Hayride," the "Renfro Valley Barn Dance," and the "Wheeling Jamboree" in order to raid their rising stars.

A War-time crowd for the Grand Ole Opry.
credit: Courtesy of the Grand Ole Opry

Milestones

- On January 1, lacking an agreement to play ASCAP tunes, broadcasters institute a ten-month ban on the ASCAP catalog, turning to BMI and its increasing hillbilly and folk catalog.
- Henson Cargill born in Oklahoma City, Oklahoma, on February 5.
- Bobby Goldsboro born in Marianna, Florida, on January 18.
- Harmonica ace Charlie McCoy born in Oak Hill, West Virginia, on March 28.
- Singer-songwriter Sonny Throckmorton born in Carlsbad, New Mexico, on April 2.
- Johnny Paycheck (Donald Eugene Lytle) born in Greenfield, Ohio, on May 31.
- Connie Smith (Constance June Meadows) born in Elkhart, Indiana, on September 14.
- Dickey Lee (D. Lipscomb) born in Memphis, Tennessee, on September 21.
- David Frizzell born in Texas on September 26.
- The "Grand Ole Opry" organizes the first "Camel Country" tour in October, taking country music to servicemen.
- Earl Thomas Conley born in Portsmith, Ohio, on October 17.
- Doug Sahm (of Texas Tornadoes) born November 6.
- Guy Clark born in Rockport, Texas, on November 6.
- Jody Miller born in Phoenix, Arizona, on November 29.
- Partners in the Singing Pals duo, Wilma Leigh Leary and Dale Troy "Stoney" Cooper, marry.

Most Important Records

"There's A Star Spangled Banner Waving Somewhere" Elton Britt / Bluebird
"My Life's Been a Pleasure"/"Please Don't Leave Me" Bob Wills / Okeh
"The Honey Song" Louise Massey & the Westerners / Okeh
"Wreck on the Highway"/"Fireball Mail" Roy Acuff / Okeh
"Tweedle-O-Twill" Gene Autry / Okeh

Milestones

- Mac Davis born in Lubbock, Texas, on January 21.
- Jerry Jeff Walker (Paul Crosby) born in Oneonta, New York, on March 14.
- Billy Joe Royal born in Valdosta, Georgia, on April 3.
- Margo Smith (Betty Lou Miller) born in Dayton, Ohio, on April 9.

1942

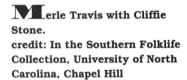

Merle Travis with Cliffie Stone.
credit: In the Southern Folklife Collection, University of North Carolina, Chapel Hill

↜ Virginia Wynette Pugh (Tammy Wynette) born in Itwamba County, Mississippi, on May 5.
↜ Billy Swan born in Cape Girardeau, Missouri, on May 12.
↜ T.G. Shepard (Bill Browder) born on June 20.
↜ Singer-songwriter Steve Young born in Noonan, Georgia, on July 12.
↜ The musicians union strikes on August 1 in what is called the Petrillo ban, forbidding their members from taking part in recording sessions until labels agree to support a fund to benefit musicians put out of work by airplay and jukeboxes. Small independent country labels are first to sign the agreement. The shortage of new "pop" tunes gives the edge to country artists.
↜ B.J. Thomas born in Hugo, Oklahoma, on August 7.
↜ K.T. (Kay Toinette) Oslin born in Crossitt, Arkansas, on August 15.
↜ Mel McDaniel born in Checotah, Oklahoma, on September 6.
↜ Acuff-Rose Publications formed on October 3, with Fred Rose chief of creative activities and Mildred Acuff in charge of business matters.
↜ Lee Greenwood born in Los Angeles, California, on December 27.

Most Important Records

"Pistol Packin' Mama" Al Dexter / Okeh
"Born To Lose"/"No Letter Today" Ted Daffan / Okeh
"Night Train To Memphis"/"Low and Lonely" Roy Acuff / Okeh

1943

"Home in San Antone"/"Miss Molly" Bob Wills / Okeh
"You Nearly Lose Your Mind" Ernest Tubb / Decca

Milestones

- Leona Williams born in Vienna, Missouri, on January 7.
- Of 608 active "recording artists" identified in a *Billboard* magazine survey for this year, 198 are country artists.
- Joe Stampley born in Springhill, Louisiana, on June 6.
- Tony Joe White born in Oak Grove, Louisiana, on July 23.
- Maybelle Carter carries on the family name, leading Mother Maybelle and the Carter Sisters, featuring her daughters Anita, June, and Helen. They join the cast of the "Tennessee Barn Dance" at WRVA in Richmond, Virginia.
- In September, Decca is the first label to come to terms with the musicians' union and releases "Pistol Packin' Mama" by Bing Crosby and the Andrews Sisters, covering Al Dexter's recording that had been a country hit since March.
- Richard Sterban (of Oak Ridge Boys) born in Camden, New Jersey, on April 24.
- Duane Allen (of Oak Ridge Boys) born in Taylortown, Texas, on April 29.
- Sammi Smith born in Orange, California, on September 5.
- Joe Sun born in Rochester, Minnesota, on September 25.
- Gene Watson born in Palestine, Texas, on October 11.
- John Denver (John Henry Deutschendorf) born in Roswell, New Mexico, on December 31.

Most Important Records

"Smoke On The Water" Red Foley / Decca
"So Long Pal"/"Too Late To Worry, Too Late Blue To Cry" Al Dexter / Okeh
"There's A New Moon Over My Shoulder"/"Jealous Heart" Tex Ritter / Capitol
"You're From Texas"/"We Might As Well Forget It" Bob Wills / Okeh
"Soldiers Last Letter" Ernest Tubb / Decca

Milestones

- The first issue of *Billboard* magazine for the year introduces a "folk" records jukebox chart, mixing country with jazz and blues.
- Jim Stafford born in Eloise, Florida, on January 16.
- Some 600 hillbilly music programs are on radio, creating a huge upsurge in national popularity for country music.
- Moe Bandy born in Meridian, Mississippi, on February 12.

1944

Homer and Jethro.
credit: In the Southern Folklife
Collection, University of North
Carolina, Chapel Hill

- Michael Johnson born in Alamosa, Colorado, on July 8, 1944.
- Bobbie Gentry (Roberta Streeter) born in Chickasaw County, Mississippi, on July 27.
- Eddie Raven (Edward Garvin Futch) born in Lafayette, Louisiana, on September 19.
- Kinky Friedman (leader of The Texas Jewboys) born in Rio Duckworth, Texas, on October 31.
- Eddie Rabbitt born in Brooklyn, New York, on November 27.
- Bradley Kincaid joins the "Grand Ole Opry."
- Chris Hillman (Byrds, Flying Burrito Brothers, leader of Desert Rose) born in San Diego County, California, on December 4.
- Brenda Lee (Brenda Mae Tarpley) born in Lithonia, Georgia, on December 11.

Most Important Records

"Shame On You" Spade Cooley / Okeh
"You Two Timed Me One Time Too Often" Tex Ritter / Capitol
"At Mail Call Today" Gene Autry / Okeh
"Oklahoma Hills" Jack Guthrie / Capitol
"I'm Losing My Mind Over You" Al Dexter / Okeh

1945

Milestones

- Michael Martin Murphey born in Dallas, Texas, on March 14.
- Gary Stewart born in Letcher County, Kentucky, on May 28.
- Singing cowboy Rex Allen joins the cast of the WLS "National Barn Dance."
- Statler Brothers' Don Reid born in Staunton, Virginia, on June 5.
- Anne Murray born in Springhill, Nova Scotia, on June 20.
- A September survey of European listeners to Armed Forces Overseas Radio Network's "Munich Morning Report" draws 3,700 votes for most popular recording artist. Roy Acuff outpolls Frank Sinatra by 600 votes.
- Jeannie C. Riley (Jeanne Carolyn Stephenson) born in Anson, Texas, on October 19.

Most Important Records

1946

"Guitar Polka" Al Dexter / Columbia
"New Spanish Two-Step"/"Roly-Poly" Bob Wills / Columbia
"Divorce Me C.O.D." Merle Travis / Capitol
"Rainbow at Midnight" Ernest Tubb / Decca
"Sioux City Sue" Zeke Manners / Victor

Milestones

- Naomi Judd (Diana Ellen Judd) born in Ashland, Kentucky, on January 11.
- Ronnie Milsap born in Robbinsville, North Carolina, on January 16.
- Dolly Parton born in Sevierville, Tennessee, on January 19.
- Howard Bellamy (Bellamy Brothers) born in Darby, Florida, on February 2.
- Johnny Lee (J.L. Ham) born in Texas City, Texas, on July 3.
- Linda Ronstadt born in Tucson, Arizona, on July 15.
- John Conlee born in Versailles, Kentucky, on August 11.
- Jo-El Sonnier born in Rayne, Louisiana, on October 2.

Most Important Records

"I'll Hold You in My Heart 'Til I Can Hold You in My Arms"
Eddy Arnold / RCA
"Smoke! Smoke! Smoke! (That Cigarette)"[1] Tex Williams /
Capitol
"It's A Sin" Eddy Arnold / RCA
"So Round, So Firm, So Fully Packed" Merle Travis / Capitol
"What Is Life Without Love?" Eddy Arnold / RCA

Milestones

- Emmylou Harris born in Birmingham, Alabama, on April 2.
- Jessi Colter (Miriam Johnson) born in Phoenix, Arizona, on
  May 25.
- Rex Allen Jr. born in Chicago, Illinois, on August 23.
- Freddy Weller born in Atlanta, Georgia, on September 9.
- Eddy Arnold quits the "Grand Ole Opry" in September.

1. "Smoke! Smoke! Smoke! (That Cigarette)" was Capitol's first million-
selling record. Ironically, the song's composer and purveyor, Tex Williams,
died of lung cancer in 1985.

1947

The 1940s were not all modern honky-tonk, bluegrass, and patriotic cowboys. The rube image continued to work for many radio stars and touring acts, including the most popular hillbilly novelty radio act of the late 1930s and 1940s, The Hoosier Hot Shots. The act consisted of Ft. Wayne natives Paul "Hezzie" Trietsch, Rudy Trietsch, Gabe Ward, and Frank Kettering. Based at Chicago's WLS from 1933 to 1942, and appearing regularly on the "National Barn Dance," the Hot Shots turned novelty tunes and pop standards inside out with humorous flair. Starting with a guitar, bass, and clarinet, they generally goofed it up with purposeful exaggeration on slide whistle and a variety of homemade percussion instruments played by "Hezzie."

The Trietsch brothers and Gabe started together on vaudeville stages in the late 1920s with Ezra Buzzington's Rube Band. Their music was not country in any traditional sense, but rural and urban audiences alike loved their wacky mix of Dixieland, fox-trots, and jitterbug instrumentals with excellent four-part harmonies played for laughs on signature songs like "I Like Bananas (Because They Have No Bones)," "Rural Rhythms," and "'Taint Nobody's Business What I Do." Touring under the WLS aegis, the Hot Shots played multiple shows in single-day stands in theaters and fairs and were paid from $3,000 to $5,000 a day in the 1940s. The spirit of the act is perhaps best captured in a piece of their own promotional copy, circa 1949:

From deep inside Indiana's corn belt, 17 years ago a weird sound fell upon the anxious ears of America. Was it a message from Mars? No—it wasn't that. Nor was it the wail of the wind through the crags, the whine of a coyote, the blood-chilling cry of a banshee or the call of a hungry wolf. It was all of these, and more. Nobody really knew, at the time, what it was. All they knew was that suddenly, out of nowhere, they would hear a voice call: "Are you ready, Hezzie?" [though most generally the phrase was reversed], followed by a wonderful tintinnabulation heretofore unheard by mortal ears.

Starting in Arcadia, Illinois, as pot and pan prodigies, their road led them to the heights in radio, recordings [Decca, ARC, and Columbia], and motion pictures. They are the originators of their style, and, though imitated by many others, they still remain the number one, highest-paid novelty group in America. But don't let the washboards, the horns, the slide-whistle, etc., fool you; for the boys are all accomplished musicians, playing a total of 26 instruments between them."

Their biggest selling recording of the 1940s was "Sioux City Sue," which went to #2 on the 1946 *Billboard* chart. Though the act faded from mainstream popularity in the mid-1950s, the Hoosier Hot Shots name continued in various configurations until the last original member, Ward Gabe, died in January 1992.

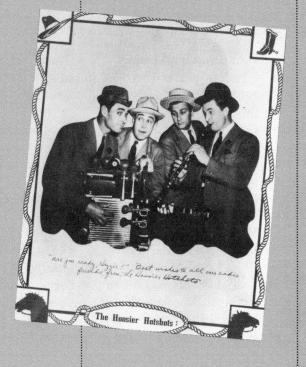

Hoosier Hotshots.
credit: In the Southern Folklife Collection, University of North Carolina, Chapel Hill

- Lynn Anderson born in Grand Forks, North Dakota, on September 26.
- Ernest Tubb hosts two nights of country music at Carnegie Hall, featuring Minnie Pearl, Rosalie Allen, Radio Dot and Smokey Swann, the Short Brothers, Limmie and Leon, with George D. Hay as emcee.
- Wilma Lee and Stoney Cooper make their recording debut on Rich-R-Tone records and join the cast of the "Wheeling Jamboree" at WWVA.
- East Coast promoter Connie B. Gay produces the first public country music extravaganza at Constitution Hall in Washington D.C., on October 31, starring Eddy Arnold, Minnie Pearl and Rod Brasfield, T. Texas Tyler, Cowboy Copas, and Kitty Wells. At $6 a head, Senators, Congressmen, cabinet members, and important lobbyists fill the massive D.A.R. hall by invitation only, disproving the theory that only the poor, ignorant, and powerless enjoyed the "Grand Ole Opry."
- Janie Fricke born in South Whitney, Indiana, on December 19.

Most Important Records

"Bouquet of Roses" Eddy Arnold / RCA
"Humpty-Dumpty Heart" Hank Thompson / Capitol
"One Has My Name (The Other Has My Heart)" Jimmy Wakely / Capitol
"Tennessee Saturday Night" Red Foley / Decca
"Anytime" Eddy Arnold / RCA

Milestones

- Dan Seals born in McCamey, Texas, on February 8.
- The "Louisiana Hayride" debuts on KWKH, Shreveport, on April 3, featuring the Bailes Brothers, and Johnny & Jack (with Kitty Wells).
- Gail Davies born in Broken Bow, Oklahoma, on April 4.
- Larry Gatlin born in Seminole, Texas, on May 2.
- Joe Bonsell (of Oak Ridge Boys) born in Philadelphia, Pennsylvania, on May 18.
- Olivia Newton-John born in Cambridge, England, on September 26.
- Mother Maybelle and the Carter Sisters become members of the "Grand Ole Opry."
- Chris LeDoux born in Biloxi, Mississippi, on October 2.
- Lacy J. Dalton (Jill Byrem) born in Bloomsburg, Pennsylvania, on October 13.
- Gary Morris born in Fort Worth, Texas, on December 7
- Barbara Mandrell born in Houston, Texas, on December 25.

1948

If ever there was an aptly nicknamed radio program, it was "Cradle of the Stars," the "Louisiana Hayride." Debuting on Shreveport station KWKH in the spring of 1948, serving Louisiana and East Texas, the "Louisiana Hayride" lured its first two stars away from its competitor to the north, WSM's "Grand Ole Opry." Thereafter, the stream of country music talent primarily went the other way, as the "Hayride" proved important in finding and developing talented newcomers, but was never large enough to keep them.

Country legends who went on to become "Opry" stars after they got their start on the "Hayride" include Hank Williams, Floyd Cramer, Sonny James, Webb Pierce, Jim Reeves, the Wilburn Brothers, Faron Young, The Browns, Jimmy C. Newman, Red Sovine, the Carlisles, and Goldie Hill.

But the "Louisiana Hayride" had stars it kept, as well: the Blue Sky Boys, Maddox Brothers and Rose, Jimmy Martin, Slim Whitman, Mac Wiseman, Johnny Horton, T. Texas Tyler, and Leon Payne. Merle Kilgore, as a youngster, was a hanger-on who once got to carry Hank Williams' guitar case up the stairs from the street to the studio.

The biggest threat to the "Louisiana Hayride" came not only from the drain of talent to Nashville, but from the rock 'n' roll revolution. In 1954–1955, when Elvis Presley was making a name for himself on the country charts, nicknamed "the Hillbilly Cat," he performed several times on the "Hayride." After his third performance, the regular "Hayride" audience was muscled out by screaming teenaged Presley fans.

"Hayride" regulars blackballed Presley from the show. Country music buckled under the weight of rock 'n' roll in the late 1950s, and by 1960 the original "Louisiana Hayride" was off the air.

The Maddox Brothers, featuring Sister Rose.
credit: In the Southern Folklife Collection, University of North Carolina, Chapel Hill

Eddy Arnold was born in a sharecropper's shack in Chester County, Tennessee, but the music with which he convincingly dominated country charts from 1945 to 1955 was hardly identifiable with any hillbilly or Western sound. He was a homegrown crooner who had worked in radio in Jackson and Memphis, Tennessee, before joining Pee Wee King's Golden West Cowboys at $25 per week in early 1939. Touring with King on the Camel Caravan circuit gave Arnold wide exposure. By 1944, Arnold had outgrown the Golden West Cowboys.

Recording for RCA Victor, Arnold waxed "Cattle Call" in 1945, a song whose haunting yodel made it Arnold's theme song and best remembered record. In 1947 he had his first #1 hit with "What Is Life Without You," in which he began veering away from a down-home musical style and toward a more pop-sounding country style. By 1948, he had outgrown the "Grand Ole Opry," too, and, chafed by the Saturday night rule, quit the show.

Arnold had his own daily syndicated radio program sponsored by Purina Mills (proving his continued popularity with rural audiences despite his emerging crooner style). Alone among country singers, he made appearances on nearly every big-time radio variety show of the day. By the mid-1950s he had, in the minds of trade chart analysts, outgrown country music entirely, though his many fans never thought so. Television in the 1950s spread his cosmopolitan country sound even further into urban enclaves. He may not have pleased the haystack traditionalists, but his undeniable impact on country music beyond his own impressive success was evidenced by Jim Reeves and the whole Nashville Sound movement of Chet Atkins and company.

Eddie Arnold.
credit: In the Southern Folklife Collection, University of North Carolina, Chapel Hill

Most Important Records

"Slippin' Around" Jimmy Wakely & Margaret Whiting / Capitol
"Lovesick Blues" Hank Williams / MGM
"Don't Rob Another Man's Castle" Eddy Arnold / RCA
"Candy Kisses" George Morgan / Columbia
"Wedding Bells" Hank Williams / MGM

Milestones

- Merle Watson, son and partner to "Doc" Watson, born on February 8.
- Stella Parton born in Sevierville, Tennessee, on May 4.
- Hank Williams Jr. (Randall Hank Williams) born in Shreveport, Louisiana, on May 26.
- Russell Smith (leader of Amazing Rhythm Aces, solo artist) born in Nashville, Tennessee, on June 17.
- Jeff Cook (Alabama) born in Ft. Payne, Alabama, on August 27.
- Donna Fargo (Yvonne Vaughan) born in Mount Airy, North Carolina, on November 10.
- Randy Owen (Alabama) born in Ft. Payne, Alabama, on December 13.

1949

Red Foley.
credit: In the Southern Folklife
Collection, University of North
Carolina, Chapel Hill

THE 1950S

As the 1950s dawned, Bluelick, Kentucky, singer Clyde Julian "Red" Foley was already a star. He'd been a regular on the "National Barn Dance" and the "Renfro Valley Barn Dance" with the Cumberland Ridge Runners through the 1930s. He got his own network radio show, "Avalon Time," with Red Skelton in 1939. He recorded for Decca through the 1940s, when he joined the "Grand Ole Opry." But he graduated from stardom to what we now call "superstardom" in 1950 with the country swing-flavored national crossover hit, "Chattanoogie Shoeshine Boy," followed by "Birmingham Bounce," "Peace In The Valley" (the first million-selling gospel record), and the enormously popular duets with Ernest Tubb, "Goodnight, Irene" and "Too Old To Cut The Mustard."

Most Important Records

"I'm Movin' On"[1] Ernest Tubb / Decca
"Chattanoogie Shoeshine Boy" Red Foley / Decca
"Why Don't You Love Me (Like You Used To Do)" Hank Williams / MGM
"Long Gone Lonesome Blues" Hank Williams / MGM
"I'll Sail My Ship Alone" Moon Mullican / King
"Birmingham Bounce" Red Foley / Decca
"Goodnight, Irene" Red Foley & Ernest Tubb / Decca

1. "I'm Movin' On" by Ernest Tubb was the top country record of the decade, topping the *Billboard* list a full 21 weeks.

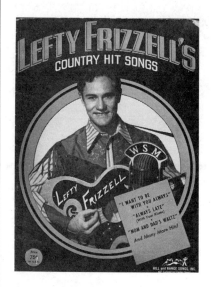

Lefty Frizzell.
credit: Archives of Robert K. Oermann

It was "Happy Trails" for Roy Rogers, who left the country charts but remained the King of the TV cowboys through the 1950s.
credit: In the Southern Folklife Collection, University of North Carolina, Chapel Hill

"If You've Got The Money Honey, I've Got The Time" Lefty Frizzell / Columbia
"Rudolf, The Red Nosed Reindeer" Gene Autry / Columbia
"Blue Christmas" Ernest Tubb / Decca

Debut Artist: Lefty Frizzell

Nineteen-year-old West Texas country singer William Orville "Lefty" Frizzell never really had the time to polish his song-writing skills until he spent six months (1947–1948) in the county jail for "fighting and carrying on." That period of invol-untary woodshedding gave Frizzell a chance to pen a letter to his young wife, the words of which would become the lyrics to "I Love You In A Thousand Ways." Frizzell's impact on country music was much greater than the sum of his five #1 records— "If You've Got The Money Honey, I've Got The Time," "I Love You A Thousand Ways," "Always Late," "I Want To Be With You Always," and "Saginaw, Michigan." His laconic soulfulness inspired singers from George Jones, Merle Haggard, and John Anderson to a host of others. Many of the best honky-tonk singers to follow would cite the Hank Williams repertoire and the Lefty Frizzell vocal style for drawing them toward country music as a career.

Milestones

- On February 4, Roy Rogers, singing "Stampede" with the Sons of the Pioneers, charts the last hit record of his career. He would continue making films and soon star in his own TV show with wife Dale Evans and former Sons of the Pioneers singer Pat Brady.
- Sam Phillips establishes the Memphis Recording Services studios in downtown Memphis.
- Roy Acuff is hired to headline the first in a series of Hadacol Caravan tour packages. Entirely underwritten by patent medicine king Dudley LeBlanc, the Hadacol tour becomes a rolling party of booze and beauty queens for many, and a financial bath for LeBlanc.
- Hank Snow and the Carter Family (Maybelle and her daughters Helen, June, and Anita) join the "Grand Ole Opry"; Chet Atkins is the group's fiddler.
- Rodney Crowell born in Houston, Texas, on August 7.
- David Bellamy born in Darby, Florida, on September 16.
- Red Foley's "Chattanoogie Shoeshine Boy" crosses over to become a pop hit.

"The Old Pea Picker," Ernie Ford, was born and reared in the state that gave him his nickname—Tennessee. Fascinated with radio, he got his first announcing job in 1937 in Knoxville. He studied voice at the Cincinnati Conservatory the following year, then returned to radio where he worked the next three years. World War II military service in California led him to work at KXLA in Pasadena, where he eventually began performing on Cliffie Stone's seminal West Coast daily variety show, "Dinner Bell Roundup," and Saturday night program, "Hometown Jamboree."

Capitol was the big West Coast–based label, so it was natural that Stone, who produced for the label, would help his protege land a recording deal there in 1948. Ford made quite a splash in his debut year, 1949, recording a Top 15, three Top 10s, and a #1 single, "Mule Train." In 1950, Ford had a second #1 with "Shot Gun Boogie." He also had a big hit in the pseudo-hillbilly treatment of "Ain't Nobody's Business But My Own," a duet with pop singer Kay Starr.

Ford's comfortable and easy manner and deep bass voice were complemented by a comedic talent that brought him his own network radio shows from 1950 to 1955, followed by his own television show on NBC. His talent for hillbilly character acting earned him an appearance as Lucille Ball's singing country cousin in an "I Love Lucy" episode.

In 1955, Ford had his biggest-selling record with a Merle Travis tune originally recorded in 1947. "Sixteen Tons," as recorded by Ford, featured a modest rock 'n' roll beat and generated sales topping 4 million copies. It was the best-selling crossover record of the early rock era, but Ford was not really adaptable to the rockabilly/rock 'n' roll trend country was going through in the late 1950s. Turning to inspirational music, he was awarded the first gospel gold record in 1959 for his album, "Hymns," and earned a Grammy for his album "Great Gospel Songs" in 1964.

Though he retired a number of times starting in the early 1960s, he always came back to host another television show. Inducted into the Country Music Hall of Fame in 1990, Ford died of cancer the following year.

In 1951 Dallas was attracting major labels and gearing up to compete with Nashville and Hollywood as the country music recording capital. Jim Beck built his first studio downtown, just a block from the offices of the *Dallas Times Herald*. He assembled a first rate stable of session pickers and "discovered" West Texas honky-tonk singer Lefty Frizzell. Frizzell's success for Columbia brought RCA and Decca to Dallas to try Beck's studio. Beck was smart enough to get his name on several of Frizzell's early tunes, but neglected to clean the heads of his recorders in a well-ventilated room. Several years later, Beck allegedly died of liver poisoning caused by fumes from cleaning fluid—also killing plans by Columbia and Decca to establish their country recording headquarters in Dallas.

Most Important Records

"Slow Poke" Pee Wee King / RCA
"Shot Gun Boogie" Tennessee Ernie Ford / Capitol
"Always Late (With Your Kisses)" Lefty Frizzell / Columbia
"I Want To Be With You Always" Lefty Frizzell / Columbia
"There's Been A Change in Me" Eddy Arnold / RCA

1951

A TEXAS CONNECTION

"I Wanna Play House With You" Eddy Arnold / RCA
"Let Old Mother Nature Have Her Way" Carl Smith / Columbia
"Rhumba Boogie" Hank Snow / RCA
"Hey, Good Lookin'" Hank Williams / MGM
"Cold, Cold Heart" Hank Williams / MGM

Debut Artist: Carl Smith

Carl Smith was born in Roy Acuff country, Maynardsville, Tennessee. He started his career in radio in the 1940s on WROL in Knoxville, working with Molly O'Day and Archie Campbell. He then moved to Nashville and WSM in 1950, where he was signed by Don Law to Columbia. Influenced by Hank Williams and a protege of Ernest Tubb, Smith was a key bridge between country's rural traditions and its emerging urban identity. Once married to June Carter, he is the father of Carlene Carter. His 1951 hits were "Let's Live A Little," "Mr. Moon"/"If Teardrops Were Pennies," and "Let Old Mother Nature Have Her Way." He retired from show business in 1977 and lives on his Middle Tennessee farm with his wife since 1957, ex-country singer Goldie Hill.

Milestones

- Crystal Gayle (Brenda Gail Webb) born in Paintsville, Kentucky, on January 9.
- Pee Wee King's "Tennessee Waltz" makes the charts in February. Though the song would become one of the best-selling and most-played country tunes in history after Peggy Lee covers it for the pop market, the song only reaches #6—not as good a showing as the band's 1949 hit, "Tennessee Polka."
- Ray Benson (leader of Asleep at the Wheel) born in Philadelphia, Pennsylvania, on May 16.
- John Dittrich (Restless Heart) born in Syracuse, New York, on April 7.
- Hank Williams, Minnie Pearl, and (on selected dates) Bob Hope are headliners for this year's Hadacol Caravan national tour.
- Hank and Audrey Williams open a Western wear shop in downtown Nashville.
- Martha Carson joins the "Grand Ole Opry"; Lefty Frizzell ignores Hank Williams' advice that he do the same.
- Johnny Rodriguez born in Sabinol, Texas, on December 10.

Pee Wee King.
credit: Bob Millard Collection

Carl Smith.
credit: In the Southern Folklife Collection, University of North Carolina, Chapel Hill

Of the generation immediately following Hank Williams—those such as George Jones, Webb Pierce, Stonewall Jackson, Ray Price, and Carl Smith who were drawn into a country music career by Hank's music and legend—Faron Young was the first to become a star. A Shreveport native, he was in his early teens when Hank was a local hero on the "Louisiana Hayride." Young hung around the KWKH studio, trying to get a hearing. He met Hank Williams and Webb Pierce, among others. Pierce hired him as a backing singer and recorded him with no success on his own Pacemaker Records label. It got Young exposure, however, and whetted his appetite for stardom.

Young was drafted during the Korean War and served as an entertainer in Special Services until 1954. He managed to record during leaves and cut his first hit, "Goin' Steady," in 1953. Young had the dubious honor of having one of his girlfriends stolen by Hank Williams on a double date in 1952—she was Billie Jean Eshlimar, who would become Williams' second wife. Once out of the Army, Young returned to the "Grand Ole Opry" and enjoyed a string of Top 5 hits, including "If You Ain't Lovin' (You Ain't Livin')."

Young's good looks earned him film roles in the 1950s in "Hidden Guns," "Daniel Boone," and "Raiders of Old California." His nickname, "The Singing Sheriff," came from "Hidden Guns." Another dubious footnote in an otherwise notable career is Young's having co-starred with Ferlin Husky and June Carter in "Country Music Holiday," generally considered the worst country music movie ever made.

Initially something of a Hank Williams imitator, but later a full-throated modern honky-tonk singer, Young wrote many of the tunes he recorded. He also gambled on tunes by unknown composers, scooping up classics such as Don Gibson's "Sweet Dreams" and Willie Nelson's "Hello Walls." Young entered a second hot streak with "Wine Me Up" in 1969. His last chart-topper was "It's Four In The Morning" in 1971. His Top 10 success as a recording artist ran clear through the mid-1970s and he stayed in the Top 40 until 1979. By then, good business investments allowed him the luxury of becoming an outspoken and unrepentant elder statesman of the modern honky-tonk movement.

Faron Young.
credit: In the Southern Folklife Collection, University of North Carolina, Chapel Hill

1952

THE FINAL DECLINE OF HANK WILLIAMS

Hank Williams' recording career was at its peak, but his life was in shambles in 1952. Divorced from Audrey and banished from the "Grand Ole Opry," he retreated for a time to Shreveport, where he rejoined the "Louisiana Hayride" and drank heavily, mixing booze with "uppers" and "downers." That summer, he met pretty 19-year-old Billie Jean Jones Eshlimar, whom he married in two public ceremonies that October onstage at the New Orleans Municipal Auditorium, charging fans to see the spectacle. Hank's style of music, honky-tonk, was hot that year, but Hank seemed hell-bent on dying as 1952 dawned, recording a song called "I'll Never Get Out Of This World Alive" as if issuing a tongue-in-cheek prophesy.

Most Important Records

"The Wild Side of Life" Hank Thompson / Capitol
"Jambalaya" Hank Williams / MGM

Hank Williams.
credit: Bob Millard Collection

"(When You Feel Like You're In Love) Don't Just Stand There"
Carl Smith / Columbia
"It Wasn't God Who Made Honky-Tonk Angels" Kitty Wells / Decca
"Back Street Affair" Webb Pierce / Decca
"Don't Let The Stars Get In Your Eyes"[2] Skeets McDonald /
Capitol
"Don't Let The Stars Get In Your Eyes" Slim Willet / Four Star
"Wondering" Webb Pierce / Decca
"A Full Time Job" Eddy Arnold / RCA
"Give Me More, More, More (Of Your Kisses)" Lefty Frizzell /
Columbia
"That Heart Belongs To Me" Webb Pierce / Decca

Debut Artist: Webb Pierce

Louisiana native Webb Pierce struggled to make his mark in
music working days as a salesman at Sears, Roebuck before
becoming a "Louisiana Hayride" star in the early 1950s. He
recorded for his own small regional Pacemaker label, but had
never reached the *Billboard* chart until he signed with Decca.
His first band included Faron Young, Floyd Cramer, and
Jimmy Day. A savvy businessman, he became an original
partner with "Grand Ole Opry" executive Jim Denny at the
Cedarwood Publishing Company in Nashville. He had three hit
records in 1952, all peaking at #1, including "Back Street
Affair," the quintessential country cheatin' song.

Milestones

- Ricky Van Shelton born in Grit, Virginia, on January 12.
- Teddy Gentry (Alabama) born in Ft. Payne, Alabama, on
  January 22.
- Hank Williams is fired from the "Grand Ole Opry."
- Juice Newton born on February 18.
- A summer replacement, Eddy Arnold hosts the "Perry Como
  Show" on NBC-TV.
- Uncle Dave Macon dies on March 22.
- George Strait born in Pearsall, Texas, on May 18.

Webb Pierce.
**credit: In the Southern Folklife
Collection, University of North
Carolina, Chapel Hill**

2. It was not uncommon from the 1920s through the 1960s for a major
label to "cover" a great song recorded by a lesser label, in effect stealing a
hit. "Don't Let Stars Get In Your Eyes" became, in late 1952, a battle
between one-hit wonders. Small time Texas honky-tonk singer Winston
Lee Moore, who worked under the stage name Slim Willet, achieved a
rapidly red-hot #1 hit in late 1952 with "Don't Let The Stars Get In Your
Eyes." Capitol jumped his claim to fame (it was the only charting record of
Willet's career) with West Coast–based television singer Enos William
"Skeets" McDonald a month later. Between the two artists' versions, the
tune was #1 for four weeks. Perry Como would have a #1 pop cover of the
tune in 1953. Interestingly, stealing Willet's hit didn't keep McDonald in
the spotlight long. He didn't chart another record for eight years.

- June Carter, billed as a "singing comedienne," marries Carl Smith on July 9 in Alcoa, Tennessee.
- Slim Whitman makes his chart debut with "Indian Love Call."
- Roy Rogers and Dale Evans' three-year-old daughter dies of the mumps on August 23; they adopt a child later in the year and Evans writes the book *Angel Unaware*.
- Hank Williams records "Take These Chains From My Heart" and "Your Cheatin' Heart" on September 23—his last recording session.
- Rabon Delmore of the Delmore Brothers dies December 4.
- In December, Columbia drops Roy Acuff after 20 years.

Kitty Wells

Kitty Wells, born Muriel Deason, never intended to be a country music star, much less the leader of an entire generation of women in country music. She sang gospel as a teenager, and got a job on WSIX's "Old Country Store" program at 17. In 1938, at 18, she married itinerant musician/mechanic Johnny Wright and dutifully followed Wright and singing partner Jack Anglin around the Southeast as they struggled from radio station to radio station trying to become stars. She generally sang an inspirational tune on Johnny and Jack shows, but cared more about her children than a singing career.

In 1952, Johnny and Jack (having already given Muriel her stage name from the title of an old folk song), got a job on the "Grand Ole Opry." Kitty wasn't a velvet-voiced singer. She wailed mournfully in an unadorned, pure-country, fashion that made her one-of-a-kind. She wasn't particularly interested in singing a quickly-written response song to Hank Thompson's honky-tonk hit, "Wild Side of Life," but she did it when Johnny insisted. The tune, "It Wasn't God Who Made Honky-Tonk Angels," made Kitty an overnight star, bigger than

Johnny and Jack by a longshot. Within a couple of years, the tune had sold over a million copies and Kitty was dubbed "Queen of Country Music," the only female artist of the era to rival Roy Acuff, the acknowledged "King," in popularity.

A star almost by accident, Kitty made a name for herself in the early and mid-1950s, singing women's retorts to cheating honky-tonk songs, including "Paying For That Back Street Affair," the 1953 response to one of Webb Pierce's breakthrough hits; "Hey Joe," for Carl Smith's hit by the same title; "Release Me"; and "Cheatin's a

Sin." She also sang several duets with Red Foley, including the 1954 #1, "One By One." Because of Kitty's phenomenal success, doors opened for a whole generation of female country singing stars, such as Wilma Lee Cooper, Jean Shepard, Skeeter Davis, Patsy Cline, Jan Howard, and Wanda Jackson.

She continues to perform occasionally with her husband and with her son, Bobby, who was an actor in the old "McHale's Navy" television series. Kitty and Johnny operate a museum near their Madison, Tennessee, home.

Kitty Wells.
credit: In the Southern Folklife Collection, University of North Carolina, Chapel Hill

Thrown out of his house and divorced by Audrey, banned from appearing on the "Grand Ole Opry" because of his uncontrolled alcoholism, Hank Williams seemed to shrink. Through 1952, he drank steadily, except when he faced a recording session. He missed more and more show dates until his Drifting Cowboys band deserted him to work the road with his Nashville roommate, Ray Price. The Drifting Cowboys agreed to back him in Canton, Ohio, on New Years' night 1953, to start the year on what was wistfully hoped would be a new footing, but it snowed and half the band didn't show up. Neither did Hank. Only 29 years old, he died sometime after midnight, insensible from alcohol and pills, in the backseat of his last powder blue Cadillac, somewhere south of Oak Hill, West Virginia.

Most Important Records

"Kaw-Liga" Hank Williams / MGM
"There Stands The Glass" Webb Pierce / Decca
"Mexican Joe" Jim Reeves / Abbott
"I Forgot More Than You'll Ever Know" Davis Sisters / RCA
"It's Been So Long" Webb Pierce / Decca

Hank Williams.
credit: Archives of Robert K. Oermann

"Hey, Joe" Carl Smith / Columbia
"A Dear John Letter" Ferlin Huskey & Jean Shepard / Capitol
"Your Cheatin' Heart" Hank Williams / MGM
"Take These Chains From My Heart" Hank Williams / MGM
"No Help Wanted" The Carlisles / Mercury

Debut Artist: Jim Reeves

Reeves earns kudos not only for having a #1 record with his first chart entry in 1953, but for doing so with an independent label, Abbott Records. A Texan, Reeves was playing baseball for a St. Louis Cardinals' farm team when a leg injury ended a promising career. He turned to announcing at KWKH in Shreveport, where he sang in small local clubs almost as a hobby. Unprepared for the sudden hit that "Mexican Joe" was, Reeves nevertheless became a regular on the "Louisiana Hayride" program, and scored a second #1 hit early in 1954 with "Bimbo." His smooth, deep voice was from the Eddy Arnold school, and his demeanor got him dubbed "Gentleman Jim." *Billboard* magazine declared Reeves and Elvis Presley tied for top new country artist of 1953.

Jim Reeves.
credit: Courtesy of the Grand Ole Opry

Milestones

- Hank Williams dies on January 1.
- In February, thinking Hank Williams had died with little money, Johnny and Jack arrange for the royalties from their tribute record, "Hank Williams Will Live Forever," to go to his estate.
- Hal Ketchum born in Greenwich, New York, on April 9.
- Ronnie Dunn (Brooks & Dunn) born in Coleman, Texas, on June 1.
- Tex Ritter sings the theme song to the movie "High Noon" on the Academy Awards' first televised show.
- Martha White Flour sponsors Flatt & Scruggs on WSM radio, bringing the act back to Nashville.
- Marty Robbins makes his "Grand Ole Opry" debut.
- Webb Pierce becomes an "Opry" regular as his hit "Back Street Affair" is named best-selling jukebox record of the year by the Amusement Machine Operators of America. Other new members to the "Opry" include Del Wood, the Carlisles, and the Wilburn Brothers.
- Virginia Patterson marries Gerald Cline and begins performing on the "Louisiana Hayride" under her nickname, Patsy.

Wilburn Brothers.
credit: In the Southern Folklife Collection, University of North Carolina, Chapel Hill

Two small-town East Kentucky girls, B.J. (Betty Jack) Davis and Mary Francis Penick (Skeeter Davis) grew up in the 1940s together, listening to the folk, gospel, and traditional country artists of the "Grand Ole Opry." They formed a duo and began singing around Lexington in the late 1940s, landing a slot on WLAX in 1949. Despite the near absence of female country music acts outside the cowgirl mold, the Davis Sisters barnstormed successfully from Detroit to Wheeling before finding the nerve to go to New York and ask RCA for a chance to record. Their preternaturally close harmonies would chart a course that another East Kentucky duo, The Judds, would follow three decades later, but tragedy was to be their end almost as soon as they had begun.

Their first single, "I Forgot More Than You'll Ever Know," was a resounding success, reaching #1 in early August 1952. But on tour with the likes of Hank Snow, Ernest and Justin Tubb, and Hank Cochran, the sisters fell victim to the ultimate bane of traveling show people—a car wreck. B.J. was killed and Skeeter was critically injured. Skeeter tried to keep the act going for a while, replacing B.J. with her sister, Georgia Davis, but Skeeter could never emotionally adjust to the change and the act foundered in 1955.

Skeeter's solo career began a slow changeover from traditional country to pop singer under the tutelage of Chet Atkins. Her signature hits of the 1960s included "The End Of The World," "Gonna Get Along Without You Now," and "Sun Glasses." Once married to country radio and television personality Ralph Emery, Skeeter found religion in her later career as a "Grand Ole Opry" regular. Currently married to Joey Spampinato of the classy, wacky rock 'n' roll bar band, NRBQ, she is still an "Opry" regular.

Justin Tubb, Betty Jack Davis, Hank Locklin, Skeeter Davis and Hank Snow on tour.
credit: In the Southern Folklife Collection, University of North Carolina, Chapel Hill

Practically unnoticed, a synthesis was taking place in Memphis, mixing elements so disparate that they had never before been lumped together: the sensual rhythms of R&B, the visceral energy of Pentecostal Southern gospel, and a hopped-up beer hall beat only hinted at in Hank Williams' "Settin' The Woods On Fire." It appeared that Bill Monroe's mournful "Blue Moon of Kentucky" was starting to dance with Big Mama Hornton's "Hound Dog," and neither one yet knew it. Sam Phillips ran the Memphis Recording Service. He had produced records for the Chicago blues label, Chess Records, but they allegedly cheated him, forcing him to open his own label—Sun Records. He had perfected "slapback" echo and, about this time, was supposed to have uttered that fateful phrase, "If I could only find a white boy who could sing like a negro I could make me a million dollars." What he was about to do, in short order, was "discover" Elvis Presley, Johnny Cash, Jerry Lee Lewis, and Carl Perkins. Honky-tonk reigned in 1954, but commercial country music was about to be shaken, rattled and rolled to its very foundation.

Most Important Records

"I Don't Hurt Anymore" Hank Snow / RCA
"Slowly" Webb Pierce / Decca
"More And More" Webb Pierce / Decca
"Bimbo" Jim Reeves / RCA
"Wake Up Irene" Hank Thompson / Capitol
"Oh Baby Mine (I Get So Lonely)" Johnny and Jack / RCA
"Even Though" Webb Pierce / Decca
"I Really Don't Want To Know" Eddy Arnold / RCA
"One By One" Kitty Wells & Red Foley / Decca
"I'll Be There (If You Ever Want Me)" Ray Price / Columbia

Debut Artist: Elvis Presley

Despite greater first-record chart action by Porter Wagoner in 1954, Elvis Presley's appearance as a blip on the regional country charts was to augur an unprecedented earthquake on the country music landscape. Unable to get work in a Southern gospel quartet, Elvis turned to the country market with a mix of Arthur Cruddup and Big Mama Thornton riffs and Bill Monroe tunes. Though his debut records on Memphis-based blues label Sun Records were country hits only in isolated markets such as Memphis, Richmond, New Orleans, and Dallas during this year, his electrifying Texas, Mississippi, Louisiana, and Alabama concerts with Hank Snow, Johnny Cash, Carl Perkins, and assorted other "Louisiana Hayride" and "Grand Ole Opry" acts blasted a hole in country music big enough to drive a pink Cadillac through. Country's establishment rejected him as fast as it could—his audience found almost no overlap

1954

STRANGE BREW

Hank Thompson.
credit: Bob Millard Collection

with theirs. Losing the majority of the rural youth, and subsequently a string of radio outlets, to the same rock 'n' roll that Presley was forced to pioneer, country music nearly didn't recover. Presley's 1954 Sun releases included "That's All Right (Mama)," "Blue Moon of Kentucky," and "Good Rockin' Tonight."

Elvis Presley
credit: Archives of Robert K. Oermann

Milestones

- Reba McEntire born near Chockie, Oklahoma, on March 28.
- Red Foley quits the "Grand Ole Opry," where he had risen to host of "The Prince Albert Show," to host his own television show, "Ozark Jubilee," from Springfield, Missouri. ("Opry" attendance begins a decline that will continue for several years due to the impact of both rock 'n' roll and television.)
- Ricky Skaggs born in Cordell, Kentucky, on July 18.
- On July 30, Elvis Presley makes his first public concert appearance at Overton Park Band Shell in Memphis, opening for Slim Whitman.

- Most major market country deejays announce they will no longer play 78 rpm records, except for oldies; the 45 rpm has taken over.
- Gretsch markets its first Chet Atkins signature electric guitar.
- On October 2, Elvis Presley makes his first and last guest appearance on the "Grand Ole Opry" and sings "Blue Moon of Kentucky." He has been in front of an audience only two months and, as legend has it, is told to "go back to driving a truck in Memphis."
- Gregg Jennings (Restless Heart) born near Oklahoma City, Oklahoma, on October 2.
- On October 16, Elvis Presley makes his debut on the "Louisiana Hayride." He is asked back and becomes, for a brief time, a regular.
- T. Graham Brown born in Arabi, Georgia, on October 30.
- Late in 1954, Johnny Cash attends his first sessions for Sun Records, recording "Wide Open Road" and "You're My Baby," both self-written.

The stage was always crowded at the Grand Ole Opry
credit: Courtesy of the Grand Ole Opry, photo by Les Leverett

- Fred Rose dies on December 1.
- Paul Gregg (Restless Heart) born near Oklahoma City, Oklahoma, on December 3.
- John Anderson born in Apopka, Florida, on December 13.
- Steve Wariner born in Noblesville, Indiana, on December 25.

Country Music on Television

Red Foley and Cliffie Stone led the invasion of country music personalities to major regional exposure on regularly scheduled television shows in the early to mid-1950s as television was beginning to gradually edge out radio as the medium of choice. The "Stars of the Grand Ole Opry" syndicated series was filmed in the Bradley Brothers' studio, the first studio on what would become Nashville's Record Row. That show, Foley's "Ozark Jubilee," and Stone's West Coast programs were forerunners of network shows to be hosted by Tennessee Ernie Ford, Eddy Arnold, and Jimmie Dean, among others, as well as the Johnny Cash, Barbara Mandrell, Mac Davis, Everly Brothers, Glen Campbell, and "Hee Haw" shows of the 1960s and 1970s; and today, The Nashville Network. Among the more popular of the innumerable small-time early morning shows were Ralph Emery's "Opry Almanac" and "Smilin'" Eddy Hill's "Country Junction" out of Nashville featuring the cut-ups of singer-songwriter Carmol Taylor that made him a star in Alabama and Mississippi.

Of course, radio was already flush with local country programs by the beginning of the 1950s, from the 15-minute dawn farm reports and noon gospel shows to the four-hour barn dances. Actually, country music had been seen on television in it's earliest days when event song composer Red River Dave McEnery appeared in experimental broadcasts at the 1939 New York World's Fair. For the most part, though, country was kept in the "farm hour" slots.

Pee Wee King left WSM and the "Opry" in 1947 to host four different weekly country variety programs in four different local TV markets in the Midwest, anchored by his own show at WAVE-TV and the "Midwestern Hayride" program on WLW-TV in Cincinnati. In June 1948, West Coast bandleader Spade Cooley got his own show on KTLA-TV in Los Angeles. His guests were a mixed lot, including such non-country names as Frank Sinatra, Jerry Lewis, and Sarah Vaughan. The most successful shows hosted by big-time country artists did lean rather heavily to pop and pop-country guests.

The daddy of country on network TV was East Coast promoter Connie B. Gay. Gay produced a country special in the DAR's Constitution Hall in Washington, D.C., in 1948 that went to all five cities in the infant NBC-TV network: Washington, D.C., New York, Boston, Philadelphia, and Baltimore. Shortly after that, Gay started the first syndicated country music television show, "Town and Country Time."

That same year NBC-TV introduced two series, "Village Barn Dance" and "Saturday Night Jamboree." In 1949, the ABC-TV network aired the "ABC Barn Dance." In December of that year, Eddy Arnold broke ground by appearing on "The Perry Como Show," followed in 1950 by a string of appearances on nearly every network musical variety show on the air.

Today, TV has taken over. Until Emery stepped down it was almost impossible to break a new country act without an appearance on Ralph Emery's popular "Nashville Now" show and a series of music videos running constantly on TNN and CMT. Back in the mid-1950s, pop-country singers getting television exposure was a major breakthrough.

Following World War II, Southerners with rural roots, whether they lived in small Alabama towns or in Detroit, were subjected to pressures of increased mobility, urbanization, and dissolving social traditions. Home and mama, key themes of pre-war country music lyrics, gave way to the new realities of a soaring divorce rate and a dispersal of families. Honky-tonk lyrics addressed these new realities, giving country fans a mirror of the new social order, or disorder, in which they found themselves. Even Tennessee Ernie Ford's rock-beat version of Merle Travis' 1947 coal camp anthem, "Sixteen Tons," spoke to the rural heart still beating in a people drawn to the city by employment opportunities, and often pulled apart by the fast-paced life they found there.

Most Important Records

"In The Jail House Now" Webb Pierce / Decca
"I Don't Care"/"Your Good For Nothing Heart" Webb Pierce / Decca
"Sixteen Tons" Tennessee Ernie Ford / Capitol
"Love, Love, Love" Webb Pierce / Decca
"Loose Talk" Carl Smith / Columbia
"I Forgot To Remember To Forget"/"Mystery Train" Elvis Presley / Sun
"A Satisfied Mind" Porter Wagoner / RCA
"Live Fast, Love Hard, Die Young" Faron Young / Capitol
"Let Me Go, Lover" Hank Snow / RCA
"The Cattle Call" Eddy Arnold / RCA

1955

A New Social Order

Hank Snow in the studio. credit: In the Southern Folklife Collection, University of North Carolina, Chapel Hill

Debut Artists: George Jones/ Johnny Cash

George Jones.
credit: In the Southern Folklife Collection, University of North Carolina, Chapel Hill

The arrival of George Jones and the debut of Johnny Cash in 1954 were equally significant. Jones' first charting record, "Why, Baby, Why" was released late in the year, eventually reaching the #4 position on the *Billboard* chart and continuing as a hit through the winter of 1956. Jones had been recording on "Pappy" Daily's Starday label since 1953, including rockabilly cuts under the names "Hank Smith" and "Thumper Jones," building a Texas-Louisiana following but without cracking the national charts. During his Starday years he appeared on the "Houston Jamboree" radio program and worked part-time as a deejay on KTRM in nearby Beaumont. With this hit and a short string of Top 10s that followed before he signed with Mercury Records at the end of 1956, Jones became a regular on Shreveport's "Louisiana Hayride."

Cash had a new bride and a new baby (Rosanne) and was struggling to make a living selling appliances door to door in Memphis when he became a regional sensation with his first Sun Records release, "Cry, Cry, Cry" in 1955. Working with distinctive guitarist Luther Perkins and bassist Marshall Grant and an occasional drummer as the Tennessee Three, Cash toured weekends, sometimes in Sun Records package tours, through Alabama, Mississippi, Louisiana and Texas during the next six months, before his first #1 record, "I Walk The Line." His second Sun release, "So Doggone Lonesome," was backed with his original version of "Folsom Prison Blues," which would become a #1 hit in a live version in 1968.

Milestones

- Flatt and Scruggs, the Louvin Brothers, Hawkshaw Hawkins, and Jim Reeves join the "Grand Ole Opry."
- Jimmy Fortune (Statler Brothers) born in Newport News, Virginia, on March 11.
- Kix Brooks (Leon Eric Brooks III) born in Shreveport, Louisiana on May 12.
- Rosanne Cash born in Memphis, Tennessee, on May 24.
- Keith Whitley born in Sandy Hook, Kentucky, on July 1.
- Col. Tom Parker first becomes involved in Elvis Presley's career, acting as booking agent and tour promoter. Presley is booked for summer shows opening for Andy Griffith and Ferlin Huskey, and Hank Snow, the Louvin Brothers, and Cowboy Copas. He steals the show at every stop.
- Ray Price and his Cherokee Cowboys are voted Best New Big Dance Band and the #4 Show Band in the nation by a *Downbeat* magazine reader's poll.
- Waylon Jennings works as a disc jockey in Lubbock, where he meets an ambitious local musician named Buddy Holly.

- Floyd Cramer moves to Nashville.
- Carlene Carter born in Madison, Tennessee, on September 26.
- Earl Scruggs critically injured in a car crash. The subsequent life-long back injury will eventually contribute to the breakup of Flatt and Scruggs.
- In October, Elvis Presley is headlining his own country music tour. The Elvis Presley Jamboree features Jimmy C. Newman, Jean Shepard, Bobby Lord, Johnny Cash, and Floyd Cramer.

The Folk Music Revival

In post-war America, much of what is celebrated as "good old mountain music" became passe to a country music–buying public enthralled with electrified instruments and honky-tonk rhythms. Acts that came from Appalachian traditions, especially latter-day configurations of acts such as the Carter Family and the Stoneman Family made famous in Ralph Peer's 1927 Bristol, Tennessee, sessions had a difficult time finding work. By the time Elvis Presley began to reshape popular music in 1954 and 1955, bluegrass giants such as Bill Monroe, Flatt and Scruggs, and the Stanley Brothers were suffering along with the string band traditionalists. The bluegrass gospel duo, the Louvin Brothers, adapted to more modern sounds and became mainstream country stars by 1956, but those who clung to the truly old-time rural sounds or who continued to drive bluegrass needed a miracle to survive by the mid-1950s. These hillbilly heroes got their miracle from the least likely source—upscale, highly-educated urban professionals.

The folk music revival that lifted Southern traditional acoustic music on its second wave beginning in the mid-1950s got its academic start with song collectors such as John Avery Lomax and his son Alan in the mid-1930s. They brought Huddy "Leadbelly" Ledbetter to New York to record for American Recording Company labels and to write a book about his life and music. Columbia University in Manhattan was a tiny, but important, beacon of folk music study and celebration. In Greenwich Village, a young Pete Seeger would eventually hook up with other folk-performing heartland immigrants: Cisco Houston, Woody Guthrie, and Leadbelly. Manhattan was where it began, expanding to reach the rest of the country with the Weavers' 1950–1951 pop hit of Leadbelly's "Goodnight Irene," which was soon covered by such country artists as Ernest Tubb and Red Foley.

Still a staple in 1955 of numerous radio programs such as the "Grand Ole Opry," the "Midwest Hayride," and the "Renfro Valley Barn Dance," traditional string bands and mountain music had lost out to cowboy-suited contemporary electric ensembles in the record and touring business. The Carter Family brand of "folk music" of Guthrie and Seeger, if not bluegrass, became identified with progressive political ideals, but enlarging its appeal with down-to-earth honesty, energy, and different rhythms and harmonies. To a growing audience of big city professionals, it was refreshingly new and nostalgic all at once.

"It was sometime around 1955 that I began to notice a change in our audiences," said Roni Stoneman, then a central character of the Stoneman Family act. "I started looking out there and seeing doctors and lawyers and such. They'd say, 'do you play that folk music?' I said, 'Well, I guess we do—we're folk, ain't we?'"

Mother Maybelle and the Carter sisters were quite popular on this developing circuit. Flatt and Scruggs became a huge hit on college campuses, especially after they became known for writing and performing theme songs for the early 1960s television series "The Beverly Hillbillies" and the soundtrack of the film *Bonnie and Clyde*. TV variety programs such as "Hootenanny" sprung up in the early 1960s, combining acts like Johnny Cash and the Chad Mitchell Trio, spawning a trend on college campuses nationwide for local hootenannies and guitar pulls. Thanks to urban interest, these acoustic branches of country music survived and even thrived through times when their rural base may not have been sufficient to see them through.

THE LOUVIN BROTHERS BREAK THROUGH

In 1956 rural gospel harmonies were introduced to the mainstream. The Louvin Brothers, Charlie and Ira, Section, Alabama, boys with gospel and bluegrass running through their veins, were popular gospel artists on Capitol when they shifted to Decca and proved they could swing with secular country music and conventional instrumentals. They joined the "Grand Ole Opry" in 1955 and enjoyed their first #1 hit single with "I Don't Believe You've Met My Baby" in 1956. They could write, harmonize, and sell their heartfelt songs with genuine emotion. Their impact and influence on bluegrass is evident in their 1956–1957 hit, "Cash On The Barrel Head." When the Everly Brothers came along, they were widely seen as a younger version of the Louvins. Emmylou Harris acknowledges their influence. Though they would break-up in 1962, and Ira would die in 1965, the Louvin Brothers were alive and kicking in 1956, and notching hits to prove it. They were on top of the world.

Louvin Brothers with Roy Acuff backstage at the Opry. credit: In the Southern Folklife Collection, University of North Carolina, Chapel Hill

Most Important Records

"Crazy Arms" Ray Price / Columbia
"Heartbreak Hotel" Elvis Presley / RCA
"Singing The Blues" Marty Robbins / Columbia
"Don't Be Cruel" Elvis Presley / RCA
"I Walk The Line" Johnny Cash / Sun
"Why Baby Why"[3] Red Sovine & Webb Pierce / Decca
"Hound Dog" Elvis Presley / RCA
"Blue Suede Shoes"[4] Carl Perkins / Sun
"I Want You, I Need You, I Love You" Elvis Presley / RCA
"I Don't Believe You've Met My Baby" Louvin Brothers / Capitol

Debut Artist: Johnny Horton

Born April 30, 1925 in Los Angeles and reared in Tyler, Texas, Johnny Horton was a college scholarship athlete. After graduation, he worked in Alaska as a professional fisherman where he took his original performing nickname "The Singing Fisherman." He first recorded for tiny Cormac Records when he began as a regular on the "Louisiana Hayride" in 1951, then for Dot, Abbott and Mercury, but didn't chart until he signed with Columbia where his 1956 debut records, "Honky-Tonk Man" and "I'm A One Woman Man" both hit the Top 10. ("Honky-Tonk Man" was successfully revived by Dwight Yoakam in 1986.) Within a few years he would be a big star for history-based story sings such as "The Battle of New Orleans," "Johnny Reb," "Sink The Bismark" and "North To Alaska." His 1959 hit, "When It's Springtime In Alaska (It's 40 Down Below)," started a trend of country saga songs at Columbia, followed by Johnny Cash's "Don't Take Your Guns To Town," etc., and Horton's own followup hits. Married to Billie Jean Jones Eshlimar Williams, widow of Hank Williams, Horton died in an auto accident in 1960.

Milestones

- Mark Collie born in Waynesboro, Tennessee, on January 18.
- Mark Herndon (Alabama) born in Springfield, Massachusetts, on May 11.

3. "Why, Baby, Why" was co-written by George Jones and Darrell Edwards, and first released by Jones for his first hit on the Starday label in 1955. It has been recorded many times since, including in 1993 by Palomino Road.

4. Perkins' "Blue Suede Shoes" was a triple threat, topping *Billboard's* pop, country, and R&B charts. Had Perkins not been nearly killed and subsequently sidelined for a year by a car wreck on his way to appear on the "Perry Como Show" to receive the gold record for this tune, he might have been as big a superstar as Presley.

It would be an understatement simply to say that Marty Robbins was versatile. Through his long career he convincingly represented honky-tonk, Hawaiian, rockabilly, teen-style pop, jazz, and his own brand of Western gunfighter ballads. Few singers could spread themselves over so much stylistic ground without losing themselves in the process, but Robbins was the exception to the rule.

Born Martin David Robinson (with a twin sister) and reared near Glendale, Arizona, Robbins had a childhood of poverty and instability. His father drank heavily, and when he got angry he more often than not took it out on Marty. One of the few pleasant memories he garnered from his first six years was of listening to songs and stories by his grandfather, Texas Bob Heckle, a retired medicine show performer. Between Heckle and Gene Autry movies, Marty fell in love early with The Old West of romance and adventure.

Grandpa Heckle died when Robbins was 6, and when his parents divorced in 1937, he moved into Glendale with his mother. There, he became a veritable juvenile delinquent, always in trouble with the police, often turning to petty theft for his spending money. World War II gave him a sanctioned outlet for his aggression and he joined the Navy in 1943, at the age of 17. He learned to play guitar in the South Pacific.

Returning to Arizona after the war, Robbins played at music until 1948, when he married Marizona Baldwin and joined KPHO as host of the early morning "Chuck Wagon Time" program. When KPHO launched the state's first TV station, Robbins hosted "Country Caravan," though the thought of appearing on-screen terrified him so deeply that he almost quit.

In 1951, Little Jimmy Dickens was a guest on "Country Caravan" and "discovered" Robbins. Robbins recorded four songs for Columbia's Art Satherly that fall, but they all stiffed miserably. Though his star rose steadily over this decade, he remained a temperamental personality. His temper got him fired from the "Grand Ole Opry" for one week in 1958, and in 1979 Robbins got into another row with "Opry" management about their banning of horns on stage. He was known backstage at the "Opry" as an inveterate practical joker.

Robbins' chart debut in 1952 was a #1, "I'll Go Alone," and he had reasonable success in the intervening years, but he lacked an image as an artist until 1954, when he scored his second #1, "Singing The Blues." In 1955, rolling with trends, he fell into a lackluster rut of covering rock 'n' roll hits for the country market (including Chuck Berry's "Mabellene" and Elvis Presley's "That's All Right (Mama)." He would record in New York under Mitch Miller to establish himself as a teen market artist with both country and pop-rock appeal in the late 1950s when the lines between the genres were blurred, providing such light fare as his chart-topping "White Sport Coat (And A Pink Carnation)," "Teenage Dream," and "She Was Only Seventeen (He Was One Year Older)." It wasn't until 1959 that he established himself with the musical image he would carry through the 1960s, as a singer of Western and gunslinger tunes that began with the electrifying ballad "El Paso," his last hit (seven weeks at #1) of the 1950s.

Marty Robbins.
credit: Courtesy of the Grand Ole Opry

- Doug Stone born in Atlanta, Georgia, on June 19.
- Johnny Cash, George Jones, Jimmy C. Newman, and Stonewall Jackson join the "Grand Ole Opry."
- Dwight Yoakam born in Pikesville, Kentucky, on October 23.
- June Carter takes six weeks of acting lessons in New York prior to making her television acting debut in an episode of "Gunsmoke."
- Sylvia (Sylvia Kirby Allen) born in Kokomo, Indiana, on December 9.
- Leroy Parnell born in Abilene, Texas, on December 21.
- Suzy Bogguss born in Aledo, Illinois, on December 30.

Sam Phillips was surprised when a combination of RCA, Hill & Range Songs, and Col. Tom Parker met his demand late in 1956 for $35,000 to take over Elvis Presley's recording contract—but he was not unhappy. Sun had to pay cash to press and ship his growing string of hot-selling hits, but retailers, sensing Sun's financial precariousness, were slow-walking payment to Phillips. The more records Presley sold, the closer Phillips came to bankruptcy. In 1957, Phillips took the money from RCA and invested in his other developing artists, mainly Johnny Cash, Carl Perkins, and Jerry Lee Lewis. Years later, in retrospect of the fabulous success Presley had at RCA, Phillips stood by his original decision. "If I've been asked once, I've been asked a thousand times, did I regret it? No. I did not, I do not, and I never will." For Phillips, Presley was the goose who'd laid a golden egg that was too large to be hatched.

1957

SUN SHINES
WITHOUT ELVIS

Johnny Cash and his Tennessee Two, Luther Perkins on guitar and Marshall Grant on bass. credit: In the Southern Folklife Collection, University of North Carolina, Chapel Hill

Most Important Records

"Gone" Ferlin Husky / Capitol
"Young Love" Sonny James / Capitol
"Wake Up Little Susie" Everly Brothers / Cadence
"Four Walls" Jim Reeves / RCA
"Bye Bye Love" Everly Brothers / Cadence
"A White Sport Coat (And A Pink Carnation)" Marty Robbins / Columbia
"There You Go" Johnny Cash / Columbia
"My Special Angel" Bobby Helms / Decca
"Fraulein" Bobby Helms / Decca
"Whole Lot Of Shakin' Goin' On" Jerry Lee Lewis / Sun

Debut Artist: Bobby Helms

Born September 15, 1933 in Bloomington, Indiana, Bobby Helms found a unique niche, singing to two generations of American G.I.s stationed in post-war Germany. The tune, "Fraulein," topped

Porter Wagoner and Chet Atkins.
credit: In the Southern Folklife Collection, University of North Carolina, Chapel Hill

Don and Phil Everly are a prime example of rock 'n' roll history with country roots. They grew up in Muhlenburg County, Kentucky, in a musical family. Parents, Ike and Margaret, were notable part-time country entertainers in the South and Midwest. The brothers toured with them from an early age each summer, learning to harmonize to gospel and country standards. Ike and Margaret retired when the boys graduated from high school, clearing the path for the Everly Brothers to travel their own road, closely watched by Mom and Dad.

They came to Nashville and were asked to join the "Grand Ole Opry." They recorded for a year for Columbia, but had no success until they signed with Cadence Records and hooked up with Nashville songwriters Felice and Boudleaux Bryant, who gave them "Wake Up Little Suzie," "All I Have To Do Is Dream," "Bird Dog," and "Bye Bye Love." Their own songwriting talents emerged later, including Phil's timeless "When Will I Be Loved." The Everly Brothers' records became classics of both country and rock 'n' roll.

In the early 1960s the Everly Brothers relocated to the West Coast, signing a 10-year, $1 million contract with Warner Brothers Records with hopes of getting a break in movies. They quit touring to take acting lessons, "fired" their manager, Wesley Rose after a series of lawsuits, and then enlisted in the Marine Corps, which took them out of the market at precisely the time the British Invasion groups were beginning to dominate the pop charts. They reunited in the mid-1960s but, like Rick Nelson, remained popular primarily as a nostalgia act. They continued to make reasonably successful records for many years, but were unable to recapture their original trend-setting glory, despite new country-oriented appearances on the "Johnny Cash Show" and the "Glen Campbell Goodtime" Hour.

The Everly Brothers split publicly at Knott's Berry Farm in 1973. Don had already indicated his dissatisfaction with life on the "oldies-but-goodies" circuit with a tune called "I'm Tired Of Singing My Songs In Las Vegas." Phil made the act's final appearance more dramatic by throwing down his guitar and walking off stage, leaving an astonished younger brother holding the bag for two more performances.

Phil went solo, and Don toured for years under the aegis of the Dead Cowboys Band. The brothers have since gotten back together, recording a particularly successful reunion album at London's Albert Hall. They make a widely renowned annual benefit appearance called "The Everly Brothers Homecoming" in Central City, Kentucky, generally featuring John Prine, whose family roots are also in that county he immortalized in his popular composition, "Paradise."

Everly Brothers, Phil and Don. credit: In the Southern Folklife Collection, University of North Carolina, Chapel Hill

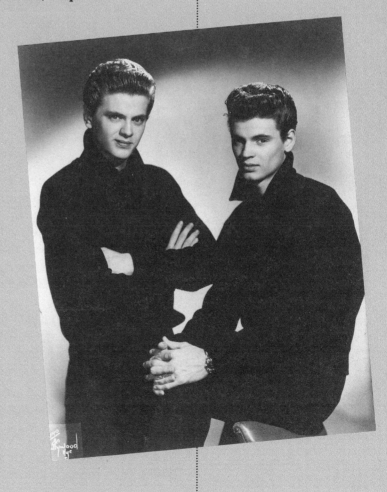

the charts. He followed it with a pair of records that reached the Top 10 in the pop charts, including "My Special Angel." Helm's country fame was short-lived—he managed country Top 10s in only two years. He is best remembered for that quintessential Christmas record he cut in 1957, "Jingle Bell Rock."

Milestones

- Patty Loveless (Patricia Ramey) born in Pikesville, Kentucky, on January 4.
- The Everly Brothers, Porter Wagoner, Stonewall Jackson, Ferlin Huskey, and Doug and Rusty Kershaw join the "Grand Ole Opry."
- Competing on "Arthur Godfrey's Talent Scouts," Patsy Cline wins with "Walkin' after Midnight."
- Vince Gill born in Norman, Oklahoma, on April 12.
- "Rev." Blind Andrew Jenkins dies on April 25.
- Badly shaken by a telephoned death threat, Ernest Tubb mistakenly takes a wild pistol shot at *Billboard's* Nashville office manager, Bill Williams. He is arrested and charged only with public drunkenness.
- Pam Tillis born in Plant City, Florida, on July 24.
- Twelve-year-old Dolly Parton comes to Nashville with family friends, Carl and Pearl Butler, and bluffs her way onto WSM's "Friday Night Frolics" radio program, making her Nashville singing debut with a George Jones song.
- Holly Dunn born in San Antonio, Texas, on August 22.
- Lyle Lovett born in Klein, Texas, on November 1.

1958

A Crossover Year

In this pop-rock/country crossover year all ten of the "Most Important Records" in country were simultaneously major pop or rock 'n' roll hits. The rural side of commercial country music was in danger of being crowded out by a quickly shifting format. Hank Snow had a Top 5 and a Top 10 record, but Ernest Tubb had only one Top 10 record in 1958. Hank Thompson couldn't break into the Top 10 with either of his two releases, Lefty Frizzell didn't even chart, and Roy Acuff, still the top star of the "Grand Ole Opry," marked his tenth year without making the charts. Nashville wasn't hurting—the records topping *Billboard's* country charts were doing phenomenally well—but the definition of "country" was slipping away from the traditionalists.

Most Important Records

"City Lights" Ray Price / Columbia
"Alone With You" Faron Young / Capitol
"Ballad Of A Teenage Queen" Johnny Cash / Sun

"Guess Things Happen That Way" Johnny Cash / Sun
"Oh Lonesome Me" Don Gibson / RCA
"Bird Dog" Everly Brothers / Cadence
"The Story Of My Life" Marty Robbins / Columbia
"All I Have To Do Is Dream" Everly Brothers / Cadence
"Just Married" Marty Robbins / Columbia
"Great Balls Of Fire" Jerry Lee Lewis / Sun

Debut Artist:
Stonewall Jackson

It looked for a while that Stonewall Jackson (a descendent of famed Confederate General Thomas "Stonewall" Jackson) might have a military career. He served in the Navy from 1949 to 1954, but he bought a guitar and was soon entertaining the troops. The day he arrived in Nashville in 1956, he tried to sell songs to Acuff-Rose Publications. Instead, three days later, he was on the "Grand Ole Opry" and on his way to a record deal. His first hit, a George Jones composition called "Life To Go," reached #2 and remained on the charts for nearly half a year. Jackson is best known for his pounding 2 million-selling 1959 crossover hit, "Waterloo," and "I Washed My Hands In Muddy Water." He has remained a stalwart of his era's music on the "Grand Ole Opry" for more than 35 years.

Awards

GRAMMY WINNERS

BEST COUNTRY AND WESTERN PERFORMANCE—"Tom Dooley" The Kingston Trio

GOLD RECORDS

"Hard Headed Woman" G/S Elvis Presley / RCA

Milestones

- Owen Bradley hired full-time as A&R man for Decca in Nashville.
- Elvis Presley enters the Army on March 24.
- Johnny Cash quits the "Opry" and "casts his lot with Los Angeles," the trade papers report.
- Shelly West born in Cleveland, Ohio, on May 23.
- The Glaser Brothers, three brothers who learned to sing while riding tractors across the Nebraska corn fields, move to Nashville to seek fame and fortune.
- "Opry" comic Rod Brasfield, 48, dies on September 12.
- Marty Stuart born in Philadelphia, Mississippi, on September 30.
- The "Grand Ole Opry" hires Don Gibson, Roy Drusky, and Archie Campbell as cast members.
- Tanya Tucker born in Seminole, Texas, on October 10.
- Mark Miller (lead singer/songwriter for Sawyer Brown) born in Dayton, Ohio, on October 25.
- Country Music Association founded in November.
- Arkansas singer Harold Jenkins names himself after two little Southern towns, Conway, Arkansas and Twitty, Texas, and has his first #1 on the pop charts with "It's Only Make Believe."
- When Johnny Cash performs his first free concert for the inmates at San Quentin Prison, Merle Haggard is there—as an inmate.
- Near Rome, an Italian mugger tries to strong-arm Roy Acuff, who is on tour, and gets a surprise instead. The "Opry" icon wheels on his heels and socks the would-be robber in the jaw.
- Joe Diffie born in Duncan, Oklahoma, on December 28.

The pop-style production touch that Chet Atkins had been perfecting came together with beautiful, simple, meaningful country melodies and lyrics by Don Gibson in 1958 to produce a two-sided hit single, "Oh Lonesome Me"/"I Can't Stop Loving You." This, critics generally agree, was the first fully-realized example of "The Nashville Sound."

Stereophonic records came into millions of American homes in 1958, and Atkins' pop-influenced records were produced with much the same attention to detail as pop stereo productions of that year. Decca producer Owen Bradley, himself a former pop orchestra piano player and arranger, adapted Brenda Lee and Patsy Cline, among others, to this

Nashville Sound idea. Soon, every producer in Nashville who could figure it out was trying the new pop-flavored approach. Traditional honky-tonk music, which had been losing radio outlets to the point of near-extinction, took a back seat to a new form that kept country viable in the larger market.

The Nashville Sound used violins instead of fiddles, and the sound of a smooth, jingling six-string rhythm guitar. It would prove a lifesaver for country music, which was being crushed beneath the weight of the "child" it put out for adoption—rock 'n' roll. Smooth vocal backing by the Jordonaires or the more generic Anita Kerr Singers contributed to vastly more sophisticated and

subtle arrangements that earned country a new hearing in the national market.

The best of the Nashville Sound was gorgeous, high-quality music. The classic power of those Don Gibson RCA records, Patsy Cline's Decca sessions, and the late Jim Reeves represents the best of that sound, called in turns "metropolitan country" and "countrypolitan music." Much of Dottie West's early catalog seems to represent the worst excesses of the sound. Even Chet Atkins repented partially for soaking country music too generously with what became alien instrumental overlays. But no serious student of popular music can deny its utility in saving country music from the scrapheap of history.

Don Gibson.
credit: In the Southern Folklife Collection, University of North Carolina, Chapel Hill

1959

FLATT AND SCRUGGS ARRIVE

After three years of poor wages and near-constant touring with Bill Monroe's Blue Grass Boys, Lester Flatt and Earl Scruggs struck out on their own in 1948. Furious, Monroe blackballed them from the "Grand Ole Opry," relegating Flatt and Scruggs and their Foggy Mountain Boys to secondary radio markets in rural mountain regions. Adding an element of entertainment to their act, they were back in Nashville, on WSM, with Martha White Flour as a sponsor in 1953. Bluegrass was hurt badly by the emergence of rock 'n' roll. Flatt and Scruggs didn't get their string of hit records started until 1959, when "Cabin on the Hill" reached the Top 10. In the early 1960s, fueled by their theme song for the national TV series, the "Beverly Hillbillies," they were discovered by the urban folk revival audience, taking their popularity to new heights.

Most Important Records

"Battle Of New Orleans" Johnny Horton / Columbia
"The Three Bells" The Browns / RCA
"El Paso" Marty Robbins / Columbia
"Don't Take Your Guns To Town" Johnny Cash / Columbia
"White Lightning" George Jones / Mercury
"Waterloo" Johnny Horton / Columbia
"Billy Bayou" Jim Reeves / RCA
"Country Girl" Faron Young / Capitol
"Same Old Me" Ray Price / RCA
"When It's Springtime In Alaska (It's 40 Down Below)" Johnny Horton / Columbia

Flatt & Scruggs and their Foggy Mountain Boys on the set of their show, "Martha White Biscuit Time."
credit: In the Southern Folklife Collection, University of North Carolina, Chapel Hill

Buck Owens (r.) and Jimmy
Dean.
credit: Bob Millard Collection

Debut Artist: Buck Owens

Alvis Edgar "Buck" Owens had recorded briefly, with limited regional success, as a rockabilly artist using the name Corky Jones in the mid-1950s. His record, "Second Fiddle," charted only briefly, but was popular along Owens' stomping grounds— Washington State to Southern California. His second Capitol Records single, "Under Your Spell Again," carried him to national prominence.

A Texas sharecropper's son largely raised in Arizona, he had worked in California as a session player for such artists as Faron Young, Sonny James, and Wanda Jackson. He took Ferlin Husky's place as Tommy Duncan's guitarist before making his own mark in the early 1960s with protege/best friend guitarist Don Rich as the leader of his Buckaroos band. Together they made punched-up, kickin', all-electric California country music a new and lively aesthetic. Owens' insistence on basing his business operations in Bakersfield and Capitol's preference that he record in their West Coast studio made the Bakersfield-Hollywood area the second most important country music center of that time. Out of that breeding ground would emerge significant artists such as Merle Haggard, Bonnie Owens, Leona Williams, and Dwight Yoakam.

Awards

GRAMMY WINNERS
BEST COUNTRY AND WESTERN PERFORMANCE—"The Battle of New Orleans" Johnny Horton

SONG OF THE YEAR (NC)—"The Battle of New Orleans" Jimmy Driftwood (writer)
BEST COMEDY PERFORMANCE, MUSICAL (NC)—"The Battle of Kooka-monga" Homer and Jethro

GOLD RECORDS
"Hymns" G/A Tennessee Ernie Ford / Capitol

Milestones

- Roger Miller, who had been working as Minnie Pearl's fiddler, has first major success as a songwriter when Jim Reeves records "Billy Bayou."
- Larry Stewart born in Paducah, Kentucky, on March 2.
- Randy Travis (Randy Bruce Trawick) born in Marshville, North Carolina, on May 4.
- Kathy Mattea born in Cross Lane, West Virginia, on June 21.
- New "Grand Ole Opry" members include Billy Grammer, Hawkshaw Hawkins, Skeeter Davis, and George Morgan (rejoining).
- Lorrie Morgan born in Nashville, Tennessee, on June 27.
- A reader poll by *Radio Mirror* reveals that the "Grand Ole Opry" is America's favorite radio program.
- Radney Foster born in Del Rio, Texas, on July 20.
- Collin Raye born in De Queen, Arkansas, on August 22.
- Dottie West inks her first recording contract, signing with Starday Records.

Bill Anderson helped shave the rural edge off country music starting in the late 1950s, thus vitalizing the genre for the next two decades. Anderson came by his relative sophistication honestly. A University of Georgia journalism graduate in the early 1950s, he was already a successful radio announcer and songwriter ("City Lights" and "That's What It's Like To Be Lonesome" for Ray Price) when he got his first big break as a recording artist by covering Price's recording of his own song, "That's What It's Like To Be Lonesome." It became a respectable Top 15 hit

for Anderson, even after Price's hit several months earlier. "Whisperin' Bill," as he was called for his soft-spoken recitations, noodled along for several years, until he slammed "Mama Sang a Song" and "Still" into the top of the charts for seven weeks apiece in 1962 and 1963.

Beginning in the late 1970s, Anderson's road show was one of the earliest to attempt larger-than-life visual elements that mark today's concert packages. It was pretty small by rock 'n' roll standards of even 10 years earlier, but the colored lights and large screen projections of native Americans

and Hank Williams represented an important development in country entertainment.

Anderson epitomizes longevity —charting for nearly 30 straight years—in part because he wrote many of his own songs. His best-remembered hit singles include "Tips Of My Fingers" (revived for another hit by Steve Wariner in 1992), "I Love You Drops," and "Wild Week-End." Anderson still gives concerts, but lately has been seen by most country fans as a television show host for The Nashville Network.

Bill Anderson.
credit: Bob Millard Collection

Marty Robbins.
**credit: In the Southern Folklife
Collection, University of North
Carolina, Chapel Hill**

THE 1960S

1960

GUNFIGHTER BALLADS

Marty Robbins became a country recording star in 1953. He entered his teen-idol stage in 1957 with "White Sport Coat (And A Pink Carnation)." With the release in late 1959 of "El Paso," from his million-selling album, *Gunfighter Ballads & Other Trail Songs*, he moved up another notch to superstar. Written by Robbins himself, "El Paso" was inspired by his grandfather, a former medicine show singer who had enjoyed telling his small grandson tales of the Old West. The song's plotting and dramatic tension, flavored by gut-string Spanish guitar sounds, combined to make it one of the most popular story songs of all time. Starting a new trend in country music, it wasn't based on any real incident, as previous million-selling country story songs such as Vernon Dalhart's "The Ballad of Floyd Collins" or Johnny Horton's history-based saga songs had been. Robbins perfected the three-minute musical novel.

Most Important Records

"He'll Have To Go" Jim Reeves / RCA
"Please Help Me I'm Falling" Hank Locklin / RCA
"Alabam" Cowboy Copas / Starday
"Wings of a Dove" Ferlin Husky / Capitol
"Above And Beyond" Buck Owens / Capitol
"Last Date" Floyd Cramer / RCA
"Am I Losing You" Jim Reeves / RCA
"Just One Time" Don Gibson / RCA
"The Window Up Above" George Jones / Mercury
"Big Iron" Marty Robbins / Columbia

Debut Artist: Loretta Lynn

There is no life story more "country" than Loretta Lynn's. As her best-selling autobiography, *Coal Miner's Daughter*, explains, she was raised in dirt-poor Butcher Holler, Kentucky, married to an older man (Mooney Lynn) at age 13, and having babies before she herself was ready to put away her dolls.

Mooney gave her a guitar for her 18th birthday and was tireless in trying to get her a singing career in the Northwest, where he'd relocated to find work. Not having access to Nashville tunesmiths, she wrote her own songs. She found a local investor to put out her first several records on an ad hoc label called Zero Records. Mooney and Loretta piled the kids into the family car and started out on the bread-and-baloney-in-the-back-seat promotional tour of country radio. Despite no money or major label muscle to push the record, they still managed to score a Top 20 with "Honky-Tonk Girl" on Zero Records, and see most of the country in so doing. Loretta showed spunk and pluck, not to mention talent, on that rag-tag tour.

Ernest Tubb and Loretta Lynn.
credit: In the Southern Folklife Collection, University of North Carolina, Chapel Hill

Awards

GRAMMYS

BEST COUNTRY AND WESTERN PERFORMANCE—"El Paso" Marty Robbins

GOLD RECORDS

"Elvis Presley" G/A Elvis Presley / RCA

Milestones

- Patsy Cline joins the "Opry" cast on January 9.
- Former Sun Records engineer and hit songwriter Jack Clements is hired as A&R assistant to Chet Atkins at RCA Victor.
- Ralph Peer dies of pneumonia at age 67 in Los Angeles on January 19.
- In the wake of on-going Congressional investigations into the pop radio payola scandal, Sam Phillips switches his radio stations to all-girl staffs and "good music" formats, banning his most popular Sun Records artists—Elvis Presley, Johnny Cash, Carl Perkins and Jerry Lee Lewis.
- Eddy Arnold releases "Johnny Reb—That's Me," a continuation of a Civil War theme in country music that will include Johnny Horton's "Johnny Reb," Johnny Cash's "The Rebel—Johnny Yuma," Claude King's "The Burning of Atlanta," and Hoyt Axton's "Georgia Hoss Soldier."
- In February, the Everly Brothers leave Cadence Records for a 10-year $1 million contract with Warner Brothers Records that includes movie opportunities. Later this year, the brothers forsake their tour career to attend a Hollywood acting school for six months.
- In March, Elvis Presley returns to the United States and to civilian life. In quick succession, he records three albums in marathon, one-day sessions in Nashville, but will have to hire a policeman to keep spectators out of the studio by the third one.
- WLS is bought out by the ABC Radio Network and converted to an all-pop format. After 36 years on the air, the "National Barn Dance" does its last broadcast at WLS the first week in May.
- Chet Atkins hosts "Nashville Night" at the Newport Jazz Festival on July 4th, showcasing his band, which features Buddy Harmon (drums), Hank Garland (additional guitar), Gary Burton (vibes), Floyd Cramer and Brenton Banks (piano), and Bob Moore (bass). It is the first time Southern music, other than Dixieland, is featured at Newport.
- New "Grand Ole Opry" members include George Hamilton IV, Hank Locklin, Bobby Lord, and Billy Walker.
- On August 27, the "Louisiana Hayride" is canceled after nearly 14 continuous years. It will later return to the air.

- Owen Bradley produces three consecutive #1 pop singles for Brenda Lee in his Nashville studio.
- Hawkshaw Hawkins and long-time stage partner Jean Shepard are married on-stage at the Forum in Wichita, Kansas, following their show.
- On November 5, Johnny Horton is killed in a car wreck near Milano, Texas, while returning from a concert in Austin. His manager Tillman Franks and guitarist Tommy Tomlinson are injured.
- A.P. Carter dies in Kingsport, Tennessee, of heart disease on November 7.
- Off-the-wall Southern hipster comic Brother Dave Gardner, a protege of Col. Tom Parker, has a pair of smash-hit, left-field comedy albums for RCA, then mysteriously disappears. Says *Billboard* magazine on December 19: "Chet Atkins is ready, willin', and able to cut a new Brother Dave Gardner album if Dave can be located."
- Marty Roe (lead singer for Diamond Rio) born in Dayton, Ohio, on December 28.

Hitsville U.S.A.

The Nashville Sound, as produced by Chet Atkins and Owen Bradley for RCA and Decca, respectively, made Nashville's two major studios magnets for hit pop recordings. *Billboard* magazine explained: "At RCA alone, for example, more than half of last year's pop hits emanated from what used to be considered the country music capital." Major pop/country hits by Brenda Lee, the Everly Brothers, Don Gibson, Bobby Helms, Mark Denning, The Browns, Bob Beckham, Conway Twitty, Marty Robbins, Johnny Cash, Connie Francis, Johnny Tillotson, and others often came from Nashville-based songwriters but were especially beholden to the first-rate Nashville session musicians drawn by steady work at the RCA and Bradley studios.

"Mostly these men are jazz musicians," Atkins explained. "But instead of sneering at country music, they understand it and love it."

Session players such as Harold Bradley, Floyd Cramer, Hank Garland, Grady Martin, Bob Moore, and Buddy Harmon are joined by a pair of top-notch, back-up vocal groups on nearly every hit record cut in Nashville during this period: the ex-gospel Jordanaires and the Anita Kerr Quartet. The Jordanaires are credited with perfecting a shorthand notation system called the Nashville Number System that gave maximum efficiency and flexibility to Nashville session players. Session players used the system to do skeletal "head arrangements" that they could then flesh out during the actual recording. The old joke about Nashville players was that "they can read music, but it hasn't hurt their playing much."

As Atkins noted about the laid back cooperation and spontaneity that marked Nashville sessions: "A New York record always sounds mechanical. The musicians are inhibited by the sheet music in front of them. . . Down here we have arrangements but we never write them down. Every musician offers suggestions, so we have seven or eight creative minds at work for every record."

The particular style known as the Nashville Sound is no longer in vogue. Nashville's best recording musicians still operate with the Nashville Number System, though, and contribute their own ideas to every song recorded.

Patsy Cline.
credit: Archives of Robert K.
Oermann

Patsy Breaks Free

Patsy Cline's early recording career has to be one of the worst cases of wasted potential in country music history. Stuck in a contract with Four Star Records, she scored only one hit in about five years, "Walkin' After Midnight," the only decent song made available to her during that period. Four Star owner Bill McCall wouldn't let Owen Bradley record anything but songs he picked from the Four Star Music Catalog, which contained a lot of bad rockabilly and yodel numbers that Patsy was compelled to cut at a flat rate per side. Her contract ran out in 1960. Owen Bradley convinced her to come out of semi-retirement and signed her at Decca. Free at last to pick from the best songs available in Nashville, her string of hits began in 1961 with "I Fall To Pieces" and "Crazy."

Most Important Records

"Just Walk On By" Leroy Van Dyke / Mercury
"Don't Worry (Like All The Other Times)" Marty Robbins / Columbia

"Hello Walls" Faron Young / Capitol
"Tender Years" George Jones / Mercury
"North To Alaska" Johnny Horton / Columbia
"Heartbreak USA" Kitty Wells / Decca
"Big, Bad John" Jimmy Dean / Columbia
"I Fall To Pieces" Patsy Cline / Decca
"Foolin' Around" Buck Owens / Capitol
"Po' Folks" Bill Anderson / Decca

Debut Artist: Claude King

Shreveport native Claude King learned to play guitar well before he could shave, but by 1948, when the "Louisiana Hayride" was started at KWKH, King was at the University of Idaho on a baseball scholarship. He returned home and began playing on the "Louisiana Hayride" in 1952. His path crossed fellow-Shreveport denizen Merle Kilgore at the radio station, and their fates would become entwined in the early 1960s. King scored a pair of Top 10 singles ("Big River, Big Man" and "The Comancheros," inspired by the John Wayne movie of the same title) in 1961. Having quit his disk jockey job to pursue a career as recording artist and songwriter himself, Kilgore penned a song called "Wolverton Mountain" that gave King a nine-week ride atop the country charts in 1962 and a Top 10 pop hit as well—his biggest record ever. King continued, with mixed success, to record for Columbia through the early 1970s.

Awards

GRAMMYS
BEST COUNTRY AND WESTERN RECORDING—"Big, Bad John" Jimmy Dean

GOLD RECORDS
"Big, Bad John" G/A Jimmy Dean / Columbia
"Blue Hawaii" G/A Elvis Presley / RCA
"Elvis' Golden Records" G/A Elvis Presley / RCA

Milestones

- The Everly Brothers, approaching the age of majority, bide their time. In May they form a record label, Calliope Records, and by November they have all but quit the concert business. Finally, in a futile bid to escape the control of parents and managers, they enlist in the Marines.
- Gene Autry buys the remainder of Bill McCall's Four Star Record Company for $75,000, but Patsy Cline is already gone.
- Bill Anderson joins the "Grand Ole Opry" cast.

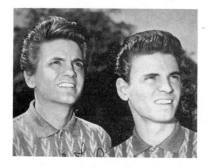

Everly Brothers.
credit: Bob Millard Collection

- Ray Pillow is discovered as a contestant on the Pet Milk "Grand Ole Opry" Talent Contest this year.
- On June 14, just as "I Fall To Pieces" reaches #1, Patsy Cline is seriously injured in an automobile accident in Madison, Tennessee.
- Webb Pierce debuts his famous Silver Dollar Pontiac, a convertible trimmed with hundreds of silver dollar coins, 13 pistols, and three rifles.
- Michelle Wright born in Chatham, Ontario, Canada, on July 1.
- In late summer meetings the CMA board of directors approves plans for establishing a Country Music Hall of Fame, approving a $1,500 budget to cast bronze plaques honoring the first three inductees: Jimmie Rodgers, Fred Rose, and Hank Williams.
- Billy Ray Cyrus born in Flatwoods, Kentucky, on August 25.
- k.d. lang born in Consort, Alberta, Canada, on November 2.
- Carrie Rodgers, widow of Jimmie Rodgers and a long-time sponsor of various struggling newcomers, most notably Ernest Tubb, dies of cancer on November 28 in San Antonio, Texas.
- Grandpa Jones steals the show as "Grand Ole Opry" stars, including Minnie Pearl, Patsy Cline, Bill Monroe, and the Jordanaires, perform at Carnegie Hall in New York on November 29.
- Military buyers report that 65 percent of European PX record sales are country, saying, "We could have sold more if we had had the records."

Jimmy Dean

If ever a country boy was made for television, it was cherub-cheeked Jimmy Dean. His crossover pop and country hit, "Big, Bad John" sold more than two million copies, snared a Grammy, and helped put Dean on network television in the mid-1960s.

Dean, born Seth Ward in Plainview, Texas, on August 10, 1928, was dirt poor but ambitious for a better life. Through his mother's early encouragement he took up piano, guitar, accordion, and harmonica. Stationed at an Air Force base near Washington, D.C., in 1948, Dean filled in with the Tennessee Haymakers, a service group started by friends. They played service clubs and local nightspots. Dean formed his own Texas Wildcats band in 1952 and recorded his first hit record, "Bumming Around," for Four Star, the California label that later launched Patsy Cline.

Hit records were not to be his calling card. Though he recorded with decent success for Columbia in the late 1950s, he didn't hit the *Billboard* Top 30 charts again for nine more years. By 1955, Dean hosted Connie B. Gay's East Coast TV show, "Town and Country Time." Dean's outgoing personality and cornball humor led to his being tapped to host "The Jimmy Dean Show" on CBS-TV in 1957, originating from Washington, D.C., again under the aegis of Gay.

Dean was a popular TV performer, but he got back to recording in a big way with "Big, Bad John." The song itself launched various flash-in-the-pan parodies. With follow-up hits like "P.T. 109" he was a pop-country star of high standing by the time he landed his second network TV show on ABC from 1963 to 1966, a show that was instrumental in broadening the popularity of country music in the mid-1960s.

1962

MUSIC CITY U.S.A.

Nashville's success as a recording center was largely due to it being the base for extremely flexible musicians who could play pop, jazz, and country with equal virtuosity. Owen Bradley and Chet Atkins, both musicians, were the main record producers at the Bradley Brothers and RCA studios, the only major studios in town until 1962, when Starday and Sun-Phillips opened Nashville's third and fourth master-quality recording rooms. (It now has at least 60.) Things really came together on the 800 blocks of 16th and 17th Avenues South in Nashville in 1962. Columbia bought Bradley's famous quonset hut studio and built offices around it. Decca commissioned a major office complex across from Columbia. Capitol moved its country division from Hollywood to newly-built offices one block from RCA. And Mercury-Smash-Philips launched a country division in Nashville.

From right to left: Jo Walker (Meador), executive director of the Country Music Association, Jimmy Dean, and Frances Preston, then BMI vice president in charge of the Nashville office. credit: Bob Millard Collection

Billboard magazine began calling this busy couple of Nashville blocks Music Row, and opened its first Nashville bureau a few blocks away. The U.S. Senate declared the week of the Country Music Association convention in November as "Country Music Week" in America. There were four network television salutes to country music aired that same week, and the CMA opened permanent offices with its first full-time executive director, Jo Walker (Meador). City officials, who had previously refused to recognize country music as an integral part of the fabric of the city, now publicly embraced it as Mayor Ben West approved the first road signs reading "Welcome To Nashville, Home of the Grand Ole Opry—Music City U.S.A."

Most Important Records

"Don't Let Me Cross Over" Carl & Pearl Butler / Columbia
"Wolverton Mountain" Claude King / Columbia
"Devil Woman" Marty Robbins / Columbia
"Mama Sang A Song" Bill Anderson / Decca
"She Thinks I Still Care" George Jones / Mercury
"She's Got You" Patsy Cline / Decca
"I've Been Everywhere" Hank Snow / RCA
"Charlie's Shoes" Billy Walker / Columbia
"I Can't Stop Loving You" Ray Charles / ABC/Paramount
"A Wound Time Can't Erase" Stonewall Jackson / Columbia

Debut Artist: Willie Nelson

Though Willie Nelson's quirky, jazz-influenced phrasing had prevented him from charting records before 1962, he had written a string of hits for other artists, including Faron Young's "Hello Walls" and Patsy Cline's "Crazy." He finally broke through as an artist in his own right, hitting the Top 10 with "Touch Me" for Liberty Records. It would take Nelson 15 years to crack the Top 10 again, or even the Top 20 on a regular basis, but 1962 was the year that Nelson, one of country music's most unique stylists and songwriters, first tasted success as a recording artist.

credit: Bob Millard Collection

Willie Nelson.
credit: photo by Les Leverett

Awards

GRAMMYS

BEST COUNTRY AND WESTERN RECORDING—"Funny Way of Laughin'"
Burl Ives

GOLD RECORDS

"Nearer The Cross" G/A Tennessee Ernie Ford / Capitol
"Star Carol" G/A Tennessee Ernie Ford / Capitol
"Can't Help Falling in Love" G/S Elvis Presley / RCA

Milestones

- Clint Black born in Long Branch, New Jersey, on February 4.
- Garth Brooks born in Tulsa, Oklahoma, on February 7.
- R&B artist Ray Charles expanded his own audience and that of contemporary country music with a pair of albums called *Modern Sounds of Country Music—Vols. 1 and 2*. Covering Don Gibson's "I Can't Stop Loving You," Eddy Arnold's "You Don't Know Me," and Hank Williams' "Your Cheatin' Heart," Charles enjoys his best-selling records to date, selling more than 1.5 million copies of "I Can't Stop Loving You" by the end of the year.
- Billy Dean born in Quincy, Florida, on April 12.
- In April, the National Association of Record Merchandisers names "Big, Bad John" the nation's Best-Selling Hit Single. Jimmy Dean brings Big, Bad John back to life in his single "Cajun Queen."
- Country music artists hit the campaign trail en mass to support Frank Clement and George Wallace in gubernatorial races in Tennessee and Alabama, respectively.

Carl and Pearl Butler

When native East Tennessean Carl Butler, who had been a "Grand Ole Opry" member for 14 years, added his wife, Pearl, to the act in 1962, his success really began.

Carl had been recording since 1951 for Capitol and Columbia, and had been successful writing hits for other artists, including Roy Acuff, Earl Scruggs, Bill Monroe, Carl Smith, and Flatt and Scruggs. Featuring tight vocal harmonies, Carl and Pearl scored a tremendous 11-week, chart-topping record, "Don't Let Me Cross Over," followed by a string of reasonably successful records through the decade.

The pair was immortalized in the country music movie *Second Fiddle to a Steel Guitar*, and continued to record and tour throughout North America through the 1970s as gospel music became an ever more important part of their repertoire. Genuine "country" entertainers in an era of pop-tinged urban cowboys, they were rediscovered in the 1980s by the Southern grass roots music movement and became extremely popular on that folk festival circuit until Pearl died in 1988.

Carl and Pearl Butler.
credit: Bob Millard Collection

There were hard losses for the "Grand Ole Opry" in 1963. On March 5, Patsy Cline, her pilot Randy Hughes, Cowboy Copas, and Hawkshaw Hawkins were returning in a light plane from a Kansas City benefit concert for country deejay/entertainer Cactus Jack Call when their plane crashed into a rocky hillside just outside of Nashville, killing all aboard. It was only by chance that Roy Acuff had turned down Hughes' offer of a ride home from the show. Friends were called in to help locate the crash site and reportedly Roger Miller was one of the first on the scene. Then, Jack Anglin, of Johnnie and Jack fame, ran his car off the road and was killed on his way to Patsy's funeral a few days later. As if it couldn't get any worse for country music in 1963, Texas Ruby, Curley Fox's wife and former musical partner, died in a fire that destroyed their trailer home while Curley was performing on WSM's "Friday Night Frolics." Ironically, Patsy Cline's biggest hit, "Sweet Dreams," made its debut just one week after her untimely death.

1963

TRAGEDY STRIKES THE OPRY

Patsy Cline on the Opry stage. credit: Courtesy of the Grand Ole Opry, photo by Les Leverett

Flatt and Scruggs on the set of the Beverly Hillbillies with Jed Clampett (Buddy Ebsen).

Most Important Records

"Love's Gonna Live Here" Buck Owens / Capitol
"Ring Of Fire" Johnny Cash / Columbia
"Still" Bill Anderson / Decca
"Abilene" George Hamilton IV / RCA
"Act Naturally" Buck Owens / Capitol
"Lonesome 7-7203" Hawkshaw Hawkins / King
"The Ballad of Jed Clampett" Flatt and Scruggs / Columbia
"Talk Back Trembling Lips" Ernie Ashworth / Hickory
"Ruby Ann" Marty Robbins / Columbia
"Sweet Dreams" Patsy Cline / Decca

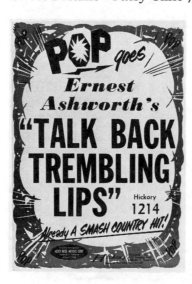

Debut Artist: David Houston

A Bossier City, Louisiana, native, David Houston began working in country music when he was 12, joining the "Louisiana Hayride." Despite a splashy #2 chart hit debut in 1963 with "Mountain of Love," Houston became better known for "Almost Persuaded," his 1966 #1 (one of seven chart toppers in his career) and as a journeyman duet singer. Houston harmonized most successfully with Tammy Wynette from 1968 to 1975, and to significantly lesser results with Calvin Crawford through 1981. From 1970 to 1974 he also scored two Top 10s and four Top 40 singles, singing in tandem with Barbara Mandrell.

David Houston.
credit: Bob Millard Collection

Awards

GRAMMYS
BEST COUNTRY AND WESTERN RECORDING—"Detroit City" Bobby Bare
BEST INSTRUMENTAL ARRANGEMENT (NC)—"I Can't Stop Loving You" Count Basie (artist); Quincy Jones (arranger)

GOLD RECORDS
"Elvis' Christmas Album" G/A Elvis Presley / RCA
"G.I. Blues" G/A Elvis Presley / RCA
"Girls, Girls, Girls" G/A Elvis Presley / RCA

Milestones

- Red Foley appears as a regular in the Fess Parker television series "Mr. Smith Goes to Washington," and Sheb Wooley becomes a regular on the "Rawhide" series.
- In January, the legacy of Jimmie Rodgers reappears when Grandpa Jones earns a Top 10 hit covering "T For Texas."
- In February, Ned Miller scores a hit with "From a Jack to a King"; nearly 30 years later, the song becomes a hit for Ricky Van Shelton.
- In March, *Billboard* notes that Jim Reeves has earned his pilot's license and "is reported shopping for an air chariot to carry him and his Blue Boys on future engagements."
- Texas Ruby Owens dies in a house trailer fire on March 29.
- Mark Chesnutt born in Beaumont, Texas, on September 6.
- The National Life and Accident Insurance Company purchases the Ryman Auditorium for $200,000 in late September, renaming it the Grand Ole Opry House.
- Robin Lee born in Nashville, Tennessee, on November 7.
- Lampooning the current international pop hit, "Tie Me Kangaroo Down, Sport," popular late 1940s artist Arthur "Guitar Boogie" Smith stages a brief comeback, with a Top 30 parody, "Tie My Hunting Dog Down, Jed."

- Roy Clark signs with Capitol Records.
- BMI breaks ground for its first permanent offices on Music Row.
- Hank Williams Jr., 14, signs a recording contract in November with MGM Records, the same label his father recorded for. His first release will be the Hank Sr. tune, "Long Gone Lonesome Blues."
- ASCAP opens a Nashville office.
- After seeing him perform in a Montana country nightspot, Red Sovine urges Charley Pride to come to Nashville.
- New additions to the "Grand Ole Opry" cast include The Browns and Marion Worth.
- Charlie and Ira disband the Louvin Brothers, and each goes solo.

Roy Clark signs with Capitol Records' Ken Nelson.
credit: Bob Millard Collection

Bobby Bare: Songs of the Southern Diaspora

The industrial buildup leading to World War II drew a whole generation of Southern men and women from their homes to alien places. A sense of loss grew like a prickly rose in the hearts of those displaced Southerners, as the Northern migration to factory towns like Flint and Detroit, Michigan, drew poor Southern rural people to the promise of good jobs at high wages.

That promise didn't always come through, and even if it did, there was a corresponding longing for home that Bobby Bare, like no other artist of his time, successfully conveyed. Bare debuted on the country charts with "Shame On Me" in 1962, but he really found his niche in 1963, singing a moving tune of this Southern diaspora, "Detroit City." The song had been a moderate hit for "Grand Ole Opry" regular Billy Grammer earlier in the year, released as "I Wanna Go Home," but Bare's sadeyed sincerity hit homesick listeners like an existential ninepound hammer. He followed it with "500 Miles Away From Home," again mining the theme of lost home. Nostalgic songs about family and home are rife in the historical country repertoire, but in the early 1960s Bare alone was able to tap the deep emotion inherent in this social phenomenon.

In 1964, he repeated the theme of melancholy wanderlust with "Four Strong Winds" and in 1966 had a moderate Top 40 record with "Homesick," but no one—including Bare—ever underscored the loneliness of the culturally dispossessed better or with more understated passion than with those two songs from 1963.

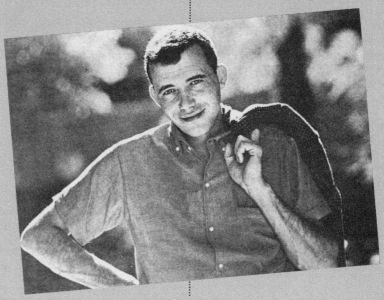

Bobby Bare.
credit: Bob Millard Collection

With urban folk acts like the Kingston Trio and Burl Ives considered "country" by the Grammy voters, it seemed only a matter of time before a real country artist tapped into the urban folk repertoire. Steeped in black-dirt Arkansas folk and gospel traditions, Johnny Cash became that experimental soul, cutting Bob Dylan's "It Ain't Me Babe" in 1964. Bobby Bare followed Cash's lead in 1964 with a hit cover of the Ian & Sylvia folk-pop hit, "Four Strong Winds." These meldings of related genres would encourage a dabbling relationship in this decade between country and such folk artists as Dylan, Buffy St. Marie, Judy Collins, and Joan Baez, not to mention seminal experiments with country-rock by The Byrds. Cash's relationship with Dylan grew during this decade, culminating several years later in a fabulous duet performance on Dylan's *Nashville Skyline* album.

Johnny Cash.
credit: In the Southern Folklife Collection, University of North Carolina, Chapel Hill

Lefty Frizzell.
credit: Bob Millard Collection

Most Important Records

"Once A Day" Connie Smith / RCA
"My Heart Skips A Beat" Buck Owens / Capitol
"I Guess I'm Crazy" Jim Reeves / RCA
"Dang Me" Roger Miller / Smash
"Understand Your Man" Johnny Cash / Columbia
"I Don't Care Just As Long As You Love Me" Buck Owens / Capitol
"Saginaw, Michigan" Lefty Frizzell / Columbia
"Begging To You" Marty Robbins / Columbia
"Together Again" Buck Owens / Capitol
"B.J. The D.J." Stonewall Jackson / Columbia

Debut Artist: Connie Smith

Connie Smith seemed a happy-go-lucky 23-year-old when Bill Anderson discovered her, wrote "Once A Day" for her first big hit, and put her on the road to major stardom. In truth, she was emotionally scarred by a difficult childhood. Her father was an alcoholic who beat her and her 13 brothers and sisters, moving repeatedly and keeping them in poverty. When success came so suddenly, Smith had no foundation. She was unable to make savvy decisions or stick by the ones she did make, and ultimately was unable to remain, as John Lennon once put it, "on the merry-go-round." As she told *Country Music* magazine in the early 1970s, by which time she was basically retired, enjoying the fruits of a religious conversion and happily raising her growing family, "I couldn't face the reality of life, and I became bitter when people I admired didn't act the way I expected them to off the stage. . . I came to mistrust everybody." Smith has since become a regular performer on the "Grand Ole Opry" and seems not to miss those whirlwind days in late 1964 when her very first record, "Once a Day," began a phenomenal eight-week ride atop the country charts.

Awards

GRAMMYS

BEST COUNTRY AND WESTERN SINGLE—"Dang Me" Roger Miller

BEST COUNTRY AND WESTERN ALBUM—"Dang Me/Chug-A-Lug" Roger Miller

BEST COUNTRY AND WESTERN PERFORMANCE, FEMALE—"Here Comes My Baby" Dottie West

BEST COUNTRY AND WESTERN PERFORMANCE, MALE—"Dang Me" Roger Miller

BEST COUNTRY AND WESTERN SONG—"Dang Me" Roger Miller

BEST NEW COUNTRY AND WESTERN ARTIST—Roger Miller

BEST GOSPEL OR OTHER RELIGIOUS RECORDING (MUSICAL) (NC)—"Great Gospel Songs" Tennessee Ernie Ford

GOLD RECORDS
"Johnny Horton's Greatest Hits" G/A Johnny Horton / Columbia
"Oh, Pretty Woman" G/A Roy Orbison / Capitol

Milestones

- Tennessee Governor Frank Clement designates February "Eddy Arnold Month" in honor of Arnold's 20th anniversary with RCA Victor.
- Travis Tritt born in Marietta, Georgia, on February 9.
- Jimmy Martin's "Widow Maker" hits the charts, setting off a series of truck driver songs.
- Bluegrass artist Bill Clifton garners country music's first response to the onset of Beatlemania in America with a talking blues novelty tune entitled "Beatle Crazy."
- Brenda Lee's first baby, Julie Leana Shacklett, is born on April 1, four weeks early. The baby remains in the hospital "in serious, but not critical condition."
- Alton Delmore, 56, the last surviving Delmore Brother, dies on June 8 in Huntsville, Alabama. He was the father of Lionel Delmore, who was a co-writer with John Anderson of the 1980s smash hit "Swingin'."
- Following up their hit theme song to TV's "The Beverly Hillbillies" series, Flatt and Scruggs write and record the theme to the "Petticoat Junction" TV sitcom.
- Wynonna Judd (Christina Ciminella) born in Ashland, Kentucky, on May 30.
- Jim Reeves and his pianist, Dean Manuel, are killed when the light plane Reeves is piloting goes down in bad weather a few miles shy of the Nashville Airport. Friends helping to search for them include Chet Atkins, Eddy Arnold, Ernest Tubb, and Stonewall Jackson. Because the crash occurred in a heavily wooded area, they are not found for two days. Reeve's funeral in Carthage, Tennessee, a week later is one of the largest in the history of that community.
- Marty Robbins accepts a post as Southern director for "Stars for Barry," a celebrity auxiliary supporting the U.S. presidential candidacy of Arizona Senator Barry Goldwater.
- Trisha Yearwood born in Monticello, Georgia, on September 19.
- New artists signed as regulars on the "Grand Ole Opry" include Dottie West, Ernie Ashworth, the Osborne Brothers, Jim and Jesse McReynolds, and Willie Nelson.
- Popular Nashville TV and radio personality Ralph Emery quits his "Opry Star Spotlight" program to devote himself to his newfound career as a Mercury Records artist. Wisely hedging his bets, Emery keeps his local early morning TV show, "Opry Almanac."
- Switching from middle-of-the-road pop guests to contemporary country hit acts, the "Jimmy Dean Show," a mid-year

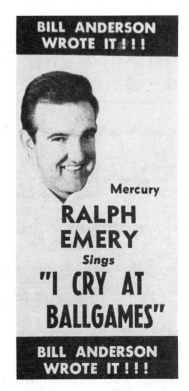

BILL ANDERSON WROTE IT!!!

Mercury
RALPH EMERY
Sings
"I CRY AT BALLGAMES"

BILL ANDERSON WROTE IT!!!

Ralph Emery, host of TNN's *Nashville Now*, as a recording artist in the mid-'60s.
credit: Bob Millard Collection

credit: Bob Millard Collection

replacement musical variety program, increases its ratings and gets renewed for the rest of the season. It becomes the key outlet for exposure of new country music in America.

➤ On November 4, MGM's loosely biographical movie of Hank Williams, *Your Cheatin' Heart*, debuts in Montgomery, Alabama.

➤ Having previously relaxed requirements that members perform a minimum of 26 Saturdays to retain membership, the "Grand Ole Opry" suddenly fires a dozen top stars, including Chet Atkins, Stonewall Jackson, Ray Price, Don Gibson, Kitty Wells, George Morgan, Ferlin Huskey, and the Jordanaires. Rather than be fired, Minnie Pearl goes on a one-year sabbatical. Publicly embarrassing the WSM management, Chet Atkins protests his firing by pointing out that, except as a sideman for The Carter Family, he was never a member in the first place.

Texas born and Oklahoma reared, Roger Miller never exactly fit the country star mold. But rather than missing the country or pop marks, he managed to hit the bull's eye on both, and a few others before he was through. Miller's mother was widowed when he was one year old, and he was subsequently raised by an uncle on a small farm near a not-much-bigger town. His sense of humor saved him, and eventually proved one of his most valuable assets as a songwriter and entertainer.

Miller was a Korean War vet who used his military service to broaden his horizons. His budding musical talents got him out of the fox holes, however. In the Special Services, he learned guitar, fiddle, and drums. Back in the States, he met a brother of Jethro Burns. This connection led him to Nashville, where, after a few false starts, he found alternating work as a fiddler behind Minnie Pearl, a drummer for Faron Young, and a utility man for Ray Price. Price cut Miller's "Invitation To The Blues," the first hit of a songwriting career that would include

"Billy Bayou," "When Two Worlds Collide," "Home," and "Half a Mind."

In retrospect, Miller's clean, dimpled good looks might make him seem an unlikely regular down at Tootsie Bess's Orchid Lounge on Lower Broadway, just below the Ryman Auditorium. Nevertheless, in the early 1960s he was fast pals with "outlaws" like Waylon Jennings, Willie Nelson, and others who made the unfashionable watering hole *the* hangout for struggling country writers and entertainers. Tootsie's was like a union hall that would run a bar tab, the kind of place where a country musician could eventually find work if he was any good, and Miller was good.

Ironically, Miller's big break came just after the death of one of his best friends, Patsy Cline. Miller landed a recording deal with Mercury's Smash Records subsidiary and quickly began writing and recording a string of quirky, wacky hit records that sounded nothing like the country or pop records of the time, which is probably why they were so

successful in both realms. In 1964, "Dang Me" brought Miller five Grammys. In 1965, he won six Grammy awards, including non-country categories, for "King of the Road." The hits kept on coming, as Miller created such gems as "Engine Engine #9," "England Swings,"and "Husbands and Wives." NBC snapped him up to host "The Roger Miller Show" in 1966, precisely because his music and sparkling wit cut across many boundaries.

Miller's streak of hits ended in 1971, though he continued releasing records through the mid-1980s. He worked as many concert and symphonic pop dates as he wanted to and generally enjoyed life in California. He stormed back into the winner's circle in 1985, winning five Tony Awards for his score to *Big River*, the Broadway adaptation of Mark Twain's *Huck Finn*. It was named Best Musical for that year. Cancer had been diagnosed by then, and though he seemed for a time to have beaten the disease, Miller died in late 1992.

Roger Miller.
credit: Archives of Robert K. Oermann

1965

THE BIG COUNTRY BOOM

Grand Ole Opry cast.
credit: photo by Les Leverett

Aided by crossover hits and the tireless efforts of CMA stalwarts Tex Ritter, Connie B. Gay, and Wesley Rose, country music gained numerous converts in radio, including stations reaching the greater New York and Chicago markets. "The Ernie Ford Show" featured Minnie Pearl repeatedly throughout 1965, and Jimmy Dean's ABC-TV series was a huge success with mainstream contemporary country stars as guests. A plethora of syndicated country music shows sprung up in Dean's wake, including shows hosted by Bill Anderson and Porter Wagoner. Both Stu Philips and Carl Smith hosted on popular Canadian TV shows featuring country music. Country artists became popular with variety and talk show hosts from Johnny Carson to Lloyd Thaxton, and appeared on such pop shows as "Shindig" and "Hootenanny." More country artists performed overseas and on USO tours than ever before, as the mid-1960s introduced new country stars such as Loretta Lynn, David Houston, Tammy Wynette, Conway Twitty, Connie Smith, the Statler Brothers, and others. This period is now understood to have been one of the genre's most fertile periods.

Most Important Records

"Before You Go" Buck Owens / Capitol
"King Of The Road" Roger Miller / Smash
"I've Got A Tiger By The Tail" Buck Owens / Capitol
"You're The Only World I Know" Sonny James / RCA
"Make The World Go Away" Eddy Arnold / RCA
"Is It Really Over?" Jim Reeves / RCA
"The Girl On The Billboard" Del Reeves / UA
"Hello Vietnam" Johnny Wright / Decca
"May The Bird Of Paradise Fly Up Your Nose" Jimmy Dickens / Columbia
"What's He Doing In My World?" Eddy Arnold / RCA

Debut Artist:
The Statler Brothers

"Flowers on the Wall" by the Statler Brothers reached #2 on the national charts for four weeks, its profound combination of ironic lyrics and minor/major key shifts conspiring to make this tune a huge pop and country hit. Subsequently, it launched this former gospel quartet on one of the longest-lived continuously charting periods in country music after years as Johnny Cash's backing group. The song's writer, Lew DeWitt, left the group in the early 1980s due to poor health. Replacement Jimmy Fortune generated a string of revitalizing hit songs for the Statlers before older members of the group mysteriously quashed his lead singing role. The group now hosts its own cable series for The Nashville Network.

"Little" Jimmy Dickens.
credit: In the Southern Folklife Collection, University of North Carolina, Chapel Hill

The original Statler Brothers; clockwise from top l., Phil Balsley, Don Reid, Harold Reed, and Lew DeWitt.
credit: Archives of Robert K. Oermann

Awards

GRAMMYS

BEST COUNTRY AND WESTERN SINGLE—"King of the Road" Roger Miller

BEST COUNTRY AND WESTERN ALBUM—"The Return of Roger Miller" Roger Miller

BEST COUNTRY AND WESTERN PERFORMANCE, FEMALE—"Queen of the House" Jody Miller

BEST COUNTRY AND WESTERN PERFORMANCE, MALE—"King of the Road" Roger Miller

BEST COUNTRY AND WESTERN SONG—"King of the Road" Roger Miller

BEST NEW COUNTRY AND WESTERN ARTIST—Statler Brothers

BEST CONTEMPORARY (R&R) SINGLE (NC)—"King of the Road" Roger Miller

BEST CONTEMPORARY PERFORMANCE GROUP (VOCAL OR INSTRUMENTAL) (NC)—"Flowers on the Wall" single Statler Brothers

GOLD RECORDS

"Ring Of Fire" G/A Johnny Cash / Columbia

"King Of The Road" G/S Roger Miller / Smash

"Return Of Roger Miller" G/A Roger Miller / Smash

"Gunfire Ballads & Trail Songs" G/A Marty Robbins / Columbia

ACADEMY OF COUNTRY MUSIC AWARDS

MALE VOCALIST—Buck Owens

FEMALE VOCALIST—Bonnie Owens

VOCAL DUET/GROUP—Bonnie Owens & Merle Haggard

NEW MALE VOCALIST—Merle Haggard

NEW FEMALE VOCALIST—Kaye Adams

TOURING BAND—Buckaroos (Buck Owens)

DISC JOCKEY—Biff Collie

CLUB—Palomino (North Hollywood, California)

MAN OF THE YEAR—Roger Miller

SONGWRITER—Roger Miller

PUBLICATION—*Billboard*

TV PERSONALITY—Billy Mize

PUBLISHER—Central Songs

TALENT MANAGEMENT—Jack McFadden (Buck Owens)

PRODUCER/A&R MAN—Ken Nelson (Capitol/Hollywood)

INSTRUMENTALISTS: fiddle, Billy Armstrong; keyboard, Billy Liebert; bass, Bob Morris; drums, Muddy Berry; guitar, Phil Baugh; steel guitar, Red Rhodes

Milestones

- After a long and successful career as a singing cowboy in the movies, Tex Ritter joins the "Grand Ole Opry" fueled by the success of his current hit single, "I Dreamed of a Hill-Billy Heaven."
- In January, Leo Fender, 59 and founder of Fender Guitars, sells his California company to a subsidiary of Columbia

Records for a reported $13 million. His guitars had been favorites of country musicians since electrification began in the early 1930s. During CMA Week in the autumn, CMA head Tex Ritter gives Fender the President's Award for "outstanding contributions to the sound of country music."

- A trend of country singers becoming television actors continues, with Webb Pierce appearing in "The Virginian," "Suspense Theatre," and "Wagon Train." Sheb Wooley adds "Death Valley Days" episodes to his list of acting credits. Jim Reeves' acting debut is posthumously hailed when his film *Kimberley Jim* debuts in March.

- Ira Louvin is killed in a car crash near Jefferson City, Missouri, on June 20.

- New cast members for the "Grand Ole Opry" include Bobby Bare, Norma Jean (as part of Porter Wagoner's band), Connie Smith, and Bob Luman.

- Popular announcer for the "Renfro Valley Barn Dance," Roy Starkey, 51, dies of a heart attack on October 2. He had previously been the "voice" of the WLS "Barn Dance" and WLW's "Boone County Jamboree."

- Johnny Cash is banned from the "Grand Ole Opry" for smashing the footlights on stage with a microphone and walking off in the middle of a song while high on pills. On October 5, he is arrested in the El Paso, Texas, airport and charged in Federal Circuit Court with illegal possession of 668 dexedrine and 475 equanil pills. Pleading guilty in late December, he receives a $1,000 fine and 30-day suspended jail term.

- Bill Black, 39, bass player in Elvis Presley's original touring and recording band, dies in Memphis of brain cancer.
- New syndicated country music shows join Jimmy Dean and Ernie Ford network programs on-air this year. The strangest by far is on WOR-TV, New York City. Its debut of a one-hour colorcast called "Country A Go-Go" features a dizzying mix of top-name country, hard rock, and gospel music, discotheque, Tahitian hula, and square dancing.
- In November, Roy Acuff Jr. comes out of the mailroom at Acuff-Rose Publications to release a debut single, a remake of his father's "Wabash Cannonball." Said Roy Sr., "I didn't know he could sing." Said country radio, "He can't."
- In the year's most bizarre country music crime story, George Jones, his agent, and entire band are held for lie detector tests in connection with a Houston murder investigation in December. Polygraphs clear them all.

Harlan Howard: The Songwriter's Songwriter

Few country songwriters have careers and repertoires that span the Nashville era of commercial country music as representatively as do those of Harlan Howard. Son of Southern migrants in Detroit, Howard grew up in the farm communities that surround the industrial Mecca. He was surrounded by the music of his ancestors, and, in 1939, at age 12, he was introduced to the records of Ernest Tubb.

"I'd try to copy down what he was singing, and as soon as he was done I'd turn the radio off and memorize the melodies," Howard recalled. "Sometimes I couldn't write down the words as fast as he would sing them, so I started making up my own words." Those words turned out to be nearly as good as what Tubb had sung, thus starting one of the most prolific composing careers in country music.

Harlan Howard began writing country songs in the military and tried his hand at making money from it on the West Coast as early as 1954. He received encouragement from Johnny Bond, Tex Ritter, and Wynn Stewart. Meeting Buck Owens was a turning point: Owens' first #1 was a Harlan Howard song, "Above and Beyond." Howard and Owens began collaborating on tunes, and their hits together would include Kitty Wells' "Mommy For A Day" and the Buck Owens smash, "Tiger By The Tail."

Howard moved to Nashville in 1960, where collaboration soon became a way of life, especially on Nashville's Music Row. Still, it has been that common, simple brilliance of Howard's work that is visible in each tune that bears his name. The Harlan Howard hits from the mid-1950s through today are numerous and include some of the classics of the genre. These hits include "Busted" (Ray Charles and John Conlee), "Foolin Around" (Buck Owens), "Why Not Me" (The Judds), "Little Band of Gold" (Ernest Tubb), "Heaven Help The Working Girl" (Norma Jean), "The Chokin' Kind" (Joe Simon and Waylon Jennings), "Heartaches by The Number" (Ray Price and Guy Mitchell), "I Fall To Pieces" (Patsy Cline), "She's A Little Bit Country" (George Hamilton IV), "She's Gone, Gone, Gone" (Lefty Frizzell), "Too Many Rivers" (Brenda Lee and The Forester Sisters), "Somewhere Tonight" (Highway 101), "Life Turned Her That Way" (Mel Tillis and Ricky Van Shelton), "Pick Me Up On Your Way Down" (Billy Walker), "The Streets of Baltimore" (Bobby Bare), "No Charge" (Melba Montgomery and Shirley Ceasar), "Sally Was a Good Ole Girl" (Hank Cochran), "Bummin' Around" (Rex Allen and Jimmy Dean), "She Called Me Baby" (Charlie Rich), "Second Hand Rose" (Teresa Brewer). . . and the list just goes on.

Buck Owens paid the ultimate tribute to a songwriter by recording an album called *Buck Owens Sings Harlan Howard*.

Grateful for the help he got from Jimmie Rodgers' widow, Carrie, in starting his own career, Ernest Tubb often tried to help others get their careers going, providing exposure for many on his "Midnight Jamboree" radio program. In the case of Jack Greene, though, Tubb had to be cruel to be kind. Greene had worked as a journeyman musician all over the South through the 1950s, joining Tubb's Texas Troubadours in 1962. When Tubb arranged for the band to cut their own record for Decca in 1965, Greene's vocal number was the most popular. Greene, nicknamed "the Jolly Green Giant" because he stood well over six feet tall, tried to develop his solo career from within Tubb's band, but Ernest eventually fired him, thereby forcing Greene to become a star in his own right. In 1966, Greene had his career-launching #1 hit, "There Goes My Everything." When he was inducted into the cast of the "Grand Ole Opry" at the end of 1967, it was his old boss Ernest Tubb who made the introduction.

1966
CRUEL TO BE KIND

credit: Bob Millard Collection

Most Important Records

"Almost Persuaded" David Houston / Epic
"There Goes My Everything" Jack Greene / Decca
"Waitin' In Your Welfare Line" Buck Owens / Capitol
"Giggyup Go" Red Sovine / Starday
"Think Of Me" Buck Owens / Capitol
"I Want To Go With You" Eddy Arnold / RCA
"Distant Drums" Jim Reeves / RCA
"Open Up Your Heart" Buck Owens / Capitol
"Somebody Like Me" Eddy Arnold / RCA
"Take Good Care Of Her" Sonny James / RCA

Debut Artist: Jeannie Seely

Pennsylvanian Jeannie Seely worked on live radio shows from age 11. She moved from Los Angeles, where she was a songwriter, and became the Norma Jean replacement (before Dolly Parton) in the Porter Waggoner Show in 1965. "Don't Touch Me" never quite topped the charts, but hung in at #2 for three consecutive weeks, probably ultimately selling more records than many #1's. It was a powerful message for women, vulnerable, yet strong in its demand not to be taken advantage of. Unfortunately, she lacked the follow-up records to fully capitalize on her smash debut. Seely went to work with the "Jack Greene Show" and had a strong duet single with him, "Wish I Didn't Have To Miss You," in 1969. She remains a regular on the "Grand Ole Opry" cast.

Awards

GRAMMYS

BEST COUNTRY AND WESTERN RECORDING—"Almost Persuaded" David Houston

BEST COUNTRY AND WESTERN PERFORMANCE, FEMALE—"Don't Touch Me" single Jeannie Seely

BEST COUNTRY AND WESTERN PERFORMANCE, MALE—"Almost Persuaded" David Houston

BEST COUNTRY AND WESTERN SONG—"Almost Persuaded" Billy Sherrill and Glenn Sutton, writers

BEST SACRED RECORDING (MUSICAL) (NC)—"Grand Ole Gospel" Porter Wagoner & The Blackwood Brothers

GOLD RECORDS

"My World" G/A Eddie Arnold / RCA
"Battle Of New Orleans" G/A Johnny Horton / Columbia
"Dang Me" G/A Roger Miller / Smash
"Golden Hits" G/A Roger Miller / Smash
"Roy Orbison's Greatest Hits" G/A Roy Orbison / Monument
"Elvis Presley" G/A Elvis Presley / RCA

"Elvis' Golden Hits Vol. 2" G/A Elvis Presley / RCA
"Elvis' Golden Hits Vol. 3" G/A Elvis Presley / RCA
"The Best Of Jim Reeves" G/A Jim Reeves / RCA

ACADEMY OF COUNTRY MUSIC AWARDS
SONG OF THE YEAR—"Apartment #9" Johnny Paycheck, Fern Foley, "Fuzzy" Owen, writers
MALE VOCALIST—Merle Haggard
FEMALE VOCALIST—Bonnie Guitar
VOCAL DUET/GROUP—Bonnie Owens & Merle Haggard
NEW MALE VOCALIST—Billy Mize
NEW FEMALE VOCALIST—Kathy Taylor
NEW VOCAL DUET/GROUP—Bob Morris & Faye Hardin
TOURING BAND—Buckaroos (Buck Owens)
DISC JOCKEY—(tie) Bob Kingsley/Biff Collie
CLUB—Palomino
MAN OF THE YEAR—Dean Martin
PUBLICATION—*Billboard*
TV PERSONALITY—Billy Mize

On that cold, windy Friday night of March 25, 1966, when Buck Owens played Carnegie Hall, a Capitol Records sound truck was reeling in the sound, and in so doing captured the drawling, prowling energy of an electrifying country artist at the height of his powers. Owens was hardly the first country artist to perform at the prestigious New York venue. Ernest Tubb had done that 20 years earlier, and Flatt and Scruggs released the first country album ever recorded there in 1962. The significance of Owens' performance is the quality of both the show and the recording. It was the best "live" album by a country artist to that day, and many critics maintain that, along with Johnny Cash's prison concert albums, it still is.

In 1966, country artists didn't release "live" albums, as a rule. They were part of tour bands, rarely polished as studio musicians, making their personal appearances seldom as sharp and defined as their records. The nature of the honky-tonks, state fairs, and the low-budget country labels meant a live country album would almost invariably be the worst of a bad situation. They were typically only recorded for their low production costs. Later, Owens' own slapdash "live" albums from London, Las Vegas, and Japan fell into that pile. "The Carnegie Hall Concert with Buck Owens and his Buckaroos" represented two crucial exceptions to the rule.

The Buckaroos of that time—guitarist/bandleader Don Rich, steel player Tom Brumley, drummer Willie Cantu, and bassist Doyle Holly—were Owens's recording *and* touring band. They had been together for two years and, though Merle Haggard's Strangers might have been their equal, a better electric country unit didn't exist. The acoustical perfection of Carnegie Hall made recording the concert almost a can't-fail proposition. Owens' kicking alternative to the spongy Nashville Sound records then in vogue crisply and energetically tore through "Act Naturally," "Together Again," "Love's Gonna Live Here," "Waitin' In Your Welfare Line," "I've Got A Tiger By The Tail," and the band's signature instrumental number, "Buckaroo." Medleys covered several other Owens'

hits, and when the album was reissued in 1988 by the Country Music Foundation, additional material from the concert, lost in vaults since then, was added. "Twist and Shout," a Beatles' hit from an Isley Brothers original, was covered for comedy by Buck and the band in these additional original tracks. They even donned Beatle wigs to do it. Of course, The Beatles were covering Buck's hit, "Act Naturally," for a #1 pop hit, so the turnabout was more than fair play.

Owens joined the TV cast of "Hee Haw" in the late 1960s and lost his right-hand man, Don Rich, in a motorcycle accident in 1974. Owens turned his attention to radio stations, publishing companies, small newspapers, and real estate, becoming more interested in business than in performing. The ease of the cornball television series and the deep personal loss of Rich's death took the edge off Owens' music permanently. He was never sharper or more incisive than he was that chilly, windy night in New York in 1966. Fortunately, that magic night is preserved.

credit: Bob Millard Collection

PUBLISHER—Central Songs

TALENT MANAGEMENT—Jack McFadden

PRODUCER/A&R MAN—Ken Nelson

INSTRUMENTALISTS: fiddle, Billy Armstrong; keyboard, Billy Liebert; bass, Bob Morris; drums, Jerry Wiggins; guitar, Jimmy Bryant; steel guitar, (tie) Tom Brumley/Ralph Mooney

Milestones

- Bill Browder of Memphis records with little success as Brian Stacy for Atlantic Records. He will have better luck in 1974 when he employs the stage name T.G. Shepard.
- Minnie Pearl returns in January to the "Grand Ole Opry" after a one-year absence.
- Proving country music's strength among locals in Europe, Billy Walker takes time during a successful USO tour and records a country album in phonetic German.
- Flatt and Scruggs continue to be popular with television producers; they record the theme for the 1966 sitcom, "Green Acres."
- Pop stars discover country as Rick Nelson records his first all-country album, *Bright Lights & Country Music*.
- Dolly Parton's first release is a pop market remake of "Happy Birthday, Baby" for Monument Records. She has better success turning to country for her debut solo hit, the cagily titled "Dumb Blonde." She has even better luck joining forces with Porter Wagoner.
- The "Jimmie Dean Show" is canceled; fans and the CMA mount a massive letter-writing campaign to get it back. Dick Clark produces "Swingin' Country," which soon replaces Dean's program as the nation's leading venue for country exposure.

Sultry Mississippi-born Bobbie Gentry's "Ode To Billie Joe" came out in September, too late to influence the Country Music Association Awards that made their debut this year, but her two gold records and four Grammys reflected a new, California-produced, pop/country crossover trend. Gentry and Glen Campbell had tremendous success on both the pop and country charts in 1967, and both called Capitol Records' Studio C in Hollywood, not Nashville, their musical headquarters.

Between "Ode To Billie Joe" and Campbell's "Gentle On My Mind" (with more than 5 million airplays logged as of December, 1992, one of the most frequently-played country tunes of all time) and the popular Campbell-Gentry duets that followed, West Coast country-pop in 1967 broadened the appeal of country music. It did so at a moment when rising

1967

A HOLLYWOOD YEAR

Bobbie Gentry and Glen
Campbell.
credit: In the Southern Folklife
Collection, University of North
Carolina, Chapel Hill

sentiment against the war in Vietnam was about to identify the
more traditional country artists with the sort of conservative,
anti-intellectual, pro-war stance that was coloring country
music negatively for the urban Baby Boom generation. The
West Coast country axis of Campbell and Gentry bridged that
social gap, keeping country music in the minds of a generation
that would outgrow psychedelia and be swept up by a country
and western dance club craze a dozen years later.

Most Important Records

"Gentle On My Mind" Glen Campbell / Capitol
"Ode To Billie Joe" Bobbie Gentry / Capitol
"I Walk The Line" Johnny Cash / Columbia
"There Goes My Everything" Jack Greene / Decca
"I Don't Wanna Play House" Tammy Wynette / Epic
"By The Time I Get To Phoenix" Glen Campbell / Capitol
"All The Time" Jack Greene / Decca
"Where Does The Good Times Go" Buck Owens / Capitol

"Sam's Place" Buck Owens / Capitol
"It's The Little Things" Sonny James / Capitol

Debut Artist: Tammy Wynette

Virginia Wynette Pugh came up the hard way during the 1940s in Mississippi delta cotton country outside Tupelo. Her father died before her first birthday. Her mother followed work to the war factories in Birmingham, Alabama, leaving Tammy on the farm with her grandfather. In rural Itawamba County, she developed her voice singing country folk tunes and religious songs in the Sacred Harp, or shape note tradition. She married, divorced, worked in a beauty parlor in Birmingham, and in 1966 went to Nashville.

In Nashville, Wynette quickly established herself as a woman of considerable talent, both as a singer and as a songwriter. Producer Billy Sherrill found country melodies for her in old Baptist hymnals, and used the natural catch in her voice to maximum emotional effect through a series of hits that included "Apartment #9," "Your Good Girl's Gonna Go Bad," "I Don't Wanna Play House," and "My Elusive Dreams," the later a chart-topping duet with David Houston.

Thanks in no small part to the trail blazed before her by strong and independent female country singers Patsy Cline and Loretta Lynn, even a vulnerable personality like Wynette's was able to assert itself through a voice that more than hinted at inner strength, combined with the fusion of a sultry country sensuality with roiling emotional tension.

Awards

GRAMMYS

BEST COUNTRY AND WESTERN RECORDING—"Gentle On My Mind" Glen Campbell

BEST COUNTRY AND WESTERN SOLO VOCAL PERFORMANCE, FEMALE—"I Don't Wanna Play House" Tammy Wynette

BEST COUNTRY AND WESTERN SOLO PERFORMANCE, MALE—"Gentle On My Mind" Glen Campbell

BEST COUNTRY AND WESTERN PERFORMANCE, DUET, TRIO, OR GROUP (VOCAL OR INSTRUMENTAL)—"Jackson" Johnny Cash and June Carter

BEST COUNTRY AND WESTERN SONG—"Gentle On My Mind" John Hartford, writer

BEST VOCAL PERFORMANCE, FEMALE (NC)—"Ode To Billie Joe" single Bobbie Gentry

BEST VOCAL PERFORMANCE, MALE (NC)—"By The Time I Get To Phoenix" single Glen Campbell

BEST INSTRUMENTAL PERFORMANCE (NC)—"Chet Atkins Picks The Best" Chet Atkins

BEST NEW ARTIST (NC)—Bobbie Gentry

BEST CONTEMPORARY FEMALE SOLO VOCAL PERFORMANCE (NC)—"Ode To

Billie Joe" Bobbie Gentry

BEST CONTEMPORARY MALE SOLO PERFORMANCE (NC)—"By The Time I Get To Phoenix" Glen Campbell

BEST ARRANGEMENT ACCOMPANYING VOCALIST(S) OR INSTRUMENTALIST(S) (NC)—"Ode To Billie Joe" Bobbie Gentry, artist; Jimmie Haskell, arranger

BEST ALBUM NOTES (NC)—"Suburban Attitudes In Country Verse" John D. Loudermilk

GOLD RECORDS

"I Walk The Line" G/A Johnny Cash / Columbia
"Ode To Billy Joe" G/S Bobbie Gentry / Capitol
"Ode To Billy Joe" G/A Bobbie Gentry / Capitol
"Yackety Sax" G/A Boots Randolph / Monument

COUNTRY MUSIC ASSOCIATION AWARDS

ENTERTAINER OF THE YEAR—Eddy Arnold
FEMALE VOCALIST—Loretta Lynn
MALE VOCALIST—Jack Greene
SONG OF THE YEAR—"There Goes My Everything" Dallas Frazier, writer
SINGLE OF THE YEAR—"There Goes My Everything" Jack Greene
ALBUM OF THE YEAR—"There Goes My Everything" Jack Greene
VOCAL GROUP—The Stoneman Family
MUSICIAN OF THE YEAR—Chet Atkins
INSTRUMENTAL GROUP OF THE YEAR—The Buckaroos
COMEDIAN OF THE YEAR—Don Bowman

ACADEMY OF COUNTRY MUSIC AWARDS

SONG OF THE YEAR—"It's Such A Pretty World Today" Wynn Stewart, writer
SINGLE RECORD OF THE YEAR—"Gentle On My Mind" Glen Campbell, artist
ALBUM OF THE YEAR—"Gentle On My Mind" Glen Campbell
MALE VOCALIST—Glen Campbell
FEMALE VOCALIST—Lynn Anderson
VOCAL DUET—Bonnie Owens and Merle Haggard
NEW MALE VOCALIST—Jerry Inman
NEW FEMALE VOCALIST—Bobbi Gentry
VOCAL GROUP—Sons of the Pioneers
TOURING GROUP—Buckaroos (Buck Owens)
TV PERSONALITY—Billy Mize
DISC JOCKEY—Bob Kingsley
MAN OF THE YEAR—Joey Bishop
CLUB—Palomino
INSTRUMENTALISTS: fiddle, Billy Armstrong; keyboard, Earl Ball; bass, Red Wooten; drums, Pee Wee Adams; guitar, Jimmy Bryant; steel guitar, Red Rhodes

Bobbie Gentry was born Roberta Streeter in rural Chicasaw County, Mississippi, in 1944. She was raised in poor surroundings in and around Greenwood, Mississippi, partly by her grandparents, who lacked indoor plumbing. Her parents traded a cow for her first piano.

She was a self-taught musician who learned to play guitar, banjo, and bass after the family moved to Palm Springs, California, when she was 13 years old. She became a college-educated musician and worked a stint as a Las Vegas show dancer before she caught Capitol Records' attention with her self-penned "Ode To Bille Joe" in 1967. Her debut record, it would prove to be one of the most powerfully evocative story songs in the history of country music, rivaling "The Long Black Veil."

Though it is certainly a country record, it was a bigger hit on the pop charts (#1) than on country charts (Top 20) as its popularity spilled over into 1968. Ironically, Bobbie Gentry was all but a one-hit artist, despite, or maybe even because of, the colossal and universal popularity of "Ode To Billie Joe." Her second release, "Louisiana Man," bombed on both country and pop radio. Her third, "Fancy," was a Top 30 country hit, but the song itself would prove vastly more successful in country charts in 1992 when covered by Reba McEntire.

In 1969, Gentry scored a pair of Top 20 duet hits with Glen Campbell. "All I Have To Do Is Dream" from that pairing in 1970 was to be her last charting single and her only other Top 10 country record. Despite troubles duplicating her artistic success in America, she had her own television show in England for a time in the late 1960s.

Gentry married singer/songwriter/television performer Jim Stafford in 1978. She would forever be known for the haunting, deep Mississippi-accented classic, "Ode To Billie Joe."

Milestones

- The Country Music Hall of Fame Museum opens in Nashville.
- Former Rhodes scholar Kris Kristofferson works as a night janitor at Columbia Records and as a daytime bartender at a Music Row "dive" as an entre to the music business.
- Tom T. Hall signs his first recording contract with Mercury Records.
- Dolly Parton replaces Norma Jean in the "Porter Wagoner" TV show.
- David Allan Coe, released from prison, heads to Nashville in an old car, determined to become a professional singer.
- Elvis Presley and Priscilla Beaulieu marry on May 1.
- Tommy Duncan, a singer with the Lightcrust Doughboys from 1932 to 1933 and with Bob Wills' Texas Playboys from 1933 to 1948, dies of a heart attack on July 24.
- Woody Guthrie dies of Huntington's chorea on October 3.
- Sisters Maxine and Bonnie Brown quit The Browns, leaving brother Jim Ed to sign with RCA as a solo.
- Lynn Anderson becomes a regular on television's "Lawrence Welk" show and signs her first recording contract with independent Chart Records.
- Rick Nelson, the 1950s teen idol and television star, lays further foundation for the country rock movement by forming his first country-rock band, which includes James Burton, Glen D. Hardin, and Clarence White, and records another country album, *Country Fever*.

Already a successful story-telling songwriter, Tom T. Hall became a recording artist in 1967.
credit: Bob Millard Collection

- Just as Roy Orbison is getting over his wife's tragic death two years earlier in a motorcycle accident, beginning to write songs, and itching to record again, two of his three children are killed in a fire at his house in Hendersonville, Tennessee.
- RCA releases *The Unbelievable Guitar and Voice of Jerry Reed*, a prophetically-titled first album.
- After 34 years of success as a singing cowboy film and recording artist, Tex Ritter has his last Top 20 single, "A Working Man's Prayer."
- Kenny Rogers and Mike Settle, two former singers with the New Christy Minstrels, form The First Edition rock group, whose hits would include the Mel Tillis-penned "Ruby, Don't Take Your Love To Town."
- Hank Williams Jr. is featured in the MGM movie *A Time To Sing*.
- New "Grand Ole Opry" members include Stu Phillips, Charlie Walker, Jeannie Seely, Jack Greene, The 4 Guys, and, as a member of the "Porter Wagoner" show, Dolly Parton.

1968

FRESH BLOOD

A trio of new country artists burst onto the scene with smash-hit records in 1968; each one was different and each scored one of the biggest records of the year. Henson Cargill, Jeannie C. Riley, and Bobby Goldsboro seemed to come out of nowhere this year and, in truth, Riley actually did. Goldsboro had toured with Roy Orbison since 1962 and Cargill had performed with the West Coast-based Kimberleys in the mid-1960s. Riley was actually a gospel-loving Anson, Texas, girl named Jeanne Carolyn Stephenson, with a service station attendant husband who ignored her and a Nashville secretary's job that was leading her nowhere until producer Shelby Singleton put her in his studio with a Tom T. Hall song. "Harper Valley P.T.A." was written from an incident Hall recalled from his own rural home-town. Jeannie was such a mild-mannered young lady that record man Singleton had to needle her until she got angry in the studio to get the fiery performance that made the song a #1 record, a six-million seller, and the basis for a later movie and television series. Singleton molded her image—from her sassy, sexy anger to the miniskirts she loathed wearing—but she eventually rebelled and turned to gospel music. Though she is often dismissed as a one-shot artist and not even listed in most country music reference works, Riley scored six more Top 10 hits and two Top 20s over the next eight years and in 1981 released a best-selling autobiography, *Jeannie C. Riley—From Harper Valley To The Mountain Top*.

Most Important Records

"Skip A Rope" Henson Cargill / Monument
"Folsom Prison Blues" Johnny Cash / Columbia
"Mama Tried" Merle Haggard / Capitol
"Harper Valley P.T.A." Jeannie C. Riley / Plantation
"Stand by Your Man" Tammy Wynette / Epic
"D-I-V-O-R-C-E" Tammy Wynette / Epic
"Honey" Bobby Goldsboro / UA
"I Want To Live" Glen Campbell / Capitol
"A World Of Our Own" Sonny James / RCA
"Wichita Lineman" Glen Campbell / Capitol

Debut Artist: Henson Cargill

Henson Cargill came from a prominent Oklahoma family. His grandfather had been mayor of Oklahoma City in the 1930s. He was drawn to country music early and dropped out of college to become a nightclub singer. He joined The Kimberleys, with whom Waylon Jennings recorded in the mid-1960s. "Skip A Rope," though firmly within a trend of songs built around kid's games and play songs (Tammy Wynette's early repertoire was almost entirely in this vein), was too strongly worded for

Jeannie C. Riley.
credit: Archives of Robert K. Oermann

most country artists. Cargill cut it, but was turned down by every major label in Nashville before Fred Foster's Monument Records gave him a shot. Luckily, Cargill had gotten a 90-day exclusive license on the tune. By then, Cargill had the year's biggest record—a pop smash as well as a country chart topper—and 22 others had it in the can, just in case his version faltered. "My career was a disaster from that point," Cargill explains. "One record company after another was going down and me with them." In the mid-1970s, he walked away from the business and returned to the family's 2,800-acre ranch and other commercial interests near Oklahoma City.

Awards

GRAMMYS

BEST COUNTRY PERFORMANCE, FEMALE—"Harper Valley P.T.A." Jeannie C. Riley

BEST COUNTRY PERFORMANCE, MALE—"Folsom Prison Blues" single Johnny Cash

BEST COUNTRY PERFORMANCE, DUO OR GROUP, VOCAL OR INSTRUMENTAL—"Foggy Mountain Breakdown" Flatt and Scruggs

BEST COUNTRY SONG—"Little Green Apples" Bobby Russell, writer

ALBUM OF THE YEAR (NC)—"By The Time I Get To Phoenix" Glen Campbell

SONG OF THE YEAR (NC)—"Little Green Apples" Bobby Russell

BEST ENGINEERED RECORDING (NC)—"Wichita Lineman" Glen Campbell, artist; Joe Polito and Hugh Davis, engineers

BEST ALBUM NOTES (NC)—"Johnny Cash at Folsom Prison" Johnny Cash, annotator

GOLD RECORDS

"The Best Of Eddy Arnold" G/A Eddy Arnold / RCA

"By The Time I Get To Phoenix" G/A Glen Campbell / Capitol

"Gentle On My Mind" G/A Glen Campbell / Capitol

"Johnny Cash At Folsom Prison" G/A Johnny Cash / Columbia

"Modern Sounds In Country & Western Music, Vol. 2" G/A Ray Charles / ABC

"Honey" G/S Bobby Goldsboro / UA

"Honey" G/A Bobby Goldsboro / UA

"Best Of Buck Owens" G/A Buck Owens / Capitol

"How Great Thou Art" G/A Elvis Presley / RCA

"Loving You" G/A Elvis Presley / RCA

"Distant Drums" G/A Jim Reeves / RCA

"Harper Valley P.T.A." G/S Jeannie C. Riley / Plantation

"Harper Valley P.T.A." G/A Jeannie C. Riley / Plantation

COUNTRY MUSIC ASSOCIATION AWARDS

ENTERTAINER OF THE YEAR—Glen Campbell

FEMALE VOCALIST OF THE YEAR—Tammy Wynette

MALE VOCALIST OF THE YEAR—Glen Campbell
SONG OF THE YEAR—"Honey" Bobby Goldsboro
SINGLE OF THE YEAR—"Harper Valley P.T.A." Jeannie C. Riley
ALBUM OF THE YEAR—"Johnny Cash At Folsom Prison" Johnny Cash
VOCAL GROUP OF THE YEAR—Porter Wagoner and Dolly Parton
MUSICIAN OF THE YEAR—Chet Atkins
INSTRUMENTAL GROUP OF THE YEAR—The Buckaroos
COMEDIAN OF THE YEAR—Ben Colder (stage name of singer Sheb Wooley)

ACADEMY OF COUNTRY MUSIC AWARDS
SONG OF THE YEAR—"Wichita Lineman" Jimmy Webb, writer
SINGLE RECORD OF THE YEAR—"Little Green Apples" Roger Miller
ALBUM OF THE YEAR—"Glen Campbell & Bobbie Gentry"
MALE VOCALIST—Glen Campbell
FEMALE VOCALIST—Cathie Taylor
VOCAL DUET/GROUP—Johnny & Jonie Mosby
NEW MALE VOCALIST—Ray Sanders
NEW FEMALE VOCALIST—Cheryl Poole
TOURING BAND—Buckaroos (Buck Owens)
NON-TOURING BAND (CLUB)—Billy Mize's Tennesseans
DISC JOCKEY—(tie) Larry Scott/Tex Williams
CLUB—(tie) Golden Nugget/Palomino
TV PERSONALITY—Glen Campbell
MAN OF THE YEAR—Tommy Smothers
SPECIAL DIRECTORS' AWARD—Nudie Cohen
PIONEER AWARD—"Uncle" Art Satherly
INSTRUMENTALISTS: fiddle, Billy Armstrong; keyboard, Earl Ball; bass, Red Wooten; drums, Jerry Wiggins; guitar, Jimmy Bryant; steel guitar, Red Rhodes

Milestones

— Ernestine Dickens, wife of Little Jimmy Dickens, dies in a car wreck in Sherman, Texas, on New Years' Day.

— Glen Campbell quits his lucrative Los Angeles career as a session musician to become a solo artist. He immediately begins recording hits and is tapped as the summer replacement host for "The Smothers Brothers Show."

— Hank Williams Jr. commercially breaks with his mother, Audrey, separating his management, booking, and publishing interests from her Nashville business activities.

— Cree Indian folk singer Buffy St. Marie records her first country-flavored album in Nashville.

— Kenny Rogers and the First Edition have a pop hit, "I Just Dropped In (To See What Condition My Conditions Was In)."

— In early April, the Friday and Saturday "Opry" performances are canceled for the first time in history, due to

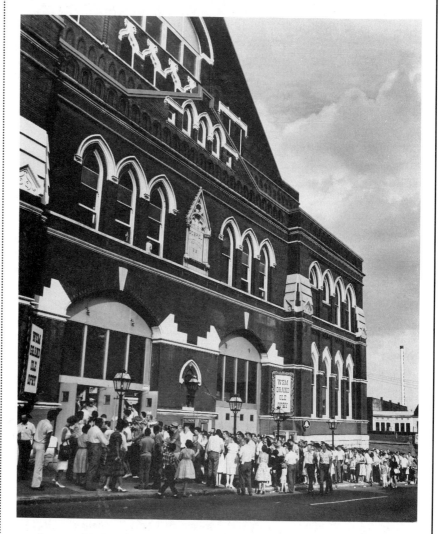

Ryman Auditorium, long-time home of the Grand Ole Opry, jammed with fans on Saturday night.
credit: Courtesy of the Grand Ole Opry

fears of racial violence in downtown Nashville following the assassination of civil rights leader Dr. Martin Luther King Jr. The fears proved unfounded.

↞ Lynn Anderson marries producer/songwriter Glenn Sutton.

↞ Nashville songwriter Beasley Smith, 66, writer of "God's Country," "Lucky Old Sun," "The Old Master Painter," and "Night Train To Memphis," dies on May 14 of a cerebral hemorrhage.

↞ Johnny Cash marries June Carter.

↞ Tom T. Hall marries *Music City News* fan magazine staffer Dixie Deen.

↞ Jerry Lee Lewis, having recorded his first "traditional country" record in 1961 with Hank Williams' "Cold, Cold Heart," successfully redirects his sagging career into the country market with "Another Place, Another Time" and "What Made Milwaukee Famous (Has Made A Loser Out of Me)."

↞ After 28 years, The Wilburn Brothers quit touring together. Doyle announces that he wants to concentrate on publishing and book agency matters, but soon slips off to Hol-

RCA/Nashville chief Chet Atkins must have been laughing behind his poker face when he first played Charley Pride's first recordings for label brass in Los Angeles prior to giving the singer a recording contract. "He played it for them, and they liked it, but then he said, 'Now wait a minute. This guy is black.' Of course I think it was 'colored' or 'negro' then, but he says there was a kind of a pause and they all looked back at each other. But they all said, 'We're gonna sign him anyway.'"

Pride's Sledge, Mississippi, childhood was typical of delta cotton patch poverty. The Pride household was suffused with country music from the family radio because Pride's father, a

powerful force in his life, found blues morally reprehensible. Eventually, young Pride migrated to Helena, Montana, where race was less an issue than in the South. He worked at an aluminum plant, played semi-pro baseball, and sang the music he'd been raised on at nights in a country dance hall.

Red Sovine and Red Foley met Pride in Montana and encouraged him to come to Nashville. Pride himself was "colorblind" to the potential ironies of a "man of color" singing "white man's music." "See, it wasn't until I got to Nashville that it was pointed out to me, "Hey, you're the first." But by the early 1970s, Pride was earning more gold records at RCA than any other artist except Elvis Presley.

Pride made Dallas, Texas, his home, primarily for the educational opportunities and relative lack of racial tension he found there for his children. By and large, the language of Dallas was money, and Pride, becoming a major real estate and banking mogul, learned to speak it fluently.

Though black country artists such as O.B. McClinton, Stoney Edwards, Big Al Downing, and, more recently, Cleve Francis, have followed Pride into the country music arena, black country singers remain a rarity and are essentially fringe players, basically because they lack Pride's enormous talent.

Charley Pride.
credit: In the Southern Folklife Collection, University of North Carolina, Chapel Hill

lywood to take acting lessons. He rejoins his brother in concerts by the first of the next year.

- Dewey Grooms' Longhorn Ballroom in Dallas, once managed by Jack Ruby, undergoes an expansion and has a grand opening as the world's largest dance hall.
- Elton Britt kicks off a major revival of Jimmie Rodgers' music with an LP titled *Jimmie Rodgers Blues*.
- The Nitty Gritty Dirt Band appears in the film *Paint Your Wagon*.
- "Grand Ole Opry" cast members are featured at the Newport Folk Festival for the first time. On the bill are Roy Acuff, George Hamilton IV, Ralph Stanley and the Clinch Mountain Boys, and Kenneth Threadgill performing as Jimmie Rodgers.
- Ernest V. "Pop" Stoneman, 75, dies on June 14 after a long illness.
- Red Foley dies on September 19.
- Ronnie Robbins makes his recording debut as Marty Robbins Jr.
- In December, Pee Wee King officially disbands his Golden West Cowboys band.

1969

THE MAN IN BLACK

Johnny Cash had been steadily recovering from those dark days in the mid-1960s when a drug possession conviction had threatened his career as surely as drug addiction had threatened his life. His second marriage, to June Carter the year before, seemed to bring new strength and focus to this tortured artist. In an explosion of creativity and recording activity, he reached a new plateau of humor, social conscience, folk infusion, and mainstream gospel-washed country all at the same time. He appeared on television, on radio, at the winner's podium on one awards show after another, topping it with the CMA's Entertainer of the Year. From here, he became even more committed to widening his musical horizons and would eventually use his "Johnny Cash Show" to explore the compatibility of cutting edge Southern rock and electric folk music with country. As the decade raced to an end, the last 12 months in country music clearly bore the stamp of The Man in Black.

Most Important Records

"Daddy Sang Bass" Johnny Cash / Columbia
"A Boy Named Sue" Johnny Cash / Columbia
"Okie From Muskogee Merle Haggard / Capitol
"I'm So Afraid Of Losing You Again" Charley Pride / RCA
"Running Bear" Sonny James / RCA
"Since I Met You, Baby" Sonny James / RCA

ohnny and June Carter Cash.
credit: Archives of Robert K. Oermann

"Galveston" Glen Campbell / Capitol
"Only The Lonely" Sonny James / RCA
"Statue Of A Fool" Jack Greene / Decca
"The Ways To Love A Man" Tammy Wynette / Epic

Debut Artist: Freddy Weller

Freddy Weller's Southern roots were showing when he left Atlanta
to become a replacement member of the popular teen-idol group
Paul Revere and the Raiders in 1967, but he was never content in
a tri-cornered hat, doing the Paul Revere kick dance for teenybop-
pers. In 1969 he released a country-laced version of "Games
People Play," a pop hit by his Atlanta pal Joe South, which
debuted on country charts in the #2 slot for two weeks. He solidified his niche with a string of pop hits arranged for the country
market, including "Down In The Boondocks," "Indian Lake," "The
Promised Land," "Nadine," and "Too Much Monkey Business."

Awards

GRAMMYS

BEST COUNTRY PERFORMANCE, FEMALE—"Stand By Your Man"
album Tammy Wynette
BEST COUNTRY PERFORMANCE, MALE—"A Boy Named Sue" single
Johnny Cash

BEST COUNTRY PERFORMANCE, DUO OR GROUP—"MacArthur Park"
Waylon Jennings & The Kimberlys

BEST COUNTRY INSTRUMENTAL PERFORMANCE—"The Nashville Brass
Featuring Danny Davis Play More Country Sounds" Danny
Davis & The Nashville Brass

BEST COUNTRY SONG—"A Boy Named Sue" Shel Silverstein, writer

BEST GOSPEL PERFORMANCE (NC)—"In Gospel Country" Porter Wagoner & The Blackwood Brothers

BEST ALBUM NOTES (NC)—"Nashville Skyline" Bob Dylan artist;
Johnny Cash, annotator

GOLD RECORDS

"Rudolph The Red-Nosed Reindeer" (reissue) G/S Gene Autry
/ Columbia

"Galveston" G/S Glen Campbell / Capitol

"Galveston" G/A Glen Campbell / Capitol

"Glen Campbell—Live" G/A Glen Campbell / Capitol

"Hey Little One" G/A Glen Campbell / Capitol

"Wichita Lineman" G/S Glen Campbell / Capitol

"A Boy Named Sue" G/S Johnny Cash / Columbia

"Johnny Cash's Greatest Hits" G/A Johnny Cash / Columbia

"Johnny Cash At San Quentin" G/A Johnny Cash / Columbia

"Nashville Skyline" G/A Bob Dylan / Columbia

"Gentry/Campbell" G/A Bobbie Gentry & Glen Campbell /
Capitol

"Elvis TV Special" G/A Elvis Presley / RCA

"From Vegas To Memphis" G/A Elvis Presley / RCA

"His Hand In Mine" G/A Elvis Presley / RCA

"In The Ghetto" G/S Elvis Presley / RCA
"Suspicious Minds" G/S Elvis Presley / RCA
"Boots With Strings" G/A Boots Randolph / Monument
"Gitarzan" G/S Ray Stevens / Monument
"Hank Williams' Greatest Hits" G/A Hank Williams / MGM
"Your Cheatin' Heart" G/A Hank Williams MGM

COUNTRY MUSIC ASSOCIATION AWARDS
ENTERTAINER OF THE YEAR—Johnny Cash
FEMALE VOCALIST OF THE YEAR—Tammy Wynette
MALE VOCALIST OF THE YEAR—Johnny Cash
SONG OF THE YEAR—"Carroll Country Accident" Bob Ferguson, writer
SINGLE OF THE YEAR—"A Boy Named Sue" Johnny Cash
ALBUM OF THE YEAR—"Johnny Cash At San Quentin" Johnny Cash
VOCAL GROUP OF THE YEAR—Johnny Cash and June Carter
MUSICIAN OF THE YEAR—Chet Atkins
INSTRUMENTAL GROUP OF THE YEAR—Danny Davis & the Nashville Brass
COMEDIAN OF THE YEAR—Archie Campbell

ACADEMY OF COUNTRY MUSIC AWARDS
SONG OF THE YEAR—"Okie From Muskogee" Merle Haggard, writer
SINGLE RECORD OF THE YEAR—"Okie From Muskogee" Merle Haggard, artist
ALBUM OF THE YEAR—"Okie From Muskogee" Merle Haggard
MALE VOCALIST—Merle Haggard
FEMALE VOCALIST—Tammy Wynette
VOCAL DUET/GROUP—The Kimberlys
NEW MALE VOCALIST—Freddy Weller
NEW FEMALE VOCALIST—Donna Fargo
COMEDY ACT—Roy Clark
TOURING BAND—The Strangers (Merle Haggard)
DISC JOCKEY—Dick Haynes
CLUB—Palomino
TV PERSONALITY—Johnny Cash
MAN OF THE YEAR—(tie) Joe Peppiatt/John Aylesworth
PIONEER AWARD—Bob Wills
JIM REEVES MEMORIAL AWARD—Joe B. Allison
INSTRUMENTALISTS: fiddle, Billy Armstrong; keyboard, Floyd Cramer; bass, Billy Graham; drums, Jerry Wiggins; guitar, (tie) Jerry Inman/Al Bruno; steel guitar, Red Rhodes; banjo, John Hartford
ARTIST OF THE DECADE AWARD—Marty Robbins

Milestones

↜ Only 15 years old, Ricky Skaggs is hired to play with Ralph Stanley's Clinch Mountain Boys.

Country music's early efforts regarding the war in Vietnam rode a bandwagon of patriotism. Women stuck to personal issues while men sang out their political convictions. That would change, though, as America's involvement became more controversial, costly, and obviously fruitless, until only singers with strong personal feelings—male or female—would dare sing about the war.

At first, as President Johnson began his military buildup in 1964 and 1965, country artists responded with unilateral patriotic songs. This trend began with a late 1965, three-week #1 hit by Johnny Wright about a professional soldier's stoic acceptance of war, steeped in mild Cold War rationale, "Hello Vietnam." As always, a hit spawned imitators, and soon country deejays were flooded with Vietnam songs. Wright followed his first war hit with "Keep The Flag Flying." Ernest Tubb scalded war protesters with "It's America (Love It Or Leave It)." Songwriter Tom T. Hall made a cottage industry out of Vietnam war songs, supplying Wright with "Hello Vietnam," Dave Dudley with "What We're Fighting For," and later his own more thoughtful, "Mama Bake a Pie."

But it didn't take long for flag waving to subside and other human interest angles to emerge. Memphis lounge singer Dean Cross put out a comin' home war song called "Hello Frisco, Goodbye Vietnam," while Split Records artists Joyce and Linda New warbled "I'm The Girl He Left Behind."

Kris Kristofferson, who would later compose entire albums opposing covert American military involvement in Central America, had just come back from flying helicopters in Vietnam when he wrote "The Viet Nam Blues" for Jack Sanders, released at about the same time.

In 1966 *Billboard* magazine wrote, "Since the first of the year, well over 100 Vietnam records have been released. . . a dozen making *Billboard's* country charts." The 100 included Loretta Lynn's "Dear Uncle Sam," Elton Britt's remake of Bob Miller's World War II hit, "There's A Star Spangled Banner Waving Somewhere," and Kitty Hawkins' Capra Records release, "Goodbye Vietnam."

The biggest hit of the pro-war songs, though, was an across-the-board pop and country smash by Staff Sgt. Barry Sadler, "The Ballad of the Green Berets." Sadler followed it with "The 'A' Team" and "Letter From Vietnam," but they packed far less wallop. After his death, RCA released Jim Reeves' war song, "Distant Drums." Ernest Tubb, who had sung patriotically in the 1940s during America's "last good war," issued "It's For God and Country and You, Mom" and "Soldier's Prayer in Viet Nam." Stonewall Jackson rode the wave with one of Harlan Howard's lesser efforts, "The Minute Men Are Turning In Their Graves," a nasty swipe at war protesters, and the trend, exhausted in the marketplace, mercifully fell off. Howard's personal interest in it, unfortunately, did not. He had two adopted stepsons in that war, one of whom was later killed in action. His wife, Jan Howard, had the poignant misfortune to have her self-penned war letter record, *My Son*, released the same week Jimmy Howard was killed in action.

By the end of the decade, the nation was torn over the war, and songs were different. Mel Tillis' powerful story of a disabled Korean War vet, "Ruby, Don't Take Your Love To Town," was revived by Kenny Rogers and the First Edition for a Top 40 country hit (#6 pop) in 1969. That and Tom T. Hall's "Mama Bake A Pie" were closer to John Prine's starkly poetic "Sam Stone" than any other mainstream country take on the human tragedy of the forgotten vet. Arlene Hardin sniped at military training in general for turning her loving man into a desensitized automaton in "Congratulations (You Sure Made A Man Out of Him)" in 1971.

Johnny Cash was consistent in his musical messages, if not in his politics. Only one verse in "Man In Black" referred to current events in Vietnam, but it was one of the most powerful repudiations of war. Being shelled on a base during a harrowing USO tour produced Johnny's Cash's overtly pacifist "Singin' In Vietnam Talkin' Blues," a Top 20 country hit in 1971. Nonetheless, Cash continued to publicly support President Nixon's escalation of the war, hoping it would bring lasting peace. Skeeter Davis, on the other hand, took Nixon to

Merle Haggard.
credit: Bob Millard Collection

task for his broken campaign promise to end the conflict early with her bouncy-yet-scathing "When You Gonna Bring Our Soldiers Home?"

Merle Haggard spoke for blind conservatism at the end of the decade, issuing "Okie From Muskogee," which blasted draft card burners in 1969. He followed that with his vitriolic "The Fightin' Side of Me." Both hits were more defensive of his working man's view that equated criticism of national mistakes with disloyalty to the motherland, rather than being truly pro-war.

The most controversial Vietnam War song was Terry Nelson's defense of the My Lai Massacre officer in "The Battle Hymn of Lt. Calley." It caused numerous barroom fist fights due to jukebox play and sold a million records.

The last word in country music on Vietnam was also Haggard's. He had a solid Top 5 hit in 1971, remaking Ernest Tubb's World War II weeper, "Soldier's Last Letter." As a pull on the emotions, it worked closer to Dalton Trumbo's poignant film *Johnny Got His Gun* than to Barry Sadler's cheap jingoism in "The Ballad of the Green Berets."[1]

1. For all his musical glorification of war, Staff Sgt. Barry Sadler was not a combatant in Vietnam. Following a tour of duty in the U.S. Air Force from 1958 to 1962, Sadler served in the Army's Special Forces (Green Berets) as a medical corpsman. In 1988, while in Guatemala to train Contra rebels to fight in El Salvador, he was shot in the head. He survived for one year.

- Tammy Wynette marries George Jones on the spur of the moment in Ringgold, Georgia, on February 16.
- Mel Tillis, Dolly Parton, Tammy Wynette, and George Jones are made regular "Grand Ole Opry" members.
- The first week in March, Johnny Cash joins Bob Dylan in Columbia's Nashville studios to record a dozen duets. In the end, only "Girl From The North Country" and Cash's award-winning liner notes will appear on Dylan's album, *Nashville Skyline.*
- After the obligatory round of lawsuits with Acuff-Rose Publications, Hank Williams Jr. gains access to a sheaf of half-finished lyrics left by his father. Hank Jr. finishes the songs and records the album *Songs My Father Left Me: The Poetry of Hank Williams Set to Music and Sung by Hank Williams Jr.* The album soon tops the *Billboard* album charts.
- Syndicated television show "Hee Haw," produced in the studios of a Nashville television station at first, debuts on national TV.
- Hank Cochran marries Jeannie Seely in Renfro Valley, Kentucky.
- Marty Robbins suffers his first major heart attack in August. He recovers, but ignores his doctor's advice not to return to race cars and a heavy touring schedule.
- West Coast country-rock bands play Carnegie Hall for the first time in September, including the Byrds, the Flying Burrito Brothers, and The Holy Modal Rounders.
- Songwriter Mac Davis makes his debut as a singer at the International Hotel in Las Vegas in October.
- Clearing up a long-running feud between Audrey Williams and Billie Jean Jones, a federal court establishes that Billie Jean is, in fact, the legal widow of Hank Williams. Billie Jean had sued the producers of the film *Your Cheatin' Heart* for $4 million for indicating otherwise.

Sonny James.
credit: Bob Millard Collection

THE 1970S

Sonny James had four multiweek #1 records in 1970 for a combined reign atop the charts of 14 weeks, the longest of any artist. The soft-spoken James, born Jimmie Loden into a show business family in Hackleburg, Alabama, in 1929, spent much of his childhood on the road. He was a seasoned radio performer by the time he reached high school and had his first Top 10 country hit in 1953. He might be best remembered for "Young Love," which topped the pop charts and was #1 on the country lists for nine weeks in 1956. Sixteen consecutive #1 singles between 1967 and 1971 stood as a record in country music until the group Alabama came along and claimed 21 in a row, discounting a Christmas single that only reached #35. James, an RCA roster alumni and a good sport, graciously attended Alabama's celebration for "breaking" his record. It wasn't for nothing that they called him "The Southern Gentleman."

Most Important Records

"Rose Garden" Lynn Anderson / Columbia
"Hello Darlin" Conway Twitty / Decca
"It's Just A Matter Time" Sonny James / RCA
"The Fightin' Side Of Me" Merle Haggard / Capitol
"He Loves Me All The Way" Tammy Wynette / Epic
"Sunday Morning Coming Down" Johnny Cash / Columbia
"I Wonder Could I Live There Anymore" Charley Pride / RCA
"Fifteen Years Ago" Conway Twitty / Decca
"Coal Miner's Daughter" Loretta Lynn / Decca
"Snowbird" Anne Murray / Capitol

Anne Murray.
credit: Bob Millard Collection

Debut Artist: Anne Murray

A rosy-cheeked young girl from a Nova Scotia mining town, Anne Murray made her country chart debut in the best way possible—with a smash hit. "Snowbird" failed to top either the country or pop charts, but it earned a gold record and never has entirely faded from radio. "Danny's Song," which came two and a half years later, allowed her to finally make good money, but the touring wore her out. Despite a string of hits, she quit show business altogether between 1975 and 1978 to marry and have children. When she returned, she did it with class, relaunching herself with an aptly titled hit, "Walk Right Back," followed by nine of her ten #1 records. After 23 years, Murray remains a tremendously popular entertainer with pop and country audiences. Savvy and outspoken, she is nobody's patsy.

Awards

GOLD RECORDS
"Try A Little Kindness" G/A Glen Campbell/Capitol
"Hello, I'm Johnny Cash" G/A Johnny Cash / Columbia
"Okie From Muskogee" G/A Merle Haggard / Capitol
"Don't Come Home A Drinkin'" G/A Loretta Lynn / Decca
"Snowbird" G/S Anne Murray / Capitol
"Don't Cry Daddy" G/S Elvis Presley / RCA
"From Elvis In Memphis" G/A Elvis Presley / RCA
"The Wonder Of You" G/S Elvis Presley / RCA
"The Best Of Charley Pride" G/A Charley Pride / RCA
"Tammy's Greatest Hits" G/A Tammy Wynette / Epic

GRAMMYS

BEST COUNTRY VOCAL PERFORMANCE, FEMALE—"Rose Garden" Lynn Anderson

BEST COUNTRY VOCAL PERFORMANCE, MALE—"For The Good Times" Ray Price

BEST COUNTRY PERFORMANCE, DUO OR GROUP—"If I Were A Carpenter" Johnny Cash & June Carter

BEST COUNTRY INSTRUMENTAL PERFORMANCE—"Me & Jerry" Chet Atkins & Jerry Reed

BEST COUNTRY SONG—"My Woman, My Woman, My Wife" Marty Robbins, writer

BEST GOSPEL PERFORMANCE (OTHER THAN SOUL GOSPEL) (NC)—"Talk About Good Times" The Oak Ridge Boys

BEST CONTEMPORARY VOCAL PERFORMANCE, MALE (NC)—"Everything Is Beautiful" single Ray Stevens

COUNTRY MUSIC ASSOCIATION AWARDS

ENTERTAINER OF THE YEAR—Merle Haggard

FEMALE VOCALIST—Tammy Wynette

MALE VOCALIST—Merle Haggard

SONG OF THE YEAR—"Sunday Morning Coming Down" Kris Kristofferson

SINGLE OF THE YEAR—"Okie From Muskogee" Merle Haggard

ALBUM OF THE YEAR—"Okie From Muskogee" Merle Haggard

VOCAL DUO OF THE YEAR—Porter Wagoner and Dolly Parton

VOCAL GROUP OF THE YEAR—The Glaser Brothers

INSTRUMENTALIST OF THE YEAR—Jerry Reed

INSTRUMENTAL GROUP OF THE YEAR—Danny Davis and the Nashville Brass

COMEDIAN OF THE YEAR—Roy Clark

ACADEMY OF COUNTRY MUSIC AWARDS

SONG OF THE YEAR—"For The Good Times" Kris Kristofferson, writer

SINGLE RECORD OF THE YEAR—"For The Good Times" Ray Price, artist

ALBUM OF THE YEAR—"For The Good Times" Ray Price

ENTERTAINER—Merle Haggard

MALE VOCALIST—Merle Haggard

FEMALE VOCALIST—Lynn Anderson

VOCAL DUET/GROUP—Kimberlys

NEW MALE VOCALIST—Buddy Alan

NEW FEMALE VOCALIST—Sammi Smith

COMEDY ACT—Roy Clark

TOURING BAND—The Strangers

NON-TOURING BAND—Tony Booth Band

DISC JOCKEY—Corky Mayberry

RADIO STATION—KLAC, Los Angeles, CA

Lynn Anderson.
credit: Bob Millard Collection

Dolly Parton owes her start in country music to her long association with Porter Wagoner.

In 1970 Parton finally outgrew Wagoner and began a concerted effort to establish herself as a solo star. She dug into the old Jimmie Rodgers catalog and updated his "Blue Yodel No. 8" as "Muleskinner Blues" for her first big hit, a strong Top 5 record. From her own pen came her first #1 late in the year, "Joshua." Another story from her East Tennessee mountains childhood became the basis for the touching "Coat of Many Colors" that marked the sweeter side of her developing catalog.

In late 1973, on the verge of making a permanent and not very friendly break with Porter Wagoner, Dolly released "Jolene" and started a run of #1 solo hits, including "Love Is Like A Butterfly," "I Will Always Love You," and "The Bargain Store," which ran consecutively through 1975. Her solo popularity even carried her 1974 duet with Wagoner,

"Please Don't Stop Loving Me," to the top of the charts, the first time in their long collaboration.

With manager Sandy Gallen, Parton built an empire of publishing and production companies, and opened a successful East Tennessee theme park, Dollywood. She hosted a couple of TV series, with mixed results, and expanded her talents into film acting, again with mixed results. Her appearances in *The Best Little Whorehouse In Texas* with Burt Reynolds and in *9-to-5* with Lillie Tomlin and Jane Fonda were raving smashes, spinning off successful soundtrack albums in the process. Her *Rhinestone Cowboy* with Sylvester Stallone was the most publicized flop among country music movies of the 1980s. Unflappable, Dolly just kept going. Her 1980s collaborations with Kenny Rogers ("Islands In The Streams,") and "Trio" with Linda Ronstadt and Emmylou Harris were 180 degrees apart in style, but both earned RIAA certifications and awards.

Porter Wagoner and Dolly Parton.
credit: Bob Millard Collection

From the beginning, Dolly Parton knew what her calling card would be. "It takes a lot of money to look this cheap," she says with a laugh, making more bosom jokes about herself than Johnny Carson ever did. Her repertoire, much of the best of which she has written, is a mixture of genuine heart songs and sexy twaddle, and she has somehow pulled it all off with the same self-assured grace.

CLUB—Palomino
TV PERSONALITY—Johnny Cash
MAN OF THE YEAR—Hugh Cherry
PIONEER AWARD—Tex Ritter
JIM REEVES MEMORIAL AWARD—Bill Boyd
NEWS PUBLICATION—*Billboard*
INSTRUMENTALISTS: fiddle, Billy Armstrong; keyboard, Floyd Cramer; bass, (tie) Billy Graham/Doyle Holly; drums, Archie Francis; guitar, Al Bruno; steel guitar, J.D. Maness

Milestones

⇥ Minnie Pearl's newly published cookbook proves a popular-selling Christmas item.

⇥ "The Johnny Cash Show," a popular summer 1969 replacement, debuts as a regular on ABC-TV in January. Indicative of Cash's eclectic tastes, first-night guests include Arlo Guthrie, Jose Feliciano, and Bobbie Gentry.

- Marty Robbins undergoes triple bypass heart surgery.
- In Nashville in March, the first of a proposed chain of motels called King of the Road Motor Inns, after Roger Miller's hit song, opens downtown on the east side of the Cumberland River. The lounge becomes a magnet for entertainers and soon features a blind piano-playing R&B singer, recently arrived from the Memphis lounges, Ronnie Milsap.
- Loretta Lynn's sister, Crystal Gayle (Brenda Gail Webb), makes her chart debut, but will struggle for five years before she has a hit.
- New Jersey songwriter Eddie Rabbitt signs his first Nashville recording contract with tiny independent Royal American Records.
- A pioneer in Decca's early country A&R activities in Nashville, Paul Cohen, 63, dies in Bryan, Texas, on April 1.
- Ray Stevens is summer guest host for NBC-TV's "Andy Williams Show."
- Tex Ritter runs in the Republican primary for U.S. Senator from Tennessee. He is defeated by Bill Brock, who unseats Al Gore Sr. in the election in November.
- The first Country Radio Seminar is held in Nashville.
- Luther Perkins, lead guitarist in Johnny Cash's original Tennessee Two, dies in a house fire.

1971

SONGWRITER

Rhodes scholar and Vietnam vet Kris Kristofferson arrived in Nashville in 1965. He swept floors at Columbia studios and wrote songs. His songs were deeper and more serious than typical country music fare, but in 1970 his songs began to stick on the charts with a new, more adult, kind of sound. "Sunday Morning Coming Down," Johnny Cash's stark, yet image-filled, song of the reality of life as an addict, came from Kristofferson's pen. Of 37 career releases, Sammi Smith is remembered solely for her 1971 Kristofferson chart topper, "Help Me Make It Through The Night." Ray Price had a huge hit in 1970 with Kristofferson's "For The Good Times." Janis Joplin and Roger Miller made Kristofferson's "Me and Bobbie McGee" a pervasive anthem of life on the road in a difficult time. Kristofferson's songwriting success helped country music become relevant to a sophisticated urban adult audience in the 1970s.

Most Important Records

"Easy Lovin'" Freddie Hart / Capitol
"When You're Hot, You're Hot" Jerry Reed / RCA
"Kiss An Angel Good Morning" Charley Pride / RCA
"I'm Just Me" Charley Pride / RCA

Kris Kristofferson.
credit: Bob Millard Collection

"Empty Arms" Sonny James / RCA
"Help Me Make It Through The Night" Sammi Smith / Mega
"I'd Rather Love You" Charley Pride / RCA
"After The Fire Is Gone" Conway Twitty and Loretta Lynn / Decca
"I Won't Mention It Again" Ray Price / Columbia
"The Year That Clayton Delaney Died" Tom T. Hall / Mercury

Debut Artist: Freddie Hart

Freddie Hart had been recording country music since 1959, but for all the success he had enjoyed prior to "Easy Lovin'," he might as well have come from nowhere in 1971. Born Fred Segrest in Lochapoka, Alabama, Hart enlisted underaged and fought overseas during World War II before he was discovered and shipped home. He worked in Arizona with Lefty Frizzell in the glory days of 1951 and 1952. Managed within the Buck Owens organization until "Easy Lovin'," with 17 releases on Columbia, Kapp, and Capitol over a dozen years, he twice barely made the Top 20. The record preceding "Easy Lovin'" hit the chart at #68 and bounced off. He took over his own management after the hit and was able to follow with a series of chart toppers, including "My Hang-Up Is You," "Bless Your Heart," "Got The All Overs For You (All Over Me)," "Super Kind of Woman," and "Trip To Heaven," not to mention a matching set of Top 5's. His string of hits faded in the late 1970s, and Hart devolved onto a series of independent labels. He is now semi-retired in North Ridge, California and still does occasional personal appearances.

Freddie Hart.
credit: Bob Millard Collection

Awards

GOLD RECORDS

"Rose Garden" G/S Lynn Anderson / Columbia
"Rose Garden" G/A Lynn Anderson / Columbia
"The World Of Johnny Cash" G/A Johnny Cash / Columbia
"Take Me Home Country Road" G/S John Denver / RCA
"The Fightin' Side Of Me" G/S Merle Haggard / Capitol
"Easy Lovin'" G/S Freddie Hart / Capitol
"On Stage February 1970" G/A Elvis Presley / RCA
"For The Good Times" G/A Ray Price / Columbia
"Charley Pride's 10th Album" G/A / Charley Pride / RCA
"Charley Pride In Person" G/A Charley Pride / RCA
"Just Plain Charley" G/A Charley Pride / RCA
"Amos Moses" G/S Jerry Reed / RCA
"Help Me Make It Through The Night" G/S Sammi Smith / Mega

GRAMMYS

BEST COUNTRY VOCAL PERFORMANCE, FEMALE—"Help Me Make It Through The Night" Sammi Smith
BEST COUNTRY VOCAL PERFORMANCE, MALE—"When You're Hot, You're Hot" Jerry Reed
BEST COUNTRY PERFORMANCE, DUO OR GROUP—"After The Fire Is Gone" Conway Twitty and Loretta Lynn
BEST COUNTRY INSTRUMENTAL PERFORMANCE—"Snowbird" single Chet Atkins
BEST COUNTRY SONG—"Help Me Make It Through The Night" Kris Kristofferson, writer
BEST SACRED PERFORMANCE (NC)—"Did You Think To Pray" Charley Pride
BEST GOSPEL PERFORMANCE (OTHER THAN SOUL GOSPEL) (NC)—"Let Me Live" Charley Pride

COUNTRY MUSIC ASSOCIATION AWARDS

ENTERTAINER OF THE YEAR—Charley Pride
FEMALE VOCALIST—Lynn Anderson
MALE VOCALIST—Charley Pride
SONG OF THE YEAR—"Easy Lovin'" Freddie Hart
SINGLE OF THE YEAR—"Help Me Make It Through The Night" Sammi Smith
ALBUM OF THE YEAR—"I Won't Mention It Again" Ray Price / Columbia
VOCAL DUO OF THE YEAR—Porter Wagoner and Dolly Parton
VOCAL GROUP OF THE YEAR—The Osborne Brothers
INSTRUMENTALIST OF THE YEAR—Jerry Reed
INSTRUMENTAL GROUP OF THE YEAR—Danny Davis and the Nashville Brass

ACADEMY OF COUNTRY MUSIC AWARDS

SONG OF THE YEAR—"Easy Lovin'" Freddie Hart, writer

SINGLE RECORD OF THE YEAR—"Easy Lovin'" Freddie Hart, artist

ALBUM OF THE YEAR—"Easy Lovin'" Freddie Hart

ENTERTAINER—Freddie Hart

MALE VOCALIST—Freddie Hart

FEMALE VOCALIST—Loretta Lynn

VOCAL DUET/GROUP—Conway Twitty and Loretta Lynn

NEW MALE VOCALIST—Tony Booth

NEW FEMALE VOCALIST—Barbara Mandrell

COMEDY ACT—Roy Clark

TOURING BAND—The Strangers

NON-TOURING BAND—Tony Booth Band

DISC JOCKEY—Larry Scott

RADIO STATION—KLAC, Los Angeles, CA

CLUB—Palomino

TV PERSONALITY—Glen Campbell

MAN OF THE YEAR—Walter Knott

PIONEER AWARD—Stuart Hamblin, Bob Nolan, and Tex Williams

JIM REEVES MEMORIAL AWARD—Roy Rogers

INSTRUMENTALISTS: fiddle, Billy Armstrong; keyboard, Floyd Cramer; bass, Larry Booth; drums, Jerry Wiggins; guitar, Al Bruno; steel guitar, J.D. Maness

Milestones

- In February, Loretta Lynn and Conway Twitty strike with "After The Fire Is Gone," the first of a decade-long string of hit duets that spawns a new trend of male-female country duets.

- The "Grand Ole Opry" and the Country Music Association sponsor the first Country Music Fan Fair in Nashville.

- The "Grand Ole Opry" at the Ryman Auditorium adds a second Saturday night performance. Before the year is out, the "Opry" will experience its first sell-out weekend, with all 3,000 seats sold for all four Friday and Saturday night shows.

- The massacre by American troops of villagers in the Vietnamese village of My Lai climaxes in the court-martial trial of Lt. Rusty Calley. Plantation Records issues a controversial pro-Calley record called "The Battle Hymn of Lt. Calley." It becomes the biggest-selling country song about the war. *Billboard* reports that the record on jukeboxes "is actually causing fist fights in bars and headaches for the nation's jukebox operators." An "answer song" is released shortly thereafter, telling the story of a soldier who refused orders to kill civilians at My Lai, titled "The Coward (?) of My Lai."

- In July, after a 23-year estrangement, Lester Flatt joins Bill Monroe on stage for the finale of Monroe's annual Bean Blossom Bluegrass Festival.

- Glen Campbell, his "Good Time Hour" a top TV variety series, breaks records for gate receipts at large concert halls all over the country.
- The Missouri town of Marceline (boyhood residence of Walt Disney) opens a major country music entertainment complex, called Codyland after developer Buck Cody.
- Smokey Bleacher, 50, long-time country radio comedian, dies in late September at his Pennsylvania home near Wheeling, West Virginia. Bleacher worked with the original Lonzo & Oscar show, with the Hawkshaw Hawkins show, and with Doc Williams on the WWVA "Wheeling Jamboree."
- An unknown singer, Earl T. Conley, has his first country release on Prize Records with "The Night They Drove Old Dixie Down."
- Kentucky-born, Chicago-raised contemporary country-folk singer/songwriter John Prine plays the Bitter End in New York, with "City of New Orleans" writer Steve Goodman, and acquires his first trade review. "It is obvious Prine is a writer to watch," writes *Billboard*, which misidentifies the writer of Don Williams' "Love Is On A Roll" and Lynn Anderson's "Paradise" as "Tom Prine."
- Country flavor in rock records, from the Nitty Gritty Dirt Band to the Rolling Stones, from Poco to Linda Ronstadt, is credited with a rise in acoustic stringed instrument sales. Musical instrument industry reports show that, between 1969 and the end of 1970, sales of guitars, banjos, pedal steel guitars, and dobros increase from $106 million to $160 million.
- In November, ground is broken for construction of the new Opry House at Opryland complex, already under construction.
- *Country Music* magazine debuts.

Jerry Reed Gets Hot

When session guitarist Jerry Reed was signed to RCA by Chet Atkins in the mid-1960s, he and labelmates Ed Bruce and John Hartford were initially pitched to a college audience in a program taking its name from Reed's album "Underground Nashville." Reed made a decent living as a guitar stylist and singer of oft-humorous story songs such as "Alabama Wildman" and "Amos Moses" until his 1971 breakthrough hit, "When You're Hot, You're Hot," became a self-fulfilling prophesy. Five weeks at #1, the song put Reed on the map. He re-released "Alabama Wild Man," topped the charts again in 1973 with "Lord, Mr. Ford," but soon became as well known as a film actor as a singing star and musician.

Reed teamed with Burt Reynolds in the road chase comedies *Smokey & The Bandit*, *Gator*, and *High Ballin'*. He appeared in *Bat 21* and other dramatic roles, but was best received in comic characterizations such as *W.W. and the Dixie Dance Kings* and *Smokey & The Bandit 2*.

The major hits in Reed's musical repertoire were also comedic. "She Got The Gold Mine (I Got The Shaft)" led to a television special for him, but his interest in films and the television series "Concrete Cowboys" and "Nashville 99" cut off his career as a hit singles artist by 1983. In 1992, Reed put the emphasis back on his guitar work, recording a third album of instrumental duets with Chet Atkins, titled *Sneakin' Around*, for Sony Music.

- Willie Nelson releases "Yesterday's Wine," country music's first "concept album."
- A Federal ban on cigarette advertising on television creates a windfall of tobacco sponsorship of country concert tours not seen since the Camel Caravan days of the early 1950s.
- Kris Kristofferson appears at Carnegie Hall in New York on December 30, with a band featuring Norman Blake, Donnie Fritz, Billy Swann, and ex-Lovin' Spoonful guitarist Zal Yanofsky.

1972

AN A-TEAM PICKER COMES INTO HIS OWN

Charlie McCoy.
credit: Courtesy of Charlie McCoy

West Virginia-born harmonica ace Charlie McCoy got his start as a dance combo leader while breaking into the Nashville sessions scene in the early 1960s. He took a shot at recording as a vocalist with a tune called "Cherry Wine" in the mid-1960s but soon became legendary as an instrumentalist. In addition to his trademark harmonica, he developed skills with guitar, bass, vibraphone, and trumpet. He was an A-Team picker in Nashville from the late 1960s on, a regular on Elvis Presley's Nashville and Hollywood sessions, and once played trumpet and bass simultaneously on a Bob Dylan album. He led the country-rock experiments in Nashville as part of the Area Code 615 and Barefoot Jerry groups and started his solo recording career in 1971. In 1972, he earned extraordinary public notice for a country instrumentalist, earning a Grammy and the first of two CMA awards for his instrumental prowess.

Most Important Records

"My Hang Up Is You" Freddie Hart / Capitol
"The Happiest Girl In The Whole USA" Donna Fargo / Dot
"Chantilly Lace" Jerry Lee Lewis / Mercury
"Carolyn" Merle Haggard / Capitol
"It's Gonna Take A Little Bit Longer" Charley Pride / RCA
"Funny Face" Donna Fargo / Dot
"I've Got The All Overs For You (All Over Me)" Freddy Hart / Capitol
"I Ain't Never" Mel Tillis / MGM
"One's On The Way" Loretta Lynn / Decca
"Woman (Sensuous Woman)" Don Gibson / Hickory

Debut Artist: Donna Fargo

A debut year that features a pair of three-week #1's is impossible to ignore. That's what former Mount Airy, North Carolina, high school teacher Donna Fargo accomplished with "The Happiest Girl In The Whole USA" and "Funny Face." The chirpy, upbeat singer/songwriter collected country music awards from every organization that handed them out for "The Happiest Girl In The Whole USA." She became a popular concert and television performer, and even had her own syndicated TV show in the mid-1970s, but fate intervened to slow her career significantly in the late 1970s. She was hospitalized for tests in 1978 and was diagnosed with multiple sclerosis, the crippler of young adults. Fargo became despondent and her music suffered. She turned to gospel music for a time, attained a condition of at least temporary remission in her fight with M.S., and made her last comeback attempt as a mainstream country recording artist in the late 1980s. Proper diet and adequate rest allow her to pursue a limited performing career.

Donna Fargo.
credit: Bob Millard Collection

Awards

GOLD RECORDS

"Glen Campbell's Greatest Hits" G/A Glen Campbell / Capitol
"Baby Don't Get Hooked On Me" G/S Mac Davis / Columbia
"The Happiest Girl In The Whole USA" G/S Donna Fargo / Dot
"The Best Of Merle Haggard" G/A Merle Haggard / Capitol
"Easy Loving" G/A Freddy Hart / Capitol
"Loretta Lynn's Greatest Hits" G/A Loretta Lynn / Decca
"Burning Love" G/S Elvis Presley / RCA
"Elvis As Recorded At Madison Square Garden" G/A Elvis Presley / RCA
"Charley Pride Sings Heart Songs" G/A Charley Pride / RCA
"Kiss An Angel Good Mornin'" G/S Charley Pride / RCA
"The Best Of Charley Pride" G/A Charley Pride / RCA
"Hello Darlin'" G/A Conway Twitty / Decca

GRAMMYS

BEST COUNTRY VOCAL PERFORMANCE, FEMALE—"The Happiest Girl In The Whole USA" single Donna Fargo
BEST COUNTRY VOCAL PERFORMANCE, MALE—"Charley Pride Sings Heart Songs" album Charley Pride
BEST COUNTRY PERFORMANCE, DUO OR GROUP—"Class Of '57" single The Statler Brothers
BEST COUNTRY INSTRUMENTAL PERFORMANCE—"Charlie McCoy/The Real McCoy" album Charlie McCoy
BEST COUNTRY SONG—"Kiss An Angel Good Mornin'" Ben Peters, writer
BEST ALBUM NOTES (NC)—"Tom T. Hall's Greatest Hits" Tom T. Hall, annotator
BEST INSPIRATIONAL PERFORMANCE (NC)—"He Touched Me" Elvis Presley

COUNTRY MUSIC ASSOCIATION AWARDS

ENTERTAINER OF THE YEAR—Loretta Lynn
FEMALE VOCALIST OF THE YEAR—Loretta Lynn
MALE VOCALIST OF THE YEAR—Charley Pride
SONG OF THE YEAR—"Easy Lovin'" Freddie Hart
SINGLE OF THE YEAR—"The Happiest Girl In The Whole USA" Donna Fargo
ALBUM OF THE YEAR—"Let Me Tell You About A Song" Merle Haggard
VOCAL DUO OF THE YEAR—Conway Twitty and Loretta Lynn
VOCAL GROUP OF THE YEAR—The Statler Brothers
INSTRUMENTALIST OF THE YEAR—Charlie McCoy
INSTRUMENTAL GROUP OF THE YEAR—Danny Davis & the Nashville Brass

ACADEMY OF COUNTRY MUSIC AWARDS

SONG OF THE YEAR—"The Happiest Girl In The Whole USA" Donna Fargo, writer

SINGLE RECORD OF THE YEAR—"The Happiest Girl In The Whole USA" Donna Fargo, artist

ALBUM OF THE YEAR—"The Happiest Girl In The Whole USA" Donna Fargo

ENTERTAINER—Roy Clark

MALE VOCALIST—Merle Haggard

FEMALE VOCALIST—Donna Fargo

VOCAL DUET/GROUP—The Statler Brothers

NEW MALE VOCALIST—Johnny Rodriguez

NEW FEMALE VOCALIST—Tanya Tucker

TOURING BAND—The Strangers

NON-TOURING BAND—Tony Booth Band

DISC JOCKEY—Larry Scott

RADIO STATION—KLAC, Los Angeles, CA

CLUB—Palomino

TV PERSONALITY—Roy Clark

MAN OF THE YEAR—Lawrence Welk

PIONEER AWARD—Gene Autry and Cliffie Stone

JIM REEVES MEMORIAL AWARD—Thurston Moore

INSTRUMENTALISTS: fiddle, Billy Armstrong; keyboard, Floyd Cramer; bass, Larry Booth; drums, Jerry Wiggins; guitar, Al Bruno; steel guitar, Buddy Emmons

Milestones

→ In January, Hollywood record producer Jimmy Bowen sets up his first offices in Nashville. His demanding standards concerning studio sound revolutionize the way country records are made.

→ The first annual Dripping Springs Reunion, a new idea of combining rock and country artists on the same stage, takes place in January in Dripping Springs, Texas. Oriented to the Austin music scene, this first concert loses money.

→ Johnny Rodriguez hires on as Tom T. Hall's guitarist, but by the end of the year he becomes a star in his own right with "Don't Pass Me By."

→ Opryland theme park opens; first year attendance is 1.4 million. Opryland officials announce that the old Ryman Auditorium will be torn down and its bricks used to build a chapel in the new theme park. Public outcry leads Opryland to preserve the Ryman, instead.

→ Joe Stampley, a 1960s Louisiana swamp rocker with The Uniques, has his first country hits with "If You Touch Me (You've Got To Love Me)" and "Soul Song."

→ New "Grand Ole Opry" members include Barbara Mandrell and David Houston. Rev. Jimmie Rodgers Snow, Hank's son, hosts a new post-Friday night "Opry" radio show called "Grand Ole Gospel." Featuring top country stars singing spiritual music, it is an immediate hit.

Starting out as a quirky West Coast act originally called the Illegitimate Jug Band, the Nitty Gritty Dirt Band had evolved through personnel and musical changes into one of the nation's premier country-folk-rock acts by 1972. Immediately after the million-selling album containing Jerry Jeff Walker's "Mr. Bojangles," the group followed their hearts into folk-country. The band's first countryesque album, *All The Good Times*, was released early in 1972, featuring sparkling renditions of the Cajun country favorites "Jam-balaya" and "Diggy-Diggy-Lo." Their debut on the country charts was a guest shot with Roy Acuff in 1971. Their second album was an astounding creative risk, a merging of the folksier veins of old country, new country, and modern folk-country.

Their experiment in melding the talents of country music elder statesmen like Maybelle Carter and Roy Acuff with the Earl Scruggs Revue members, Merle Travis, Doc Watson, and themselves yielded a landmark album entitled *Will The Circle Be Unbroken?* Its success shook Nashville's music establishment, eventually helping to open doors for other folk-country and country-rock musical influences and representatives from the West Coast. More importantly for the Dirt Band, it opened doors to mainstream country radio to them a decade later. Their 1980 pop hit, "An American Dream," a vocal collaboration with Linda Ronstadt, did poorly in the country charts but opened ears at country radio, rapidly being invaded by former rock and Top 40 disc jockeys receptive to the energies of non-traditional country-rock.

Nitty Gritty Dirt Band.
credit: photo by Allen Messer

- Don Williams, former member of the folk-pop vocal group The Pozo Seco Singers, bows on the country charts as a solo artist with "The Shelter of Your Eyes," a Top 20 record. It is the first production success for a young Allen Reynolds.
- The first annual International Country Music Fan Fair draws 10,000 fans to Nashville.
- On June 8 and 10, Elvis Presley plays the first New York City concert dates of his career. He performs three shows at Madison Square Garden. The concerts are filmed and recorded live. The record is gold by the end of the year.
- The first annual Kerrville Folk Festival is held in Kerrville, Texas, where Jimmie Rodgers built his "Yodeler's Paradise" home in 1930. Michael Martin Murphey, Mance Lipscomb, John Lomax Jr., and Allen Damron are on the bill June 1–3.
- Elton Britt, 54, dies in Crystal Springs, Pennsylvania, of a heart attack on June 23.
- Country music goes abroad as nine acts are sponsored by the United Nations to perform in Australia, New Zealand, and Japan. Among the stars on the bill are Tex Ritter, Tom T. Hall, and Connie Smith.
- The Oak Ridge Boys, a gospel quintet featuring Duane Allen, William Lee Golden, and Noel Fox, begin to play more country events, including appearances on the "Grand Ole Opry."
- At 13 years old, Marty Stuart goes on the road with Lester Flatt and draws much attention as a promising performer.
- In December, Chet Atkins steps down as head of RCA/Nashville to devote more time to recording and production. Jerry Bradley, son of Music Row pioneer Owen Bradley, takes over the label.

Charlie Rich, a shy loner with a drinking problem and a lifelong guilt complex ingrained by his religious upbringing, had popped up twice before. A great pianist and rheumy vocalist whose musical roots include gospel, blues, and especially jazz, he'd hit in late 1959 with "Lonely Weekends," an Elvis-style rocker on Sun Records. In the mid-1960s, he had a pop hit with "Mohair Sam," then seemed to disappear again into dingy Memphis clubs. In 1968, he began a painful five-year transition to commercial country singer without ever really leaving his jazz and blues behind. In 1973, he scored a career-making hit, "Behind Closed Doors," in a style that didn't exactly suit him, personally, but suited his voice to a tee. It brought a level of public attention that was hard for a him to bear. He is said to have self-destructed through the rest of the decade, all the while having one fine, musically sophisticated country smash after another, including "A Very Special Love Song," "She Called Me Baby," "My Elusive Dreams," and "Rollin' With The

1973

BEHIND CLOSED DOORS

Flow." By 1982, he had disappeared from commercial country music charts, taking a closet full of Grammys, gold records, and the CMA Entertainer of the Year glass bullet with him.

Most Important Records

"If We Make It Through December" Merle Haggard / Capitol
"Satin Sheets" Jeanne Pruett / MCA
"The Most Beautiful Girl" Charlie Rich / Epic
"You've Never Been This Far Before" Conway Twitty / MCA
"Behind Closed Doors" Charlie Rich / Epic
"Everybody's Had The Blues" Merle Haggard / Capitol
"We're Gonna Hold On" George Jones and Tammy Wynette / Epic
"What's Your Mama's Name" Tanya Tucker / Columbia
"Louisiana Woman, Mississippi Man" Conway Twitty and Loretta Lynn / MCA
"Why Me" Kris Kristofferson / Monument

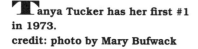

Tanya Tucker has her first #1 in 1973.
credit: photo by Mary Bufwack

Debut Artist:
Olivia Newton-John

How an Australian pop singer, granddaughter of a German Nobel Prize-winning physicist, became the toast of country radio by way of England is a long, involved story, but Olivia Newton-John's arrival in American country and pop charts was unmistakable in 1973. Lots of previous artists had charted country and pop with the same song, but usually one audience liked the music noticeably better than the other. With Newton-John, the numbers were virtually the same for the first three years. "Let Me Be There," her Top 10 1973 debut, announced her arrival as a pop-country phenomenon, inaugurating a string of hits, an acting career that included the female lead in the movie *Grease*, and a lot of resentment from country traditionalists.

Olivia Newton-John—pop or country?
credit: Bob Millard Collection

Awards

GOLD RECORDS

"Baby Don't Get Hooked On Me" G/A Mac Davis / Columbia
"Funny Face" G/A Donna Fargo / Dot
"The Happiest Girl In The Whole USA" G/A Donna Fargo / Dot
"Jesus Was A Capricorn" G/A Kris Kristofferson / Monument
"The Silver Tongued Devil & I" G/A Kris Kristofferson / Monument
"Why Me" G/S Kris Kristofferson / Monument
"Snowbird" G/A Anne Murray / Capitol
"Wm. E. McEuen Presents: Will The Circle Be Unbroken" G/A The Nitty Gritty Dirt Band / UA
"Elvis—Aloha From Hawaii Via Satellite" G/A Elvis Presley / RCA
"Elvis—That's The Way It Is" G/A Elvis Presley / RCA
"World Wide 50 Gold Award Hits, Vol. 1" G/A Elvis Presley RCA
"From Me To You" G/A Charley Pride / RCA
"The Country Way" G/A Charley Pride / RCA
"The Sensational Charley Pride" G/A Charley Pride / RCA
"Behind Closed Doors" G/S Charlie Rich / Epic
"Behind Closed Doors" G/A Charlie Rich / Epic
"The Most Beautiful Girl" G/S Charlie Rich / Epic
"Dueling Banjos/Deliverance" G/A Soundtrack / Warner Brothers
"Dueling Banjos" G/S Eric Weissberg / Warner Brothers

GRAMMYS

BEST COUNTRY VOCAL PERFORMANCE, FEMALE—"Let Me Be There" Olivia Newton-John

BEST COUNTRY VOCAL PERFORMANCE, MALE—"Behind Closed Doors" single Charlie Rich
BEST COUNTRY PERFORMANCE, DUO OR GROUP—"From The Bottle To The Bottom" Kris Kristofferson & Rita Coolidge
BEST COUNTRY INSTRUMENTAL PERFORMANCE—"Dueling Banjos" Eric Weissberg and Steve Mandell
BEST COUNTRY SONG—"Behind Closed Doors" Kenny O'Dell, writer

COUNTRY MUSIC ASSOCIATION AWARDS
ENTERTAINER OF THE YEAR—Roy Clark
FEMALE VOCALIST OF THE YEAR—Loretta Lynn
MALE VOCALIST OF THE YEAR—Charlie Rich
SONG OF THE YEAR—"Behind Closed Doors" Kenny O'Dell, writer
SINGLE OF THE YEAR—"Behind Closed Doors" Charlie Rich
ALBUM OF THE YEAR—"Behind Closed Doors" Charlie Rich
VOCAL DUO OF THE YEAR—Conway Twitty and Loretta Lynn
VOCAL GROUP OF THE YEAR—The Statler Brothers
INSTRUMENTALIST OF THE YEAR—Charlie McCoy
INSTRUMENTAL GROUP OF THE YEAR—Danny Davis & the Nashville Brass

ACADEMY OF COUNTRY MUSIC AWARDS
SONG OF THE YEAR—"Behind Closed Doors" Kenny O'Dell, writer
SINGLE RECORD OF THE YEAR—"Behind Closed Doors" Charlie Rich, artist
ALBUM OF THE YEAR—"Behind Closed Doors" Charlie Rich
ENTERTAINER—Roy Clark
MALE VOCALIST—Charlie Rich
FEMALE VOCALIST—Loretta Lynn
VOCAL DUET/GROUP—Brush Arbor
NEW MALE VOCALIST—Dorsey Burnette
NEW FEMALE VOCALIST—Olivia Newton-John
TOURING BAND—Brush Arbor
NON-TOURING BAND—Sound Company
DISC JOCKEY—Craig Scott
RADIO STATION—KLAC, Los Angeles, CA
CLUB—Palomino
PIONEER AWARD—Hank Williams
JIM REEVES MEMORIAL AWARD—Sam Lovullo
INSTRUMENTALISTS: fiddle, Billy Armstrong; keyboard, Floyd Cramer; bass, Larry Booth; drums, Jerry Wiggins; guitar, Al Bruno; steel guitar, Red Rhodes

Milestones

→ "Delta Dawn" proves a potent chart debut for a spunky 13-year-old Seminole, Texas, girl, Tanya Tucker. The tune reaches the #6 chart position on the country charts, #72 on the pop lists.

- Elvis Presley and The Stamps quartet perform in Honolulu, in a concert shown via satellite in 38 countries to an estimated worldwide audience of one billion. The NBC-TV special is a hit in the United States, and the double record album set, *Elvis: Aloha From Hawaii*, advances more than a million copies.
- JMI Records pioneers the country music video concept, producing a 3-minute film to go along with Don Williams' debut, "The Shelter of Your Eyes."
- The Oak Ridge Boys record a gospel song with Johnny Cash in an effort to expand their fan base into the country arena.
- Stuart Hamblen hosts a popular West Coast religious program, "Cowboy Church of the Air," on KLAC in Los Angeles.
- Jerry Lee Lewis makes his debut on the "Grand Ole Opry" and performs for 55 minutes, due to audience demand. His performance preempts the Ernest Tubb show that normally follows the "Opry" broadcast.
- In Dallas, the "Big D Jamboree" returns and is wildly successful. In Richmond, Virginia's "Old Dominion Barn Dance," popular from the late 1940s through the late 1950s, tries for a comeback as a live radio show and flops miserably after only three weeks.
- The sister in TV's Osmond Family singers, 13-year-old Marie Osmond, records her debut country album in Nashville with Sonny James producing, scoring a #1 hit with the title tune, "Paper Roses."
- The Hillbilly Jamboree Theatre becomes one of the first country venues built in Branson, Missouri. The building owners, The Baldknobbers band, are the house act.
- Southwest folkie Michael (Martin) Murphey makes his radio debut with "Cosmic Cowboy." Unfortunately for him, The Nitty Gritty Dirt Band releases the Murphey-penned song the same week. Country radio passes on both versions.
- Former Nashville *Billboard* reporter Jimmy Buffett makes his country recording debut with a poor-showing single, "Great Filling Station Hold-up." The flip-side, "Why Don't We Get Drunk And Screw," becomes a raging hit on newly emerging Underground-FM album rock stations across the nation, connecting Buffett with his best audience.
- Honky-tonk legend Lefty Frizzell, destitute, is hospitalized in Nashville's Memorial Hospital with pneumonia in March.
- New members of the "Grand Ole Opry" include comedian Jerry Clower, the Tammy Wynette and George Jones duet team, and Jeanne Pruett. Skeeter Davis is suspended from the "Opry" for making personal political-religious statements on the air.
- A high energy combo from Ft. Payne, Alabama, Wild Country, entertains young vacation crowds at Myrtle Beach, South Carolina. In about five years, the band will change its name to Alabama.

Theoretically, it should never have worked, the combination of country music's most outspoken feminist and a former rock 'n' roll balladeer who defined his music as jukebox Hallmark cards that could do the romantic speaking for any man to any woman. But when Loretta Lynn and Conway Twitty sang together, not only did the voices blend, there was a special body language. For a male-female duet to work more than once, there has to be a sexual tension portrayed, and Conway and Loretta portrayed it well for 11 hit-making years.

Both were established stars when the idea of collaboration arose. Starting in 1973 with "(There's Nothing Cold As Ashes) After The Fire Is Gone," Conway and Loretta sang of the joy of physical passion in such up-tempo tunes as "Louisiana Woman, Mississippi Man" and "I Can't Love You Enough," and of its pains in "Feelin's."

Their duets not only joined in spine tingling harmonies, but they traded lines to sing to each other, as well as with each other, adding to the impression that this was a couple, a sort of Mr. & Mrs. Country Music Everyman. In a decade that saw pop crossover once again muscle the rural Southern element for primacy, Conway and Loretta stood their ground in down-to-earth "Opry" style and were tremendously successful in reinforcing their solo careers while they did it.

By pre-arrangement (Twitty was long seen as one of the more business-minded country stars) they released only one duet per year, though there were popular-selling duet albums in the market from time to time. The only year they strayed from their one-a-year program was in their final year, when "Lovin' What Your Lovin' Does To Me" and "I Still Believe In Waltzes" were Top 10 and #2, respectively.

Loretta Lynn and Conway Twitty—the top country duet of the 1970s.
credit: photo by Alan Mayor

- Loretta Lynn becomes the first woman to win the CMA's Entertainer of the Year Award, and lands on the cover of *Newsweek*.
- Country-rock pioneer Gram Parsons, 26, dies in Joshua Tree, CA on September 17 of heart failure due to drugs. His work with The Byrds, the Flying Burrito Brothers, and with Emmylou Harris were important links between West Coast rock and country music in the 1970s. Fellow former-Byrd, Clarence White, dies in a car wreck two months earlier.

→ With Newgrass Revival as his backup band, infamous rock 'n' roll legend Leon Russell records at Nashville's Bradley's Barn studios. The album, *Hank Wilson's Back*, yields a pair of moderate country hits in "I'm So Lonesome I Could Cry" and "Roll In My Sweet Baby's Arms." This effort suggests Russell's later #1 collaboration with Willie Nelson in 1979, "Heartbreak Hotel."

→ In October, teenager John Anderson loses everything he owns in a house trailer fire in Nashville. He had moved there to live with his sister Donna, who was the first in the family to try to make a career singing in Nashville.

→ Country comedian/banjo player David "Stringbean" Akeman and his wife Estelle are murdered in a robbery as they return home from an "Opry" performance on November 10. The killers are later caught and convicted.

For some time, commercial country music had been developing competing subgenres, primarily a "countrypolitan" pop-flavored style. In 1974, the general acceptance by trade press and trade organizations, like the CMA and ACM, of Texas-style progressive country music, urban West Coast-based country-rockers, and eclectic jazz and Western big bands caused considerable grumbling in the ranks of rural-based country entertainers. The last straw for the Nashville traditionalists was top CMA awards for well-financed popsters Olivia Newton-John and John Denver, and the sixth consecutive country instrumental group award going to RCA A&R executive and former New Yorker Danny Davis for his Nashville Brass unit. More than 50 top names bolted the CMA to found the ACE (Association of

1974

A COUNTRYPOLITAN
PROTEST

Paul and Linda McCartney meet Porter Wagoner and Dolly Parton in Nashville.
credit: photo by Les Leverett

Country Entertainers) to protest loosening definitions of country music by the trade association and the charts. Among prominent ACE agitators were George Jones, Tammy Wynette, Porter Wagoner, Hank Snow, George Morgan, Dolly Parton, and Jan Howard. The controversy caused bad feelings in the Nashville music community for months, but there was no legislating the boundaries of country music.

Most Important Records

"A Very Special Love Song" Charlie Rich / Epic
"I Can Help" Billy Swan / Monument
"I Love" Tom T. Hall / Mercury
"Please Don't Tell Me How The Story Ends" Ronnie Milsap / RCA
"He Thinks I Still Care" Anne Murray / Capitol
"No Charge" Melba Montgomery / Elektra
"Hello Love" Hank Snow / RCA
"Back Home Again" John Denver / RCA
"Jolene" Dolly Parton / RCA
"The Streak" Ray Stevens / Barnaby

Debut Artist: Eddie Rabbitt

Eddie Rabbitt's background is hardly typical in the ranks of country singers. He was born in Brooklyn, New York, and raised in East Orange, New Jersey, with an innate love for Irish music and an acquired taste for jukebox country. He moved to Nashville as a singer/songwriter in 1968 and gained a foothold when Elvis Presley cut his tune "Kentucky Rain." Giving the song to Presley instead of recording it himself brought Rabbitt a financial stability he had lacked, but delayed his recording career another four years. In 1974, "You Get To Me" cracked the Top 40, setting up a string of #1 and Top 10 hits including "Drinkin' My Baby (Off My Mind)," "Drivin' My Life Away," and his duet with Crystal Gayle, "You And I." Rabbitt has been a prolific composer. He helped write nearly all his music. His string of hits was uninterrupted until a self-imposed hiatus in the late 1980s, coinciding with the death of Rabbitt's young son, Timmy, and Rabbitt's breakup with long-time writing partner Even Stevens.

Awards

GOLD RECORDS
"Stop & Smell The Roses" G/A Mac Davis / Columbia
"Annie's Song" G/S John Denver / RCA
"Back Home Again " G/A John Denver / RCA
"Sunshine On My Shoulder" G/S John Denver / RCA
"The Best Of The Best Of Merle Haggard" G/A Merle Haggard / Capitol

"Me & Bobby McGee" G/A Kris Kristofferson / Monument
"Sundown" G/S Gordon Lightfoot / Reprise
"Sundown" G/A Gordon Lightfoot / Reprise
"I Honestly Love You" G/S Olivia Newton-John / MCA
"If You Love Me (Let Me Know)" G/S Olivia Newton-John / MCA
"If You Love Me (Let Me Know)" G/A Olivia Newton-John / MCA
"Let Me Be There" G/S Olivia Newton-John / MCA
"Let Me Be There" G/A Olivia Newton-John / MCA
"There Won't Be Anymore" G/A Charlie Rich / RCA
"Very Special Love Songs" G/A Charlie Rich / Epic
"Spiders & Snakes" G/S Jim Stafford / MGM
"I Can Help" G/S Billy Swan / Monument

GRAMMYS
BEST COUNTRY VOCAL PERFORMANCE, FEMALE—"Love Song" album Anne Murray
BEST COUNTRY VOCAL PERFORMANCE, MALE—"Please Don't Tell Me How The Story Ends" single Ronnie Milsap
BEST COUNTRY PERFORMANCE, DUO OR GROUP—"Fairytale" track The Pointer Sisters
BEST COUNTRY INSTRUMENTAL PERFORMANCE—"The Atkins-Travis Traveling Show" album Chet Atkins & Merle Travis
BEST COUNTRY SONG—"A Very Special Love Song" Norro Wilson & Billy Sherrill
BEST INSPIRATIONAL PERFORMANCE (NC)—"How Great Thou Art" track Elvis Presley
BEST GOSPEL PERFORMANCE (NC)—"The Baptism of Jesse Taylor"
BEST ALBUM NOTES* (NC)—"For The Last Time" Bob Wills and His Texas Playboys, artists; Charles R. Townsend, annotator
* (NOTE—there was a tie in this category)

COUNTRY MUSIC ASSOCIATION AWARDS
ENTERTAINER OF THE YEAR—Charlie Rich
FEMALE VOCALIST OF THE YEAR—Olivia Newton-John
MALE VOCALIST OF THE YEAR—Ronnie Milsap
SONG OF THE YEAR—"Country Bumpkin" Don Wayne
SINGLE OF THE YEAR—"Country Bumpkin" Cal Smith
ALBUM OF THE YEAR—"A Very Special Love Song" Charlie Rich
VOCAL DUO OF THE YEAR—Conway Twitty and Loretta Lynn
VOCAL GROUP OF THE YEAR—The Statler Brothers
INSTRUMENTALIST OF THE YEAR—Don Rich
INSTRUMENTAL GROUP OF THE YEAR—Danny Davis & the Nashville Brass

ACADEMY OF COUNTRY MUSIC AWARDS
SONG OF THE YEAR—"Country Bumpkin" Don Wayne, writer
SINGLE RECORD OF THE YEAR—"Country Bumpkin" Cal Smith, artist

ALBUM OF THE YEAR—"Back Home Again" John Denver
ENTERTAINER—Mac Davis
MALE VOCALIST—Merle Haggard
FEMALE VOCALIST—Loretta Lynn
VOCAL DUET/GROUP—Conway Twitty and Loretta Lynn
NEW MALE VOCALIST—Mickey Gilley
NEW FEMALE VOCALIST—Linda Ronstadt
TOURING BAND—The Strangers
NON-TOURING BAND—Palomino Riders
DISC JOCKEY—Larry Scott
RADIO STATION—KLAC, Los Angeles, CA
CLUB—Palomino
PIONEER AWARD—Tennessee Ernie Ford, Merle Travis, and Johnny Bond
JIM REEVES MEMORIAL AWARD—Merv Griffin
INSTRUMENTALISTS: fiddle, Billy Armstrong; keyboard, Floyd Cramer; bass, Billy Graham; drums, Jerry Wiggins; guitar, Al Bruno; steel guitar, J.D. Maness

Milestones

- On January 2, Tex Ritter dies of a heart attack at the Nashville Criminal Justice Center, where he had gone to bail a band member out of jail.
- Thirteen-year-old daughter of "Opry" member George Morgan, Loretta Lynn (Lorrie) Morgan, makes her first appearance on the "Opry."
- The Ryman Auditorium hosts an "Old Timers" show featuring Fiddlin' Sid Harkreader, Pee Wee King and Redd Stewart, and Deford Bailey in its last "Grand Ole Opry" broadcast on Friday, March 15. The following night President Richard M. Nixon, close to impeachment in the Watergate scandal, appears as musical guest as the new Opry House hosts its first "Opry" broadcast.
- The Arab oil embargo causes an overnight quadrupling of oil prices and subsequent gas shortages that seriously hurt the country tour business. Related vinyl shortages restrict record pressing.
- Nelson King dies on March 16, the day the new "Grand Ole Opry" opens. An important country radio announcer (WCKY, 1946–1961; WCLU 1961–1970), he founded the Country Music Deejays Association and organized the first country music disk jockey's convention in Nashville, forerunners of the Country Radio Seminar and Fan Fair.
- Willie Nelson's 1st Annual Fourth of July Picnic concert, the rebirth of the Dripping Springs Reunion concert, draws 100,000 people over three days in May. The event's success heralds Austin, Texas, as headquarters of the "progressive country music" scene.

Hoyt Axton's was a musical family. His mother, Mae Boren Axton, was co-writer of Elvis Presley's first major hit, "Heartbreak Hotel." Though Axton's mother offered the connections to the country music community, Axton chose to blaze his own trail as a West Coast-based, folk-rock artist. Essentially conservative, he found little welcome among radical East Coast folksingers, but in the late 1950s and early 1960s he built a name for himself in Southern California folk and rock nightclubs with a sandy, nasal baritone and a subtle sense of humor.

Axton scored his first success as co-writer of the Kingston Trio's big hit "Greenback Dollar" in 1962. He wrote numerous hits for rock acts of the 1960s, including Steppenwolf's anti-drug song, "(God Damn) The Pusher," which was featured in the soundtrack for the popular counterculture film *Easy Rider*. Axton cranked out a handful of memorable humor-laced and anti-drug songs including "The No-No Song" for Ringo Starr and "Mama Told Me Not To Come" for Three Dog Night. Three Dog Night also hit with Axton's "Joy To The World" and "Never Been To Spain."

Though he always capitalized on his down home Oklahoma country roots, Axton's sophistication came through in his music. He was already a category-defying star when he made an all-too-brief impact on the country charts. He scored two smash hits, both released in 1974, and among the most memorable records of that year. "When The Morning Comes" featured vocals by Linda Ronstadt. The brilliantly-produced novelty number, "Boney Fingers," was a duet with Renee Armand.

Axton organized his own label, Jeremiah Records, and continued to generate country releases through the early 1980s, including Top 20 hits "Della and the Dealer" and "Rusty Old Halo."

→ In separate, but related, musical developments, eclectic country-based, youth-oriented acts including Poco, Commander Cody and His Lost Planet Airmen, New Riders of the Purple Sage, and Dan Hicks and the Hot Licks earn consistent notice in the trade press as new-wave country acts, stirring simmering resentment among Nashville traditionalists. Meanwhile, the addition as a "country oldie" at some radio stations of Crosby Stills & Nash's 1970 record "Teach Your Children Well," featuring decidedly non-traditional pedal steel guitar work by the Grateful Dead's Jerry Garcia, further alienates Nashville's establishment.

→ Ex-Beatle Paul McCartney, who had previously recorded country-inspired tunes "Act Naturally," "Matchbox," "Everybody's Trying To Be My Baby," "Honey Don't," "Rocky Raccoon," "I've Just Seen A Face," "Don't Pass Me By," and "I'm Looking Through You" with the Beatles, releases a non-charting single titled "Country Dreamer" (Apple #1869). He subsequently spends six weeks in Nashville in June and July observing the country music scene, writing and recording with local musicians. The result is an album, *Junior's Farm*, and a charting single, "Sally G," written about Heaven Lee, a burlesque queen from Nashville's famed Printer's Alley.

→ Dolly Parton formally dissolves her musical partnership with Porter Wagoner on July 15. Her autobiographical solo LP, *In My Tennessee Mountain Home*, becomes country music's second concept album.

→ Buckaroos bandleader Don Rich, 33, is killed on July 17 in a motorcycle accident. Despite lingering grief and depression, Buck Owens continues recording and touring, but never recovers the joy of making music. Owens never again reaches the Top 10 and essentially retires in 1981.

- Ignoring doctors' advice, Marty Robbins continues racing stock cars, taking 32 stitches following a crash during the Charlotte 500.
- Bitter and protracted lawsuits herald the breakup of the long-standing business relationship between Loretta Lynn and the Wilburn Brothers.
- Announcing "hippy folkie" John Denver as Entertainer of the Year on the CMA show, a disgusted Charlie Rich sets fire to the winner's envelope on national TV.

1975

COUNTRY ROCK TAKES ROOT

Emmylou Harris.
credit: The Archives of Robert K. Oermann

The convergence of country and rock music in the early 1970s was, for the same cultural reasons that caused their original rift in the late 1950s, initially resisted by radio on both sides. In Nashville, the original experimenters were bands called Area Code 615, Barefoot Jerry (essentially the same group as Area Code 615), and the Amazing Rhythm Aces, country boys playing rock with a deep Dixie flavor. On the West Coast it was post-war babies bringing rock aesthetics to country songs—The Byrds, Flying Burrito Brothers, The Buffalo Springfield, and Linda Ronstadt's backup band, who became known as the Eagles. The East Coast folk scene contributed Emmylou Harris as harmony singer with Gram Parsons' band. In 1975 the breakthrough began. Ronstadt and Harris bowed as outsiders but became legitimate country singers. The Eagles were scoring rock radio hits with country-rock records that would become the most pervasive oldies on country airwaves throughout the 1980s, including "Desperado," "Lyin' Eyes," "Take It Easy," and "Tequila Sunrise."

Most Important Records

"Convoy" C.W. McCall / MGM
"Rhinestone Cowboy" Glen Campbell / Capitol
"Blue Eyes Crying In The Rain" Willie Nelson / Columbia
"Before The Next Teardrop Falls" Freddy Fender / ABC/Dot
"Thank God I'm A Country Boy" John Denver / RCA
"Are You Sure Hank Done It This Way" Waylon Jennings / RCA
"When Will I Be Loved" Linda Ronstadt / Capitol
"Wasted Days and Wasted Nights" Freddy Fender / ABC/Dot
"Another Somebody Done Somebody Wrong Song" B. J. Thomas / ABC
"Third Rate Romance" Amazing Rhythm Aces / ABC

Debut Artist: Freddy Fender

South Texas has always had South of the Border music spicing its other ethnic dance sounds, including Bohemian polkas, Western swing, and honky-tonk country. In 1975, following the first Mexican-American country artist, Johnny Rodriguez, Freddy Fender became an instant star. Fender originally recorded "Wasted Days and Wasted Nights" in 1959. Its New Orleans triplets beat and Fender's Tex-Mex delivery made it a regional rock 'n' roll hit, but a Louisiana marijuana conviction put Fender's career on ice from 1960 to 1963. "Before The Next Teardrop Falls" mixed verses in Spanish and English to appeal to the two Southwestern music audiences. Fender's last Top 10 hit was "The Rains Came," a 1977 remake of a Sir Douglas Quintet recording. In recent years, Fender has joined former Sir Douglas mainstays Doug Sahm and Augie Meyers, with internationally-famed accordionist Flaco Jimenez, to form The Texas Tornadoes.

Freddy Fender.
credit: Bob Millard Collection

Awards

GOLD RECORDS
"Rhinestone Cowboy" G/S Glen Campbell / Capitol
"Rhinestone Cowboy" G/A Glen Campbell / Capitol

"Fire On The Mountain" G/A Charlie Daniels Band / Kama Sutra

"An Evening With John Denver" G/A John Denver / RCA

"Back Home Again" G/S John Denver / RCA

"I'm Sorry" G/S John Denver / RCA

"Rocky Mountain Christmas" G/A John Denver / RCA

"Thank God I'm A Country Boy" G/S John Denver / RCA

"Windsong" G/A John Denver / RCA

"Before The Next Teardrop Falls" G/S Freddy Fender / Dot

"Before The Next Teardrop Falls" G/A Freddy Fender / Dot

"Wasted Days and Wasted Nights" G/S Freddy Fender / Dot

"Kris & Rita—Full Moon" G/A Kris Kristofferson and Rita Coolidge / A&M

"Blue Sky—Night Thunder" G/A Michael Martin Murphey / Epic

"Wildfire" G/S Michael Martin Murphey / Epic

"Clearly Love" G/A Olivia Newton-John / MCA

"Have You Never Been Mellow" G/S Olivia Newton-John / MCA

"Have You Never Been Mellow" G/A Olivia Newton-John / MCA

"Please Mister Please" G/S Olivia Newton-John / MCA

"Elvis—A Legendary Performer—Vol. 1" G/A Elvis Presley / RCA

"(Country) Charley Pride" G/A Charley Pride / RCA

"Did You Think To Pray" G/A Charley Pride / RCA

"Don't Cry Now" G/A Linda Ronstadt / Asylum

"Heart Like A Wheel" G/A Linda Ronstadt / Capitol

"Prisoner In Disguise" G/A Linda Ronstadt / Asylum

"Another Somebody Done Somebody Wrong Song" G/S B.J. Thomas / ABC

GRAMMYS

BEST COUNTRY VOCAL PERFORMANCE, FEMALE—"I Can't Help It If I'm Still In Love With You" single Linda Ronstadt

BEST COUNTRY VOCAL PERFORMANCE, MALE—"Blue Eyes Crying In The Rain" single Willie Nelson

BEST COUNTRY PERFORMANCE, DUO OR GROUP—"Lover Please" single Kris Kristofferson and Rita Coolidge

BEST COUNTRY INSTRUMENTAL PERFORMANCE—"The Entertainer" track Chet Atkins

BEST COUNTRY SONG—"Another Somebody Done Somebody Wrong Song" Chips Moman and Larry Butler, writers

BEST ARRANGEMENT ACCOMPANYING VOCALISTS (NC)—"Misty" Ray Stevens, artist and arranger

COUNTRY MUSIC ASSOCIATION AWARDS

ENTERTAINER OF THE YEAR—John Denver

FEMALE VOCALIST—Dolly Parton

MALE VOCALIST—Waylon Jennings

SONG OF THE YEAR—"Back Home Again" John Denver

SINGLE OF THE YEAR—"Before The Next Teardrop Falls" Freddy Fender

ALBUM OF THE YEAR—"A Legend In My Time" Charlie Rich

VOCAL DUO OF THE YEAR—Conway Twitty and Loretta Lynn

VOCAL GROUP OF THE YEAR—The Statler Brothers

INSTRUMENTALIST OF THE YEAR—Johnny Gimble

INSTRUMENTAL GROUP OF THE YEAR—Roy Clark and Buck Trent

ACADEMY OF COUNTRY MUSIC AWARDS

SONG OF THE YEAR—"Rhinestone Cowboy" Larry Weiss, writer

SINGLE RECORD OF THE YEAR—"Rhinestone Cowboy" Glen Campbell, artist

ALBUM OF THE YEAR—"Feelings" Conway Twitty and Loretta Lynn

ENTERTAINER—Loretta Lynn

MALE VOCALIST—Conway Twitty

FEMALE VOCALIST—Loretta Lynn

VOCAL DUET/GROUP—Conway Twitty and Loretta Lynn

NEW MALE VOCALIST—Freddy Fender

NEW FEMALE VOCALIST—Crystal Gayle

TOURING BAND—The Strangers

NON-TOURING BAND—Palomino Riders

DISC JOCKEY—Billy Parker

RADIO STATION—KLAC, Los Angeles, CA

CLUB—Palomino

PIONEER AWARD—Roy Rogers

JIM REEVES MEMORIAL AWARD—Dinah Shore

INSTRUMENTALISTS: fiddle, Billy Armstrong; keyboard, Jerry Lee Lewis; bass, Billy Graham; drums, Archie Francis; rhythm guitar, Jerry Inman; lead guitar, Russ Hansen; steel guitar, J.D. Maness

Milestones

- In January, Eddie Rabbitt signs with Asylum Records, his first major label.
- Billie Jo Spears releases "Blanket on the Ground," to be her only chart topping record in 20 years of recording in the United States.
- The vinyl shortage and recession cause a sharp cutback in the number of records pressed. There is a sharp fall off in older records kept in active catalog.
- In the spring, Tammy Wynette files for divorce from George Jones. She takes the house and the band, The Jones Boys, and renames them The Country Gentlemen.
- Hank Williams Jr. has a momentous year. In February he disbands his musical show, made up mostly of musicians who formerly played in his father's Drifting Cowboys band, and moves from Nashville to Cullman, Alabama, to work on his music and form a new band. On August 9, while moun-

Billie Jo Spears.
credit: Bob Millard Collection

tain climbing outside Missoula, Montana, with friends, he falls more than 500 feet and is nearly killed. During his long and painful recovery, his mother dies.

↦ Chuck Glaser, of the Glaser Brothers, suffers partial paralysis from a stroke, but recovers sufficiently to resume his booking and management enterprises.

↦ March rains flood the Cumberland River at Opryland, causing $5 million in damages and forcing the "Grand Ole Opry" into Nashville's Municipal Auditorium. For the first time in years, everyone who wants to get in attends the "Opry" performances in the 9,600-seat arena.

↦ In remote Perdenales, Texas, in April, Willie Nelson completes *Red Headed Stranger*, his revolutionary self-produced masterpiece, a concept album mixing characters of the Old West with the reincarnation philosophy of the Near East.

↦ Oscar Davis, "The Baron of the Box Office," 72, important early country music booking agent and promoter, dies of a heart attack the first week in April. He promoted Hank Williams' notorious wedding shows in New Orleans in 1952.

↦ Johnny Cash finishes writing his autobiographical *Man In Black*.

↦ George Morgan, 50, dies on July 7 following his third major heart attack.

↦ Lefty Frizzell, 47, suffers a massive stroke and dies in Nashville on July 17.

↦ Former WLS "Barn Dance" star Lulu Belle Wiseman is elected to the state legislature in North Carolina.

↦ Marty Robbins, running at Talladega, suffers his third stock car racing accident in two years and vows to quit the racing game.

↦ Nashville's City Council votes to rename several streets in the Music Row area. Sixteenth Avenue South becomes Music Square East; Seventeenth Avenue South becomes Music Square West.

↦ Tom T. Hall and Dolly Parton each lay plans to host nationally-syndicated TV variety shows, putting a positive spin on country music. Director Robert Altman's darkly irreverent film, *Nashville*, is released in the autumn, prompting mass indignation from the country entertainers who see too much of themselves in Altman's unflattering portrait of the country music capital.

↦ Conway Twitty sings "Hello Darlin'" in phonetic Russian for the orbiting rendezvous of Soviet and American space capsules.

↦ Elvis Presley goes on a month-long campaign of bizarre behavior during his summer tour, shooting out a motel television in Ashville, North Carolina, impulsively giving fans and bandmembers nearly $50,000 worth of jewelry during concerts, and buying 14 Cadillacs in midnight shopping sprees for friends, associates, and total strangers. He performs three concerts of a scheduled two-week Las Vegas stint, collapses on August 21, is flown to Memphis, and is hospitalized for severe fatigue and constipation.

→ Guitarist Sam McGee, 81, the oldest musician on the "Grand Ole Opry," dies on August 21 from injuries sustained in a tractor accident at his Williamson County, Tennessee, farm. McGee was a sideman for Uncle Dave Macon in the 1920s.

→ After 28 years of hosting his "Midnight Jamboree" radio program, Ernest Tubb hands the show over to son Justin Tubb.

→ Audrey Williams, 52, former wife of Hank Williams and mother of Hank Williams Jr., dies at her Nashville home on November 3, the night before the IRS is scheduled to seize her house for back taxes.

→ Veteran "Opry" comedian and musician James Clell Summey, 61, a sideman in Roy Acuff's original Smokey Mountain Boys in the late 1930s, dies on August 18 in Nashville. He is best known as Cousin Jody.

→ Earl Scruggs narrowly escapes death when his private plane crash lands outside Nashville.

→ Lester Flatt recovers from open heart surgery and a month later is back on stage at the "Grand Ole Opry."

B.J. Thomas: The Country Years

With a golden balladeer's voice, Texan B.J. Thomas was able to establish himself as a star first in pop, then country, then gospel music. His soulful pop hits dripped with Southern working-class sex appeal. He had scored a pop hit with Hank Williams' "I'm So Lonesome I Could Cry" before he decided to cast his lot in the country market. His Burt Bacharach movie themes transcended all boundaries, so his repertoire of hits such as "Just Can't Help Believin'" were hardly unfamiliar or anathema to country fans. In 1975, it was only a matter of sending copies of his single "(Hey Won't You Play) Another Somebody Done Some body Wrong Song" to country stations for ABC Records to rack up a #1 pop and country hit for Thomas.

However, Thomas was in no position to capitalize on his chart topper. Drug addiction and marital problems wrecked his private life, leading to a religious conversion and a gospel career. He wrote a best-selling Christian confessional autobiography, *Home Where I Belong*. Thomas was an early star in what became known as the contemporary Christian field. Choosing to mix his secular hits with his religious music caused enormous problems for the entertainer, and he was rejected for years in both markets.

During that period, Thomas' secular records were played on country radio, but he didn't have another country hit until 1983. Produced by Nashville veteran Pete Drake, Thomas had several major hits, including *Whatever Happened to Old Fashioned Love* and *Two Car Garage*. He had a successful duet with pop and country soulmate Ray Charles in 1984, *Rock And Roll Shoes*, but his recording career was hurt by more personal problems and business complications. CBS Records forced Thomas to quit working with Drake almost as soon as the hits started. Other producers failed to match Drake's successes.

The "outlaw" movement, typified by Waylon Jennings, Jessi Colter, and producer Jack Clement, was in full swing as progressive country music shook up the Nashville establishment.
credit: photo by Alan Mayor

1976

Comin' Back Atcha Good Buddy

From their heyday in the 1920s, emotionally-charged story songs have held a place in country fans' hearts. In 1976, Red Sovine, a middle-aged journeyman late in his career, did what he had always done best, recording a good old-fashioned tear-jerking narration, "Teddy Bear." It represented something of a comeback for Sovine, who had never been off the charts but hadn't had a Top 10 for a decade. He started his recording career with a bang—three major duet hits with Webb Pierce in 1955 and 1956. Over a 25-year career, many of his releases, and all three of his best remembered solo hits, "Teddy Bear" included, were songs about truck drivers.

Most Important Records

"Good Hearted Woman" Waylon Jennings and Willie Nelson / RCA

"Teddy Bear" Red Sovine / Starday
"Somebody Somewhere (Don't Know What He's Missin' Tonight)"
Loretta Lynn / MCA
"One Piece At A Time" Johnny Cash / Columbia
"El Paso City" Marty Robbins / Columbia
"(I'm A) Stand By My Woman Man" Ronnie Milsap / RCA
"I Don't Want To Have To Marry You" Jim Ed Brown and Helen
Cornelius / RCA
"I'll Get Over You" Crystal Gayle / UA
"Drinkin' My Baby (Off My Mind)" Eddie Rabbitt / Elektra
"Don't The Girls All Get Prettier At Closing Time" Mickey Gilley
/ Playboy

Debut Artists: Oak Ridge Boys

Originally forming in 1940 as a gospel group, the Oak Ridge
Boys evolved through personnel changes for more than 35
years before the lineup of Duane Allen, William Lee Golden,
Richard Sterban, and Joe Bonsell applied their four-part gospel
harmonies to mainstream country lyrics in 1976. Coming on

Oak Ridge Boys, top gospel
group turned country hitmakers,
playing 21 with Lee Greenwood,
Las Vegas dealer-turned country
entertainer.
credit: Courtesy of the Las Vegas
News Bureau

the heels of two years of angling toward a wider market, their 1976 debut was not spectacular; "Family Reunion" barely charted. Their second record, "Y'All Come Back Saloon," was released in 1977 and ignited a career of lively gospel-style country performances. Their best-loved hits, among a string of #1's and Top 5's that spanned the 1980s, are "Elvira" and "Bobby Sue," both of which are predicated on tenor and bass strengths—exactly the same strengths that make gospel popular. In the mid-1980s, the Oak Ridge Boys had a run of chart toppers that established them as the vocal group of the decade.

Awards

GOLD AND PLATINUM RECORDS
"That Christmas Feeling" G/A Glen Campbell / Capitol
"All The Love In The World" G/A Mac Davis / Capitol
"Spirit" G/A John Denver / RCA
"Spirit" P/A John Denver / RCA
"Wanted: The Outlaws" G/A Waylon Jennings, Willie Nelson, Jessi Colter, Tompall Glaser / RCA
"Wanted: The Outlaws" P/A Waylon Jennings, Willie Nelson, Jessi Colter, Tompall Glaser / RCA
"A Star Is Born" G/A Kris Kristofferson and Barbra Streisand / Columbia
"Summertime Dream" G/A Gordon Lightfoot / Reprise
"Black Bear Road" G/A C.W. McCall / MGM
"Red Headed Stranger" G/A Willie Nelson / Columbia
"Come On Over" G/A Olivia Newton-John / MCA
"Don't Stop Believin'" G/A Olivia Newton-John / MCA
"Hasten Down The Wind" G/A Linda Ronstadt / Asylum
"Hasten Down The Wind" P/A Linda Ronstadt / Asylum
"Teddy Bear" G/S Red Sovine / Gusto
"You've Never Been This Far Before" G/A Conway Twitty / MCA

GRAMMYS
BEST COUNTRY VOCAL PERFORMANCE, FEMALE—"Elite Hotel" album Emmylou Harris
BEST COUNTRY VOCAL PERFORMANCE, MALE—"I'm A Stand By My Woman Man" single Ronnie Milsap
BEST COUNTRY PERFORMANCE, DUO OR GROUP—"The End Is Not In Sight (The Cowboy Tune)" single Amazing Rhythm Aces
BEST COUNTRY INSTRUMENTAL PERFORMANCE—"Chester & Lester" album Chet Atkins and Les Paul
BEST COUNTRY SONG—"Broken Lady" Larry Gatlin, writer
BEST GOSPEL PERFORMANCE (NC)—"Where The Soul Never Dies" The Oak Ridge Boys

COUNTRY MUSIC ASSOCIATION AWARDS
ENTERTAINER OF THE YEAR—Mel Tillis
FEMALE VOCALIST—Dolly Parton

MALE VOCALIST—Ronnie Milsap

SONG OF THE YEAR—"Rhinestone Cowboy" Larry Weiss

SINGLE OF THE YEAR—"Good Hearted Woman" Waylon Jennings and Willie Nelson

ALBUM OF THE YEAR—"Wanted—The Outlaws" Waylon Jennings, Willie Nelson, Jessi Colter, and Tompall Glaser

VOCAL DUO OF THE YEAR—Waylon Jennings and Willie Nelson

VOCAL GROUP OF THE YEAR—The Statler Brothers

INSTRUMENTALIST OF THE YEAR—Hargus "Pig" Robbins

INSTRUMENTAL GROUP OF THE YEAR—Roy Clark and Buck Trent

ACADEMY OF COUNTRY MUSIC AWARDS

SONG OF THE YEAR—"Don't The Girls All Get Prettier At Closing Time" Baker Knight, writer

SINGLE RECORD OF THE YEAR—"Bring It On Home" Mickey Gilley, artist

ALBUM OF THE YEAR—"Gilley's Smoking" Mickey Gilley

ENTERTAINER—Mickey Gilley

MALE VOCALIST—Mickey Gilley

FEMALE VOCALIST—Crystal Gayle

VOCAL DUET/GROUP—Conway Twitty and Loretta Lynn

NEW MALE VOCALIST—Moe Bandy

NEW FEMALE VOCALIST—Billie Jo Spears

TOURING BAND—Red Rose Express

NON-TOURING BAND—Possum Holler Band

DISC JOCKEY—Charlie Douglas

RADIO STATION—KLAC, Los Angeles, CA

CLUB—Palomino

PIONEER AWARD—Owen Bradley

JIM REEVES MEMORIAL AWARD—Roy Clark

INSTRUMENTALISTS: fiddle, Billy Armstrong; keyboard, Hargus "Pig" Robbins; bass, Curtis Stone; drums, Archie Francis; lead guitar, Danny Michael; steel guitar, J.D. Maness

Milestones

- On January 22, in a Nashville studio, rodeo brat and Oklahoma college student Reba McEntire makes her first recordings for a major country label, Mercury Records. She cuts four songs, then drives home with her parents, who had accompanied her on the trip from Oklahoma. Later in 1976 she marries rodeo champ Charlie Battles. They spend their honeymoon driving around Texas promoting her first record, "I Don't Want To Be A One Night Stand."

- In February, B.J. Thomas files for bankruptcy in Dallas, Texas.

- David Kapp, 71, early country music producer and co-founder of Decca Records and Kapp Records, dies on March 1 in New York City.

- Vern Gosden makes a comeback as a solo artist with

The Bellamy Brothers score their first pop-goes-country hit with "Let Your Love Flow" in 1976.
credit: Courtesy of the Bellamy Brothers

"Hangin' On," a remake of the 1967 Top 40 country hit for Vern and Rex, The Gosden Brothers.

↪ *Coal Miner's Daughter*, Loretta Lynn's autobiography, is published in May.

↪ By summer, it is apparent that, together and separately, Willie Nelson and Waylon Jennings are the dominant album sellers in country music. Between them they have six albums in the Top 50.

↪ Donna Fargo is hospitalized for exhaustion. Tests later reveal that she has multiple sclerosis.

↪ Hattie Frost Stoneman, 75, who first recorded along with Ernest V. "Pop" Stoneman some 51 years earlier, dies on July 25 in Murfreesboro, Tennessee.

↪ Two of Bob Wills' original Texas Playboys die: fiddler Jesse Aslock, 61, in Austin, Texas, on August 9; and Clifford "Sleepy" Johnson, 67, on stage in April during a Bob Wills tribute concert in Turkey, Texas.

↪ New "Grand Ole Opry" members include Larry Gatlin and the Gatlin Brothers, Don Williams, and Ronnie Milsap; George Hamilton IV rejoins.

↪ Doug Sahm's first Texas Tornadoes lineup records for ABC/Dot and get rave reviews for their Tex-Mex dance music in concerts around the Southwest.

↪ The Bellamy Brothers debut on country (#21) and pop (#1) charts with "Let Your Love Flow."

The End Is (Still) Not In Sight

Nashville-born singer/song-writer Russell Smith was the leader and creative genius behind perhaps the most original country-rock-R&B band ever—The Amazing Rhythm Aces. Russell's soulful vocals, the funky Latin beat, and Byrd Burton's distinctive guitar work made the band's country debut, "Third Rate Romance," a much larger and more influential hit than it's #13 chart ranking might indicate. The record, which originated with a 20 verse song Smith cooked up to amuse the band, had an instantly recognizable groove, a combination of unforgettable beat and guitar riffs lifted by tongue-in-cheek lyrics that stripped away the maudlin pretense of previous country cheatin' songs. The Aces' impact can be measured by the fact that their follow-up hit, "The End Is Not In Sight (The Cowboy Song)" won a Grammy.

The band was formed in 1972 and continued as it originated, as a vehicle for Smith's prodigious writing and singing talents. Their third and final country hit album included "Amazing Grace (Used To Be Her Favorite Song)." Their brilliant remake of the Don Gibson chestnut, "Ashes of Love," was too syncopated for the country market of the 1970s. At best, the Aces' records were slow to catch on, so they never topped the charts, although they were generally long-running hits. The Aces' work illuminates the problems of depending entirely on chart position for assigning historical importance in country music. The tendency of radio to pigeonhole music into sharply defined formats hurt the band, as well. As Smith put it, "Nobody knew what kind of music we played." Burton quit over musical and personal differences, and Smith took the band into a more blues and R&B vein in the late 1970s.

In the early 1980s, when debts mounted, Smith disbanded the group. He settled back in Nashville as a songwriter and had two moderately successful shots as a solo country recording artist. His major contribution to country music in the 1980s and 1990s has been as a songwriter.

- *Wanted: The Outlaws*, by Willie Nelson, Waylon Jennings, Jessi Colter, and Tompall Glaser, becomes country's first platinum album certified by the RIAA.

- Passage of the Copyright Act of 1976 helps writers with a higher royalty rate for record sales and sheet music and a longer period of copyright protection. Most country labels react to the higher royalty rate by shaving the number of songs on albums from 12 to 10. RCA will later declare a 9-song album.

- In December, Reba McEntire graduates from Southeastern Oklahoma State University with a B.A. in elementary education and a minor in music.

Larry Gatlin got his professional start in 1971 as a fill-in with a big-name group singing gospel music in Las Vegas. There he met Dottie West, who encouraged him to move to Nashville. She recorded two of his songs and sent him a plane ticket to Music City, where he soon had songs recorded by Elvis Presley, Kris Kristofferson, Tom Jones, and Glen Campbell. He began his own recording career in 1974, and soon had Top 20 and Top 5 hits. In 1977 he climbed for the first time to the top of the charts, with "I Just Wish You Were Someone I Loved." Though he has always been the leader and writer for the Gatlin Brothers band, he generally credits his singing brothers Steve and Rudy as integral parts of his sound.

1977

GATLIN CLIMBS TO THE TOP

The Gatlin Brothers.
credit: Bob Millard Collection

Most Important Records

"Luckenbach, Texas (Back To The Basics of Love)" Waylon Jennings / RCA
"Here You Come Again" Dolly Parton / RCA
"Don't It Make My Brown Eyes Blue" Crystal Gayle / UA
"Heaven's Just A Sin Away" The Kendalls / Ovation
"It Was Almost Like A Song" Ronnie Milsap / RCA
"Near You" George Jones & Tammy Wynette / Epic
"Lucille" Kenny Rogers / UA
"Southern Nights" Glen Campbell / Capitol
"Rollin' With The Flow" Charlie Rich / Epic
"The Wurlitzer Prize (I Don't Want To Get Over You)" Waylon Jennings / RCA

Debut Artists: Janie Frickie and Ronnie McDowell

Janie Frickie and Ronnie McDowell were the most significant new artists in country music in 1977. Frickie (originally spelled Fricke) started modestly as a Memphis jingle singer. She moved to Nashville, a sweet, shy Hoosier, and soon became a top studio backup singer. Her best showing in her year as an artist was a Top 5 duet with Johnny Duncan, the Marty Robbins style "Come A Little Bit Closer." Always best when her vulnerability showed through in her voice and lyrics, she went on to score #1's with "Down On My Knees" (a duet with Charlie Rich), "Don't Worry 'Bout Me Baby," "It Ain't Easy Being Easy," "Tell Me A Lie," and four others before changing the spelling of her name in 1986 for her last #1, "Always Have, Always Will." She was named CMA's Female Vocalist of the Year in both 1982 and 1983.

McDowell was a protege of powerful country music publisher and record producer Buddy Killen. When Elvis Presley died in August 1977, McDowell, a talented Elvis impersonator but otherwise a total unknown, was rushed into the studio to record what became the biggest-selling Elvis tribute record, "The King Is Gone." He spent the rest of his career alternately exploiting and trying to escape his Elvis impersonator image. His hits painted him as a Romeo, though he is really a quiet family man. He scored #1 records with "Older Women" and "You're Gonna Ruin My Bad Reputation." His imitative talents have been utilized in a number of well-received TV movies based on Presley's life story. McDowell still lives in his hometown, Portland, Tennessee.

Awards

GOLD AND PLATINUM RECORDS
"Southern Nights" G/S Glen Campbell / Capitol
"Southern Nights" G/A Glen Campbell / Capitol
"The Johnny Cash Portrait/Greatest Hits, Vol. 2" G/A Johnny

Cash / Columbia
"I Want To Live" G/A John Denver / RCA
"John Denver's Greatest Hits, Vol. II" G/A John Denver / RCA
"Are You Ready For The Country" G/A Waylon Jennings / RCA
"Dreaming My Dreams" G/A Waylon Jennings / RCA
"Ol' Waylon" G/A Waylon Jennings / RCA
"Ol' Waylon" P/A Waylon Jennings / RCA
"Gord's Gold" G/A Gordon Lightfoot / Reprise
"The King Is Gone" G/S Ronnie McDowell / GRT
"Greatest Hits" G/A Olivia Newton-John / MCA
"Greatest Hits" P/A Olivia Newton-John / MCA
"Here You Come Again" G/A Dolly Parton / RCA
"Elvis—The Legendary Performer, Vol. II" G/A Elvis Presley / RCA
"Elvis Country" G/A Elvis Presley / RCA
"Elvis Sings The Wonderful World Of Christmas" G/A Elvis Presley / RCA
"Elvis Sings The Wonderful World Of Christmas" P/A Elvis Presley / RCA
"From Elvis Presley Blvd., Memphis, Tennessee" G/A Elvis Presley / RCA
"His Hand In Mine" G/A Elvis Presley / RCA
"In Concert" G/A Elvis Presley / RCA
"In Concert" P/A Elvis Presley / RCA
"Moody Blue" G/A Elvis Presley / RCA
"Moody Blue" P/A Elvis Presley / RCA
"Pure Gold" G/A Elvis Presley / RCA
"Way Down" G/S Elvis Presley / RCA
"Welcome To My World" G/A Elvis Presley / RCA
"Daytime Friends" G/A Kenny Rogers / UA
"Kenny Rogers" G/A Kenny Rogers / UA
"Lucille" G/S Kenny Rogers / UA
"Greatest Hits" P/A Linda Ronstadt / Asylum
"Simple Dreams" G/A Linda Ronstadt / Asylum
"Simple Dreams" P/A Linda Ronstadt / Asylum
"The Best Of The Statler Brothers" G/A Statler Brothers / Mercury
"A Star Is Born" P/A Kris Kristofferson and Barbara Streisand / Columbia
"Viva Terlingua" G/A Jerry Jeff Walker / MCA
"24 Greatest Hits" G/A Hank Williams / MGM

GRAMMYS
BEST COUNTRY VOCAL PERFORMANCE, FEMALE—"Don't It Make My Brown Eyes Blue" single Crystal Gayle
BEST COUNTRY VOCAL PERFORMANCE, MALE—"Lucille" single Kenny Rogers
BEST COUNTRY PERFORMANCE, DUO OR GROUP—"Heaven's Just A Sin Away" single The Kendells
BEST COUNTRY INSTRUMENTAL PERFORMANCE—"Country Instrumentalist Of The Year" album Hargus "Pig" Robbins

BEST COUNTRY SONG—"Don't It Make My Brown Eyes Blue"
Richard Leigh, writer
BEST GOSPEL PERFORMANCE (NC)—"Just A Little Talk With Jesus"
track The Oak Ridge Boys

COUNTRY MUSIC ASSOCIATION AWARDS
ENTERTAINER OF THE YEAR—Ronnie Milsap
FEMALE VOCALIST—Crystal Gayle
MALE VOCALIST—Ronnie Milsap
SONG OF THE YEAR—"Lucille" Roger Bowling and Hal Bynum
SINGLE OF THE YEAR—"Lucille" Kenny Rogers
ALBUM OF THE YEAR—"Ronnie Milsap Live"
VOCAL DUO OF THE YEAR—Jim Ed Brown and Helen Cornelius
VOCAL GROUP OF THE YEAR—The Statler Brothers
INSTRUMENTALIST OF THE YEAR—Roy Clark
INSTRUMENTAL GROUP OF THE YEAR—The Original Texas Playboys

ACADEMY OF COUNTRY MUSIC AWARDS
SONG OF THE YEAR—"Lucille" Roger Bowling and Hal Bynum, writers
SINGLE RECORD OF THE YEAR—"Lucille" Kenny Rogers, artist
ALBUM OF THE YEAR—"Kenny Rogers" Kenny Rogers
ENTERTAINER—Dolly Parton
MALE VOCALIST—Kenny Rogers
FEMALE VOCALIST—Crystal Gayle
VOCAL DUET/GROUP—The Statler Brothers
NEW MALE VOCALIST—Eddie Rabbitt
NEW FEMALE VOCALIST—Debbie Boone
TOURING BAND—(tie) Asleep at the Wheel/Sons of the Pioneers
NON-TOURING BAND—Palomino Riders
DISC JOCKEY—Billy Parker
RADIO STATION—KGBS, Los Angeles, CA
CLUB—Palomino
PIONEER AWARD—Sons of the Pioneers
JIM REEVES MEMORIAL AWARD—Jim Halsey
INSTRUMENTALISTS: fiddle, Billy Armstrong; keyboard, Hargus "Pig"
Robbins; bass, Larry Booth; drums, (tie) Archie Francis/George
Manz; guitar, Roy Clark; steel guitar, Buddy Emmons

Milestones

- In January a documentary film, *New Country*, chronicles hard-edged folk and rock influenced progressive country artists Guy Clark, Townes Van Zant, Steve Young, David Allan Coe, Larry Jon Wilson, and The Charlie Daniels Band.
- The Nashville Sound, generated through a system of close record company control of a few studios and record-makers, is unofficially dissolved as RCA shuts down its Nashville studio operations and MCA releases Owen Bradley from an exclusive production contract in January.

- Austin's "progressive country" scene is shaken as a favorite "outlaw" nightclub, Armadillo World Headquarters, files Chapter 11 bankruptcy.
- Mel Tillis helps his 19-year-old daughter, Pam, make her concert debut in Kansas City. She signs a recording contract with MCA Records.
- "Lucille" establishes Kenny Rogers as a solo country singing star.
- Dolly Parton starts a major push to establish herself among pop music fans.
- Backed by an extensive television advertising campaign, Slim Whitman becomes an enormous best-selling country artist in the United Kingdom.
- Elvis Presley, 42, dies at Graceland, on August 16. His death ignites a seemingly unquenchable market for his records. Eleven Presley records instantly re-enter the pop and country charts. RCA strains to meet the demand, putting other country records on standby. By the end of the year, Nashville record pressing plants are all working 24 hours a day manufacturing Presley records.
- Waylon Jennings is arrested for possession of cocaine in an elaborate federal smuggling investigation on August 24. His manager takes the rap; Waylon takes the cure.
- Early country singing star, Elvira June Weaver, 86, "Elviry" of the Weaver Brothers and Elviry, dies in December in Ventura, California.

Decline and Death of Elvis

Fame ultimately caused Elvis to cut himself off from the world. Fencing in Graceland and surrounding himself with family and a gaggle of friends-turned-hangers-on whom he kept on the payroll in roles that ranged from companion to gofer to bodyguard. As his business and career decisions were all made by super manager Col. Tom Parker, Presley had only to come out of hiding to make a movie, a record, or go on a tour. Keeping Las Vegas entertainer's hours, he became more and more dependent on prescribed stimulants, sleep aids, and tranquilizers to define his waking and sleeping periods.

There was a noticeable decay in his physical state during 1976 and 1977. Photos taken in that period often show a bloated man whose eyes and life seemed out of focus. Still, as he slipped from his pinnacle as rock 'n' roll hero, his country fans never abandoned him.

Beginning in 1971, his records reversed a trend and did better on the country charts than on the pop lists. "Way On Down," his last hit while still alive, had topped the country chart while not even breaking the Top 20 in pop. For a while, recording equipment had to be set up in the whimsical Jungle Room in his basement at Graceland because the once-outgoing and gregarious King of Rock 'n' Roll had become the reclusive Howard Hughes of pop music. He didn't want to leave the house to record anymore.

No one close to Presley ever seriously tried to deal with his chemical dependency as a problem. In the end, drug-induced dissipation and bad diet loosened his once sexy figure and facial tone below marketability in Hollywood. His concert performances became undependable. He forgot or slurred the words to his own greatest hits. Maybe in the end he was beginning to realize his own decline. He was trying desperately to lose weight in the week prior to a planned early fall concert tour. He had just finished an energetic midnight racquetball game in his gym behind the house when he died suddenly of cardiac arrest in his private quarters at Graceland.

1978

WILLIE'S BLUE SKIES

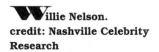 Willie Nelson.
credit: Nashville Celebrity
Research

The big problem with Willie Nelson in the 1960s was his quirky phrasing. Instead of flavoring his music with pedal steel he played gut string guitar like 1930s' French jazz great D'jango Reinhart and sang his country songs more like a European cabaret jazz man than a hillbilly. As long-haired cowboys touting a 1970s rebellion against hypocritical "family values" and the musical limitations of the Nashville establishment, Willie, Waylon Jennings, Tompall Glaser, and a few others established what was known as "the outlaw" movement in country music. But in 1978, Willie fashioned yet another new image for himself, singing cool countrified jazz treatments of 1940s pop standards. His album *Stardust* featured timeless pop tunes such as Irving Berlin's "Blue Skies," the Hoagy Carmichael classic "Stardust," and "Georgia On My Mind."

Appealing to a much broader audience, *Stardust* remained on the country album charts for several years, identifying Willie Nelson as an artist with the Midas touch, a singer whose music knew no boundaries.

Most Important Records

"Mammas Don't Let Your Babies Grow Up To Be Cowboys" Waylon Jennings and Willie Nelson / RCA
"I've Always Been Crazy" Waylon Jennings / RCA
"The Gambler" Kenny Rogers / UA
"Sleeping Single In A Double Bed" Barbara Mandrell / ABC
"Only One Love In My Life" Ronnie Milsap / RCA
"Heartbreaker" Dolly Parton / RCA
"Take This Job and Shove It" Johnny Paycheck / Epic
"Don't Break The Heart That Loves You" Margo Smith / Warner Brothers
"Georgia On My Mind" Willie Nelson / RCA
"Two More Bottles Of Wine" Emmylou Harris / Warner Brothers

Debut Artist: John Conlee

Country music, more than any other genre of popular music, often finds artists among its disk jockeys. Ernie Ford, Waylon Jennings, Jim Reeves, Merle Kilgore, and CMA's first Comedian of the Year, Don Bowman, were among the record spinners who became record makers. John Conlee was another example. Conlee was a Kentucky farm boy who worked six years in a funeral home before letting his interest in music pull him into a radio career at WLAC in Nashville in 1971. Though WLAC was then a pop music station, Conlee matriculated into the country music community in his off hours and soon began writing songs. A heavy-set man with a stout baritone voice, he wrote and sang with a barely-veiled vulnerability about emotional issues facing country War Babies fast approaching middle age. He parlayed his perspective and assets into a deal with ABC Records, culminating in his first Top 5 hit "Rose Colored Glasses," in 1978. Only when ABC called for an album did Conlee quit his day job at WLAC. Hits (most of which he wrote) that followed included "Backside of Thirty," "Common Man," "Miss Emily's Picture," "Years After You," and "Old School."

Awards

GOLD AND PLATINUM RECORDS
"I Want To Live" P/A John Denver / RCA
"When I Dream" P/A Crystal Gayle / UA
"I've Always Been Crazy" G/A Waylon Jennings / RCA
"Waylon Live" G/A Waylon Jennings / RCA

Margo Smith cracks the charts with Connie Frances' "Don't Break The Heart That Loves You."
credit: Bob Millard Collection

John Conlee.
credit: Bob Millard Collection

"Waylon & Willie" G/A Waylon Jennings and Willie Nelson / RCA
"Waylon & Willie" P/A Waylon Jennings and Willie Nelson / RCA
"Songs Of Kristofferson" G/A Kris Kristofferson / Columbia
"It Was Almost Like A Song" G/A Ronnie Milsap / RCA
"Only One Love In My Life" G/A Ronnie Milsap / RCA
"Let's Keep It That Way" G/A Anne Murray / Capitol
"Let's Keep It That Way" P/A Anne Murray / Capitol
"You Needed Me" G/S Anne Murray / Capitol
"Stardust" G/A Willie Nelson / RCA
"Stardust" P/A Willie Nelson / RCA
"The Sound In Your Mind" G/A Willie Nelson / RCA
"Hopelessly Devoted To You" G/S Olivia Newton-John / MCA
"Heartbreaker" G/A Dolly Parton / RCA
"Here You Come Again" G/S Dolly Parton / RCA
"Here You Come Again" P/A Dolly Parton / RCA
"The Best Of Dolly Parton" G/A Dolly Parton / RCA
"Take This Job And Shove It" G/A Johnny Paycheck / Epic
"A Legendary Performer—Elvis, Vol 3" G/A Elvis Presley / RCA
"My Way" G/S Elvis Presley / RCA
"Love Or Something Like It" G/A Kenny Rogers / UA
"Ten Years Of Gold" G/A Kenny Rogers / UA
"Ten Years Of Gold" P/A Kenny Rogers / UA
"The Gambler" G/A Kenny Rogers / UA
"A Retrospective" G/A Linda Ronstadt / Capitol
"Blue Bayou" G/S Linda Ronstadt / Asylum
"Entertainers On And Off The Road" G/A Statler Brothers / Mercury
"Tanya Tucker's Greatest Hits" G/A Tanya Tucker / Columbia

GRAMMYS

BEST COUNTRY VOCAL PERFORMANCE, FEMALE—"Here You Come Again" album Dolly Parton

BEST COUNTRY VOCAL PERFORMANCE, MALE—"Georgia On My Mind" single Willie Nelson

BEST COUNTRY PERFORMANCE, DUO OR GROUP—"Mammas Don't Let Your Babies Grow Up To Be Cowboys" single Waylon Jennings and Willie Nelson

BEST COUNTRY INSTRUMENTAL PERFORMANCE—"One O'Clock Jump" track Asleep At The Wheel

BEST COUNTRY SONG—"The Gambler" Don Schlitz, writer

BEST POP VOCAL PERFORMANCE, FEMALE (NC)—"You Needed Me" Anne Murray

COUNTRY MUSIC ASSOCIATION AWARDS

ENTERTAINER OF THE YEAR—Dolly Parton

FEMALE VOCALIST—Crystal Gayle

MALE VOCALIST—Don Williams

SONG OF THE YEAR—"Don't It Make My Brown Eyes Blue" Richard Leigh, writer

SINGLE OF THE YEAR—"Heaven's Just A Sin Away" The Kendalls

ALBUM OF THE YEAR—"It Was Almost Like A Song" Ronnie Milsap
VOCAL DUO OF THE YEAR—Kenny Rogers and Dottie West
VOCAL GROUP OF THE YEAR—Oak Ridge Boys
INSTRUMENTALIST OF THE YEAR—Roy Clark
INSTRUMENTAL GROUP OF THE YEAR—Oak Ridge Boys Band

ACADEMY OF COUNTRY MUSIC AWARDS
SONG OF THE YEAR—"You Needed Me" Randy Goodrum, writer
SINGLE RECORD OF THE YEAR—"Tulsa Time" Don Williams, artist
ALBUM OF THE YEAR—"Ya'll Come Back Saloon" Oak Ridge Boys
ENTERTAINER—Kenny Rogers
MALE VOCALIST—Kenny Rogers
FEMALE VOCALIST—Barbara Mandrell
VOCAL DUET/GROUP—Oak Ridge Boys
NEW MALE VOCALIST—John Conlee
NEW FEMALE VOCALIST—Christy Lane
TOURING BAND—Original Playboys Band
NON-TOURING BAND—Rebel Playboys
DISC JOCKEY—Billy Parker
RADIO STATION—KVOO, Tulsa, OK
CLUB—Palomino
PIONEER AWARD—Eddie Dean
JIM REEVES MEMORIAL AWARD—Joe Cates
INSTRUMENTALISTS: fiddle, Johnny Gimble; keyboard, Jimmy Pruett; bass, Rod Culpepper; drums, Archie Francis; guitar, James Burton; steel guitar, Buddy Emmons

Milestones

- Rodney Crowell first appears on the country charts.
- Hattie Louise "Tootsie" Bess, 63, owner and operator of the famous Tootsie's Orchid Lounge on Lower Broad in Nashville, dies of cancer on February 18 in Nashville. Because of her kindness to "Opry" stars during their struggling years, the funeral is attended by dozens of country stars; Connie Smith sings.
- Alton Delmore's unfinished autobiography is found by his son and published under the title *Truth Is Stranger Than Fiction.* It offers the most detailed, unvarnished, and personal account of the country music business in the 1930s and early 1940s.
- Reba McEntire scores her first #1 record, "Three Sheets In The Wind," a duet with Jackie Ward.
- Johnny Bond, 63, singer, songwriter, and publisher who gained prominence in numerous Gene Autry and Jimmy Wakely movies in the 1940s, dies on June 12 in Burbank, California.
- Bill Anderson scores a disco hit with "I Can't Wait Any Longer."
- British songwriter Paul Kennerly creates country music's

Barbara Mandrell has her first #1 record in 1978 with "Sleeping Single In A Double Bed." credit: Bob Millard Collection

George Jones and Tammy Wynette, a fiery duo on stage and off in the 1970s.
credit: photo by Alan Mayor

most ambitious concept album, *White Mansions*. A novel-on-vinyl from the Civil War era, it features Eric Clapton, Waylon Jennings, Jessi Colter, Bernie Leadon from the Eagles, and the Ozark Mountain Dare Devils.

- Foy Willing, 63, singer for the original Riders of the Purple Sage, dies of a heart attack on July 24 in Nashville.

- Indicative of the growth and wealth now in country music, where $100 dates were a rich rarity in 1940 for even the biggest stars, The Statler Brothers report grossing $1.1 million in 32 concerts for the first half of 1978.

- Tammy Wynette is kidnapped out of a Nashville shopping mall parking lot on October 4. She is driven into the countryside, roughed up, and released.

- Merle Haggard and singer-songwriter Leona Williams marry on October 7.

- Bobbie Gentry marries country-pop songwriter and entertainer Jim Stafford in Somerville, Tennessee, on October 15.

- Mel Street, 45, dies on October 21 at his Nashville home of a self-inflicted gunshot wound.

- Dorothy Shay, 57, whose 1947 Top 5 hit "Feudin' and Fightin'" established her as a popular West Coast nightclub performer, dies on October 22 in Santa Monica, California. Known for dressing to the nines and doing comedic renditions of popular tunes, she was known as "The Park Avenue Hillbilly."

- Maybelle Addington Carter, 69, mother of June, Anita, and Helen, grandmother of Carlene Carter, and the original member of the Carter Family, dies on October 23.
- Lee Emerson Bellamy (Lee Emerson), 50, writer of the country classic "I Thought I Heard You Calling My Name," is shot to death in Nashville in early December.
- Bob Luman, 40, dies of pneumonia in Nashville on December 27.

The Gambler

This is the tale of a song with a life of its own. Singer/songwriter Don Schlitz had just broken into the country Top 20 with his self-penned single "The Gambler" when Kenny Rogers debuted his own version of the song on "The Johnny Carson Show," and stole Schlitz's thunder. Schlitz never did become a country recording artist after that, but this massive Kenny Rogers hit did propel the talented composer on to become the most successful songwriter of his generation. No one could have guessed at the time just how big

or how long-lasting a force "The Gambler" would become.

For Rogers, the song was to double his stardom, already raised high on the wings of "Lucille" the year before. But the tune's impact on Rogers didn't stop there. Not only did the song give Rogers a three-week ride atop the charts, it became a Top 20 pop hit and the idea behind a string of made-for-TV movies stretching clear into the 1990s, all starring Rogers. Along with "Lucille," the tune became Rogers' theme song. Between the album, the single, and greatest hits packages, "The

Gambler" has rung up several million copies in sales. The song was the most-played country song in the ASCAP catalog for several consecutive years.

Schlitz was Nashville's hottest songwriter for many years after "The Gambler" first hit. "The Gambler" brought Schlitz his first Grammy as writer of the Best Country Song of the Year for 1978. It gave him the first of a record three career CMA Awards as writer of songs of the year.

Kenny Rogers with Ronnie Milsap.
credit: Photo by Alan Mayor

1979

A Rock 'n' Roll Long-Haired Country Boy

Charlie Daniels' first hit was an early 1970s pop novelty item called "Uneasy Rider," which embraced the cause of the pot-smoking hippy against beer-guzzling pool hall rednecks. He made his breakthrough to country stardom in 1979 with "The Devil Went Down To Georgia," an apolitical epic with a generous sampling of traditional fiddle themes. Very much a rock 'n' roll long-haired country boy, Daniels was a parallel to Hank Williams Jr. in many ways. He was far closer in musical tenor to Southern rocking blues artists like the Allman Brothers, Lynyrd Skynyrd, and the Marshall Tucker Band than a country-rocker in the Eagles vein. His fiddle style owed as much to contemporary blues fiddler Pappy John Creech as to Sid Harkreader or Pappy McMichen.

Most Important Records

"Amanda" Waylon Jennings / RCA
"Every Which Way But Loose" Eddie Rabbitt / RCA
"Backside of Thirty" John Conlee / ABC
"Happy Birthday Darlin'" Conway Twitty / MCA
"If I Said You Had A Beautiful Body Would You Hold It Against Me" Bellamy Brothers / Warner Brothers
"She Believes In Me" Kenny Rogers / UA
"All The Gold In California" Larry Gatlin / Columbia

Charlie Daniels.
credit: Bob Millard Collection

"It's A Cheatin' Situation" Moe Bandy with Janie Frickie / Columbia
"Tulsa Time" Don Williams / ABC
"All I Ever Need Is You" Kenny Rogers and Dottie West / UA

Debut Artist: Rosanne Cash

Rosanne Cash, first daughter of Johnny and Vivian Liberto Cash, didn't intend to follow her famous father into country music. When she attended Vanderbilt University in Nashville, she hid her identity while studying English in hopes of becoming a writer. Acting became her next goal, and she enrolled in method acting classes in Hollywood. While living in Germany, working as a factotum for CBS Records, she was talked into recording. When she hooked up with cutting-edge country writer Rodney Crowell as producer, she began to establish herself as a unique voice in country music, just as her father had done, though she sounded nothing like him. Her 1979 duet with Bobby Bare, "No Memories Hangin' Round," started a recording career that would include pop-style hit songs of veiled autobiography, including "Seven Year Ache," "Blue Moon With Heartache," and "I Don't Know Why You Don't Want Me." When she finally cut one of her father's old songs, "Tennessee Flat Top Box," it became a #1 hit. It had only risen to #11 for her father in 1962.

Rosanne Cash and Rodney Crowell.
credit: photo by Alan Mayor

Awards

GOLD AND PLATINUM RECORDS

"Million Mile Reflection" G/A Charlie Daniels Band / Epic

"Million Mile Reflection" P/A Charlie Daniels Band / Epic

"The Devil Went Down To Georgia" G/S Charlie Daniels Band / Epic

"John Denver" G/A John Denver / RCA

"Greatest Hits" G/A Waylon Jennings / RCA

"Greatest Hits" P/A Waylon Jennings / RCA

"Ronnie Milsap Live" G/A Ronnie Milsap / RCA

"New Kind Of Feeling" G/A Anne Murray / Capitol

"Willie & Family Live" G/A Willie Nelson / Columbia

"One For The Road" G/A Willie Nelson & Leon Russell / Columbia

"A Little More Love" G/S Olivia Newton-John / MCA

"Great Balls Of Fire" G/A Dolly Parton / RCA

"She Believes In Me" G/S Kenny Rogers / UA

"The Gambler" P/A Kenny Rogers / UA

"Classics" G/A Kenny Rogers & Dottie West / UA

"TNT" G/A Tanya Tucker /MCA

GRAMMYS

BEST COUNTRY VOCAL PERFORMANCE, FEMALE—"Blue Kentucky Girl" album Emmylou Harris

BEST COUNTRY VOCAL PERFORMANCE, MALE—"The Gambler" single Kenny Rogers

BEST COUNTRY PERFORMANCE, DUO OR GROUP—"The Devil Went Down To Georgia" single Charlie Daniels Band

BEST COUNTRY INSTRUMENTAL PERFORMANCE—"Big Sandy/Leather Britches" track Doc and Merle Watson

BEST COUNTRY SONG—"You Decorated My Life" Debbie Hupp and Bob Morrison

PRODUCER OF THE YEAR (NON-CLASSICAL) (NC)—Larry Butler (Kenny Rogers' producer)

COUNTRY MUSIC ASSOCIATION AWARDS

ENTERTAINER OF THE YEAR—Willie Nelson

FEMALE VOCALIST—Barbara Mandrell

MALE VOCALIST—Kenny Rogers

SONG OF THE YEAR—"The Gambler" Don Schlitz

SINGLE OF THE YEAR—"The Devil Went Down To Georgia" Charlie Daniels Band

ALBUM OF THE YEAR—"The Gambler" Kenny Rogers

VOCAL DUO OF THE YEAR—Kenny Rogers and Dottie West

VOCAL GROUP OF THE YEAR—The Statler Brothers

INSTRUMENTALIST OF THE YEAR—Charlie Daniels

INSTRUMENTAL GROUP OF THE YEAR—Charlie Daniels Band

ACADEMY OF COUNTRY MUSIC AWARDS

SONG OF THE YEAR—"It's A Cheatin' Situation" Curly Putman and Sonny Throckmorton, writers

SINGLE RECORD OF THE YEAR—"All The Gold In California" Larry Gatlin, artist

ALBUM OF THE YEAR—"Straight Ahead" Larry Gatlin and The Gatlin Brothers

ENTERTAINER—Willie Nelson

MALE VOCALIST—Larry Gatlin

FEMALE VOCALIST—Crystal Gayle

VOCAL DUET/GROUP—Moe Bandy and Joe Stampley

NEW MALE VOCALIST—R.C. Bannon

NEW FEMALE VOCALIST—Lacy J. Dalton

TOURING BAND—Charlie Daniels Band

NON-TOURING BAND—Midnight Riders

DISC JOCKEY—King Edward IV

RADIO STATION—KFDI, Wichita, KS

CLUB—Gilley's

PIONEER AWARD—Patti Page

JIM REEVES MEMORIAL AWARD—Bill Ward

TEX RITTER AWARD—*Electric Horseman* (movie)

INSTRUMENTALISTS: fiddle, Johnny Gimble; keyboard, Hargus "Pig" Robbins; bass, Billy Graham; drums, Archie Francis; guitar, Al Bruno; steel guitar, Buddy Emmons

Milestones

- Sara Carter Bayes, 80, last surviving member of the original Carter Family and ex-wife of A.P. Carter, dies on January 8 in Lodi, California, of heart disease.
- Ray Whitley, 77, popular 1940s singing cowboy who appeared in more than 50 movies, a close associate of Gene Autry and composer of Autry's 1938 theme song "Back In The Saddle Again," dies on February 21 while on vacation in Mexico. Whitley also designed Gibson Guitar's popular model SJ-200.
- Louise Mandrell marries fellow artist R.C. Bannon on February 26 in Las Vegas.
- On April 1, shooting begins in Nashville for the movie *Coal Miner's Daughter*, the autobiography of Loretta Lynn starring Sissy Spacek.
- Lester Flatt, 61, dies on May 11 in Nashville of heart disease.
- Porter Wagoner hits Dolly Parton with a $3 million lawsuit claiming she owes him 15% of her earnings since she quit working as his partner.
- The Jerry Lee Lewis hit, "Middle Age Crazy," inspires a movie by that name, to be released in 1980.

erry Lee Lewis's big 1977 hit, "Middle Age Crazy," spawned a popular movie by the same title. credit: Courtesy of Opryland USA

↠ Nat Vincent, 89, songwriter, composer of Tom Mix's cowboy movie theme, "When The Bloom Is On The Sage," and "I'm Forever Blowing Bubbles," dies on June 6 in Burbank, California.

↠ Unknown singer-songwriter Deborah Allen gets her big break singing studio overdubbed duets with the late Jim Reeves. Their string of Top 10 hits include "Don't Let Me Cross Over," "Oh How I Miss You Tonight," and "Take Me In Your Arms and Hold Me."

↠ Vernon Presley, 63, father and executor for the estate of Elvis Presley, dies on June 26 in Memphis of heart failure.

↠ Dorsey Burnette, 46, influential early rockabilly artist and composer of "It's Late" (Ricky Nelson), "You're Sixteen"

Family Tradition

Hank Williams Jr. never had much chance of being anything other than his father's son. His mother, Audrey, had had little success controlling his father, but she molded Hank Jr. into a pint-sized Hank Williams impersonator by the time he was in the third grade. Hank Jr. was headlining country concert tours at age eight, carrying on the tradition of his father's songs for fans who simply could not get enough.

Hank Jr. reached a point in his life when he had to break out on his own. It started in the late 1960s, when he reached the age of legal adulthood and sued to free his business interests from those of his mother. By the mid-1970s, Hank Jr. was beginning to play his own songs, with a boogie beat and a hard rock edge. His near-fatal fall from a Montana mountain only hardened his desire to become his own man, musically.

Hank Williams Jr. remade himself into a singer of songs mostly about his father and the life and lifestyle he feels he inherited from Hank Sr. His most famous autobiographical song was his 1979 hit "Family Tradition." In it, Hank Jr. sings of his late father and of his boozing and womanizing ways, that breaking all the rules is a family tradition and his birthright. Still, it would take the industry another decade to accept Hank Jr. for who he was and give him the Entertainer of the Year awards he rightfully deserved.

(Johnny Burnette), and "Hey Little One" (Glen Campbell), dies in Canoga Park, California, on August 19. His survivors include his son, Billy Burnette.

→ In the fall, Yukon, Oklahoma, 11th grader Garth Brooks enters a local talent contest singing a country tune. Schoolmates hoot and boo, embarrassing Brooks so much that he doesn't perform a country song in his hometown for another 10 years.

→ Jimmie Skinner, popular "Grand Ole Opry" fiddler and bluegrass artist, dies on October 28 in Nashville of a heart attack.

→ Peter Guralnik's groundbreaking book on country music artists, *Lost Highways*, is published.

THE 1980S

URBAN COWBOY

Actor John Travolta seemed to personify disposable dance fads, first with his disco movie *Saturday Night Fever*, and in August of this year, with *Urban Cowboy*. Growing out of a 1979 article in *Esquire* about alienated Houston oil refinery workers who frequented Mickey Gilley's massive Pasadena, Texas, nightclub, this popular movie spawned ersatz cowboy fashion and dance fads all over the country, with emphasis on Western wear and mechanical bulls. The movie soundtrack spun off pop hits for Kenny Rogers and Mickey Gilley, and made a star of Gilley's house band singer, Johnny Lee, with "Lookin' For Love." Chris LeDoux, himself a professional rodeo rider, recorded "The Bucking Machine," a paean to the mechanical bull. Aggregate country record sales increased by nearly 50% largely because pop-country records attracted adult contemporary listeners for the next few years. But the "bulls & boots" fad soon wore off in the wake of a national recession. Reporting record sales shrinkage to 1979 levels and the end of pop radio interest in Nashville artists, the lead story on the January 23, 1985 issue of *Variety* proclaimed, "The Urban Cowboy is definitely buried in boot hill . . ."

Mechanical bull riding at Gilley's.
credit: photo by Dean Dixon

Most Important Records

"Lookin' For Love" Johnny Lee / Full Moon
"Coward Of The County" Kenny Rogers / UA
"My Heart" Ronnie Milsap / RCA
"I Believe In You" Don Williams / MCA
"My Heroes Have Always Been Cowboys" Willie Nelson / Columbia
"I Ain't Living Long Like This" Waylon Jennings / RCA
"On The Road Again" Willie Nelson
"Tennessee River" Alabama / RCA
"He Stopped Loving Her Today" George Jones / Epic
"9 To 5" Dolly Parton / RCA
"Somebody's Knockin'" Terri Gibbs / MCA

Debut Artist: Ricky Skaggs

Ricky Skaggs was a genuine East Kentucky country boy. He played bluegrass classics with boyhood pal Keith Whitley until both joined Ralph Stanley's band in 1970. Skaggs left Stanley in 1972 and eventually became leader and front man for Emmylou Harris' Hot Band. As an established young turk of bluegrass, Skaggs made a tenuous appearance in the country charts in 1980 on independent folk label Sugar Hill Records. He jumped to Epic in 1981 and had a career defining hit with

Ricky Skaggs.
credit: Photo by Dean Dixon

his second charting release. His up-beat, electric guitar treatment of Flatt and Scruggs' "Don't Get Above Your Raising" launched the neo-traditionalist movement in commercial country music. His initial success foreshadowed a return to hardcore country sounds, from bluegrass to rockabilly and honky-tonk. Once the Urban Cowboy movement faltered, by aiming records at pop radio rather than the core country fan, Skaggs' revitalized rural root sound helped give the industry a solid new direction, along with honky-tonk and swing revivalists John Anderson and George Strait.

Awards

GOLD AND PLATINUM RECORDS
"Full Moon" G/A Charlie Daniels Band / Epic
"Full Moon" P/A Charlie Daniels Band / Epic
"Straight Ahead" G/A Larry Gatlin / Columbia
"Classic Crystal" G/A Crystal Gayle / UA
"Miss The Mississippi" G/A Crystal Gayle / UA
"Music Man" G/A Waylon Jennings / RCA
"Theme From The Dukes Of Hazzard" G/S Waylon Jennings / RCA
"What Goes Around" G/A Waylon Jennings / RCA
"Lookin' For Love" G/S Johnny Lee / Full Moon
"Summertime Dream" P/A Gordon Lightfoot / Reprise
"Greatest Hits" G/A Anne Murray / Capitol
"Greatest Hits" P/A Anne Murray / Capitol
"I'll Always Love You" G/A Anne Murray / Capitol
"Willie Nelson Sings Kristofferson" G/A Willie Nelson / Columbia
"Willie Nelson & Family Live" P/A Willie Nelson / Columbia
"Honeysuckle Rose (Soundtrack)" G/A Willie Nelson / Columbia
"Honeysuckle Rose (Soundtrack)" P/A Willie Nelson / Columbia
"Horizon" G/A Eddie Rabbitt / Elektra
"The Best Of Eddie Rabbitt" G/A Eddie Rabbitt / Elektra
"Coward Of The County" G/S Kenny Rogers / UA
"Gideon" G/A Kenny Rogers / UA
"Gideon" P/A Kenny Rogers / UA
"Greatest Hits" G/A Kenny Rogers / Liberty
"Greatest Hits" P/A Kenny Rogers / Liberty
"Kenny" G/A Kenny Rogers / Capitol
"Kenny" P/A Kenny Rogers / Capitol
"Lady" G/S Kenny Rogers / UA
"Urban Cowboy" G/A Soundtrack / Asylum
"Urban Cowboy" P/A Soundtrack / Asylum
"The Best Of Don Williams Vol. II" G/A Don Williams / MCA
"I Believe In You" G/A Don Williams / MCA

GRAMMYS
BEST COUNTRY VOCAL PERFORMANCE, FEMALE—"Could I Have This Dance" single Anne Murray

BEST COUNTRY VOCAL PERFORMANCE, MALE—"He Stopped Loving Her Today" single George Jones

BEST COUNTRY PERFORMANCE, DUO OR GROUP—"That Lovin' You Feelin' Again" single Roy Orbison and Emmylou Harris

BEST COUNTRY INSTRUMENTAL PERFORMANCE—"Orange Blossom Special/Hoedown" track Gilley's "Urban Cowboy" Band

BEST COUNTRY SONG—"On The Road Again" Willie Nelson, writer

COUNTRY MUSIC ASSOCIATION AWARDS

ENTERTAINER OF THE YEAR—Barbara Mandrell

FEMALE VOCALIST—Emmylou Harris

MALE VOCALIST—George Jones

SONG OF THE YEAR—"He Stopped Loving Her Today" Bobby Braddock and Curly Putman

SINGLE OF THE YEAR—"He Stopped Loving Her Today" George Jones

ALBUM OF THE YEAR—*Coal Miner's Daughter* Original Motion Picture Soundtrack / MCA

VOCAL DUO OF THE YEAR—Moe Bandy and Joe Stampley

VOCAL GROUP OF THE YEAR—The Statler Brothers

INSTRUMENTALIST OF THE YEAR—Roy Clark

INSTRUMENTAL GROUP OF THE YEAR—Charlie Daniels Band

ACADEMY OF COUNTRY MUSIC AWARDS

SONG OF THE YEAR—"He Stopped Loving Her Today" Curly Putnam and Bobby Braddock, writers

SINGLE RECORD OF THE YEAR—"He Stopped Loving Her Today" George Jones, artist

ALBUM OF THE YEAR—*Urban Cowboy* (soundtrack)

ENTERTAINER—Barbara Mandrell

MALE VOCALIST—George Jones

FEMALE VOCALIST—Dolly Parton

VOCAL DUET/GROUP—Moe Bandy and Joe Stampley

NEW MALE VOCALIST—Johnny Lee

NEW FEMALE VOCALIST—Terri Gibbs

TOURING BAND—Charlie Daniels Band

NON-TOURING BAND—Palomino Riders

DISC JOCKEY—Sammy Jackson

RADIO STATION—KLAC, Los Angeles, CA

CLUB—(tie) Palomino/Gilley's

PIONEER AWARD—Ernest Tubb

JIM REEVES MEMORIAL AWARD—Ken Kragen

TEX RITTER AWARD—*Coal Miner's Daughter* (movie); *Urban Cowboy* (movie)

ARTISTS OF THE DECADE (1970s)—Loretta Lynn and Conway Twitty

INSTRUMENTALISTS: fiddle, Johnny Gimble; keyboard, Hargus "Pig" Robbins; bass, Curtis Stone; drums, Archie Francis; guitar, Al Bruno; steel guitar, (tie) J.D. Maness/Buddy Emmons

Milestones

- "Wanted: The Outlaws" album becomes the first country album certified by the RIAA for double platinum, designating sales over two million units.
- Vernice "Vic" McAlpin, successful songwriter whose collaboration partners had included Hank Williams, Fred Rose, Marty Robbins, Johnny Cash, and others, dies in Nashville the last week of January.
- Ralph Sloan, 55, founder of the "Grand Ole Opry's" Tennessee Travelers folk dance ensemble, dies on March 12 in Nashville of cancer.
- At the end of a string of hit duets with Kenny Rogers, Dottie West spruces up her image and modernizes her sound. She scores her first Top 10 record in several years with "A Lesson In Leavin'."
- George Jones and Tammy Wynette record together for the first time in many years, singing the duet "Two Story House."
- *Kenny Rogers as The Gambler* is broadcast on CBS-TV, the first in a series of made-for-TV movies taken from the Don Schlitz-penned tune.
- Woodrow Wilson "Red" Sovine, 62, king of recitation and truck driver songs, dies on April 4 in Nashville as a result of a car wreck.
- After years of trying to break through as a singer, successful television character actor, advertising jingles voice, and songwriter Ed Bruce ("Mamas Don't Let Your Babies Grow Up To Be Cowboys") has his first country hit record, "Diane."

Ingratiating sweetness, multi-instrumental proficiency, grit, drive, and bottomless ambition brought Barbara Mandrell to the winner's circle and to television stardom by the early 1980s. Photogenic and likable, Mandrell had been a hard worker on stage and off. She performed in the family band in California during her teen years. She received early television exposure on the West Coast on "Town Hall Party," then wider exposure on the "Red Foley Show" and the "Johnny Cash Show." While still in her teens, she married the former drummer of the Mandrell Family Band, Ken Dudney. In 1971, she moved to Nashville.

Despite the assertion in her pop-style hit, "I Was Country When Country Wasn't Cool," Mandrell, born in Houston and reared in California, was a singer of sexy R&B covers and a string of pop-country hits generated by Nashville song-writers Kye Fleming and Dennis Morgan. With a fine sense of Las Vegas-style costuming and show-manship, Mandrell parlayed limited vocal and instrumental abilities into consecutive CMA Entertainer of the Year awards in 1980 and 1981, and a widely popular network television series co-starring her sisters Louise and Irlene. The show offered a forum for Mandrell's full repertoire: her comic skills, instrumental talents, emotional appeal via patriotic and gospel numbers, and her dance abilities. The CMA Awards were true descriptors, as she was first and foremost a terrific entertainer. After the television show was over, she mounted a glittering, energetic Vegas-style touring production, "The Lady Is A Champ," which was filmed for a network television special in early 1984.

A car wreck in late 1984 left Mandrell with permanent leg injuries that curtailed her dancing.

The long-kept secret of that episode was that Mandrell also suffered disabling mental problems caused by severe head injuries. Though she returned to recording relatively quickly, she wrestled with depression for several years. The press unfairly castigated her for suing the insurer of the young man who caused her accident, because he died in the wreck. But it was not Mandrell's fault. Her own insurance company refused to settle until courts proved the party at fault was unable to compensate for her injuries and the loss of her ability to work during her long recuperation. Loyal to her band, she kept the Do-Rites on the payroll for nearly a year even though she was unable to perform.

Mandrell eventually recovered and resumed her show business career. She remains a popular entertainer, commanding top dollar for corporate events and conventions.

Barbara Mandrell.
credit: Courtesy of Barbara Mandrell

- Tommy Caldwell, bass player and singer for the Marshall Tucker Band, dies on April 28, fives days after an automobile accident in Spartanburg, South Carolina, and a month after brother Timmy Caldwell dies in a separate car wreck.

- Domination by Epic and Columbia Records artists of the Academy of Country Music Awards creates a backlash in the country music industry. CBS is castigated for signing up more than 300 tangential employees and block-voting their ballots, a practice the ACM vows to stop.

- Bob Nolan, 72, singer and songwriter, one of the founders of the Sons of the Pioneers, dies on June 15 in Los Angeles of a heart attack. Nolan's compositions included "Tumbling Tumbleweeds" and "Cool Water."

- Agitated by the sudden Urban Cowboy craze, Don Everly names his new touring band The Dead Cowboys and tours Europe.

- A biography of Patsy Cline is published, *Remembering Patsy: The Untold Story*, by Ellis Nassour, fueling a boom in Patsy Cline record sales.

- *Honeysuckle Rose*, Willie Nelson's successful "road" movie, spawns an equally successful soundtrack album driven by the hit single "On The Road Again." Nelson subsequently renames his tour bus "Honeysuckle Rose." Other popular movies include *Middle Age Crazy*, *Take This Job and Shove It*, and *9 To 5*.

- The duet team of Jim Ed Brown and Helen Cornelius split up. Confessions of a seamy love affair between the two wreck their marriages and essentially ruin their recording careers.

John Anderson came to Nashville in his late teens with no one to champion his career and no idea of how the industry worked. He began singing in the seedy bars of Lower Broadway. His repertoire was eclectic—he sang all of Merle Haggard's hits and made Jimi Hendrix's "Purple Haze" sound like Lefty Frizzell—and his songwriting prowess slowly grew. He started recording in 1974 on the Ace of Hearts label, and moved to Warner Brothers in 1977. He was no svelte cowboy stud and would be no overnight success, but he had a drawling country soul that was not to be denied. In 1981 he cracked the Top 5 for the first time with a tongue-in-cheek, self-deprecating prophesy, "I'm Just An Old Chunk Of Coal (But I'm Gonna Be A Diamond Someday)."

1981

FROM COAL TO DIAMOND

Most Important Records

"Feels So Right" Alabama / RCA
"(There's) No Gettin' Over Me" Ronnie Milsap / RCA
"Love In The First Degree" Alabama / RCA
"Never Been So Loved (In All My Life)" Charley Pride / RCA
"Elvira" Oak Ridge Boys / MCA
"All My Rowdy Friends Have Settled Down" Hank Williams Jr. / Warner Brothers
"I Was Country When Country Wasn't Cool" Barbara Mandrell / MCA
"Old Flame" Alabama / RCA
"Blessed Are The Believers" Anne Murray / Capitol
"You're The Reason God Made Oklahoma" David Frizzell and Shelly West / Warner Brothers

Debut Artist: George Strait

George Strait may have appeared to the casual observer as just another handsome guy in tight jeans and Western garb taking advantage of the Urban Cowboy craze when his debut single, "Unwound," established him as a new country star in 1981, but he was much more. This laconic Texan was a genuine ranch hand by day and a popular regional swing-style band-leader by night in Central Texas. With no gimmicks, no flash, and no pop radio appeal, he emerged as the first in a continuing line of plain-dressed Western neo-traditionalists. Named CMA's Entertainer of the Year in 1989 and 1990, Strait's impact continues. Without changing his basic sound and musical direction in more than a dozen years, he remains one of the most popular entertainers and recording artists in country music.

George Strait.
credit: Photo by Alan Mayor

Awards

GOLD AND PLATINUM RECORDS
"Feels So Right" G/A Alabama / RCA
"Feels So Right" P/A Alabama / RCA
"My Home's In Alabama" G/A Alabama / RCA
"Saddle Tramp" G/A Charlie Daniels Band / Epic
"It's Hard To Be Humble" G/A Mac Davis / Casablanca
"Some Days Are Diamonds" G/A John Denver / RCA
"Greatest Hits" G/A Larry Gatlin / Columbia
"Blue Kentucky Girl" G/A Emmylou Harris / Warner Brothers
"Evangeline" G/A Emmylou Harris / Warner Brothers
"Luxury Liner" G/A Emmylou Harris / Warner Brothers
"Profile—The Best Of Emmylou Harris" G/A Emmylou Harris / Warner Brothers
"Roses In The Snow" G/A Emmylou Harris / Warner Brothers
"Leather & Lace" G/A Waylon Jennings and Jessi Colter / RCA
"I Am What I Am" G/A George Jones / Epic
"Greatest Hits Vol II" G/A Loretta Lynn / MCA
"The Best Of Barbara Mandrell" G/A Barbara Mandrell / ABC
"Greatest Hits" G/A Ronnie Milsap / RCA
"Greatest Hits" P/A Ronnie Milsap / RCA
"There's No Gettin' Over Me" G/A Ronnie Milsap / RCA
"Where Do You Go When You Dream" G/A Anne Murray / Capitol
"Somewhere Over The Rainbow" G/A Willie Nelson / Columbia
"Somewhere Over The Rainbow" P/A Willie Nelson / Columbia
"Willie Nelson's Greatest Hits (And Some That Will Be)" G/A Willie Nelson / Columbia
"Angel Of The Morning" G/A Juice Newton / Capitol
"Queen Of Hearts" G/S Juice Newton / Capitol
"Elvira" G/S Oak Ridge Boys / MCA
"Fancy Free" G/A Oak Ridge Boys / MCA
"9 To 5" G/S Dolly Parton / RCA
"9 To 5 And Odd Jobs" G/A Dolly Parton / RCA
"Drivin' My Life Away" G/S Eddie Rabbitt / Elektra
"Horizon" P/A Eddie Rabbitt / Elektra
"I Love A Rainy Night" G/S Eddie Rabbitt / Elektra
"Step By Step" G/A Eddie Rabbitt / Elektra

"Share Your Love" G/A Kenny Rogers / Liberty
"Share Your Love" P/A Kenny Rogers / Liberty
"The Best Of The Statler Brothers Rides Again, Vol. 2" G/A
Statler Brothers / Mercury
"The Originals" G/A Statler Brothers / Mercury
"Greatest Hits Vol. 1" G/A Conway Twitty / Decca
"Lead Me On" G/A Conway Twitty and Loretta Lynn / Decca
"Whiskey Bent & Hell Bound" G/A Hank Williams Jr. / Curb

GRAMMYS
BEST COUNTRY VOCAL PERFORMANCE, FEMALE—"9 To 5" single Dolly
Parton
BEST COUNTRY VOCAL PERFORMANCE, MALE—"(There's) No Gettin'
Over Me" single Ronnie Milsap
BEST COUNTRY PERFORMANCE, DUO OR GROUP—"Elvira" single Oak
Ridge Boys
BEST COUNTRY INSTRUMENTAL PERFORMANCE—"After All These Years"
Chet Atkins
BEST COUNTRY SONG—"9 To 5" Dolly Parton, writer
BEST RECORDING FOR CHILDREN (NC)—"Sesame Country" The Mup-
pets, Glen Campbell, Crystal Gayle, Loretta Lynn, Tanya Tucker,
artists; Jim Henson, Muppets Creator; Dennis Scott, producer

COUNTRY MUSIC ASSOCIATION AWARDS
ENTERTAINER OF THE YEAR—Barbara Mandrell
FEMALE VOCALIST—Barbara Mandrell
MALE VOCALIST—George Jones
SONG OF THE YEAR—"He Stopped Loving Her Today" Bobby Brad-
dock and Curly Putman
SINGLE OF THE YEAR—"Elvira" Oak Ridge Boys
ALBUM OF THE YEAR—"I Believe In You" Don Williams
VOCAL DUO OF THE YEAR—David Frizzell and Shelly West
VOCAL GROUP OF THE YEAR—Alabama
INSTRUMENTALIST OF THE YEAR—Chet Atkins
INSTRUMENTAL GROUP OF THE YEAR—Alabama
HORIZON AWARD—Terri Gibbs

ACADEMY OF COUNTRY MUSIC AWARDS
SONG OF THE YEAR—"You're The Reason God Made Oklahoma"
Sandy Pinkard and Larry Collins, writers
SINGLE RECORD OF THE YEAR—"Elvira" Oak Ridge Boys, artist
ALBUM OF THE YEAR—"Feels So Right" Alabama
ENTERTAINER—Alabama
MALE VOCALIST—Merle Haggard
FEMALE VOCALIST—Barbara Mandrell
VOCAL GROUP—Alabama
VOCAL DUET—David Frizzell and Shelly West
NEW MALE VOCALIST—Ricky Skaggs
NEW FEMALE VOCALIST—Juice Newton
TOURING BAND—The Strangers

NON-TOURING BAND—Desperadoes
DISC JOCKEY—Arch Yancy
RADIO STATION—WPLO, Atlanta, GA
CLUB—Billy Bob's Texas
PIONEER AWARD—Leo Fender
JIM REEVES MEMORIAL AWARD—Al Gallico
TEX RITTER AWARD—*Any Which Way You Can* (movie)
INSTRUMENTALISTS: fiddle, Johnny Gimble; keyboard, Hargus "Pig" Robbins; bass, (tie) Curtis Stone/Joe Osborn; drums, Buddy Harmon; guitar, James Burton; steel guitar, Buddy Emmons; harmonica, Charlie McCoy

Milestones

- Felton Jarvis, 46, long-time producer of Elvis Presley, dies on January 3 of a stroke in Nashville.
- Scotty Wiseman, 71, of Lulu Belle and Scotty fame from the WLS "Barn Dance" in the 1930s and 1940s, dies February 1 in Gainesville, Florida, of a heart attack.
- Mildred Acuff, 67, wife and long-time financial adviser of husband Roy Acuff and a founding partner in Acuff-Rose Publications, dies on June 17 in Nashville.
- Conway Twitty's Twitty City opens its gates for the first time to tourists during Fan Fair in June.
- *The Smithsonian Collection of Classic Country Music*, the first important retrospective on the genre, is released. It features 143 selections, ranging from "Sally Gooden" in 1922 to "Blue Eyes Cryin' In The Rain" from 1975.
- After five years with no new members, the "Grand Ole Opry" inducts John Conlee and Boxcar Willie.
- Bill Haley, 55, whose Comets were one of the earliest country acts to switch to rock 'n' roll with the hit "Rock Around The Clock," dies on February 9 in Harlingen, Texas. Haley originally called his early-1950s band the Saddlemen, mixing polka, yodeling, and Western swing with a hard-edged rhythm. He brought considerable country and western influence to rock music.
- Earl Thomas Conley scores his first Top 10 hit with "Silent Treatment" on independent Sunbird Records.
- After playing a free concert for inmates, Willie Nelson is named "Honorary Convict" at the Missouri State Penitentiary. Nelson extends his hit streak with his second collection of pop standards, *Somewhere Over The Rainbow*.
- The New Acoustic movement, a fusion of bluegrass, jazz, and rock, gets a major boost as the album *Leon Russell & Newgrass Revival—Live* is released. The success of pop-country is underscored by David Seville's use of it for his *Urban Chipmonks* album.
- "Elvira" marks a breakthrough for the Oak Ridge Boys who become country stars at last.

- Ervin Rouse, 64, composer of the country standard "Orange Blossom Special," dies on July 8 in Miami, Florida, of diabetes complications.
- Gilbert Orville Taylor, 67, bassist and vocalist for the Hoosier Hot Shots for more than 20 years, dies on July 5 in Burbank, California, of cancer.
- Hospitalized in Maui for a collapsed lung, Willie Nelson begins writing new songs for the first time in several years. These new tunes become the basis for his concept album, *Tougher Than Leather*.
- Lee Greenwood, songwriter, former Las Vegas lounge act and card dealer, debuts on the charts in September with "It Turns Me Inside Out."
- David Wendell Guinn, 88, composer of "Home On The Range," dies on October 17 in Dallas, Texas.

"The Killer"

Though Jerry Lee Lewis aligned himself with mainstream Nashville production, promotion, and booking in 1968, he never gave up his pounding Louisiana piano style or his gospel-style rock 'n' roll roots. His audience had aged with him, and he found them in major honky-tonk venues, reveling in his intensely personal treatment of his songs.

Lewis' nickname, "The Killer," haunted him in investigations of the deaths of two of his wives, though he was cleared in both events. His wild unpredictability and seeming penchant for violence (he liked to set fire to pianos during concerts) was magnified when he was apprehended in the early 1970s for brandishing a loaded pistol in the driveway of Elvis Presley's Memphis home, Graceland. Use of pills and alcohol caused him major health problems in the late 1970s and early 1980s,

resulting in stomach surgery. He also had problems with the IRS.

But, while Lewis' outrageous personal behavior and financial troubles created his legend, it was his music that spoke to his peers and fans in the 1970s and early 1980s. His monumental hit on Sonny Throckmorton's "Middle Age Crazy" in 1977 was revived in 1980 for the Bruce Dern movie of the same title. In 1979 he backed "Rockin' My Life Away" with "I Wish I Was Eighteen Again," and rolled into the new decade.

In 1981, Lewis made it into the Top 5 again for the first time in four years—since "Middle Age Crazy"—with another telling take on being an aging rockabilly star. "Thirty-Nine and Holding" declared he would never grow old. In heart and mind, he was right. If music alone can keep a man young in spirit, Jerry Lee Lewis will remain a wild 20-year-old in an aging body.

credit: Bob Millard Collection

Sylvia Kirby was a little girl of boundless friendliness, but her home life was haunted by a controlling parent. She retreated into a fantasy of singing stardom, a fantasy she played out in front of a full-length mirror in her bedroom until she moved to Nashville to become a secretary for publisher and producer Tom Collins. Though she had never sung professionally, Collins eventually saw in Sylvia's childlike demeanor something he thought would appeal to young girls, a rarely tapped segment of country music fandom. He was right. In 1982, Sylvia had a signature hit, "Nobody," and was an irresistible force in the teen-aimed country music market for several years. Her bouncy hits, from "Drifter" through "Nobody," "Like Nothing Ever Happened" and "Snapshot," were perfect foils for adolescent girls to sing along and daydream with. Since leaving RCA and mainstream country recording in the late 1980s, Sylvia's new direction has been, in fact, children's music.

1982

A Queen for Country Teens

Most Important Records

"Always On My Mind" Willie Nelson / Columbia
"She Got The Goldmine (I Got The Shaft)" Jerry Reed / RCA
"Wild and Blue" John Anderson / Warner Brothers
"Just To Satisfy You" Waylon Jennings & Willie Nelson / RCA
"Slow Hand" Conway Twitty / Elektra
"Bobbie Sue" Oak Ridge Boys / MCA
"Nobody" Sylvia / RCA
"Blue Moon With Heartache" Rosanne Cash / Columbia
"Mountain of Love" Charley Pride / RCA
"Crying My Heart Out Over You" Ricky Skaggs / Epic

Awards

GOLD AND PLATINUM RECORDS

"Mountain Music" G/A Alabama / RCA
"Mountain Music" P/A Alabama / RCA
"My Home's In Alabama" P/A Alabama / RCA
"Windows" G/A Charlie Daniels Band / Epic
"Heaven's Just A Sin Away" G/A The Kendalls / Ovation
"Lookin' For Love" G/A Johnny Lee / Full Moon
"Live" G/A Barbara Mandrell / MCA
"Christmas Wishes" G/A Anne Murray / Capitol
"Always On My Mind" G/A Willie Nelson / Columbia
"Always On My Mind" P/A Willie Nelson / Columbia
"Pretty Paper" G/A Willie Nelson / Columbia
"Willie Nelson's Greatest Hits (And Some That Will Be)" P/A
Willie Nelson / Columbia
"Juice" G/A Juice Newton / Capitol
"Quiet Lies" G/A Juice Newton / Capitol
"Bobbie Sue" G/A Oak Ridge Boys / MCA
"Christmas" G/A Oak Ridge Boys / MCA
"Elvira" P/S Oak Ridge Boys / MCA
"All Time Greatest Hits" G/A Ray Price / Columbia
"All Time Greatest Hits" G/A Marty Robbins / Columbia
"Christmas" G/A Kenny Rogers / Liberty
"Christmas" P/A Kenny Rogers / Liberty
"Love Will Turn You Around" G/A Kenny Rogers / Liberty
"Coal Miner's Daughter" G/A Soundtrack / MCA
"Christmas Card" G/A Statler Brothers / Mercury
"Nobody" G/S Sylvia / RCA
"The Pressure Is On" G/A Hank Williams Jr. / Elektra

GRAMMYS

BEST COUNTRY VOCAL PERFORMANCE, FEMALE— "Break It To Me Gently" single Juice Newton
BEST COUNTRY VOCAL PERFORMANCE, MALE—"Always On My Mind" single Willie Nelson

BEST COUNTRY PERFORMANCE, DUO OR GROUP—"Mountain Music" album Alabama

BEST COUNTRY INSTRUMENTAL PERFORMANCE—"Alabama Jubilee" track Roy Clark

BEST COUNTRY SONG—"Always On My Mind" Johnny Christopher, Mark James, and Wayne Carson, writers

SONG OF THE YEAR (NC)—"Always On My Mind" Johnny Christopher, Mark James, and Wayne Carson, writers

BEST INSPIRATIONAL PERFORMANCE (NC)—"He Set My Life To Music" album Barbara Mandrell

COUNTRY MUSIC ASSOCIATION AWARDS

ENTERTAINER OF THE YEAR—Alabama

FEMALE VOCALIST—Janie Frickie

MALE VOCALIST—Ricky Skaggs

SONG OF THE YEAR—"Always On My Mind" Johnny Christopher, Mark James, and Wayne Carson, writers

SINGLE OF THE YEAR—"Always On My Mind" Willie Nelson

ALBUM OF THE YEAR—"Always On My Mind" Willie Nelson

VOCAL DUO OF THE YEAR—David Frizzell and Shelly West

VOCAL GROUP OF THE YEAR—Alabama

INSTRUMENTALIST OF THE YEAR—Chet Atkins

INSTRUMENTAL GROUP OF THE YEAR—Alabama

HORIZON AWARD—Ricky Skaggs

ACADEMY OF COUNTRY MUSIC AWARDS

SONG OF THE YEAR—"Are The Good Times Really Over" Merle Haggard, writer

SINGLE RECORD OF THE YEAR—"Always On My Mind" Willie Nelson, artist

ALBUM OF THE YEAR—"Always On My Mind" Willie Nelson

ENTERTAINER—Alabama

MALE VOCALIST—Ronnie Milsap

FEMALE VOCALIST—Sylvia

VOCAL GROUP—Alabama

VOCAL DUET—David Frizzell and Shelly West

NEW MALE VOCALIST—Michael Martin Murphey

NEW FEMALE VOCALIST—Karen Brooks

TOURING BAND—Ricky Skaggs Band

NON-TOURING BAND—Desperadoes

DISC JOCKEY—Lee Arnold

RADIO STATION—KIKK, Houston, TX

CLUB—Gilley's

PIONEER AWARD—Chet Atkins

JIM REEVES MEMORIAL AWARD—Jo Walker-Meador

TEX RITTER AWARD—*The Best Little Whorehouse In Texas* (movie)

INSTRUMENTALISTS: fiddle, Johnny Gimble; keyboard, Hargus "Pig" Robbins; bass, Red Wooten; drums, Archie Francis; guitar, Al Bruno; steel guitar, J.D. Maness

Dolly Parton.
credit: Archives of Robert K.
Oermann

Milestones

- In January, Statler Brothers' tenor Lew DeWitt takes temporary medical leave due to regional enteritis, a painful intestinal condition. He is replaced by Jimmy Fortune. In July, DeWitt retires permanently.
- Gail Davies changes musical direction and has her first big hit with "Round The Clock Lovin'." The tune is co-written by K.T. Oslin, marking her major breakthrough in country music.
- Writers of the award-winning "You're The Reason God Made Oklahoma" lose out when a lawsuit by Felice and Boudleaux Bryant proves the melody is, slower but note-for-note, from "Rocky Top."
- Wedding bells ring at Lake Tahoe for Johnny Lee and "Dallas" actress Charlene Tilton on February 14.

- Dorris Macon, 71, son and former sideman of Uncle Dave Macon, dies February 15 in Murfreesboro, Tennessee. In addition to his father, the guitarist also performed with Roy Acuff and the Fruit Jar Drinkers during his long "Grand Ole Opry" career.
- Alabama stages the first of a series of annual charity concerts in their hometown of Ft. Payne, Alabama. Called the June Jam, the event draws 30,000.
- Graceland, home of the late Elvis Presley, is opened to the public as a memorial museum on June 7. Because of mounting expenses since Presley's death, and the fact that Presley sold all rights to his RCA records to the label for $5 million, which has long-since been spent, the estate is teetering on the brink of bankruptcy.
- The movie musical *The Best Little Whorehouse in Texas*, starring Dolly Parton and Burt Reynolds, premieres in Austin, Texas, in July.
- DeFord Bailey, 82, black harmonica wizard and one of the first stars of the WSM "Barn Dance" and the "Grand Ole Opry," dies on July 2 in Nashville.
- Bill Justis, 55, pianist and arranger who had worked with all the early Sun artists, including Elvis Presley, Jerry Lee Lewis, Johnny Cash, and Carl Perkins, before moving to Nashville as a sessions player, orchestrator, and instrumental recording artist (biggest hit, the million-selling "Raunchy," 1957), dies in Nashville on July 7.
- After 10 years of struggling, Eddy Raven scores his first Top 10 hit with "You're Playing Hard To Forget."
- Jimmy Wakely, 68, singer/actor nicknamed "The Melody Kid," player on "Gene Autry's Melody Ranch" radio series, and star of at least 70 singing cowboy western movies in

Gene Watson

Gene Watson was reared in Paris, Texas, the dusty little town made famous by the movie *The Last Picture Show*. He played clubs and honky-tonks, and was the house singer at Houston's Dynasty Club for several years in the late 1960s. His clear, smooth voice was nasal and twangy enough to make him a solid journeyman in country music in the 1970s with an occasional Top 5 hit, such as "Love In The Hot Afternoon" and "Paper Rosie." He was a man with a honky-tonk heart, as his signature hit, "Farewell Party," showed in 1979.

Watson wasn't slick, familiar with Las Vegas-style stage moves, or even particularly handsome. He was just a straight ahead singer waiting for the elements to come together in order to score big. His break came with a magnificent album in 1981. It contained "Fourteen Carat Mind," the quintessential driving lament of a poor man bled dry by a money-hungry younger woman who could not be satisfied. That record became Watson's first (and to date, only) #1 single. Also on the album was a catchy, but underrated, track, "Speak Softy (You're Talking To My Heart)." Watson had found a way to explore the depths of a working-class loser's worst nightmare of love lost, yet drove them with irresistible up-tempo rhythms. His biggest hit of 1983, "You're Out Doing What I'm Here Doing Without," mined that same vein of hillbilly lament and only barely missed topping the country charts.

Not since Roy Acuff put the band behind the "star" singer had self-contained units held sway in commercial country music. Not, that is, until Alabama hit the scene.

Country boys with a pop-rock sensibility, this combo/showband was formed in 1969 and originally called Wildcountry. It was fronted by singer Randy Owens, with his cousins Jeff Cook and Teddy Gentry on lead guitar and bass, and John Vartanian on drums. They became popular in the college-aged nightspots at Myrtle Beach, South Carolina, between 1973 and 1976, when they decided to pool their resources and try to become a recording success. Vartanian departed (to become, no doubt, the second most-disappointed drummer since the Beatles fired Pete Best) just before the band changed its name to Alabama and signed with independent label GRT Records, having hired Mark Herndon as drummer. They also recorded for independent, MDJ Records, where they recorded their first hit in 1980, a Top 20, "My Home's In Alabama" that was later re-released by RCA. Once signed to RCA, the band took off to new heights, capturing 21 consecutive #1 singles and CMA Entertainer of the Year Awards in 1982, 1983, and 1984.

The success of Alabama as a so-called self-contained unit (their musicianship was inadequate for studio work, as Gentry once confessed to *Country Music* magazine's Bob Allen) drove a trend-conscious Nashville establishment to scurry for bands to sign. Bands already working, such as the Nitty Gritty Dirt Band and Charlie Daniels Band, received renewed attention. Sixteen years after their chart debut, Alabama is still a potent musical force in commercial country music. Their legacy, aside from their many awards and multi-platinum albums, is the significant segment of the charts taken by "self-contained" country bands who came along in the wake of Alabama, including Diamond Rio, Confederate Railroad, Restless Heart, Shenandoah, Kentucky HeadHunters, and Little Texas.

Randy Owens and Jeff Cook of Alabama are joined on stage by Lionel Richie.
credit: photo by Alan Mayor

the 1940s, dies on September 23 in Mission Hills, California.

- Doyle Wilburn, 52, of the Wilburn Brothers, dies on October 16 in Nashville of cancer.
- Grady Nutt, 47, popular religious speaker and comedian on "Hee Haw," dies on November 24 in a plane crash in rural Alabama.
- Marty Robbins, 57, a country singing star for 30 years, dies on December 8 following heart surgery necessitated by a massive heart attack a few days earlier.
- *Honkytonk Man,* the Clint Eastwood movie based very loosely on elements of Hank Williams' and Jimmie Rodgers' lives, premieres on December 17. Marty Robbins' ironic role in the film is widely praised. Robbins plays a singer who is discovered in a recording session when Eastwood's character, *a la* Rodgers, lies dying on a cot in the next room, unable to finish his own recording session.
- Don Law, 80, dies on December 20 in LaMarque, Texas, after a long illness. Law was the Columbia Records executive who pioneered the Nashville division. Talent scout as well as producer, he was responsible for most influential Columbia and Epic artists from the late 1940s through the early 1960s, including Johnny Cash and Marty Robbins.
- Roger Bowling, 38, influential songwriter, composer of "Lucille" and "Coward of the County," dies on December 26 in Spruce Creek, Georgia.

Though John Anderson's first chart topper, 1981's "Wild and Blue," stayed at #1 for a week longer than "Swingin'," it was more a function of promotion than a measure of the impact that the latter tune had on Anderson's career. "Swingin'" was the first country gold-selling single in a long time. "Swingin'" was co-written by Anderson and Lionel Delmore, son of Delmore Brother, Alton. A spritely retro-rock-beat number with an unmistakably country storyline, the song featured lyrics of innocence that appealed to young and old alike. Most of all, the song was fun to sing, and there was no country song in 1983 that inspired more sing-alongs. It set Anderson up for a long-deserved CMA Award, though much irony was seen in his capturing the Horizon Award, which was generally understood to be a newcomer's category. Anderson scored a second #1 record later in 1983 with "Black Sheep," ironically co-written by Danny Darst and Robert Altman, director of the movie *Nashville,* much reviled by the country music establishment. More than any of Anderson's other hits, "Swingin'" remained popular with concert audiences.

1983

COUNTRY GOES "SWINGIN'"

The Oak Ridge Boys score a #1 hit with "American Made." credit: Photo by Alan Mayor

Most Important Records

"Islands In The Stream" Dolly Parton and Kenny Rogers / RCA
"Houston (Means I'm One Step Closer To You)" Larry Gatlin / Columbia
"Swingin'" John Anderson / Warner Brothers
"The Closer You Get" Alabama / RCA
"Highway 40 Blues" Ricky Skaggs / Epic
"Can't Even Get The Blues" Reba McEntire / Mercury
"American Made" Oak Ridge Boys / MCA
"We've Got Tonight" Kenny Rogers and Sheena Easton / Liberty
"Pancho & Lefty" Merle Haggard and Willie Nelson / Epic
"A Little Good News" Anne Murray / Capitol

Debut Artist: The Judds

With off-beat hill country names Naomi and Wynonna (stage names taken by Diana Judd and her eldest daughter, Christina Ciminella) the sudden appearance of The Judds portended a sophisticated new harmony sound that was more dominating in the country scene than anything since the Everly Brothers. Their 1983 debut, "Had A Dream," had been released as "For The Heart" by Elvis Presley in 1976, but The Judds made it an easy

loping acoustic number that typified the sound that mother Naomi had been honing around the kitchen table with her talented daughter since the late 1970s. With their second record, "Mama He's Crazy," Naomi's vision and Wynonna's vocal power and personality drove them to the top of the charts and to the promised land of duet and vocal group awards. They were the most popular country duo of the decade, remaining the obvious choice for duet awards as long as they remained an active, touring unit. Naomi blamed hepatitis for her retirement at the end of a grueling farewell tour through 1991, but continued to pursue acting, co-management of her daughter, and an increasingly active sideline as spokeswoman for her religious beliefs. Wynonna's solo career has been marked by soaring rock- and gospel-tinged ballads and up-tempo records including her magnificent debut, "She Is His Only Need." Non-singing Judd, Ashley, finished college in Kentucky, adopted the family stage name for a featured role in an episode of "Star Trek—The Next Generation," then landed a regular part on the television series "Sisters."

Awards

GOLD AND PLATINUM RECORDS
"The Closer You Get" G/A Alabama / RCA

"The Closer You Get" P/A Alabama / RCA
"Swingin'" G/S John Anderson / Warner Brothers
"Seven Year Ache" G/A Rosanne Cash / Columbia
"Greatest Hits" G/A David Allan Coe / Columbia
"Seasons Of The Heart" G/A John Denver / RCA
"Big City" G/A Merle Haggard / Epic
"Pancho & Lefty" G/A Merle Haggard and Willie Nelson / Epic
"WW II" G/A Waylon Jennings and Willie Nelson / RCA
"I Am What I Am" P/A George Jones / Epic
"Coal Miner's Daughter" G/A Loretta Lynn / MCA
"San Antonio Rose" G/A Willie Nelson and Ray Price / Columbia
"American Made" G/A Oak Ridge Boys / MCA
"Greatest Hits" G/A Dolly Parton / RCA
"A Fool Such As I" G/S Elvis Presley / RCA
"Are You Lonesome Tonight" G/S Elvis Presley / RCA

"Don't" G/S Elvis Presley / RCA
"I Got Stung" G/S Elvis Presley / RCA
"It's Now Or Never" G/S Elvis Presley / RCA
"Return To Sender" G/S Elvis Presley / RCA
"Wear My Ring Around Your Neck" G/S Elvis Presley / RCA
"Welcome To My World" G/A Elvis Presley / RCA
"20 Greatest Hits" G/A Kenny Rogers / Liberty
"20 Greatest Hits" P/A Kenny Rogers / Liberty
"Eyes That See In The Dark" G/A Kenny Rogers / Liberty
"Eyes That See In The Dark" P/A Kenny Rogers / Liberty
"We've Got Tonight" G/A Kenny Rogers / Liberty
"Islands In The Stream" G/S Kenny Rogers and Dolly Parton / RCA
"Islands In The Stream" P/S Kenny Rogers and Dolly Parton / RCA
"Highways And Heartaches" G/A Ricky Skaggs / Epic
"Waitin' For The Sun To Shine" G/A Ricky Skaggs / Epic
"Just Sylvia" G/A Sylvia / RCA
"The Very Best Of" G/A Conway Twitty / MCA
"Family Tradition" G/A Hank Williams Jr. / Elektra

GRAMMYS
BEST COUNTRY VOCAL PERFORMANCE, FEMALE—"A Little Good News" single Anne Murray
BEST COUNTRY VOCAL PERFORMANCE, MALE—"I.O.U." single Lee Greenwood
BEST COUNTRY PERFORMANCE, DUO OR GROUP—"The Closer You Get" album Alabama
BEST COUNTRY INSTRUMENTAL PERFORMANCE—"Fireball" track The New South (Ricky Skaggs, Jerry Douglas, Tony Rice, J.D. Crowe, Todd Phillips)
BEST COUNTRY SONG—"A Stranger In My House" Mike Reid, writer
BEST SOUL GOSPEL PERFORMANCE BY A DUO OR GROUP (NC)—"I'm So Glad I'm Standing Here Today" track Bobby Jones with Barbara Mandrell

COUNTRY MUSIC ASSOCIATION AWARDS
ENTERTAINER OF THE YEAR—Alabama
FEMALE VOCALIST—Janie Frickie
MALE VOCALIST—Lee Greenwood
SONG OF THE YEAR—"Always On My Mind" Johnny Christopher, Mark James, and Wayne Carson
SINGLE OF THE YEAR—"Swingin'" John Anderson
ALBUM OF THE YEAR—"The Closer You Get" Alabama
VOCAL DUO OF THE YEAR—Merle Haggard and Willie Nelson
VOCAL GROUP OF THE YEAR—Alabama
INSTRUMENTALIST OF THE YEAR—Chet Atkins
INSTRUMENTAL GROUP OF THE YEAR—Ricky Skaggs Band
HORIZON AWARD—John Anderson

ACADEMY OF COUNTRY MUSIC AWARDS

SONG OF THE YEAR—"The Wind Beneath My Wings" Jeff Silbar and Larry Henley, writers

SINGLE RECORD OF THE YEAR—"Islands In The Stream" Kenny Rogers and Dolly Parton, artists

ALBUM OF THE YEAR—"The Closer You Get" Alabama

ENTERTAINER—Alabama

MALE VOCALIST—Lee Greenwood

FEMALE VOCALIST—Janie Frickie

VOCAL GROUP—Alabama

VOCAL DUET—Dolly Parton and Kenny Rogers

NEW MALE VOCALIST—Jim Glaser

NEW FEMALE VOCALIST—Gus Hardin

TOURING BAND—Ricky Skaggs Band

NON-TOURING BAND—The Tennesseans

DISC JOCKEY—Rhubarb Jones

RADIO STATION—KRMD, Shreveport, LA

CLUB—Gilley's

PIONEER AWARD—Eddy Arnold

TEX RITTER AWARD—*Tender Mercies* (movie)

INSTRUMENTALISTS: fiddle, Johnny Gimble; keyboard, Floyd Cramer; bass, Joe Osborn; drums, Archie Francis; guitar, Reggie Young; steel guitar, J.D. Maness

Milestones

- The Nashville Network debuts on March 7.
- Bob Neal, 65, former Memphis deejay and booking agent, and Elvis Presley's first manager, dies on May 9.
- Rex Gosden, 45, brother and former singing partner of Vern Gosden, dies on May 23 in Stockbridge, Georgia, of a heart attack. The Gosden Brothers' had a hit with "Hangin' On" in 1967. They sang most of the harmony overdubs for the Byrds' country-rock album "Sweetheart of the Rodeo."
- The cover and accompanying advertising photos promoting Conway Twitty's album, "Lost In The Feeling," feature Naomi Judd making her first minor splash in Nashville's music business—as a model, admiring Twitty.
- Rachel Dennison, Dolly Parton's youngest sister, gets the role of Doralee in the ABC-TV sitcom version of "9 To 5." The show flops.
- National Life Trust, owners of insurance interests, WSM, and the "Grand Ole Opry," among other interests, is acquired by Houston-based American General Corp., which sells entertainment and hospitality properties, including the newly-launched The Nashville Network, to Oklahoma-headquartered Gaylord Broadcasting.
- *Great Balls Of Fire*, a movie based on the life of Jerry Lee Lewis, is planned. Originally, *Pope of Greenwich Village* star

Following a year when no new artists of note appeared, 1983 not only produced The Judds, but several significant new artists, including Kathy Mattea, Steve Earle, and Dan Seals.

Seals had a long history of pop success as part of England Dan and John Ford Coley. A Texan with eclectic musical tastes, a powerful voice, and instrumental skills ranging from left-handed guitar to tenor saxophone, Seals was a natural addition to a country scene that was enthralled with adult pop sounds in the early 1980s. He really caught fire in 1984, starting a long run of Top 10 and #1 songs such as "Bop," "Addicted," and "Big Wheels In The Moonlight" that continued unbroken through the end of the decade.

Steve Earle was a rockabilly rebel who cut his musical teeth in the mean clubs of Houston and San Antonio. His long hair and rock posturing alienated the Nashville establishment, but his post-Vietnam, redneck-biker attitudes represented a strong new generation of country-rock intensity. Once past his rockabilly phase, his successes included "Guitar Town" and "Copperhead Road." His career ground to a halt in the early 1990s due to drug problems, but he was reported "clean and sober" when he sat in on recording sessions by the Kentucky HeadHunters in 1993.

Popular Nashville club and studio singer Kathy Mattea started slowly with "Street Talk" in 1983, but found her feet when she teamed with producer Alan Reynolds the following year. Mining a persuasive vein of folk-country story songs in the late 1980s, she scored big with songs like "Love at the Five and Dime," "Eighteen Wheels and a Dozen Roses," and "Going Gone." She signaled a subtle change in direction with her Grammy-winning hit, "Where've You Been" in 1990. She ditched a long tour association with George Strait for a theater tour as headliner behind an album of eclectic songs she had long admired. Thereafter, more of her personal philosophy and a penchant for Celtic sounds found their way into her music. Up against a new generation of country female singers in the 1990s, Mattea has held her own.

Mickey Rourke is cast as Lewis. By the time filming starts, *Big Easy* star Dennis Quaid has the role.

- Merle Travis, 65, one of country music's most influential guitarists, dies on October 20. His finger-picking style directly influenced Doc Watson and Chet Atkins. Travis wrote "Sixteen Tons."
- Kirk McGee, 83, dies on October 24 in Franklin, Kentucky. McGee and his brother, Sam, accompanied Uncle Dave Macon in the 1920s. He was a fiddler and guitarist with the "Grand Ole Opry" and with the Fruit Jar Drinkers until his death.
- "The Gambler Part II—The Adventure Continues," starring Kenny Rogers, airs on CBS-TV in November.
- Junior Samples, 56, heavyset, deadpan, inarticulate comedian on "Hee Haw," dies on November 13 in Cumming, Georgia, of a heart attack.
- CBS and RCA record labels issue the first country compact disks in December. Other labels announce they have no definite plans to issue country CDs.

Kathy Mattea.
credit: Bob Millard Collection

Sawyer Brown.
credit: Photo by Alan Mayor

1984

A Notable Exception

A plethora of national talent contests was increasingly receptive to country music acts in the 1980s, but most winners invariably landed in obscurity. In a notable exception to this rule, the 1983 winner of television's "Star Search," country show band Sawyer Brown, was the most productive talent contest victory for a country act since Patsy Cline won raves on "Arthur Godfrey's Talent Scouts" in 1957. Lead by singer-songwriter Mark Miller, the band debuted with a Top 20 country hit, "Leona," in 1984. This high energy showband translated well for concert audiences, but radio developed a perverse resistance to Miller's droning vocals for several years. Persevering, the act eventually overcame radio's resistance and struck with a string of charting hit records.

Most Important Records

"Why Not Me" The Judds / RCA
"To All The Girls I've Loved Before" Willie Nelson and Julio Iglesias / Columbia
"City of New Orleans" Willie Nelson / Columbia
"Roll On (Eighteen Wheeler)" Alabama / RCA

"That's The Way Love Goes" Merle Haggard / Epic
"Mama He's Crazy" The Judds / RCA
"Nobody Loves Me Like You Do" Anne Murray and Dave Loggins / Capitol
"Woke Up In Love" Exile / Epic
"You Look So Good In Love" George Strait / MCA
"Elizabeth" Statler Brothers / Mercury

Debut Artist: Vince Gill

Vince Gill was 27 when RCA issued his debut mini-LP, "Turn Me Loose," and did the same in the process. Behind his fresh, cherubic face was a raft of musical experience. Gill had been in bands with Ricky Skaggs (Boone Creek) and Byron Berline, had been a member of the soft country-rock band Pure Prairie League, and had contributed to the legendary "bluegrass/new-grass" album *Here Today* with Herb Pederson and Dave Grisman. He had also put in time with Rosanne Cash and Rodney Crowell's Cherry Bombs band. Emmylou Harris had brought him "Oh Caroline," the second single from his debut album, and sang harmonies on the session. The son of an Oklahoma City attorney/judge, Gill had a regional hit with his high school band, Mountain Smoke, but at 18 went to Louisville to play bluegrass rather than to Nashville to pursue commercial country. Working through Pure Prairie League and The Cherry Bombs, his fame grew as a Telecaster guitarist and a bluegrass-style tenor of pure tones and power. Though he would struggle throughout the rest of the 1980s to break through, the promise that he would finally make it materialized with the first notes of his 1984 debut single, "Victim of Life's Circumstance."

Vince Gill.
credit: Photo by Donnie Beauchamp, Courtesy the Grand Ole Opry

Awards

GOLD AND PLATINUM RECORDS
"Feels So Right" 3M/A Alabama / RCA
"Mountain Music" 3M/A Alabama / RCA
"Roll On" G/A Alabama / RCA
"Roll On" P/A Alabama / RCA
"Roll On" 2M/A Alabama / RCA
"The Closer You Get" 2M/A Alabama / RCA
"Wild & Blue" G/A John Anderson / Warner Brothers
"Somebody's Gonna Love You" G/A Lee Greenwood / MCA
"Pancho & Lefty" P/A Merle Haggard and Willie Nelson / Epic
"To All The Girls I've Loved Before" G/S Julio Iglesias and Willie Nelson / Columbia
"Always On My Mind" 3M/A Willie Nelson / Columbia
"City Of New Orleans" G/A Willie Nelson / Columbia
"Stardust" 3M/A Willie Nelson / Columbia
"Without A Song" G/A Willie Nelson / Columbia

"Deliver" G/A Oak Ridge Boys / MCA
"What About Me" G/A Kenny Rogers / Liberty
"Once Upon A Christmas" G/A Kenny Rogers and Dolly Parton / RCA
"Once Upon A Christmas" P/A Kenny Rogers and Dolly Parton / RCA
"Don't Cheat In Our Home Town" G/A Ricky Skaggs / Epic
"Right Or Wrong" G/A George Strait / MCA
"Hank Williams Jr.'s Greatest Hits" G/A Hank Williams Jr. / Curb / Warner Brothers
"Hank Williams Jr.'s Greatest Hits" P/A Hank Williams Jr. / Curb / Warner Brothers

GRAMMYS

BEST COUNTRY VOCAL PERFORMANCE, FEMALE—"In My Dreams" single Emmylou Harris
BEST COUNTRY VOCAL PERFORMANCE, MALE—"That's The Way Love Goes" single Merle Haggard
BEST COUNTRY PERFORMANCE, DUO OR GROUP—"Mama He's Crazy" single The Judds
BEST COUNTRY INSTRUMENTAL PERFORMANCE—"Wheel Hoss" track from "Country Boy" Ricky Skaggs
BEST COUNTRY SONG—"City Of New Orleans" Steve Goodman, writer

COUNTRY MUSIC ASSOCIATION AWARDS

ENTERTAINER OF THE YEAR—Alabama
FEMALE VOCALIST—Reba McEntire
MALE VOCALIST—Lee Greenwood
SONG OF THE YEAR—"Wind Beneath My Wings" Larry Henley and Jeff Silbar
SINGLE OF THE YEAR—"A Little Good News" Anne Murray
ALBUM OF THE YEAR—"A Little Good News" Anne Murray
VOCAL DUO OF THE YEAR—Willie Nelson and Julio Iglesias
VOCAL GROUP OF THE YEAR—Statler Brothers
INSTRUMENTALIST OF THE YEAR—Chet Atkins
INSTRUMENTAL GROUP OF THE YEAR—Ricky Skaggs Band
HORIZON AWARD—The Judds

ACADEMY OF COUNTRY MUSIC AWARDS

SONG OF THE YEAR—"Why Not Me" Harlan Howard, Sonny Throckmorton and Brent Maher, writers
SINGLE RECORD OF THE YEAR—"To All The Girls I've Loved Before" Willie Nelson and Julio Igelsias, artists
ALBUM OF THE YEAR—"Roll On" Alabama
ENTERTAINER—Alabama
MALE VOCALIST—George Strait
FEMALE VOCALIST—Reba McEntire
VOCAL GROUP—Alabama
VOCAL DUET—The Judds
NEW MALE VOCALIST—Vince Gill

NEW FEMALE VOCALIST—Nicolette Larson
TOURING BAND—Ricky Skaggs Band
NON-TOURING BAND —The Tennesseans
DISC JOCKEY—Coyote Calhoun (large); Billy Parker (medium); Don Hollander (small)
RADIO STATION—WMC, Memphis, TN (large); KVOO, Tulsa, OK (medium); WLWI, Montgomery, AL (small)
CLUB—Gilley's
PIONEER AWARD—Roy Acuff
TEX RITTER AWARD—*Songwriter* (movie)
VIDEO OF THE YEAR—*All My Rowdy Friends Are Coming Over Tonight* Hank Williams Jr.
INSTRUMENTALISTS: fiddle, Johnny Gimble; keyboard, Hargus "Pig" Robbins; bass, Joe Osborn; drums, Larrie London; guitar, James Burton; steel guitar, Buddy Emmons

Milestones

- Al Dexter, 78, popular 1940s bandleader, songwriter, and recording artist, dies on January 28 in Lewisville, Texas. He composed "Pistol Packin' Mama," one of the first national country jukebox hits.
- On February 16, Jerry Lee Lewis is indicted on charges of federal tax evasion.
- Bluegrass and rock veteran, and former Rosanne Cash sideman, Vince Gill, makes his country debut with "Victim of Life's Circumstances" in February.
- Roy Hill, 61, rockabilly pioneer and co-writer of "Whole Lotta Shakin' Goin' On," dies on March 2 in Nashville of a heart attack.
- Nudie Cohen, 82, Hollywood stage costume designer and tailor since 1947, dies in Los Angeles on May 9. He created Hank Williams' first rhinestone suit and inspired the rhinestone and sequined cowboy look.
- Onie Wheeler, 62, rockabilly pioneer turned gospel artist and Roy Acuff sideman, dies on May 27 on the Opryhouse stage while performing on the "Grand Ole Gospel Show."
- *Rhinestone*, produced and directed by Dolly Parton and co-starring Dolly Parton and Sylvester Stallone, premieres. Reviewers universally dismiss the film as the worst country music movie in decades. *Billboard* calls it "an embarrassment." Parton later claims she had been a victim of depression the entire year before.
- Bill Monroe joins Ricky Skaggs in the recording and the video of *Country Boy*.
- Filming begins in Nashville for the film *Sweet Dreams*, based on Patsy Cline's life, starring Jessica Lange.
- Ernest Tubb, 70, honky-tonk pioneer and legendary country recording and performing artist, dies on September 6 in Nashville of emphysema.

- Steve Goodman, 36, singer and songwriter, dies of leukemia on September 20 in Seattle. He dies just as Willie Nelson's version of his tune "City of New Orleans," which had been a 1973 hit for Arlo Guthrie, reaches the Top 10. The single and album become #1 hits.
- Don Reno, 58, one of the foremost bluegrass banjoists, dies on October 16. He wrote "Dueling Banjos," the theme for the movie *Deliverance*.
- Johnnie Lee Wills, 72, younger brother of Bob Wills and an original Texas Playboy, dies on October 25 in Tulsa, Oklahoma, after open heart surgery. His most famous hits as a solo artist were "Rag Mop" and "Peter Cottontail" in 1950.
- Mel Tillis' much-delayed autobiography, *Stutterin' Boy*, is published. As critics point out, he leaves out "most of the good stuff."
- Gary Morris takes a sabbatical from his country recording career to appear on Broadway with Linda Ronstadt in the opera *La Boheme* in November and December.

"City of New Orleans" and Other Folkie Country Hits

If Bobby Bare, Johnny Cash, and Don Williams were the folk influences of the 1960s, Steve Goodman, John Prine, and Nanci Griffith were the equivalent in the 1980s. Goodman was most influential in mainstream country as a songwriter. He wrote the David Allan Coe hit, "You Never Even Call Me By My Name," with uncredited inspiration from his buddy Prine. Goodman's "City of New Orleans" became a tremendous crossover hit for Willie Nelson. It is the tale of a train, not a city, and it's cross-country trek inspired a nostalgia for the days when coal-fired steam engines pulled passengers across the nation. Goodman died of leukemia in 1984.

John Prine, once likened in a *Billboard* review to a latterday Bob Dylan and "a rumpled, leftover Everly Brother," actually had family roots in the same Kentucky county as the Everlys. His innocent, yet eye-opening, examination of the wreckage left of that county by strip mining big coal interests, "Paradise (Daddy, Won't You Take Me To Muhlenburg County)," was a big hit for Lynn Anderson in 1976. That combination of innocent, whimsical Lewis Carroll-like lyrics and meaningful social observation typified his best work. His "Love Is On A Roll" made a hit for Don Williams in 1983. He remains an extremely quirky, creative, and popular recording and touring act on a national scale.

Nanci Griffith, both as writer and artist, contributed seminally to the folkie flavor of some late 1980s and early 1990s commercial country music. Though her own late 1980s foray into country radio was not well received, her gifts as a stylist and composer remain singular. Among the hits her pen has contributed for other artists are "Love at the Five and Dime" for Kathy Mattea and "Outbound Plane" for Suzy Bogguss.

Mel McDaniel was a shy Oklahoma boy from a poor family whose dream of becoming an entertainer was fired by the sight of Elvis Presley on TV in the window of a small town furniture store one Sunday night. He started performing at 14 and worked in clubs in Oklahoma, Arkansas, and Kansas before moving to Alaska with his father from 1970 to 1972. He moved to Nashville in 1973, with his chart debut coming in 1976. He struggled five years for his first Top 10, "Louisiana Saturday Night," in 1980. "Big Ole Brew" made his first Top 5 in 1982, but most of his records languished in far less distinguished positions. He was a journeyman artist and club singer, a noted purveyor of blue collar party songs, but in 1985 he rode to the top of the chart for the first and last time with a simmering, sashaying groove song, "Baby's Got Her Blue Jeans On," which finally put him on the map. By the next year, his recording output was once again at journeyman levels—most below the Top 50, with a rare Top 15 single—but he was a journeyman with a #1 record in his repertoire, and no one could take that away from him.

Most Important Records

"Have Mercy" The Judds / RCA
"Forty Hour Week (For A Livin')" Alabama / RCA
"Does Ft. Worth Ever Cross Your Mind" George Strait / MCA
"Baby's Got Her Blues Jeans On" Mel McDaniel / Capitol
"Country Boy" Ricky Skaggs / Epic
"Lost In The Fifties (In The Still of the Night)" Ronnie Milsap / RCA
"Highwayman" Johnny Cash, Waylon Jennings, Kris Kristofferson, and Willie Nelson / Capitol
"Meet Me In Montana" Dan Seals and Marie Osmond / Capitol
"Step That Step" Sawyer Brown / Capitol
"Real Love" Kenny Rogers and Dolly Parton / RCA

Debut Artist: Restless Heart

Restless Heart was put together by songwriter/producer Tim DuBois from Nashville demo session musicians and singers. They scored their first hit in 1985 with "Let The Heartache Ride." Though they originated as Alabama clones, borrowing wholesale from the Eagles sound, these five relatively inexperienced "stars" soon became a band with its own direction and creative identity. As they matured, they developed a smooth pop-crossover style that occasionally made them the only Nashville act with hits on both adult contemporary and country radio. Despite attrition—lead singer Larry Stewart went solo in 1992 and keyboardist Dave Innis was kicked out in 1993—Greg Jennings, Paul Gregg, and John Dittrich remain a smooth, hit-producing act.

1985

BLUE JEANS
ON COUNTRY QUEENS

Awards

GOLD AND PLATINUM RECORDS
"40 Hour Week" G/A Alabama / RCA
"40 Hour Week" P/A Alabama / RCA
"Alabama Christmas" G/A Alabama / RCA
"Alabama Christmas" P/A Alabama / RCA
"Feels So Right" 4M/A Alabama / RCA
"Mountain Music" 4M/A Alabama / RCA
"The Closer You Get" 3M/A Alabama / RCA
"A Decade Of Hits" G/A Charlie Daniels Band / Epic
"Greatest Hits" G/A Lee Greenwood / MCA
"You've Got A Good Love Comin'" G/A Lee Greenwood / MCA
"Willie & Waylon" 2M/A Waylon Jennings and Willie Nelson / RCA
"Greatest Hits" 3M/A Waylon Jennings / RCA
"Wanted: The Outlaws" 2M/A Waylon Jennings, Willie Nelson, Jessi Colter, and Tompall Glaser / RCA
"Why Not Me" G/A The Judds / RCA
"Greatest Hits Vol. 2" G/A Ronnie Milsap / RCA
"A Little Good News" G/A Anne Murray / Capitol
"Heart Over Mind" G/A Anne Murray / Capitol
"Heart Of The Matter" G/A Kenny Rogers / RCA
"Does Fort Worth Ever Cross Your Mind" G/A George Strait / MCA
"George Strait's Greatest Hits" G/A George Strait / MCA
"Five-O" G/A Hank Williams Jr. / Warner Brothers
"Major Moves" G/A Hank Williams Jr. / Warner Brothers
"Man Of Steel" G/A Hank Williams Jr. / Warner Brothers
"Rowdy" G/A Hank Williams Jr. / Warner Brothers

GRAMMYS
BEST COUNTRY VOCAL PERFORMANCE, FEMALE—"I Don't Know Why You Don't Want Me" single Rosanne Cash
BEST COUNTRY VOCAL PERFORMANCE, MALE—"Lost In The Fifties Tonight (In The Still Of The Night)" single Ronnie Milsap
BEST COUNTRY PERFORMANCE, DUO OR GROUP WITH VOCAL—"Why Not Me" album The Judds
BEST COUNTRY INSTRUMENTAL PERFORMANCE—"Cosmic Square Dance" track from the album "Stay Tuned" Chet Atkins
BEST COUNTRY SONG—"Highwayman" Jimmy Webb, writer

COUNTRY MUSIC ASSOCIATION AWARDS
ENTERTAINER OF THE YEAR—Ricky Skaggs
FEMALE VOCALIST—Reba McEntire
MALE VOCALIST—George Strait
SONG OF THE YEAR—"God Bless The USA" Lee Greenwood & Paul Overstreet
SINGLE OF THE YEAR—"Why Not Me" The Judds

ALBUM OF THE YEAR—"Does Ft. Worth Ever Cross Your Mind"
George Strait
VOCAL DUO OF THE YEAR—Anne Murray and Dave Loggins
VOCAL GROUP OF THE YEAR—The Judds
INSTRUMENTALIST OF THE YEAR—Chet Atkins
INSTRUMENTAL GROUP OF THE YEAR—Ricky Skaggs Band
HORIZON AWARD—Sawyer Brown
MUSIC VIDEO OF THE YEAR—*All My Rowdy Friends Are Comin' Over Tonight* Hank Williams Jr.

ACADEMY OF COUNTRY MUSIC AWARDS
SONG OF THE YEAR—"Lost In The 'Fifties (In The Still Of The Night)" Mike Reid, Troy Seals and Fred Parris, writers
SINGLE RECORD OF THE YEAR—"Highwayman" Willie Nelson, Waylon Jennings, Johnny Cash, and Kris Kristofferson, artists
ALBUM OF THE YEAR—"Does Ft. Worth Ever Cross Your Mind"
George Strait
ENTERTAINER—Alabama
MALE VOCALIST—George Strait
FEMALE VOCALIST—Reba McEntire
VOCAL GROUP—Alabama
VOCAL DUET—The Judds
NEW MALE VOCALIST—Randy Travis
NEW FEMALE VOCALIST—Judy Rodman
TOURING BAND—Ricky Skaggs Band
NON-TOURING BAND—Nashville Now Band
DISC JOCKEY—Eddie Edwards
RADIO STATION—WAMZ, Louisville, KY
CLUB—Billy Bob's
PIONEER AWARD—Kitty Wells
TEX RITTER AWARD—*Sweet Dreams* (movie)
VIDEO OF THE YEAR—*Who's Gonna Fill Their Shoes* George Jones
INSTRUMENTALISTS: fiddle, Billy Armstrong; keyboard, Glen Hardin; bass, Joe Osborn; drums, Archie Francis; guitar, James Burton; steel guitar, Buddy Emmons; dobro, James Burton

Milestones

- Emmylou Harris takes a commercial risk with the concept album *The Ballad of Sally Rose*. Co-written and co-produced by her soon-to-be-husband Paul Kennerly, the album is a dramatic fictionalization of Harris' own musical and personal collaboration with the late Gram Parsons.

- Polk C. Brockman, 86, retired Atlanta furniture store manager and record dealer, dies on March 10 in Orlando, Florida. Brockman's letters to Okeh Records' Ralph Peer led to the first hillbilly field recording session, featuring moonshiner and WSB old-time star Fiddlin' John Carson in June 1923.

- Lila May Ledford, 68, writer, banjo player, founder and leader of the Coon Creek Girls, dies on July 14 in Lexington, Kentucky, following a lengthy illness.
- Timothy Rabbitt, 23 months old, the son of Eddie Rabbitt and a victim of birth defects, dies in early July following liver transplant surgery.
- Wynn Stewart, 51, best known as the writer and artist of the 1967 hit "It's Such A Pretty World Today," dies on July 17 in Hendersonville, Tennessee, of a heart attack.
- Charley Pride, complaining that RCA pays more attention to younger artists, quits the label.
- Following drug treatment and legal problems from his cocaine bust, Waylon Jennings candidly admits, "It's amazing how much you can get done when you're straight." He admits his latest effort, "Turn The Page," is the first record in 20 years he has recorded without the aid of drugs.
- At the end of September, Willie Nelson's first Farm Aid concert takes place in Champaign, Illinois, raising a reported $10 million.
- Catherine Yvonne Stone succeeds in her legal suit in Alabama to gain access to documents related to her January 6, 1953 birth and subsequent adoption by Hank Williams' mother, Mrs. W.W. Stone. She later proves Hank Williams is her father by Bobbie W. Jett, and begins using the stage name Jett Williams.
- Merle Watson, 36, son and musical partner of Doc Watson, dies of injuries when pinned beneath a tractor on October 23 on his farm near Lenoir, North Carolina.
- John Lair, 91, former talent director for the WLS "Barn Dance," organizer of the Cumberland Ridge Runners, and founder of the "Renfro Valley Barn Dance," dies on November 13 in Mount Vernon, Kentucky.
- Sweethearts of the Rodeo, sisters Kristine Arnold and Janice Gill, win the $50,000 grand prize in the Wrangler Country Showdown national talent contest. They already have a Columbia Records contract but put off recording to remain eligible for the contest.
- Elsie McWilliams, 89, sister-in-law and songwriting partner of Jimmie Rodgers, dies on December 30 in Meridian, Mississippi. She collaborated on the Rodgers' hits "Blue Yodel," "My Old Pal," and "Never No Mo' Blues."
- Late in December, Johnny Paycheck shoots a Hillsborough, Ohio, man in the head in a bar argument. He is eventually convicted and sentenced to prison.
- Rick Nelson, 45, dies on December 31 with his band and fiancee in a fiery plane crash near DeKalb, Texas. His Stone Canyon Band albums are considered forerunners of the country-rock hybrid.

Of all the so-called "outlaws" of country music in the 1970s and 1980s, Willie Nelson and Waylon Jennings were the two who worked together more often and most successfully. Their friendship started in the late 1960s, when the country music community in Nashville was still relatively small. Both craving artistic independence, they hung out in many of the same bars and shared in many of the same illicit drugs, but most of all they respected each other's music.

The story of their first significant collaboration involves the song "Good Hearted Woman," which Jennings had started to write but could not finish. Jennings shared what he had done with Willie during a poker game

and Willie stayed overnight to work on it. "I woke up the next morning writing that song. . . I told Waylon about it at the breakfast table, so we finished it after breakfast. We weren't scheduled to record, but Waylon called the studio and set up some time for that day."

"Good Hearted Woman" stayed at #1 for three weeks in 1975. Willie took a verse in Waylon's "Luckenbach, Texas (Back To The Basics of Love)" that rode the top of the charts for an amazing six weeks in 1977. Their next official duet, "Mamas Don't Let Your Babies Grow Up To Be Cowboys," was #1 for four weeks in 1978. "Just To Satisfy You" was a two-week chart topper for the pair, and their albums together include *Waylon and Willie, WWII,*

Wanted: The Outlaws (also featuring Tompall Glaser and Jessi Colter), and two Highwaymen projects that include Johnny Cash and Kris Kristofferson. In their heyday, their duel tours sold more tickets than any other country touring act.

They were always different temperamentally. Willie took success easily while Waylon chafed at losing his privacy, and Willie stayed pleasantly loaded on pot (so nonchalantly that no one ever bothered to bust him) while Waylon went overboard on cocaine. Though their lives and careers have diverged in recent years, when television feted Willie with a musical special on his 60th birthday in 1993, Waylon Jennings was on hand to sing for his old pal.

Willie Nelson and Waylon Jennings.
credit: Photo by Alan Mayor

Kentucky-born, L.A.-vetted, hip country retro-rocker Dwight Yoakam came on like Peck's Bad Boy, the guy with the skintight blue jeans and not a good word to say about the Nashville establishment. The country music establishment and many critics hated him—out loud—which may just have contributed to a generation of hip, young fans falling in love with his barely intelligible, nasal renditions of classic post-WWII honky-tonk music on his album *Guitars, Cadillacs, Etc., Etc.* Nevertheless, he made a hit out of his nouveau honky-tonk sound, covering Johnny Horton's 1956 debut record "Honky-Tonk Man" for his own 1986 debut, and taking it further up the charts than the originator. As he went along, he proved sincere in his affection for the old electric sounds of country, even to the point of nagging Buck Owens out of retirement for a sterling chart-topping duet of an earlier Owens album cut, "Streets of Bakersfield," in 1988.

Most Important Records

"Mind Your Own Business" Hank Williams Jr. / Warner Brothers
"Bop" Dan Seals / EMI America
"Grandpa (Tell Me 'Bout The Good Old Days)" The Judds / RCA
"Whoever's In New England" Reba McEntire / MCA
"That Rock Won't Roll" Restless Heart / RCA

Dwight Yoakam and Buck Owens.
credit: Photo by Alan Mayor

"On The Other Hand" Randy Travis / Warner Brothers
"Nobody In His Right Mind Would Have Left Her" George Strait / MCA
"You Can Dream of Me" Steve Wariner / MCA
"Happy, Happy Birthday Baby" Ronnie Milsap / RCA
"Rockin' With The Rhythm Of The Rain" The Judds / RCA

Debut Artist: Ricky Van Shelton

At the end of the year, when new records tend more to escape captivity than actually be released, Grit, Virginia's soon-to-be most famous son, Ricky Van Shelton, had his debut with "Wild-Eyed Dreamer." The former pipe fitter had made dozens of trips to Nashville looking for a break and finally got one when an important Nashville newspaper columnist became his first manager. Still, charting with your first single the week before Christmas is not intrinsically auspicious. It takes talent to make it work. The record made the Top 30; its follow-up, "Crime of Passion," reached the Top 10 in the summer of 1987; then Van Shelton's next four consecutive records went to #1. Indicative of a favored ploy, his fourth release, the second #1, "Life Turned Her That Way," was a remake of a hit Mel Tillis had recorded in the late 1960s. His later remakes of country classics would include the 1963 Ned Miller hit, "From a Jack to a King." He was able to croon warbling ballads even better than Narvel Felts, or belt out rockers like "I Am A Simple Man."

Ricky Van Shelton.
credit: Photo by Donnie Beauchamp, Courtesy the Grand Ole Opry

Awards

GOLD AND PLATINUM RECORDS
"Alabama's Greatest Hits" G/A Alabama / RCA
"Alabama's Greatest Hits" P/A Alabama / RCA
"My Home's In Alabama" 2M/A Alabama / RCA
"Rose Garden" P/A Lynn Anderson / Columbia
"The Bellamy Brothers Greatest Hits" G/A Bellamy Brothers / MCA
"Johnny Cash's Greatest Hits" P/A Johnny Cash / Columbia
"Johnny Cash's Greatest Hits" 2M/A Johnny Cash / Columbia
"Johnny Cash At San Quentin" P/A Johnny Cash / Columbia
"Johnny Cash At San Quentin" 2M/A Johnny Cash / Columbia
"Johnny Cash At Folsom Prison" P/A Johnny Cash / Columbia
"Johnny Cash At Folsom Prison" 2M/A Johnny Cash / Columbia
"Million Mile Reflection" 2M/A Charlie Daniels Band / Epic
"Baby, Don't Get Hooked On Me" P/A Mac Davis / Columbia
"Nashville Skyline" P/A Bob Dylan / Columbia
"The Very Best Of The Everly Brothers" G/A Everly Brothers / Warner Brothers

"Inside Out" G/A Lee Greenwood / MCA
"Pieces Of The Sky" G/A Emmylou Harris / Reprise
"Johnny Horton's Greatest Hits" P/A Johnny Horton / Columbia
"The Highwayman" G/A Waylon Jennings, Willie Nelson, Johnny Cash, and Kris Kristofferson / Columbia
"Rockin' With The Rhythm" G/A The Judds / RCA
"Rockin' With The Rhythm" P/A The Judds / RCA
"Why Not Me" P/A The Judds / RCA
"Gord's Gold" P/A Gordon Lightfoot / Reprise
"Sundown" P/A Gordon Lightfoot / Reprise
"Greatest Hits" 2M/A Ronnie Milsap / RCA
"Red Headed Stranger" P/A Willie Nelson / Columbia
"Red Headed Stranger" 2M/A Willie Nelson / Columbia
"The Troublemaker" G/A Willie Nelson / Columbia
"Willie Nelson's Greatest Hits (And Some That Will Be)" 2M/A Willie Nelson / Columbia
"Greatest Hits" P/A Dolly Parton / RCA
"Crying In The Chapel" G/S Elvis Presley / RCA
"Behind Closed Doors" P/A Charlie Rich / Epic
"Gunfighter Ballads & Trail Songs" P/A Marty Robbins / Columbia
"#7" G/A George Strait / MCA
"Something Special" G/A George Strait / MCA
"Storms Of Life" G/A Randy Travis / Warner Brothers
"Greatest Hits, Vol. 2" G/A Hank Williams Jr. / Curb/Warner Brothers
"Montana Cafe" G/A Hank Williams Jr. / Curb/Warner Brothers
"High Notes" G/A Hank Williams Jr. / Curb/Warner Brothers
"Strong Stuff" G/A Hank Williams Jr. / Curb/Warner Brothers
"The Pressure Is On" P/A Hank Williams Jr. / Curb/Warner Brothers

GOLD AND PLATINUM MUSIC VIDEOS
(RIAA began certifying gold and platinum sales for music videos in 1986. Criteria for gold is 25,000 units and/or $1 million in retail sales; platinum is double gold.)

Alabama
"Alabama's Greatest Video Hits" Gold
RCA/Columbia Pictures Home Video
RCA Video Productions

Alabama
"Alabama's Greatest Video Hits" Platinum
RCA/Columbia Pictures Home Video
RCA Video Productions

Elvis Presley
"'68 Comeback Special" Gold
Media Home Entertainment
RCA Video Productions, Inc.

Elvis Presley
"Aloha From Hawaii" Gold
Media Home Entertainment
RCA Video Productions, Inc.

Elvis Presley
"Aloha From Hawaii" Platinum
Media Home Entertainment
RCA Video Productions, Inc.

GRAMMYS

BEST COUNTRY VOCAL PERFORMANCE, FEMALE—"Whoever's In New England" single Reba McEntire

BEST COUNTRY VOCAL PERFORMANCE, MALE—"Lost In The Fifties" album Ronnie Milsap

BEST COUNTRY PERFORMANCE, DUO OR GROUP WITH VOCAL—"Grandpa (Tell 'Bout The Good Old Days)" single The Judds

BEST COUNTRY INSTRUMENTAL PERFORMANCE (ORCHESTRA, GROUP OR SOLOIST)—"Raisin' The Dickens" track from "Love's Gonna Get Ya " Ricky Skaggs

BEST COUNTRY SONG—"Grandpa (Tell Me 'Bout The Good Old Days" Jamie O'Hara, writer

BEST SPOKEN WORD OR NON-MUSICAL RECORDING (NC)—"Interviews From The Class Of '55 Recording Sessions" album Carl Perkins, Jerry Lee Lewis, Roy Orbison, Johnny Cash, Sam Phillips, Rick Nelson, and Chips Moman

COUNTRY MUSIC ASSOCIATION AWARDS

ENTERTAINER OF THE YEAR—Reba McEntire

FEMALE VOCALIST—Reba McEntire

MALE VOCALIST—George Strait

SONG OF THE YEAR—"On The Other Hand" Paul Overstreet and Don Schiltz

SINGLE OF THE YEAR—"Bop" Dan Seals

ALBUM OF THE YEAR—"Lost In The Fifties Tonight" Ronnie Milsap

VOCAL DUO OF THE YEAR—Dan Seals and Marie Osmond

VOCAL GROUP OF THE YEAR—The Judds

INSTRUMENTALIST OF THE YEAR—Johnny Gimble

INSTRUMENTAL GROUP OF THE YEAR—Oak Ridge Boys Band

HORIZON AWARD—Randy Travis

MUSIC VIDEO OF THE YEAR—*Who's Gonna Fill Their Shoes* George Jones

ACADEMY OF COUNTRY MUSIC AWARDS

SONG OF THE YEAR—"On The Other Hand" Paul Overstreet and Don Schlitz, writers

SINGLE RECORD OF THE YEAR—"On The Other Hand" Randy Travis, artist

ALBUM OF THE YEAR—"Storms Of Life" Randy Travis

ENTERTAINER—Hank Williams Jr.

MALE VOCALIST—Randy Travis

FEMALE VOCALIST—Reba McEntire

VOCAL GROUP—Forester Sisters

VOCAL DUET—The Judds

NEW MALE VOCALIST—Dwight Yoakam

NEW FEMALE VOCALIST—Holly Dunn

TOURING BAND—Ricky Skaggs Band

NON-TOURING BAND—Nashville Now Band

DISC JOCKEY—Chris Taylor

RADIO STATION—KNIX, Tempe, AZ

CLUB—Crazy Horse Steak House & Saloon, Santa Anna, CA

PIONEER AWARD—Minnie Pearl

CAREER ACHIEVEMENT AWARD—Carl Perkins

VIDEO OF THE YEAR—*Whoever's In New England* Reba McEntire

INSTRUMENTALISTS: fiddle, Mark O'Connor; keyboard, John Hobbs; bass, Emory Gordy Jr.; drums, Larrie London; guitar, Chet Atkins; steel guitar, J.D. Mannes

Milestones

+— Reba McEntire joins the "Grand Ole Opry."

+— C.W. McCall, of "Convoy" fame ten years earlier, is elected mayor of Ouray, Colorado, under his real name, Bill Fries.

+— Barbara Mandrell teams with Dolly Parton for an ambitious two month, 46-show tour marking her return to the stage after her 1984 accident.

+— On May 10, The Judds' "Grandpa (Tell Me 'Bout The Good Old Days)" hits #1.

+— Farm Aid II, organized again by Willie Nelson, takes place on July 4 in Austin, Texas.

+— Guitarist Mose Rager, 75, dies on May 4 in Drakesboro, Kentucky, of a stroke. His finger picking style influenced Merle Travis, Doc Watson, and Chet Atkins.

+— Steve Earle sheds his rockabilly persona, leaves CBS for MCA, and becomes a rebellious country rocker whose music speaks to the post-Vietnam war Southern experience. His tough-guy image is no publicity gimmick. He later takes a poke at a policeman backstage at a Dallas concert, is choked unconscious by apprehending officers, and faces felony charges in the same town that put ex-Byrd David Crosby in prison on drug charges.

It took long enough to happen. Seven years elapsed between Reba McEntire's debut in 1977 and her first #1 ("Can't Even Get The Blues") on Mercury in 1982, and by that time she had already decided secretly to sign with another record company. By the first day of 1986, McEntire had four chart toppers under her rodeo-buckled belt; she would have seven by December 31.

McEntire had grown up in the backseat of a station wagon, daughter of a touring rodeo champ, granddaughter of yet another, riding from one dust-choked rodeo to another with her family. Her mother taught her, her sister Suzie, and brother Pake a wide variety of songs to pass the time. Her first recording sessions were for Boss Records with the family trio in 1972. When she got her own touring show, she took sister Suzie along as a backup singer, and later helped brother Pake get a contract with RCA.

The longer her hit streak ran, the more confident and more determined McEntire became to have creative and business control over her career. Her blues curlicues, with myriad notes in her melodies, became so pronounced that host Billy Crystal made fun of the style on national television. No one ever mocked her publicly again, and McEntire never fully retreated from her style.

From an eager beginner in 1977, McEntire became a savvy business woman. She turned her stage show into an extravaganza of costume changes while never crossing the line to Las Vegas-style glitz-over-substance. She coveted an acting career and acquitted herself reasonably well in the film *Tremors*, and in a made-for-TV "Gambler" movie with Kenny Rogers. Perhaps with Dolly Parton as a role model, McEntire realized the financial potential in song publishing, self-management, and self-directed merchandising. Subsequently, she set up a very well-oiled, in-house empire in Nashville combining a variety of enterprises. She didn't have all these enterprises under control in 1986, but the hits were coming and she was well on the way to having it all.

Reba McEntire, a fresh-faced rodeo beauty, around 1977. credit: Archives of Robert K. Oermann

- Although already twice elected as CMA's Female Vocalist of the Year, Janie Fricke complains that few people pronounce her name correctly, and changes the spelling to Frickie.
- Benjamin Francis "Whitey" Ford, 85, comedian, storyteller, banjoist, and "Opry" legend, known as "The Duke of Paducah," dies after a lengthy illness on June 20 in Nashville. His signature exit line: "I'm goin' back to the wagon, boys, these shoes are killin' me."
- Joe Maphis, 65, flashy fiddle and guitar player, West Coast country pioneer and writer (with his wife, Rose Lee) of "Dim Lights, Thick Smoke, and Loud, Loud Music," dies on June 27 of cancer. He played the distinctive guitar licks on TV's "Bonanza" theme.
- Jennifer Strait, 13, daughter of singer George Strait, dies on June 25 in a car crash in San Marcos, Texas.
- Suzy Bogguss signs with Capitol Records. The label sticks with her through four complete album sessions before she hits.
- Carmol Taylor, 53, singer and songwriter, dies in Alabama of cancer on December 5. He wrote numerous hits for artists such as George Jones and Tammy Wynette, including "Grand Tour," plus Joe Stampley's "Red Wine and Blue Memories."

1987

K.T. Speaks to a Generation

At a time when middle age was elbowing Tammy, Loretta, and Brenda Lee out of the limelight in an increasingly youth-oriented commercial country music market, K.T. Oslin, in her mid-40s, made an astounding debut. Texas-born and reared, but long a theater and jingles maven in New York City, Oslin came to the fore as a singer/songwriter with a dramatic flair and an intelligent sense of humor about her generation. It wasn't so much that "'80s Ladies" spoke *for* her generation of urbanized country women, but that it spoke *of* them so brilliantly. On stage, her white gloves, big earrings, and knock-'em'-dead chic stage clothes were an instant antidote to the latter-day Annie Oakley-in-spandex look that still abounded at the time. An actress with Broadway experience, she had more command of her stage than anyone since Judy Garland. Her videos were better done than a lot of movies, and as long as she could find time to rest and regenerate before writing, her pop-style songs were some of the most honest, telling, and unique on country radio.

K.T. Oslin.
credit: Photo by Beth Gwinn

Most Important Records

"Forever And Ever, Amen" Randy Travis / Warner Brothers
"'80s Ladies"[1] K.T. Oslin / RCA
"Lynda" Steve Wariner / MCA
"What Am I Gonna Do About You" Reba McEntire / MCA
"All My Ex's Live In Texas" George Strait / MCA
"I Know Where I'm Going" The Judds / RCA
"Born To Boogie" Hank Williams Jr. / Warner Brothers
"Somebody Lied" Ricky Van Shelton / Columbia
"Don't Go To Strangers" T. Graham Brown / Capitol
"Whiskey, If You Were A Woman" Highway 101 / Warner Brothers

1. "'80s Ladies" was the title track of K.T. Oslin's debut album. Though it peaked at #7 in a year when 49 other tunes played musical chairs atop the *Billboard* country chart, it defined Oslin as an artist. It was the subject of an award-winning music video and was widely played on radio from 1987 to 1988. The tune was hailed as an anthem for a generation of American women, won a Grammy, and was clearly "more important" than Oslin's actual #1 single of 1987, "Do Ya'."

Debut Artist: Highway 101

The popular group Highway 101 was organized from disparate, but experienced, elements by manager Chuck Morris for debut as a quintet in 1986. Original members were Paulette Carlson, Curtis Stone (son of West Coast country pioneer Cliffie Stone), Scott "Cactus" Moser, Jack Daniels, and television actor/score composer Morgan Stoddard. Visually exciting and comprised of complimenting talents, the group made an early splash. Nevertheless, Stoddard left the group almost as soon as it began compiling hits, which spotlighted Carlson's vocal talents and included Top 10s "The Bed You Made For Me" (1987), "Whiskey, If You Were A Woman" (1987); and #1s "Cry, Cry, Cry" (1988), "(Do You Love Me) Just Say Yes" (1988), and "Who's Lonely Now" (1989). Despite ACM and CMA awards, the group suffered, as many put-together acts will, from personality and creative differences. Carlson left the group for a solo career at the end of 1990, and was replaced by Nikki Nelson, who sang lead on the group's catchiest hit to date, the sparkling pop ditty "Bing Bang Boom" in 1991.

Awards

GOLD AND PLATINUM RECORDS
"The Touch" G/A Alabama / RCA
"The Touch" P/A Alabama / RCA
"Greatest Hits" P/A Patsy Cline / MCA
"Sweet Dreams (Soundtrack)" G/A Patsy Cline / MCA
"Heartland" G/A The Judds / RCA
"Greatest Hits" G/A Reba McEntire / MCA
"What Am I Gonna Do About You" G/A Reba McEntire / MCA
"Whoever's In New England" G/A Reba McEntire / MCA
"Christmas Wishes" P/A Anne Murray / Capitol
"Country" G/A Anne Murray / Capitol
"Greatest Hits" 3M/A Anne Murray / Capitol
"New Kind Of Feeling" P/A Anne Murray / Capitol
"Something To Talk About" G/A Anne Murray / Capitol
"Half Nelson" G/A Willie Nelson / Columbia
"Trio" G/A Dolly Parton, Linda Ronstadt, and Emmylou Harris / Warner Brothers
"Trio" P/A Dolly Parton, Linda Ronstadt, and Emmylou Harris / Warner Brothers
"Won't Be Blue Anymore" G/A Dan Seals / EMI
"He Thinks He's Ray Stevens" G/A Ray Stevens / MCA
"George Strait's Greatest Hits" P/A George Strait / MCA
"Greatest Hits Vol. II" G/A George Strait / MCA
"Ocean Front Property" G/A George Strait / MCA
"Ocean Front Property" P/A George Strait / MCA
"Strait From The Heart" G/A George Strait / MCA
"Always & Forever" G/A Randy Travis / Warner Brothers

"Always & Forever" P/A Randy Travis / Warner Brothers
"Storms Of Life" P/A Randy Travis / Warner Brothers
"Hank Live" G/A Hank Williams Jr. / Curb/Warner Brothers
"Born To Boogie" G/A Hank Williams Jr. / Curb/Warner Brothers
"Guitars, Cadillacs, Etc., Etc." G/A Dwight Yoakam / Reprise
"Hillbilly Deluxe" G/A Dwight Yoakam / Reprise

GOLD AND PLATINUM MUSIC VIDEOS
There were no gold or platinum certifications for country video in 1987.

GRAMMYS
BEST COUNTRY VOCAL PERFORMANCE, FEMALE—"'80s Ladies" track from "'80s Ladies" album K.T. Oslin
BEST COUNTRY VOCAL PERFORMANCE, MALE—"Always & Forever" album Randy Travis
BEST COUNTRY PERFORMANCE, DUO OR GROUP WITH VOCAL—"Trio" album Dolly Parton, Linda Ronstadt, and Emmylou Harris
BEST COUNTRY PERFORMANCE, DUET—"Make No Mistake, She's Mine" single Ronnie Milsap and Kenny Rogers
BEST COUNTRY INSTRUMENTAL PERFORMANCE (ORCHESTRA, GROUP OR SOLOIST)—"String Of Pars" track from "10" Asleep At The Wheel

The Grammy-winning "Trio" ensemble: Linda Ronstadt, Emmylou Harris, and Dolly Parton.
credit: Photo by Alan Mayor

BEST COUNTRY SONG—"Forever And Ever, Amen" Paul Overstreet and Don Schlitz, writers

BEST ALBUM PACKAGE (NC)—"King's Record Shop" Rosanne Cash, artist; Bill Johnson, art director

COUNTRY MUSIC ASSOCIATION AWARDS

ENTERTAINER OF THE YEAR—Hank Williams Jr.

FEMALE VOCALIST—Reba McEntire

MALE VOCALIST—Randy Travis

SONG OF THE YEAR—"Forever and Ever, Amen" Paul Overstreet and Don Schiltz

SINGLE OF THE YEAR—"Forever and Ever, Amen" Randy Travis

ALBUM OF THE YEAR—"Always and Forever" Randy Travis

VOCAL DUO OF THE YEAR—Ricky Skaggs and Sharon White

VOCAL GROUP OF THE YEAR—The Judds

INSTRUMENTALIST OF THE YEAR—Johnny Gimble

HORIZON AWARD—Holly Dunn

MUSIC VIDEO OF THE YEAR—*My Name Is Bocephus* Hank Williams Jr.

ACADEMY OF COUNTRY MUSIC AWARDS

SONG OF THE YEAR—"Forever and Ever, Amen" Don Schlitz and Paul Overstreet, writers

SINGLE RECORD OF THE YEAR—"Forever and Ever, Amen" Randy Travis, artist

ALBUM OF THE YEAR—"Trio" Emmylou Harris, Dolly Parton, and Linda Ronstadt

ENTERTAINER—Hank Williams Jr.

MALE VOCALIST—Randy Travis

FEMALE VOCALIST—Reba McEntire

VOCAL GROUP—Highway 101

VOCAL DUET—The Judds

NEW MALE VOCALIST—Ricky Van Shelton

NEW FEMALE VOCALIST—K.T. Oslin

TOURING BAND—The Strangers

NON-TOURING BAND (CLUB)—Nashville Now band

DISC JOCKEY—Jim Tabor WMC, Memphis, TN

RADIO STATION—KNIX, Tempe, AZ

CLUB—Crazy Horse Steak House & Saloon

PIONEER AWARD—Roger Miller

VIDEO OF THE YEAR—*'80s Ladies* K.T. Oslin

INSTRUMENTALISTS: fiddle, Johnny Gimble; keyboard, (tie) John Hobbs/Ronnie Milsap; bass, (tie) David Hungate/Emory Gordy Jr.; drums, Archie Francis; guitar, Chet Atkins; steel guitar, J.D. Maness; mandolin, Ricky Skaggs; dobro, Jerry Douglas

Milestones

- "Grand Ole Opry" regular Skeeter Davis, who tours and records the previous year with quintessential '70s New York bar band NRBQ, marries NRBQ band member Joey Spampinato January 27.
- Wendy Holcomb, 23, winsome banjoist who became a national sweetheart with an appearance at 12 years old on the Sunday morning children's TV show "Big Blue Marble," dies February 14 of a heart disorder that had forced her early retirement three years before.
- Kathy Mattea and songwriter Jon Vezner ("Where've You Been") marry in Nashville on February 14, Valentine's Day.
- June Carter Cash's second book of family and career memories, *From The Heart*, is published. The first was *Among My Klediments*, a religiously-framed biography published in 1979.
- Boudleaux Bryant, 67, dies June 25 in Knoxville, Tennessee of cancer. Bryant and wife Felice moved to Nashville in the early '50s and became the city's first full-time professional commercial country songwriters. Bryant wrote such hits as "Devoted To You," "All I Have To Do Is Dream," "Love Hurts," and "Let's Think About Living." With his wife he wrote "Bye Bye Love," "Wake Up Little Susie," "Hey Joe," and "Rocky Top."
- Years of bottled up personality and creative differences between Oak Ridge Boys Duane Allen and William Lee Golden result in Golden leaving the group. He is replaced with Steve Sanders, a member of the group's band.
- Kenny Price, 56, singer and "Hee Haw" comedian, dies August 4 of heart disease in Florence, Kentucky.
- Archie Campbell, 72, "Grand Ole Opry" comedian and '60s comedy recording star, dies August 29 following a heart attack in Knoxville, Tennessee. Campbell started his career on Knoxville radio in 1936, and was instrumental in developing the "Catskills in the Smokies" country entertainment theater strip in Pigeon Forge, Tennessee.
- Obie Burnett "O.B." McClinton, 45, dies of cancer September 23 in Nashville. A talented, but never-quite-successful, black country singer, he dubbed himself "The Chocolate Cowboy."
- H.W. "Pappy" Daily, 85, pioneering honky-tonk-era Texas record distributor and founder of Starday Records dies December 5. Daily had been involved in the careers of George Jones, Melba Montgomery, the Big Bopper, Hank Lochlin, Webb Pierce and others.

Two years before, the CMA seemed to be making a peace gesture to Hank Williams Jr. by honoring his *All My Rowdy Friends Are Coming Over Tonight* with its Video of the Year Award. "I make a little audio, too," he quipped as he accepted the award which, after all, really went to the filmmaker. Hank had a rowdy image that the CMA didn't like. In truth, however, he didn't do much that many country artists hadn't done or didn't still do, he just did it openly, proudly, as a flag of his identity. He drew a crowd that was younger, drunker, and less polite than the "Opry" crowd, as well. So, when it came to awards time, despite his artistic achievements and his enormous body of gold records and record-setting concert grosses, the CMA pretended that Hank Williams Jr. didn't exist.

Some say it was the Academy of Country Music's recognition, six months earlier, of Williams as best entertainer that triggered the CMA's about-face in 1987, crowning Williams as Entertainer of the Year. Others say Williams finally promised to stop bad-mouthing everyone at the "Opry" for firing his father and to become a promoter of country music in general. Of course, with more than half a dozen LPs on the Top 50 chart at one time in the decade, overlooking him was getting a little ridiculous, and everybody knew it. In 1987, Williams was at his absolute apex, or maybe even a little past it, but giving him his due for his accomplishments, if not his personal life, was long overdue. Whatever the reasons, Hank Williams Jr. got his official kudos in 1987.

Williams, of course, was hardly humble about it, but he managed not to alienate the country music establishment over the next 12 months and was again given the Entertainer of the Year awards from the CMA and ACM in 1988.

Then, like all who reached those peaks before him, he was overtaken by another shining star whose day had come. His show, for more than a decade a taut, dynamic, sweaty three-part marathon, cooled off in the early 1990s. His 1992 Budweiser-sponsored mega tour opened in Memphis with a flabby performance that was long on bluff and bravado and short on musical commitment.

Like Elvis in his later years, Hank had reached the point where he was no longer young enough or interested enough to rock all night. Also like Elvis, Hank Jr. must have realized that the fans would always respond to the stock declarations and moves, the few legend-invoking songs, and celebrate simply being in the same room with a legend, even if that legend seemed more than a little drunk and less than enthusiastic in his performance.

Hank Williams Jr.
credit: Photo by Beth Gwinn

Figuring there was no advantage to clouding the issue, Patty Loveless, born Patricia Ramey, daughter of a coal miner in Pikeville, Kentucky, never made much of the fact that she was Loretta Lynn's cousin. Like her famous cousin, she got a start in Nashville by writing for the Wilburn Brothers, but she turned to a Top 40 copy band to earn a living. Inspired by The Judds and other new country artists, Loveless turned once again to country music in her mid-20s. After three years of struggling, her East Kentucky roots came through early in 1988 when she revived a stone country number that had been a minor George Jones hit in 1967, "If My Heart Had Windows." Ever since cracking the Top 10, she has been piling up one hit after another.

1988

HEART WITH WINDOWS

Patty Loveless.
credit: Photo by Alan Mayor

Most Important Records

"Eighteen Wheels and a Dozen Roses" Kathy Mattea / Mercury
"I Told You So" Randy Travis / Warner Brothers
"I'll Leave This World Loving You" Ricky Van Shelton / Columbia
"When You Say Nothing At All" Keith Whitley / RCA
"Addicted" Dan Seals / Capitol
"Turn It Loose" The Judds / RCA
"I'll Always Come Back" K.T. Oslin / RCA
"Streets of Bakersfield" Dwight Yoakam and Buck Owens / Reprise
"Bluest Eyes In Texas" Restless Heart / RCA
"Life Turned Her That Way" Ricky Van Shelton / Columbia

Debut Artist: k.d. lang

Like poet e.e. cummings, Alberta native Kathy Dawn Lang spells her name in lowercase. Though she had sung a Grammy-winning movie soundtrack duet with Roy Orbison ("Crying") the year before, her country chart debut, "I'm Down To My Last Cigarette," came in May of 1988. Flamboyantly rollicking around in a country repertoire, she attracted a hip, young audience that didn't really care for mainstream country. Her irrepressible style was grouped with such difficult to define artists of the time as Rosie Flores, Dwight Yoakam, and Lyle Lovett as "cowpunk," or worse yet, in lang's case, "Canadian cowpunk." Dressed and coiffed like a man, she was never particularly well received in Nashville, and the establishment essentially considered it a slap in the face when NARAS awarded lang a Grammy as best female country singer in 1989. When she joined with Nashville's legendary producer Owen Bradley to pay tribute to Patsy Cline with the "Absolute Torch and Twang" album, the establishment finally came to respect her.

Awards

GOLD AND PLATINUM RECORDS
"Alabama Live" G/A Alabama / RCA
"Just Us" G/A Alabama / RCA
"Quarter Moon In A Ten Cent Town" G/A Emmylou Harris / Warner Brothers
"The Judds Greatest Hits" G/A The Judds / RCA
"Reba" G/A Reba McEntire / MCA
"The Last One To Know" G/A Reba McEntire / MCA
"'80s Ladies" G/A K.T. Oslin / RCA
"This Woman" G/A K.T. Oslin / RCA
"Aloha From Hawaii Via Satellite" P/A Elvis Presley / RCA
"Aloha From Hawaii Via Satellite" 2M/A Elvis Presley / RCA

"Elvis As Recorded At Madison Square Garden" P/A Elvis Presley / RCA

"Elvis Sings The Wonderful World Of Christmas" 2M/A Elvis Presley / RCA

"Elvis' Golden Records" P/A Elvis Presley / RCA

"Pure Gold" P/A Elvis Presley / RCA

"Roustabout" G/A Elvis Presley / RCA

"Wheels" G/A Restless Heart / RCA

"Loving Proof" G/A Ricky Van Shelton / Columbia

"Wild-Eyed Dream" G/A Ricky Van Shelton / Columbia

"Greatest Hits Vol. II" P/A George Strait / MCA

"If You Ain't Lovin' (You Ain't Livin')" G/A George Strait / MCA

"Strait Country" G/A George Strait / MCA

"Forever & Always" 3M/A Randy Travis / Warner Brothers

"Old 8 x 10" G/A Randy Travis / Warner Brothers

"Old 8 x 10" P/A Randy Travis / Warner Brothers

"Storms Of Life" 2M/A Randy Travis / Warner Brothers

"Conway Twitty's Greatest Hits Vol. II" G/A Conway Twitty / MCA

"Number Ones" G/A Conway Twitty / MCA

"The Very Best Of" G/A Conway Twitty and Loretta Lynn / MCA

"We Only Make Believe" G/A Conway Twitty and Loretta Lynn / MCA

"Born To Boogie" P/A Hank Williams Jr. / Curb/Warner Brothers

"Hank Williams Jr.'s Greatest Hits" 2M/A Hank Williams Jr. / Curb/Warner Brothers

"Wild Streak" G/A Hank Williams Jr. / Curb/Warner Brothers

GOLD AND PLATINUM MUSIC VIDEOS
George Strait
"George Strait Live" Gold
MCA Home Video
MCA Records

GRAMMYS
BEST COUNTRY VOCAL PERFORMANCE, FEMALE—"Hold Me" track from "This Woman" K.T. Oslin

BEST COUNTRY VOCAL PERFORMANCE, MALE—"Old 8 x 10" album Randy Travis

BEST COUNTRY PERFORMANCE, DUO OR GROUP WITH VOCAL—"Give A Little Love" track from "Greatest Hits" The Judds

BEST COUNTRY VOCAL COLLABORATION—"Crying" single Roy Orbison and k.d. lang

BEST COUNTRY INSTRUMENTAL PERFORMANCE (ORCHESTRA, GROUP OR SOLOIST)—"Sugarfoot Rag" track from "Western Standard Time" Asleep At The Wheel

BEST BLUEGRASS RECORDING (VOCAL OR INSTRUMENTAL)—"Southern Flavor" album Bill Monroe

BEST COUNTRY SONG—"Hold Me" K.T. Oslin, writer

COUNTRY MUSIC ASSOCIATION AWARDS

ENTERTAINER OF THE YEAR—Hank Williams Jr.

FEMALE VOCALIST—K.T. Oslin

MALE VOCALIST—Randy Travis

SONG OF THE YEAR—"'80s Ladies" K.T. Oslin

SINGLE OF THE YEAR—"Eighteen Wheels and a Dozen Roses" Kathy Mattea

ALBUM OF THE YEAR—"Born To Boogie" Hank Williams Jr.

VOCAL EVENT OF THE YEAR—"Trio" Emmylou Harris, Dolly Parton, and Linda Ronstadt

VOCAL DUO OF THE YEAR—The Judds

VOCAL GROUP OF THE YEAR—Highway 101

MUSICIAN OF THE YEAR—Chet Atkins

HORIZON AWARD—Ricky Van Shelton

MUSIC VIDEO OF THE YEAR—No winner

ACADEMY OF COUNTRY MUSIC AWARDS

SONG OF THE YEAR—"Eighteen Wheels and a Dozen Roses" Paul Nelson and Gene Nelson, writers

SINGLE RECORD OF THE YEAR—"Eighteen Wheels and a Dozen Roses" Kathy Mattea, artist

ALBUM OF THE YEAR—"This Woman" K.T. Oslin

ENTERTAINER—Hank Williams Jr.

MALE VOCALIST—George Strait

FEMALE VOCALIST—K.T. Oslin

VOCAL GROUP—Highway 101

VOCAL DUET—The Judds

NEW MALE VOCALIST—Rodney Crowell

NEW FEMALE VOCALIST—Suzy Bogguss

TOURING BAND—Desert Rose Band

NON-TOURING BAND—Nashville Now Band

DISC JOCKEY—(tie) Dandalion/Jon Conlon

RADIO STATION—WSIX, Nashville, TN

CLUB—Crazy Horse Steak House & Saloon

PIONEER AWARD—Buck Owens

VIDEO OF THE YEAR—*Young Country* Hank Williams Jr.

INSTRUMENTALISTS: fiddle, Mark O'Connor; keyboard, John Hobbs; bass, Curtis Stone; drums, Steve Duncan; guitar, Al Bruno; steel guitar, J.D. Maness

Milestones

Riders in the Sky.
credit: Courtesy of Riders in the Sky

- John Dopyera, 94, dies January 3 at Grand Pass, Oregon. Dopyera invented the Dobro guitar in 1925, manufactured in partnership with his brothers. The instrument takes its name from Dopyera Brothers, the company moniker.
- The Western trio Riders in the Sky debut *Riders Radio Theater*, a syndicated radio program in a style combining Gene Autry's "Melody Ranch" program with comedic versions of

the weekly B-movie serials of the '30s. In 1993, the show was being carried on 171 stations around the nation.

- Sidney "Fiddlin' Sid" Harkreader, 90, dies March 19 in Nashville. Harkreader started his career in 1921, and shortly thereafter became Uncle Dave Mason's first sideman. In all likelihood, he was the first man to play country music on Nashville radio, performing on the city's first station, WDAD, when it opened in 1921. He was a regular on the WSM "Barn Dance" and the "Grand Ole Opry" from 1926 on, performing on the Opry the week before he died.

- On May 21, a generation of new country stars headline the bill at a jam-packed Madison Square Garden in New York. The performers are Alabama, Randy Travis, George Strait and the Judds.

- Herman Crook, 89, the last living link to the original "Grand Ole Opry" cast, dies June 10. He played harmonica with the Crook Brothers, the last old-time stringband on the Opry.

- Jo-El Sonnier has a Top 10 hit with "Tear Stained Letter," reasserting the appeal of Cajun patois and zydeco accordion to the country music audience that hadn't heard it since Doug and Rusty Kershaw in the 1960s. The tune's popularity brought Doug Kershaw out later in the year in a duet called "Cajun Baby" with Hank Williams Jr.

- Pete Drake, 55, writer, publisher and influential steel guitar player, dies July 29 in Nashville. Particularly influential in his liaison with the rock titans of the '60s and '70s, he played steel for George Harrison's "All Things Must Pass" album and on Bob Dylan's milestone country-folk album "Nashville Skyline."

- Leon McAuliffe, 71, dies August 20 in Tulsa, Oklahoma. He personified Western swing steel guitar and vocals, leaving the Light Crust Doughboys in 1935 to join Bob Wills' Texas Playboys. McAuliffe wrote "Steel Guitar Rag" and co-wrote "San Antonio Rose" with Wills. He left Wills' ensemble in 1942 and continued to lead his own bands into the '80s.

- Nat Stucky, 54, singer and songwriter, dies August 24 in Nashville of cancer. Among his compositions was the Buck Owen's hit, "Waitin' In Your Welfare Line."

- Garth Brooks signs with Capitol Records in mid-September.

- A fantasy movie about Elvis Presley, *Heartbreak Hotel*, premieres in Nashville September 21 staring David Keith, with Elvis' vocals dubbed by Ronnie McDowell. The film is critically acclaimed.

- On November 14, Mel Tillis loses his $2 million, 6,000-piece log home in rural Tennessee in a fire that originates in a pan of burning pork chops.

- Roy Orbison, 52, dies December 6 at his home in Hendersonville, Tennessee of a heart attack. At the time of his death he was being widely lionized for his early country-rockabilly music in an all-star TV special, and was involved in several successful rock music projects, including his contribution as a member of the Travelling Wilburys.

Keith Whitley: Close to the Edge

As 1988 wound to a close, 32-year-old Sandy Hook, Kentucky, native Keith Whitley seemed to have life by the tail. He was on the verge of becoming a country star at last—or falling victim to a private hell few people knew about. It could have gone either way, and in less than six months the issue would be settled once and for all.

Reared in a musical corner of East Kentucky, he had grown up on bluegrass music. He'd made his first appearance on radio with Buddy Starcher when he was 8, and at 13 he and Ricky Skaggs started a band called the East Kentucky Mountain Boys. At 15, they were hired together into

Ralph Stanley's Clinch Mountain Boys, where Whitley remained after Skaggs moved on. Whitley recorded with traditionalist bluegrass bands New Tradition, Country Store, and J.D. Crowe and New South. But money was hard to come by playing festivals on the lower East Coast, so Whitley migrated to Nashville. He wooed and wed Lorrie Morgan, the daughter of the late "Grand Ole Opry" regular George Morgan in 1986. Neither of them had much going for them at the time, though Whitley had already been recording for a couple of years for RCA Records. Whitley did score a pair of Top 10 records that year, however, with "Ten Feet Away"

and "Homecoming '63."

The year 1988 saw his records, "Don't Close Your Eyes" and "When You Say Nothing At All," break through to #1. He was just starting to establish the face with the voice among fans when his worst weakness did him in. Whitley was a binge drinker. When he drank, he drank vast quantities as fast as he could. At home alone one afternoon, he drank a whole lot of something, presumably moonshine, although the bottle was never found. It paralyzed Whitley and stopped his heart. His death was tragic, ending the life of a talented baritone and traditionalist who in 1988 stood on the brink of greatness.

Keith Whitley, Lorrie Morgan, her daughter by a previous marriage and their newborn baby.
credit: Photo by Alan Mayor

Travis Tritt and Marty Stuart.
credit: Photo by Alan Mayor

Travis Tritt worked hard for six years on the small-time night-club circuit before coming to Nashville, but things moved fairly quickly after that. The son of a Georgia laborer, he was a long-haired, blue-collar electric Southern boogie fan who longed to, as one of his later songs put it, put some drive in his country. His signing with Warner Brothers Records on the first try and the Top 10 hit in 1989 with "Country Club," his first release, sounds deceptively easy. But, in fact, he was a long shot from the get-go. His producer, Greg Brown, had no track record: He was just an ambitious guy from the Warner Brothers mailroom. Brown and Tritt were the would-be producer and would-be artist in the unenviable position of having to deliver the goods early or not at all. Tritt came through. "Country Club," a Conway Twitty-style novelty number, soon became the theme song for countless country radio station giveaway promotions. He followed his initial success with more serious music, on his own and with honky-tonk soulmate Marty Stuart. No pretty boy popster, the leather-clad Tritt infuses his music with an edgy intensity, creating a Southern-style, in-your-face kind of country music for the 1990s.

Most Important Records

"Is It Still Over" Randy Travis / Warner Brothers
"Two Dozen Roses" Shenandoah / Columbia
"Better Man" Clint Black / RCA
"Killin' Time" Clint Black / RCA
"The Church On The Cumberland Road" Shenandoah / Columbia
"I'm No Stranger To The Rain" Keith Whitley / RCA
"A Woman In Love" Ronnie Milsap / RCA
"Young Love" The Judds / RCA
"If Tomorrow Never Comes" Garth Brooks / Capitol
"From A Jack To A King" Ricky Van Shelton / Columbia

Clint Black and Roy Rogers.
credit: Photo by Alan Mayor

Debut Artist: Clint Black

Houston-reared club singer Clint Black made high marks in 1989, when his debut single, "Better Man," topped the charts, followed by the equally successful "Killin' Time." Certainly, it helps when you have both talent and a lot of money behind you. Black had hooked up with Z.Z. Top's manager, Bill Hamm, who reportedly put $1 million on the table to match RCA's efforts in breaking this smooth-voiced cowboy. It worked. Artists usually have to struggle for several years before they build enough career momentum to earn the CMA's Horizon Award, but Black did it in his freshman year.

Awards

GOLD AND PLATINUM RECORDS
"40 Hour Week" 2M/A Alabama / RCA
"Alabama's Greatest Hits" 3M/A Alabama / RCA
"Roll On" 3M/A Alabama / RCA
"Southern Star" G/A Alabama / RCA
"Killin' Time" G/A Clint Black / RCA
"Greatest Hits" 2M/A Patsy Cline / MCA
"A Decade Of Hits" P/A Charlie Daniels Band / Epic

"The Devil Went Down To Georgia" P/S Charlie Daniels Band / Epic
"His Epic—The First Eleven—To Be Continued" G/A Merle Haggard / Epic
"Christmas Time With The Judds" G/A The Judds / RCA
"Heartland" P/A The Judds / RCA
"River Of Time" G/A The Judds / RCA
"The Judds Greatest Hits" P/A The Judds / RCA
"Greatest Hits" P/A Reba McEntire / MCA
"Sweet Sixteen" G/A Reba McEntire / MCA
"Pretty Paper" P/A Willie Nelson / Columbia
"Take It To The Limit" G/A Willie Nelson / Columbia
"In Dreams: Greatest Hits" G/A Roy Orbison / Virgin
"Mystery Girl" G/A Roy Orbison / Virgin
"Mystery Girl" P/A Roy Orbison / Virgin
"'80's Ladies" P/A K.T. Oslin / RCA
"This Woman" P/A K.T. Oslin / RCA
"Greatest Hits Vol. II" G/A Johnny Paycheck / Epic
"Once Upon A Christmas" 2M/A Kenny Rogers and Dolly Parton / RCA
"Loving Proof" P/A Ricky Van Shelton / Columbia
"Wild-Eyed Dream" P/A Ricky Van Shelton / Columbia
"I Have Returned" G/A Ray Stevens / MCA
"Beyond The Blue Neon" G/A George Strait / MCA
"No Holdin' Back" G/A Randy Travis / Warner Brothers
"Greatest Hits III" G/A Hank Williams Jr. / Curb/Warner Brothers
"Greatest Hits III" P/A Hank Williams Jr. / Curb/Warner Brothers
"Tammy's Greatest Hits" P/A Tammy Wynette / Epic
"Buenas Noches From A Lonely Room" G/A Dwight Yoakam / Reprise
"Guitars, Cadillacs, Etc., Etc." P/A Dwight Yoakam / Reprise

GOLD AND PLATINUM MUSIC VIDEOS
The Judds
"Heartland" Gold
MPI Home Video
Tall Pony Productions

George Strait
"George Strait Live" Platinum
MCA Home Video
MCA Records

GRAMMYS
BEST COUNTRY VOCAL PERFORMANCE, FEMALE—"Absolute Torch And Twang" album k.d. lang
BEST COUNTRY VOCAL PERFORMANCE, MALE—"Lyle Lovett and His Large Band" album Lyle Lovett
BEST COUNTRY PERFORMANCE, DUO OR GROUP WITH VOCAL—"Will The

Circle Be Unbroken, Volume Two" album The Nitty Gritty Dirt Band

BEST COUNTRY VOCAL COLLABORATION—"There's A Tear In My Beer" single Hank Williams Sr. and Hank Williams Jr.

BEST COUNTRY INSTRUMENTAL PERFORMANCE (ORCHESTRA, GROUP OR SOLOIST)—"Amazing Grace" track from "Will The Circle Be Unbroken, Volume Two" Randy Scruggs

BEST BLUEGRASS RECORDING—"The Valley Road" track from "Will The Circle Be Unbroken, Volume Two" Bruce Hornsby and The Nitty Gritty Dirt Band

BEST COUNTRY SONG—"After All This Time" Rodney Crowell, writer

RECORD OF THE YEAR (NC)—"Wind Beneath My Wings" Bette Midler; Arif Mardin, producer (The tune, written by Music Row tunesmiths Larry Henley & Jeff Silbar, had originally been a # 1 country hit for Gary Morris)

SONG OF THE YEAR (NC)—"Wind Beneath My Wings" Larry Henley and Jeff Silbar, writers (noted because it was a country hit for Gary Morris in 1983)

COUNTRY MUSIC ASSOCIATION AWARDS

ENTERTAINER OF THE YEAR—George Strait

FEMALE VOCALIST—Kathy Mattea

MALE VOCALIST—Ricky Van Shelton

SONG OF THE YEAR—"Chiseled In Stone" Max D. Barnes and Vern Gosden

SINGLE OF THE YEAR—"I'm No Stranger To The Rain" Keith Whitley

ALBUM OF THE YEAR—"Will The Circle Be Unbroken, Volume Two" Nitty Gritty Dirt Band

VOCAL EVENT OF THE YEAR—Hank Williams Sr. and Hank Williams Jr.

VOCAL DUO OF THE YEAR—The Judds

VOCAL GROUP OF THE YEAR—Highway 101

MUSICIAN OF THE YEAR—Johnny Gimble

HORIZON AWARD—Clint Black

MUSIC VIDEO OF THE YEAR—*There's a Tear In My Beer* Hank Williams Sr. and Hank Williams Jr.

ACADEMY OF COUNTRY MUSIC AWARDS

SONG OF THE YEAR—"Where've You Been" Jon Vezner and Don Henry, writers

SINGLE RECORD OF THE YEAR—"Better Man" Clint Black, artist

ALBUM OF THE YEAR—"Killin' Time" Clint Black

ENTERTAINER—George Strait

MALE VOCALIST—Clint Black

FEMALE VOCALIST—Kathy Mattea

VOCAL GROUP—Restless Heart

VOCAL DUET—The Judds

NEW VOCAL DUET OR GROUP—Kentucky HeadHunters

NEW MALE VOCALIST—Clint Black

NEW FEMALE VOCALIST—Mary-Chapin Carpenter

TOURING BAND—Desert Rose Band

NON-TOURING BAND—Nashville Now Band

DISC JOCKEY—Jon Conlon

RADIO STATION—WSIX, Nashville, TN

CLUB—Crazy Horse Steak House & Saloon

VIDEO OF THE YEAR—*There's A Tear In My Beer* Hank Williams Sr. and Hank Williams Jr.

INSTRUMENTALISTS: fiddle, Mark O'Connor; keyboard, Skip Edwards; bass, Michael Rhodes; drums, Steve Duncan; guitar, Brent Rowan; steel guitar, J.D. Maness

Milestones

- Hank Williams Jr. locates a kinescope (early form of video) of what is reputed to be the last Hank Williams Sr. performance not yet issued on record, overdubs additional instrumentation and his own voice, and produces the video of the year, *There's A Tear In My Beer.*

- Jethro Burns, 69, dies of cancer in Evanston, Illinois February 4. Deadpan comic and accomplished mandolin player, Burns was partner with Homer Haynes in the Homer and Jethro comedy team. The duo won a Grammy in 1959 for "The Battle of Kookamonga," a take off on Johnny Horton's "Battle of New Orleans."

- The Country Music Foundation issues a special historic collection "Get Hot or Go Home: Vintage RCA Rockabilly 1956–1959." The collection includes performances by Pee Wee King, Martha Carson and Roy Orbison.

- Stuart Hamblen, 80, dies in Santa Monica, California on February 28 following surgery for a brain tumor. Hamblen was a mainstream West Coast country singer in the early '30s who, in 1934, became one of the first country signees to Decca America. In the early '50s, he turned his attention and talents to gospel music, writing classic country gospel tunes "This Old House" and "What God Can Do."

- The Nitty Gritty Dirt Band coordinate sessions for "Will The Circle Be Unbroken, Volume II," a followup to the popular 1972 original.

- Clyde Moody, 73, dies in Nashville April 7 after a long illness. Nicknamed "The Hillbilly Waltz King," Moody had a 1940s million-seller, "Shenandoah Waltz." He was a former member of the "Grand Ole Opry," "The New Dominion Barn Dance," Mainer's Mountaineers, and Bill Monroe's Blue Grass Boys.

- Keith Whitley, 33, RCA recording artist and husband of Lorrie Morgan, dies on May 9 of an accidental alcohol overdose at the couple's home in Nashville. Ironically, his single, "I'm No Stranger To The Rain" was falling off the chart that week, just as Morgan's poignant "Dear Me" was on the rise.

New traditionalists gave new life to the classic sounds of honky-tonk country through the 1980s, but generally the new artists put a hip spin on the sound, updating it with a wink. Not Randy Travis. His earnest charisma was gentle, but pool hall sexy, his countenance small-town simple, so hard-looking that he was handsome. His baritone could twist with classic nasal whine around George Jones' style or dip into bass to cover Brook Benton's "It's Just a Matter of Time." When he sang straight ahead country, there wasn't a trace of recreation of older styles. Randy Travis *was* hardcore country, a recessive gene popping up unexpectedly to reinvigorate the genre.

His story starts as a post-World War II country epic about the Traywick brothers, juvenile delinquent sons of Marshville, North Carolina's, most explosive bully. Randy and one of his brothers were in trouble for drugs and joyriding other people's cars before Randy was old enough to be tried as an adult. That his brother was barely old enough to do time broke up the brothers' musical act and put young Randy in the house of Lib Hatcher, the older woman who promised to keep him out of trouble, if not her bed.

Leaving her husband to move to Nashville with the youngster, Hatcher believed in Travis' talents. She wound up managing the Nashville Palace nightclub, with Randy working in the kitchen and occasionally coming out to sing in the main room, where the club owner let "Opry" "stars" run long dinner tabs. She saved enough money to bankroll a custom "live" album for him, recorded in the club, and sold as *Randy Traywick Live at the Nashville Palace*. It was incredible.

Travis' debut single, "On The Other Hand," stiffed, but was reissued for a #1 following "1982." His first album for Warner Brothers, *Storms of Life*, sold more than 1 million copies in 1986—almost as fast as the label could manufacture them. Never prone to cowboy hats or Las Vegas glitz, Travis put the hardcore ambience missing for so long in commercial country music on a brand new pedestal.

Rarely has an artist's over-protective lover proved to be an effective manager, but Hatcher's handling of Travis' talent and career has earned her more credit than she is generally given. The relationship was not publicly acknowledged for the first six years of Travis' career. Travis and Hatcher married in 1991.

Randy Travis.
credit: Photo by Donnie Beauchamp, Courtesy the Grand Ole Opry

- Signaling an end to a nearly 30-year era, Capitol Records becomes the first country label to discontinue selling 7-inch vinyl disks, except for promotional copies, while MCA Nashville drops the 12-inch vinyl album in favor of cassette and CD configurations. Within a year, no hit country singles are available in 45 rpm single format, and 33⅓ rpm "record albums" are difficult to find.

- Reba McEntire marries Narvel Blackstock, her personal manager, June 3 in Lake Tahoe, Nevada.

- Bradley Kincaid, 94, dies September 23 in a nursing home in Springfield, Ohio. The early "WLS Barn Dance" star was a pioneer commercial artist/folk song collector, sticking to the genuine folk tunes of his native East Kentucky. His long career included successful recordings and concerts, largely built on the fame he engendered as a radio performer and songbook seller.

- Barry Sadler, 49, composer and artist who made "The Ballad of The Green Berets" famous during the Vietnam War, dies of heart failure in Murfreesboro, Tennessee, October 31. Sadler had suffered a debilitating head wound while training Contra rebels in Central America the previous year.

- Connie B. Gay, 75, dies December 4 in McLean, Virginia, a suburb of Washington, D.C. Gay was a pioneer in getting country acts on network television, and in promoting country package shows in major East Coast cities in the 1940s and 1950s.

Garth Brooks.
credit: photo by Donnie
Beauchamp; Courtesy of The
Grand Ole Opry

THE 1990S

Garth Brooks hit the country music scene like he once hit the high school football field—playing for keeps, with an intensity that roiled beneath the surface, just barely contained. Brooks and Clint Black were born a few days apart, got their record debuts a few days apart, and were compared to each other repeatedly in 1989. Brooks' success built more slowly, but while Black peaked in 1990, Brooks just kept on getting bigger. His rise in popularity coincided with major changes in *Billboard*'s chart methodology, which put him at the top of the Hot 100 pop charts as well as atop the country lists, bringing national media attention he might not have gotten had he only been noticed by the country press. Alabama, in their prime, had broken the three million album sales mark, but Brooks sold more than nine million units for each of his first two albums, "Garth Brooks" and "Ropin' The Wind." If Brooks had one creative peak, it was the rollicking, "devil-may-care," concert version of "Friends In Low Places." As unrestrained and singable as the '60s pop hit "Bottle of Wine," this record was proof that a country record could dominate the entire American music field and generate sales figures like Michael Jackson and other pop icons.

Most Important Records

"Friends In Low Places" Garth Brooks / Capitol
"Where've You Been" Kathy Mattea / Mercury

"Hard Rock Bottom Of Your Heart" Randy Travis / WB
"I've Come To Expect It From You" George Strait / MCA
"Love Without End, Amen" George Strait / MCA
"Nobody's Home" Clint Black / RCA
"Come Next Monday" K.T. Oslin / RCA
"Next To You, Next To Me" Shenandoah / Columbia
"The Dance" Garth Brooks / Capitol
"Love On Arrival" Dan Seals / Capitol

Debut Artist: Mary-Chapin Carpenter

Until 1990, few had infiltrated the commercial country field with challenging, literate songs—Lyle Lovett and Nanci Griffith come immediately to mind, but the country mainstream had never fully accepted them. Mary-Chapin Carpenter changed all that. When she sang her witty, gritty song about being an opening act on the CMA Awards Show, she won the hearts of millions of hardcore country fans. Here was a girl who worked hard like they did, was having trouble getting a break just like they were, and yet could laugh about it and keep on plugging away as hard as she knew how. Her music owes more to '60s pop and urban folk legends than to any particular white rural Southern folk sources. She was hip, smart, decidedly urban, emotionally accessible and genuine. Her debut record in 1990 didn't break the Top 40, but everyone stood up and noticed.

Mary-Chapin Carpenter with Wynonna Judd and Kathy Mattea at the taping of the 1993 CBS-TV special *Women of Country.*
credit: photo by Alan Mayor

Awards

GRAMMYS

BEST COUNTRY VOCAL PERFORMANCE, FEMALE—"Where've You Been" single Kathy Mattea

BEST COUNTRY VOCAL PERFORMANCE, MALE—"When I Call Your Name" single Vince Gill

BEST COUNTRY PERFORMANCE BY A DUO OR GROUP WITH VOCAL—"Pickin' On Nashville" album Kentucky HeadHunters

BEST COUNTRY VOCAL COLLABORATION—"Poor Boy Blues" single Chet Atkins & Mark Knopfler

BEST COUNTRY INSTRUMENTAL PERFORMANCE (ORCHESTRA, GROUP OR SOLOIST)—"So Soft, Your Goodbye" track from "Neck and Neck" Chet Atkins & Mark Knopfler

BEST BLUEGRASS RECORDING—"You've Got The Old Feeling" album Alison Krauss

BEST COUNTRY SONG—"Where've You Been" Jon Vezner & Don Henry, writers

GOLD & PLATINUM RECORDS

"Pass It On Down" G/A Alabama / RCA
"Killin' Time" P/A Clint Black / RCA
"Killin' Time" 2M/A Clint Black / RCA
"Garth Brooks" G/A Garth Brooks / Capitol
"Garth Brooks" P/A Garth Brooks / Capitol
"No Fences" G/A Garth Brooks / Capitol
"No Fences" P/A Garth Brooks / Capitol
"No Fences" 2M/A Garth Brooks / Capitol
"Diamonds & Dirt" G/A Rodney Crowell / Columbia
"Simple Man" G/A Charlie Daniels Band / Columbia
"When I Call Your Name" G/A Vince Gill / MCA
"Highway 101" G/A Highway 101 / Warner Brothers
"Here In The Real World" G/A Alan Jackson / Arista
"Still The Same Ole Me" G/A George Jones / Epic
"Pickin' On Nashville" G/A Kentucky HeadHunters / Mercury
"Pickin' On Nashville" P/A Kentucky HeadHunters / Mercury
"Absolute Torch & Twang" G/A k.d. lang / Sire
"Willow In The Wind" G/A Kathy Mattea / Mercury
"Reba McEntire Live" G/A Reba McEntire / MCA
"Rumor Has It" G/A Reba McEntire / MCA
"Stardust" 4M/A Willie Nelson / Columbia
"Willie & Family Live" 2M/A Willie Nelson / Columbia
"Big Dreams In A Small Town" G/A Restless Heart / RCA
"RVS III" G/A Ricky Van Shelton / Columbia
"Livin' It Up" G/A George Strait / MCA
"Merry Christmas Strait To You" G/A George Strait / MCA
"Always & Forever" 4M/A Randy Travis / Warner Brothers
"Heroes And Friends" G/A Randy Travis / Warner Brothers
"No Holdin' Back" P/A Randy Travis / Warner Brothers

"Country Club" G/A Travis Tritt / Warner Brothers
"The Very Best Of" P/A Conway Twitty / MCA
"Greatest Hits" G/A Keith Whitley / RCA
"I Wonder Do You Think Of Me" G/A Keith Whitley / RCA
"Best Of Don Williams Vol III" G/A Don Williams / MCA
"I Believe In You" P/A Don Williams / MCA
"Lone Wolf" G/A Hank Williams Jr. / Warner Brothers

GOLD & PLATINUM MUSIC VIDEOS

Alabama
"Pass It On Down" gold
RCA Records

Alabama
"Pass It On Down" platinum
RCA Records

Alabama
"Pass It On Down" multi-platinum (100,000)
RCA Records
The Judds
"Great Video Hits" gold
RCA Records

Reba McEntire
"Reba" gold
MCA Music Video

Ronnie Milsap
"Great Video Hits" gold
RCA Records

Elvis Presley
"Great Performances Vol I: Center Stage" platinum
Buena Vista Home Video

Elvis Presley
"Great Performances Vol I: Center Stage" multi-platinum
(150,000)
Buena Vista Home Video

Elvis Presley
"Great Performances Vol II: Man & Music" gold
Buena Vista Home Video

Elvis Presley
"Great Performances Vol II: Man & Music" platinum
Buena Vista Home Video

Kenny Rogers
"Great Video Hits" gold
RCA Records

Don Williams
"Don Williams Live" gold
RCA Records

Hank Williams Jr.
"Full Access" gold
Cabin Fever Entertainment
Hank Williams Jr. Enterprises

COUNTRY MUSIC ASSOCIATION AWARDS
ENTERTAINER OF THE YEAR—George Strait
FEMALE VOCALIST—Kathy Mattea
MALE VOCALIST—Clint Black
SONG OF THE YEAR—"Where've You Been" Jon Vezner & Don Henry
SINGLE OF THE YEAR—"When I Call Your Name" Vince Gill
ALBUM OF THE YEAR—"Pickin' On Nashville" Kentucky Head-Hunters
VOCAL EVENT OF THE YEAR—Lorrie Morgan & Keith Whitley
VOCAL DUO OF THE YEAR—The Judds
VOCAL GROUP OF THE YEAR—Kentucky HeadHunters
MUSICIAN OF THE YEAR—Johnny Gimble
HORIZON AWARD—Garth Brooks
MUSIC VIDEO OF THE YEAR—"The Dance" Garth Brooks

ACADEMY OF COUNTRY MUSIC AWARDS
SONG OF THE YEAR—"The Dance" Tony Arata, writer
SINGLE RECORD OF THE YEAR—"Friends In Low Places" Garth Brooks, artist
ALBUM OF THE YEAR—"No Fences" Garth Brooks
ENTERTAINER—Garth Brooks
MALE VOCALIST—Garth Brooks
FEMALE VOCALIST—Reba McEntire
VOCAL GROUP—Shenandoah
VOCAL DUET—The Judds
NEW VOCAL DUET OR GROUP—Pirates of the Mississippi
NEW MALE VOCALIST—Alan Jackson
NEW FEMALE VOCALIST—Shelby Lynn
TOURING BAND—Desert Rose Band
NON-TOURING BAND—Boy Howdy Band
DISC JOCKEY—Gerry House WSIX, Nashville
RADIO STATION—WSIX, Nashville, TN
CLUB—Crazy Horse Steak House & Saloon
PIONEER AWARD—Johnny Cash
VIDEO OF THE YEAR—"The Dance" Garth Brooks

INSTRUMENTALISTS: fiddle, Mark O'Connor; keyboard, John Hobbs; bass, Bill Bryson; drums, Steve Duncan; guitar, John Jorgenson; steel guitar, Jay Dee Maness; dobro, Jerry Douglas

Milestones

- On January 1, RCA joins the flight from vinyl, deleting 45 rpms from all promotional production.
- In February, former Georgia mechanic Doug Stone has a hit debut titled "I'd Be Better Off In A Pine Box."
- Branson, Missouri is finally recognized by the country music industry as a significant music and vacation destination. This small Ozarks village, with only 2,250 permanent residents, reports 3,638,000 tourists a year. Country artists with theaters bearing their names in Branson include Mel Tillis, Mickey Gilley, Boxcar Willie, Danny Davis, Freddy Fender, Roy Clark, and Cristy Lane.
- Wesley Rose, 72, influential Music Row leader, dies April 26 in Nashville after a lengthy illness. Rose had taken managerial control over Acuff-Rose Publications in the mid-'40s from his father, Fred Rose. He was active as a publisher, producer and executive of Hickory Records, managing the Everly Brothers through their most productive years.
- "When I Call Your Name" gives Vince Gill the star-making hit he has been waiting for since 1983.
- Ben Smathers, 62, for 32 years the leader of the "Grand Ole Opry" folk dance team the Stoney Mountain Cloggers, dies September 12 of heart failure in Nashville.
- On a rainy day in October, Naomi Judd calls an impromptu press conference at the empty old RCA building where she and daughter Wynonna had auditioned live in the early '80s. Tearfully, she reveals she has a potentially fatal liver disease and anounces her retirement, following an ambitious year-long farewell tour.
- Important new artists making their debut include Mark Chesnutt ("Too Cold At Home") and Aaron Tippin ("You've Got To Stand For Something"). *Billboard* reports that by mid-year, five of the Top 10 country albums are by artists who had debuted since 1989: Kentucky HeadHunters, Garth Brooks, Clint Black, Alan Jackson, and Travis Tritt. This influx of new blood creates a genuine boom in the country music industry that doubles aggregate product sales and elevates several country artists into dominant positions in the redefined pop and rock charts.

It was an odd lovematch: a gregarious West Virginia Italian and a quiet Minnesota songwriter. Kathy Mattea and Jon Vezner shared a love of music with a serious and emotional streak to it.

At first, Kathy avoided recording her husband's songs, though she liked them. "I didn't want people to say I was just cutting his songs because he was my husband," she explained. When Vezner and co-writer Don Henry told in a song the heart-rending story of love undimmed by old age and infirmity—the true story of Vezner's grandparents—Mattea could no longer resist.

The marriage of the husband's song and the wife's moving vocal performance made "Where've You Been" a special recording. It also propelled Mattea's "Willow In The Wind" LP to gold, helped earn her two consecutive CMA and ACM awards as female vocalist of the year, won each of them a Grammy and racked up song of the year awards from nearly every music organization.

Kathy Mattea and husband Jon Vezner.
credit: Courtesy of Kathy Mattea

There are occasionally years when the tide of new talent is impossible to miss—1991 was one of those years. To an established "new generation" of giants, such as Reba McEntire, George Strait, Alabama, Clint Black, Alan Jackson and Garth Brooks, came a flood of hot new acts that included Trisha Yearwood, Mark Chesnutt, Joe Diffie, Doug Stone, Aaron Tippin, Billy Dean, Hal Ketchum, and Brooks & Dunn. There were so many great new acts and developing acts, such as Suzy Bogguss and Marty Stuart, coming to the fore this year that the class of '92 would have a deuce of a time wedging through the crowd into the Top 10. It would take a veritible stick of dynamite like "Achy Breaky Heart" to crack the log jam of new acts at the top of the charts. You'd have to look at 1949–1952 when another generation of giants walked the land—Gene Autry, Ernest Tubb, Eddy Arnold, Hank Williams, Webb Pierce, Red Foley, and Lefty Frizzell—to find a comparable crop of new talent.

1991

A CROP OF NEW TALENT

Brooks & Dunn.
credit: photo by Alan Mayor

Alan Jackson.
credit: Photo by Donnette Engebrecht; Courtesy of The Grand Ole Opry

Most Important Records

"Don't Rock The Jukebox" Alan Jackson / Arista
"Down Home" Alabama / RCA
"You Know Me Better Than That" George Strait / MCA
"Shameless" Garth Brooks / Capitol
"Thunder Rolls" Garth Brooks / Capitol
"Brand New Man" Brooks & Dunn / Arista
"She's In Love With The Boy" Trisha Yearwood / MCA
"Meet In The Middle" Diamond Rio / Arista
"Down At The Twist And Shout" Mary-Chapin Carpenter / Columbia
"Somewhere In My Broken Heart" Billy Dean / Capitol

Debut Artist: Trisha Yearwood

Monticello, Georgia native Trisha Yearwood went to Nashville's Belmont College to study music business management, but it was her voice that got her in, not her degree. She made friends with Garth Brooks when the unknown singers met at demo sessions in Nashville in the late-'80s. Yearwood found "She's In Love With The Boy" in a pile of songs Wynonna Judd had meant to record but had never gotten around to. It not only became Yearwood's chart-topping debut, but it became BMI's Song of the Year. Twenty-eight in 1991 and suddenly a star, Yearwood was called everything from "the new Linda Ronstadt" to "the next Reba" as her debut album, "Trisha Yearwood," sold more than a million copies. Touring with her old pal Brooks gave her added prestige, though the whirlwind of public scrutiny and large stage shows created a number of problems, stemming from her inability to adapt to celebrity status. She was a fairly normal "civilian," as Music Row denizens put it, and she took criticism and innuendo personally, but she weathered the rumors and professional controversies to emerge as one of the most distinctive talents of the '90s with her second album, "Hearts In Armor."

Awards

GRAMMYS

BEST COUNTRY VOCAL PERFORMANCE, FEMALE—"Down At The Twist And Shout" Mary-Chapin Carpenter

BEST COUNTRY VOCAL PERFORMANCE, MALE—"Ropin' The Wind" Garth Brooks

BEST COUNTRY PERFORMANCE BY A DUO OR GROUP WITH VOCAL—"Love Can Build A Bridge" The Judds

BEST COUNTRY VOCAL COLLABORATION—"Restless" Steve Wariner, Ricky Skaggs and Vince Gill (single from "Mark O'Connor & The New Nashville Cats")

BEST COUNTRY INSTRUMENTAL PERFORMANCE (ORCHESTRA, GROUP OR SOLOIST)—"Mark O'Connor & The New Nashville Cats"

BEST BLUEGRASS RECORDING—"Spring Training" Carl Jackson & John Starling (with The Nash Ramblers)

BEST COUNTRY SONG—"Love Can Build A Bridge" Naomi Judd, John Jarvis, Paul Overstreet, writers

BEST CONTEMPORARY FOLK ALBUM (NC)—"The Missing Years" John Prine

GOLD & PLATINUM RECORDS

"Put Yourself In My Shoes" G/A Clint Black / RCA
"Put Yourself In My Shoes" P/A Clint Black / RCA
"Put Yourself In My Shoes" 2M/A Clint Black / RCA
"Garth Brooks" 2M/A Garth Brooks / Capitol
"No Fences" 3M/A Garth Brooks / Capitol
"No Fences" 4M/A Garth Brooks / Capitol
"No Fences" 5M/A Garth Brooks / Capitol
"Ropin' The Wind" G/A Garth Brooks / Capitol
"Ropin' The Wind" P/A Garth Brooks / Capitol
"Ropin' The Wind" 4M/A Garth Brooks / Capitol
"Ropin' The Wind" 5M/A Garth Brooks / Capitol
"Galveston" P/A Glen Campbell / Capitol
"Gentle On My Mind" P/A Glen Campbell / Capitol
"Glen Campbell's Greatest Hits" P/A Glen Campbell / Capitol
"Greatest Hits" 3M/A Patsy Cline / MCA
"Greatest Hits" G/A Mac Davis / Columbia
"Pocket Full Of Gold" G/A Vince Gill / MCA
"When I Call Your Name" P/A Vince Gill / MCA
"Encore" G/A Mickey Gilley / Epic
"Greatest Hits" P/A Lee Greenwood / MCA
"Okie From Muskogee" P/A Merle Haggard / Capitol
"The Best Of The Best Of Merle Haggard" P/A Merle Haggard / Capitol

Trisha Yearwood.
credit: photo by Alan Mayor

"Don't Rock The Jukebox" G/A Alan Jackson / Arista
"Don't Rock The Jukebox" P/A Alan Jackson / Arista
"Here In The Real World" P/A Alan Jackson / Arista
"Greatest Hits Vol. 2" G/A The Judds / RCA
"Love Can Build A Bridge" G/A The Judds / RCA
"Electric Barnyard" G/A Kentucky HeadHunters / Mercury
"Honky Tonk Angel" G/A Patty Loveless / MCA
"A Collection Of Hits" G/A Kathy Mattea / Merecury
"For My Broken Heart" G/A Reba McEntire / MCA
"For My Broken Heart" P/A Reba McEntire / MCA
"My Kind Of Country" G/A Reba McEntire / MCA
"Rumor Has It" P/A Reba McEntire / MCA
"Something In Red" G/A Lorrie Morgan / RCA
"Christmas Wishes" 2M/A Anne Murray / Capitol
"Greatest Hits" 4M/A Anne Murray / Capitol
"After The Rain" P/A Willie Nelson / Columbia
"Always On My Mind" G/S Willie Nelson / Columbia
"Always On My Mind" P/S Willie Nelson / Columbia
"Love In A Small Town" G/A K.T. Oslin / RCA
"Eagle When She Flies" G/A Dolly Parton / Columbia
"White Limozeen" G/A Dolly Parton / Columbia
"Memories At Christmas" G/A Elvis Presley / RCA
"Fast Movin' Train" G/A Restless Heart / RCA
"Heart Like A Wheel" P/A Linda Ronstadt / Capitol
"Heart Like A Wheel" 2M/A Linda Ronstadt / Capitol
"The Best Of" G/A Dan Seals / Capitol
"Backroads" G/A Ricky Van Shelton / Columbia
"Backroads" P/A Ricky Van Shelton / Columbia
"RVS III" P/A Ricky Van Shelton / Columbia
"The Road Not Taken" G/A Shenandoah / Columbia
"Doug Stone" G/A Doug Stone / Epic
"Beyond The Blue Neon" P/A George Strait / MCA
"Chill Of An Early Fall" G/A George Strait / MCA
"Greatest Hits" 2M/A George Strait / MCA
"If You Ain't Lovin' (You Ain't Livin')" P/A George Strait / MCA
"Livin' It Up" P/A George Strait / MCA
"Heroes And Friends" P/A Randy Travis / Warner Brothers
"High Lonesome" G/A Randy Travis / Warner Brothers
"Country Club" P/A Travis Tritt / Warner Brothers
"It's All About To Change" G/A Travis Tritt / Warner Brothers
"It's All About To Change" P/A Travis Tritt / Warner Brothers
"Trisha Yearwood" G/A Trisha Yearwood / MCA
"If There Was A Way" G/A Dwight Yoakam / Reprise
"Just Lookin' For A Hit" G/A Dwight Yoakam / Reprise

GOLD & PLATINUM MUSIC VIDEOS
Clint Black
"Put Yourself In My Shoes" gold
RCA Records

Garth Brooks
"Garth Brooks" gold
Capitol Nashville

Garth Brooks
"Garth Brooks" platinum
Capitol Nashville

Garth Brooks
"Garth Brooks" multi-platinum (200,000)
Capitol Nashville

Patsy Cline
"The Real Patsy Cline" gold
Cabin Fever Entertainment
Hallway Productions, Inc.

Charlie Daniels
"Homefolks And Highways" gold
Cabin Fever Entertainment
High Lonesome Management

Lee Greenwood
"God Bless The U.S.A." (single) gold
MCA Music Video

Lee Greenwood
"God Bless The U.S.A." (single) platinum
MCA Music Video

Alan Jackson
"Here In The Real World" gold
Arista

The Judds
"Love Can Build A Bridge" gold
MPI Home Video

The Judds
"Love Can Build A Bridge" platinum
MPI Home Video

Kentucky HeadHunters
"Pickin' On Nashville" gold
Polygram
Mercury

K.T. Oslin
"Love In A Small Town" gold
RCA Records

Ricky Van Shelton
"To Be Continued" gold
Sony Music Division

Hank Williams Jr.
"Full Access" platinum
Cabin Fever Entertainment
Hank Williams Jr. Enterprises

COUNTRY MUSIC ASSOCIATION AWARDS

ENTERTAINER OF THE YEAR—Garth Brooks

FEMALE VOCALIST—Tanya Tucker

MALE VOCALIST—Vince Gill

SONG OF THE YEAR—"When I Call Your Name" Vince Gill & Tim DuBois

SINGLE OF THE YEAR—"Friends In Low Places" Garth Brooks

ALBUM OF THE YEAR—"No Fences" Garth Brooks

VOCAL EVENT OF THE YEAR—"Mark O'Connor & The New Nashville Cats" featuring Vince Gill, Ricky Skaggs & Steve Wariner

VOCAL DUO OF THE YEAR—The Judds

VOCAL GROUP OF THE YEAR—Kentucky HeadHunters

MUSICIAN OF THE YEAR—Mark O'Connor

HORIZON AWARD—Travis Tritt

MUSIC VIDEO OF THE YEAR—"The Thunder Rolls" Garth Brooks

ACADEMY OF COUNTRY MUSIC AWARDS

SONG OF THE YEAR—"Somewhere In My Broken Heart" Richard Leigh & Billy Dean, writers

SINGLE RECORD OF THE YEAR—"Don't Rock The Jukebox" Alan Jackson, artist

ALBUM OF THE YEAR—"Don't Rock The Jukebox" Alan Jackson

ENTERTAINER—Garth Brooks

MALE VOCALIST—Garth Brooks

FEMALE VOCALIST—Reba McEntire

VOCAL GROUP—Diamond Rio

VOCAL DUET—Brooks & Dunn

NEW MALE VOCALIST—Billy Dean

NEW FEMALE VOCALIST—Trisha Yearwood

DISC JOCKEY—Gerry House WSIX, Nashville

RADIO STATION—WAMZ, Louisville, KY

CLUB—Crazy Horse Steak House & Saloon

PIONEER AWARD—Willie Nelson

VIDEO OF THE YEAR—"Is There Life Out There" Reba McEntire

INSTRUMENTALISTS: fiddle, Mark O'Connor; keyboard, Matt Rollings; bass, Roy Husky Jr.; drums, Eddie Bayers; guitar, John Jorgenson; steel guitar, Paul Franklin; dobro, Jerry Douglas

Milestones

- Hip country duet Foster & Lloyd (Bill Lloyd, Radney Foster) announce they are breaking up the act on the same January day that NARAS announces they are finalists for best country instrumental performance. Foster goes on to pursue a solo career.
- Clint Black joins the "Grand Ole Opry."
- Ohio Governor Richard Celeste releases Johnny Paycheck from prison early on the condition the singer stay away from alcohol.
- Shenandoah files Chapter 11 bankruptcy and loses its contract with Columbia over multiple lawsuits from other bands that had used the name Shenandoah before them. Eventually, they settle all claims, keep their name and sign with RCA.
- Pam Tillis, after eight years of trying, finally gets a hit: "Don't Tell Me What To Do" goes #1.
- Webb Pierce, 69, dies in February of cancer in Nashville. Pierce had started on the Louisiana Hayride, had his first hits in the ealy '50s, including "Wondering," "There Stands The Glass," "Slowly" and "I Don't Care." Famous for his flamboyant costumes and outrageously customized automobiles in the '50s, Pierce's guitar-shaped pool became a notable landmark for tourists, much to the chagrin of his neighbors. Altogether, Pierce had eight #1's and 55 Top 10 records.
- A plane crash March 16 in San Diego, California kills seven members of Reba McEntire's band and her road manager.
- Leo Fender, 82, inventer and long-time manufacturer of the Fender guitar line, dies March 21 in Fullerton, California of complications of Parkinson's disease.
- Dave Guard, 56, a founding member of the Kingston Trio, winners of the first "country" Grammy for "Tom Dooley," dies March 22 in Rollinsford, New Hampshire of lymphoma.
- Ken Curtis, 74, member during the 1940s and 1950s of the Sons of the Pioneers, dies April 28 in Fresno, California. Curtis quit the singing group to become an actor, landing the Festus Haggin role on *Gunsmoke* 1963–1975.
- In May, The Nashville Network bans Garth Brooks' video "Thunder Rolls," claiming it is too violent.
- Randy Travis and manager Lib Hatcher marry May 31 in Hawaii.
- Sarah Ophelia Colley Cannon, creator of the beloved country comic character Minnie Pearl, suffers a debilitating stroke that ends her "Grand Ole Opry" career.
- Dottie West, 58, dies September 4 of injuries received five days earlier in a car wreck while enroute to the "Grand Ole Opry."

- Tennessee Ernie Ford, 72, dies October 17 in Reston, Virginia of cancer.
- Grant Turner, 79, radio announcer, "the voice of the 'Grand Ole Opry,'" dies October 19 of a heart aneurysm, hours after finishing an Opry broadcast.
- Clint Black marries television actress Lisa Hartman.
- The Judds' final fairwell concert at Murphy Center in Murfreesboro, Tennessee is a mammoth pay-per-view cable special December 4.

1992

AN ACHY BREAKY DANCE CRAZE

The huge success of the line dance created to promote "Achy Breaky Heart" spawned a renaissance of country and western dancing in clubs across the nation in 1992. The Achy Breaky was created by Nashville choreographer Melanie Greenwood, who started out her career as a Las Vegas show dancer. Before long, country record producers began to concentrate on dance rhythm records while new line dances proliferated in the biggest boom for new dances since the Cotton-Eyed Joe in the 1940s. New dance steps hitting the hardwood in 1992 included the Boot Scootin' Boogie, the Cheatin' Heart, Breaking The Bank, the Cowboy Hip-Hop, the LeDoux Shuffle, and the Cleopatra. Virtually every major dance record came with its own new dance, though none caught on quite as well as the Boot Scootin' Boogie and the Achy Breaky. Older dances also resurfaced, including the Ski Bumpus, the Tush Push, and the Reggae Cowboy.

Country dancing—a country craze for the '90s.
credit: photo by Steve Lowry

Most Important Records

"Achy Breaky Heart" Billy Ray Cyrus / Mercury
"I Still Believe In You" Vince Gill / MCA
"She Is His Only Need" Wynonna Judd / MCA
"The Whiskey Ain't Workin'" Travis Tritt & Marty Stuart / Warner Brothers
"Sticks and Stones" Tracy Lawrence / Arista
"Boot Scootin' Boogie" Brooks & Dunn / Arista
"Is There Life Out There" Reba McEntire / MCA
"Aces" Suzy Bogguss / Capitol
"I Feel Lucky" Mary-Chapin Carpenter / Columbia
"Something In Red" Lorrie Morgan / RCA

Debut Artist: Billy Ray Cyrus

It's hard to recall an artist who has been more reviled by critics and his peers than Billy Ray Cyrus was in 1992 while he managed to sell 9 million copies of his debut album, "Some Gave All." Clear-eyed, lantern-jawed and handsome, with a weight-lifter's physique, this overly shy and self-serious Ohio River

Billy Ray Cyrus.
credit: photo by Alan Mayor

copy band singer was boosted by the year's most expensive and most creative promotional campaign based on a new dance step, a tush-shaking video, and a rock-rhythmed song that everyone (except the fans) agreed was just plain dumb. More than any country artist since Billy "Crash" Craddock in the '70s, Cyrus exuded blatant sex appeal. His simplicity and humility in the face of fame and criticism made him a sympathetic figure. When his follow-up album shipped 1.5 million copies in June of 1993, Cyrus launched his first shot back at critics who in 1992 said he would be a one-hit wonder. He titled the collection "It Won't Be The Last."

Awards

GRAMMYS

BEST COUNTRY VOCAL PERFORMANCE, FEMALE—"I Feel Lucky" Mary-Chapin Carpenter

BEST COUNTRY VOCAL PERFORMANCE, MALE—"I Still Believe In You" Vince Gill

BEST COUNTRY PERFORMANCE BY A DUO OR GROUP WITH VOCAL—"Emmylou Harris & The Nash Ramblers at the Ryman" Emmylou Harris

BEST COUNTRY VOCAL COLLABORATION—"The Whiskey Ain't Workin'" Marty Stuart & Travis Tritt

BEST COUNTRY INSTRUMENTAL PERFORMANCE (ORCHESTRA, GROUP OR SOLOIST)—"Sneakin' Around" Chet Atkins & Jerry Reed

BEST BLUEGRASS RECORDING—"Every Time You Say Goodbye" Alison Krauss & Union Station

BEST COUNTRY SONG—"I Still Believe In You" Vince Gill and John Jarvis, writers

GOLD & PLATINUM RECORDS

"American Pride" G/A Alabama / RCA
"Greatest Hits Vol. II" G/A Alabama / RCA
"Seminole Wind" G/A John Anderson / RCA
"Seminole Wind" P/A John Anderson / RCA
"The Hard Way" G/A Clint Black / RCA
"The Hard Way" P/A Clint Black / RCA
"Brand New Man" G/A Brooks & Dunn / Arista
"Brand New Man" P/A Brooks & Dunn / Arista
"Brand New Man" 2M/A Brooks & Dunn / Arista
"Beyond The Season" G/A Garth Brooks / Liberty
"Beyond The Season" P/A Garth Brooks / Liberty
"Beyond The Season" 2M/A Garth Brooks / Liberty
"Garth Brooks" 3M/A Garth Brooks / Liberty
"Garth Brooks" 4M/A Garth Brooks / Liberty
"No Fences" 6M/A Garth Brooks / Liberty
"No Fences" 7M/A Garth Brooks / Liberty
"No Fences" 8M/A Garth Brooks / Liberty

"No Fences" 9M/A Garth Brooks / Liberty
"Ropin' The Wind" 6M/A Garth Brooks / Liberty
"Ropin' The Wind" 7M/A Garth Brooks / Liberty
"Ropin' The Wind" 8M/A Garth Brooks / Liberty
"Ropin' The Wind" 9M/A Garth Brooks / Liberty
"The Chase" G/A Garth Brooks / Liberty
"The Chase" P/A Garth Brooks / Liberty
"The Chase" 5M/A Garth Brooks / Liberty
"By The Time I Get To Phoenix" P/A Glen Campbell / Capitol
"Wichita Lineman" P/A Glen Campbell / Capitol
"Wichita Lineman" 2M/A Glen Campbell / Capitol
"Come On, Come On" G/A Mary-Chapin Carpenter / Columbia
"Shooting Straight In The Dark" G/A Mary-Chapin Carpenter / Columbia
"Longnecks And Short Stories" G/A Mark Chesnutt / MCA
"Chipmonks In Low Places" G/A Chipmonks / Epic
"Greatest Hits" 4M/A Patsy Cline / MCA
"Greatest Hits" G/A Jerry Clower / MCA
"Achy Breaky Heart" G/S Billy Ray Cyrus / Mercury
"Achy Breaky Heart" P/S Billy Ray Cyrus / Mercury
"Some Gave All" G/A Billy Ray Cyrus / Mercury
"Some Gave All" P/A Billy Ray Cyrus / Mercury
"Some Gave All" 2M/A Billy Ray Cyrus / Mercury
"Some Gave All" 3M/A Billy Ray Cyrus / Mercury
"Some Gave All" 4M/A Billy Ray Cyrus / Mercury
"Some Gave All" 5M/A Billy Ray Cyrus / Mercury
"A Decade Of Hits" 2M/A Charlie Daniels Band / Epic
"Fire On The Mountain" P/A Charlie Daniels Band / Epic
"Billy Dean" G/A Billy Dean / Liberty
"Diamond Rio" G/A Diamond Rio / Arista
"Hymns" P/A Tennessee Ernie Ford / Capitol
"Star Carol" P/A Tennessee Ernie Ford / Capitol
"I Still Believe In You" G/A Vince Gill / MCA
"I Still Believe In You" P/A Vince Gill / MCA
"Pocket Full Of Gold" P/A Vince Gill / MCA
"To All The Girls I've Loved Before" P/S Willie Nelson & Julio Iglesias / Columbia
"A Lot About Livin' (And A Little About Love)" G/A Alan Jackson / Arista
"A Lot About Livin' (And A Little About Love)" P/A Alan Jackson / Arista
"Don't Rock The Jukebox" 2M/A Alan Jackson / Arista
"Super Hits" G/A George Jones / MCA
"Wynonna" G/A Wynonna Judd / RCA
"Wynonna" P/A Wynonna Judd / RCA
"Wynonna" 2M/A Wynonna Judd / RCA
"The Judds Greatest Hits" 2M/A The Judds / RCA
"Why Not Me" 2M/A The Judds / RCA
"Don't Go Near The Water" G/A Sammy Kershaw / Polygram

"Past The Point Of Rescue" G/A Hal Ketchum / Curb
"Shadowland" G/A k.d. lang / Sire
"Lyle Lovett and His Large Band" G/A Lyle Lovett / MCA
"For My Broken Heart" 2M/A Reba McEntire / MCA
"Something In Red" P/A Lorrie Morgan / RCA
"Why Lady Why" G/A Gary Morris / Warner Brothers
"Willie Nelson's Greatest Hits (And Some That Will Be)" 3M/A Willie Nelson / Columbia
"Willie Nelson Sings Kristofferson" P/A Willie Nelson / Columbia
"Honeysuckle Rose (Soundtrack)" 2M/A Willie Nelson / Columbia
"Eagle When She Flies" P/A Dolly Parton / Columbia
(RCA re-released new and updated Elvis Presley singles, full-lengths and extended play records in 1992, commemorating the 15th year of his death. Since practically everything Presley ever recorded for RCA was contained in these combined packages, it is not necessary to list them separately. Sales of these packages netted a record-setting 110 RIAA awards for Presley's estate.)
"Greatest Hits" G/A Ricky Van Shelton / Columbia
"Highways & Heartaches" P/A Ricky Skaggs / Epic
"I Thought It Was You" G/A Doug Stone / Epic
"Chill Of An Early Fall" P/A George Strait / MCA
"Does Fort Worth Ever Cross Your Mind" P/A George Strait / MCA
"Holding My Own" G/A George Strait / MCA
"Pure Country (Soundtrack)" G/A George Strait / MCA
"Pure Country (Soundtrack)" P/A George Strait / MCA
"Ten Strait Hits" G/A George Strait / MCA
"Laid Between The Lines" G/A Aaron Tippin / RCA
"An Old Time Christmas" G/A Randy Travis / Warner Brothers
"Greatest Hits Vol. I" G/A Randy Travis / Warner Brothers
"Storms Of Life" 3M/A Randy Travis / Warner Brothers
"It's All About To Change" 2M/A Travis Tritt / Warner Brothers
"T-R-O-U-B-L-E" G/A Travis Tritt / Warner Brothers
"Can't Run From Yourself" G/A Tanya Tucker / Liberty
"What Do I Do With Me" P/A Tanya Tucker / Liberty
"Hearts In Armor" G/A Trisha Yearwood / MCA
"Trisha Yearwood" P/A Trisha Yearwood / MCA

GOLD & PLATINUM MUSIC VIDEOS
Garth Brooks
"Garth Brooks" multi-platinum (300,000)
Capitol Nashville

Garth Brooks
"Garth Brooks" multi-platinum (400,000)
Capitol Nashville

Garth Brooks
"This Is Garth Brooks" gold
Liberty Records

Garth Brooks
"This Is Garth Brooks" platinum
Liberty Records

Garth Brooks
"This Is Garth Brooks" multi-platinum (400,000)
Liberty Records

Billy Ray Cyrus
"Billy Ray Cyrus" gold
Polygram Music Video

Billy Ray Cyrus
"Billy Ray Cyrus" platinum
Polygram Music Video

Billy Ray Cyrus
"Billy Ray Cyrus" multi-platinum (200,000)
Polygram Music Video

Billy Ray Cyrus
"Billy Ray Cyrus" multi-platinum (300,000)
Polygram Music Video

Vince Gill
"I Still Believe In You" gold
MCA Music Video

Alan Jackson
"Here In The Real World" gold
Arista

The Judds
"Their Final Concert" gold
MPI Home Video
Ken Stilts Company

The Judds
"Their Final Concert" platinum
MPI Home Video
Ken Stilts Company

Reba McEntire
"Reba In Concert" gold
MCA Music Video

Reba McEntire
"For My Broken Heart" gold
MCA Music Video

Reba McEntire
"For My Broken Heart" platinum
MCA Music Video

Randy Travis
"Forever And Ever" gold
Warner Music Video

COUNTRY MUSIC ASSOCIATION AWARDS
ENTERTAINER OF THE YEAR—Garth Brooks
FEMALE VOCALIST—Mary-Chapin Carpenter
MALE VOCALIST—Vince Gill
SONG OF THE YEAR—"Look At Us" Vince Gill & Max D. Barnes
SINGLE OF THE YEAR—"Achy Breaky Heart" Billy Ray Cyrus
ALBUM OF THE YEAR—"Ropin' The Wind" Garth Brooks
VOCAL EVENT OF THE YEAR—Marty Stuart & Travis Tritt
VOCAL DUO OF THE YEAR—Brooks & Dunn
VOCAL GROUP OF THE YEAR—Diamond Rio
MUSICIAN OF THE YEAR—Mark O'Connor
HORIZON AWARD—Suzy Bogguss
MUSIC VIDEO OF THE YEAR—"Midnight In Montgomery" Alan Jackson

ACADEMY OF COUNTRY MUSIC
SONG OF THE YEAR—"I Still Believe In You" Vince Gill, John Jarvis, writer
SINGLE RECORD OF THE YEAR—"Boot Scootin' Boogie" Brooks & Dunn, artist
ALBUM OF THE YEAR—"Brand New Man" Brooks & Dunn
ENTERTAINER—Garth Brooks
MALE VOCALIST—Vince Gill
FEMALE VOCALIST—Mary-Chapin Carpenter
VOCAL GROUP—Diamond Rio
VOCAL DUET—Brooks & Dunn
NEW MALE VOCALIST—Tracy Lawrence
NEW FEMALE VOCALIST—Michelle Wright
NEW VOCAL DUET/GROUP—Confederate Railroad
PIONEER AWARD—George Jones
VIDEO OF THE YEAR—"Two Sparrows In A Hurricane" Tanya Tucker
INSTRUMENTALISTS: fiddle, Mark O'Connor; keyboard, Matt Rollings; bass, Glenn Worf; drums, Eddie Bayers; guitar, John Jorgenson; steel guitar, Jay Dee Maness; dobro, Jerry Douglas

Milestones

- Music Row enters its second biggest building boom since the mid-'60s.
- Country music is such big business that *Forbes* business magazine puts Garth Brooks on the cover.
- John Anderson makes a comeback as "Straight Tequila Night," off his "Seminole Wind" LP, becomes his first #1 record since 1983.
- Hank Penny, 73, singer, bandleader and comic, dies April 17 in Camarillo, California. Penny was a West Coast country television regular on Spade Cooley and Cliffie Stone's program. His signature record was "Won't You Ride In My Little Red Wagon." In 1949 he founded the Palimino Club, one of the most important country venues in the Los Angeles area.
- Travis Tritt creates a major tempest within the country music community by criticizing Billy Ray Cyrus for turning country into "an ass-wiggling contest."
- Doug and Ricky Lee Phelps announce on TNN that they are quitting the Kentucky HeadHunters. Mark Orr and Anthony Kenney replace them.
- Carl Butler, 66, dies September 4 in Franklin, Tennessee. Carl and his wife Pearl were best known for their song "Don't Let Me Cross Over," which stayed at #1 for 11 weeks in 1962.
- Del Reeves sues Billy Ray Cyrus for a percentage of all his earnings. Reeves had been Cyrus' first Nashville manager, and had once loaned him $2,200.
- Songwriter ("Sixteenth Avenue") and former artist Thom Schuyler becomes chief of RCA/Nashville.
- Lynn Anderson spends two days in a Nashville jail October 17–18 for contempt of court for violating orders not to speak ill of her ex-husband, "Spook" Stream, to their children. "If people are jailed for saying bad things about their ex-spouses, the streets will be empty," says Anderson.
- Roger Miller, 56, dies October 25 of cancer in Los Angeles.
- Artist Sammy Kershaw ("Cadillac Style") contributes his name and bodily essence to a woman's cologne called Sammy Kershaw's Starclone. It features extract from his underarm sweat pads.
- George Strait makes his acting debut in the movie *Pure Country.*
- After 20 years of being a star, Tanya Tucker finally gets a platinum album with "What Do I Do With Me."
- Dolly Parton's tune "I Will Always Love You" is recorded by R&B/pop star Whitney Houston for the soundtrack to the movie *The Bodyguard.* Houston's record tops pop, R&B, and adult contemporary charts. Parton had twice topped country charts with versions of the tune, first in 1974, and

Tanya Tucker finally gets her due.
credit: photo by Beth Gwinn

Country fans forever love their favorites, but in an increasingly competetive business where youth is important for radio exposure, two "old-timers" stood virtually alone among their contemporaries in the '90s—George Jones and Conway Twitty.

In 1990, Jones callected a gold record for his album "Still The Same Ole Me." In 1992, he again scored gold for his "Super Hits" collection. Twitty received platinum certification for his "Very Best Of" collection in 1990.

Jones had four records in the country charts in 1992, and two were Top 40. Twitty's never-fail formula put a pair of singles in the charts in 1992, including "She's Got A Man On Her Mind," which peaked at #22. Every other artist of their generation had been forced to Branson, Las Vegas or to hosting a TNN series by time and changing audiences, but somehow the record-buying country audience, despite demographic changes, never lost its taste for these distinctive personalities and their music.

Jones's last single of 1992, "I Don't Need Your Rockin' Chair," told the whole story of a singer who had his first country hit in 1955 and was known early in his career as "the Rolls Royce of country singers." Through all his ups and downs, and there had been many, the one thing that never left Jones was his voice. His voice still defines country blues. He can still wring more out of a hopped up honky-tonk number or a cut-to-the-heart deep country sad song than any three modern artists combined.

Twitty, from his first sessions for Sun records in '57 through his last session for MCA, never lost sight of his core concept that his records were the jukebox equivalent of a romantic greeting card. Any man needing to say something directly to a woman in any juke joint in America since 1957 could plunk a coin in the slot and get Twitty to do his talking. Harold Jenkins, a Friars Point, Mississippi native who returned from the Army in the mid-'50s with a yen to sing, concocted his stage name from two Southern towns and invented his strong, silent and romantic public persona out of whole cloth. That persona, Conway Twitty, knew who his listeners and fans were, knew what they wanted and, in delivering what they wanted, earned more #1 hits (40) than any other artist in the history of country music. In his concerts, "Hello Darlin'" never failed.

When Conway Twitty died of an aortic aneurysm in Springfield, Missouri in 1993 at age 59, country music lost one of its true giants.

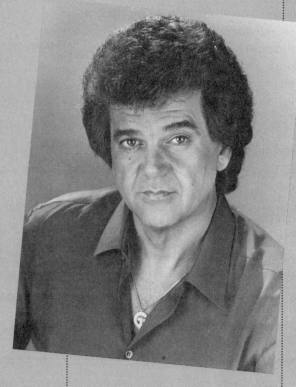

Conway Twitty had hits right to the end.
credit: Bob Millard Collection

next in the soundtrack of the film *Best Little Whorehouse in Texas* in 1984.

- Kathy Mattea and Mark Chesnutt host a charity walk and give benefit concerts to raise money and promote awareness of AIDS, becoming the first country artists to take a public stand on the issue.

- Bobby Russell, 52, songwriter and former artist, dies November 19 in Nicholasville, Kentucky. Russell's best-known compositions were "Little Green Apples," "Honey," and "Lights Went Out In Georgia."

- Marty Stuart, who first appeared on the "Grand Ole Opry" at 14 when he played with Lester Flatt, joins the Opry in November.

- Roy Claxton Acuff, 89, arguably the most visible and influential individual in country music history, dies November 23 of congestive heart disease in Nashville.

- Porter Wagoner becomes chief spokesman for the "Grand Ole Opry" and Opryland. His biography, *A Satisfied Mind*, by Steve Eng, is published.

- Bruce Kaplan, 47, founder of folk and bluegrass label Flying Fish Records, dies December 15 in Chicago, Illinois of viral meningitis.

Banks, Brenton, 117
Bannon, R. C., 211
Bare, Bobby, 46, 127, 128, *128*, 129, 137–138, 209, 244
Barker, Bob, 48
Barnes, Max D., 272, 296
Basie, Count, 127
Bate, Dr. Humphrey, *14*, 20, 25
Battles, Charlie, 195
Baugh, Phil, 136
Bayers, Eddie, 288, 296
Beatles, The, 142, 185, 232
Beck, Jim, 83
Beckham, Bob, 118
Bellamy, David, 82
Bellamy, Howard, 73
Bellamy Brothers, The, 196, *196*, 208, 251
Bennett, Tony, 62
Benson, Ray, 84
Benton, Brook, 274
Bergen, Dick, 55
Berlin, Irving, 202
Berline, Byron, 241
Berry, Chuck, 102
Berry, Muddy, 136
Bess, Hattie Louise "Tootsie," 205
Best, Pete, 232
Beverly Hillbillies, 40
Big Bopper, 261
Bill Boyd's Cowboy Ramblers, 46
Billy Bob, 225
Billy Mize's Tennesseans, 151
Bishop, Joey, 146
Black, Bill, 138
Black, Clint, 124, 269–270, *270*, 272, 277–278, 281–283, 285–286, 289–290, 292
Blackstock, Narvel, 275
Blackwood Brothers, The, 140, 156
Blake, Norman, 170
Bleacher, Smokey, 169
Blue Boys, 127
Blue Grass Boys, The, 51, 59–60, 68, 77, 110 273
Blue Sky Boys, 7, 30, 47, 53
Bob Wills and the Texas Playboys, 44
Boggs, Dock, 5
Bogguss, Suzy, 103, 244, 256, 266, 283, 291, 296
Bollick, Bill, 7, 30, 47
Bollick, Earl, 7, 30, 47
Bond, Johnny, 7, 138, 184, 205
Bonner, Captain M. J., 16
Bonsell, Joe, 76, *93*, 193

Boone, Debbie, 200
Boone Creek, 241
Booth, Larry, 168, 173, 178, 200
Booth, Tony, 163, 168, 173
Bowen, Jimmy, 173
Bowling, Roger, 200, 233
Bowman, Charlie, 21, *21*
Bowman, Don, 146, 203
Boxcar Willie, 40, 225, 282
Boy Howdy Band, 281
Boyd, Bill, 43, 50, 164
Braddock, Bobby, 218, 224
Bradley, Jerry, 175
Bradley, Owen, 108, 118–119, 122, 175, 195, 200, 264
Bradley Brothers, 96
Brady, Pat, 82
Brasfield, Rod, 67–68, 76, 108
Brewer, Teresa, 138
Brinkley, John R. (Dr. J. R.), 33, 35
Britt, Elton, 7, 31, 43, 57, *57*, 69, 155, 158, 175
Brock, Bill, 165
Brockman, Polk C., 9, 18, 247
Brooks, Garth, 124, 213, 267, 269, *276*, 277–279, 281–285, 287–289, 292–294, 296–297
Brooks, Karen, 229
Brooks, Kix, 98
Brooks & Dunn, 91, 283–284, *284*, 288, 291–292, 296
Browder, Bill, 143
Brown, Bonnie, 147
Brown, Greg, 269
Brown, Jim Ed, 44, 193, 200, 221
Brown, Maxine, 147
Brown, Milton, 5, 34, 40–41, *41*, 42, *42*, 45
Brown, T. Graham, 95, 257
Browns, The, 110, 118
Bruce, Ed, 66, 169, 219
Brumley, Tom, 142–143
Bruno, Al, 157, 164, 168, 173, 178, 184, 211, 218, 229, 266
Brush Arbor, 178
Bryant, Boudleaux, 62, 105, 230, 261
Bryant, Felice, 62, 105, 230, 261
Bryant, Jimmy, 143, 146, 151
Bryson, Bill, 282
Buckaroos, 111, 136, 141–142, *142*, 146, 151, 185–186
Buffalo Springfield, 187
Buffett, Jimmy, 179
Burnette, Billy, 213
Burnette, Dorsey, 178, 212
Burnette, Johnny, 213

Burnette, Smiley, 6
Burns, Kenneth C. "Jethro," 14
Burton, Byrd, 196
Burton, Gary, 117
Burton, James, 147, 205, 225, 243, 247
Butler, Carl, 106, 123–124, *124*, 297
Butler, Larry, 188, 210
Butler, Pearl, 106, 123–124, *124*, 297
Buzzington, Ezra, 75
Bynum, Hal, 200
Byrds, The, 72, 129, 159, 180, 187, 238

Caesar, Shirley, 138
Calahoun, Coyote, 243
Caldwell, Timmy, 221
Caldwell, Tommy, 221
Call, Cactus Jack, 125
Callahan, Bill, 30, *30*
Callahan, Joe, 30, *30*
Callahan Brothers, 30, 34, 45
Calley, Lt. Rusty, 168
Campbell, Archie, 84, 108, 157, 261
Campbell, Glen, 47, 96, 143–144, *144*, 145–147,
    149–151, 155–156, 162, 169, 172, 186, 189,
    194, 197–198, 213, 224, 285, 293
Cannon, Sarah Ophelia Colley, 289
Cantu, Willie, 142
Cargill, Henson, 69, 148–149
Carlisle, Cliff, 6, 30, 43
Carlisle Brothers, 30, 45
Carlisles, The, 77, 90–91
Carlson, Paulette, 258
Carmichael, Hoagy, 202
Carpenter, Mary-Chapin, 272, 278, *278*, 284–285,
    291–293, 296
Carroll, Lewis, 244
Carson, Fiddlin' John, 4, 9, 11, 15–16, *16*, 18, 21n,
    22, 36, 247
Carson, Johnny, 164
Carson, Martha, 15, 84, 273
Carson, Wayne, 229, 237
Carter, Alvin Pleasant (A. P.), 5, 22–23, 51, 61, 118,
    211
Carter, Anita, 71, 82, 207
Carter, Carlene, 84, 99
Carter, Ezra, 23
Carter, Helen, 71, 76, 82, 99, 207
Carter, June, 71, 82, 84, 88, 103, 145, 152, 154,
    163, 207, 261
Carter, Maybelle Addington, 6, 22, 23, 61, 82, 174,
    207
Carter, "Montana Slim" Wilf, 6, 42, 46
Carter, Sara, 5, 22, 51, 61, 211

Carter Family, The, 1, *8*, 11, 23, 27, 34, 38, 40, 45–
    47, *47*, 50, 61, *61*, 62, 82, 99, 132, 207, 211
Carter Sisters, Mother Maybelle and the, 71, 76, 99
Cash, Johnny, 22, 93, 95–96, 98–99, 101, 103,
    103, 104, 106, 107–108, 110, 117, 126, 129,
    129, 130, 135–138, 144–146, 149–152,
    154–159, 161–165, 167, 179, 190, 193,
    198–199, 209, 219, 231, 233, *236*, 244–245,
    247, 249, 251–253, 281
Cash, Rosanne, 98, 209, *209*, 228, 236, *236*, 241,
    243, 246, 260
Cash, Vivian Liberto, 209
Cates, Joe, 205
Celeste, Richard, 289
Chad Mitchell Trio, 99
Charles, Ray, 123–124, 138, 150, 191
Charlie Daniels Band, 210–211, 217, 228, 232,
    246, 251, 270, 293
Cherokee Cowboys, 98
Cherry, Hugh, 164
Cherry Bombs, The, 241
Chestnutt, Mark, 127, 282–283, 293, 299
Childre, Lew, 31, *52*
Chipmonks, 293
Christopher, Johnny, 229, 237
Clapton, Eric, 206
Clark, Dick, 143
Clark, Guy, 69, 200
Clark, Roy, 44, 128, 157, 163, 168, 173, 178, 189,
    195, 200, 205, 218, 229, 282
Clement, Frank, 124, 131
Clement, Jack, 117, 192, *192*
Clements, Vassar, 24
Clements, Zeke, 6, 51
Clifton, Bill, 131
Clinch Mountain Boys, 154, 157, 268
Cline, Gerald, 91
Cline, Patsy, 42, 88, 91, 106, 109, 117, 119, *119*,
    120–121, 123, 125, *125*, 126, 133, 138, 221,
    240, 243, 258, 264, 270, 285, 287, 293
Clower, Jerry, 179, 293
Cochran, Hank, 46, 92, 138, 159
Cody, Buck, 169
Coe, David Allan, 19, 51, 147, 200, 236, 244
Cohen, Nudie, 151, 243
Cohen, Paul, 165
Colder, Ben, 151
Coley, John Ford, 239
Colley, Spade, 96
Collie, Biff, 136, 141
Collie, Mark, 101
Collins, Judy, 129
Collins, Larry, 224

Collins, Tom, 40, 227
Colter, Jessi, 74, 192, *192*, 194, 197, 206, 223, 246, 249
Comets, 225
Commander Cody and His Lost Planet Airmen, 185
Como, Perry, 87, 96, 101*n*
Confederate Railroad, 232, 296
Conlee, John, 73, 138, 203, *203*, 205, 208, 225
Conley, Earl Thomas, 69, 169, 225
Conlon, Jon, 266, 273
Cook, Jeff, 79, 232, *232*
Cooley, Donald "Spade," 6, 73, 297
Coolidge, Rita, 178, 188
Coon Creek Girls, 248
Cooper, Dale Troy "Stoney," 31–32, 68, 69, 76
Cooper, Wilma Lee, 15, 88
Copas, Cowboy, 62, 76, 98, 115, 125
Corn Cob Crushers, 45
Cornelius, Helen, 193, 200, 221
Country Gentlemen, The, 189
Country Store, 268
Cousin Jody, 191
Craddock, Billy "Crash," 292
Cramer, Floyd, 44, 77, 87, 99, 115, 117–118, 157, 164, 168, 173, 178, 184, 238
Crawford, Calvin, 127
Crazy Mountaineers, 42
Creech, Pappy John, 208
Crook, Herman, 267
Crook Brothers, 20, 267
Crosby Stills & Nash, 185
Crosby, Bing, 45, 51, 63, 71
Crosby, David, 254
Cross, Dean, 158
Crowe, J. D., 237, 268
Crowell, Rodney, 82, 205, 209, *209*, 241, 266, 272, 279
Cruddup, Arthur, 93
Crystal, Billy, 255
Culpepper, Rod, 205
Cumberland Ridge Runners, The, 38, *38*, 81, 248
cummings, e. e., 264
Curless, Dick, 42
Curtis, Ken, 49, 289
Cyrus, Billy Ray, 121, 291, *291*, 293, 295–297

Daffan, Ted, 6, 50, 64, 70
Daily, H. W. "Pappy," 98, 261
Dalhart, Vernon, 4, 7, 12–13, *13*, 18–20, 22–23, 45, 57, 115
Dalton, Lacy J., 76, 211
Damron, Allen, 175
Damrosch, Walter, 24

Dan Hicks and the Hot Licks, 185
Daniels, Charlie, 47, 188, 200, 208, *208*, 210–211, 217–218, 223, 228, 232, 246, 251, 270–271, 279, 287, 293
Daniels, Jack, 258
Darby and Tarleton, 23
Darst, Danny, 233
Davies, Gail, 76, 230
Davis, B. J. (Betty Jack), 92
Davis, Danny, 20, 156–157, 163, 167, 172, 178, 181, 183, 282
Davis, Georgia, 92
Davis, Hugh, 150
Davis, Jimmie, 5, 29, 43–46, 50, 64
Davis, Mac, 69, 96, 159, 172, 177, 182, 184, 194, 223, 251, 285
Davis, Oscar, 55, 190
Davis, Skeeter, 40, 88, 92, *92*, 112, 158, 179, 261
Davis Sisters, 39, 89, 92
Day, Jimmy, 87
Dead Cowboys Band, 105
Dead Cowboys, The, 221
Dean, Billy, 124, 283–284, 288, 293
Dean, Dizzy, 38
Dean, Eddie, 45, 205
Dean, Jimmy, 24, 96, *111*, 120–121, *122*, 124, 131–132, 134, 138, 143
Dee, Dickey, 69
Delmore, Alton, 6, *28*, 29, 131, 205, 233
Delmore, Lionel, 131, 233
Delmore, Rabon, 6, *28*, 29, 88, 131
Delmore Brothers, 29, 45
Denning, Mark, 118
Dennison, Rachel, 238
Denny, Jim, 87
Denver, John, 13, 71, 181–182, 184, 186–188, 194, 199, 203, 210, 223, 236
Dern, Bruce, 226
Desert Rose Band, 72, 266, 273, 281
Desperadoes, 225, 229
DeWitt, Lew, 50, 135, *135*, 230
Dexter, Al, 5, 45, 53, 56, 63–64, 70–71, 73, 243
Diamond Rio, 118, 232, 284, 288, 293, 296
Dickens, Ernestine, 151
Dickens, James Cecil "Little Jimmy," 14, 31–32, 102, 135, 151
Diffie, Joe, 108, 283
Disney, Walt, 169
Dittrich, John, 84, 245
Dixon, Dorsey, 30
Dixon Brothers, 30
Dr. Bates' Possum Hunters, *14*, 20, 24
Dodds, Johnny, *38*

Dopyera, John, 266
Douglas, Charlie, 195
Douglas, Jerry, 237, 260, 282, 288, 296
Downing, Big Al, 153
Drake, Pete, 191, 267
Drifting Cowboys, *65*, 89, 189
Driftwood, Jimmy, 112
Drusky, Roy, 40, 108
DuBois, Tim, 245, 288
Dudley, Dave, 24, 158
Dudney, Ken, 220
Duncan, Johnny, 50, 198
Duncan, Steve, 266, 273, 282
Duncan, Tommy, 111, 147
Dunn, Holly, 254, 260
Dunn, Ronnie, 91
Dunny, Holly, 106
Dylan, Bob, 129, 156, 159, 170, 244, 251, 267

Eagles, The, 187, 208, 245
Earle, Steve, 239, 254
East Kentucky Mountain Boys, 268
Easton, Sheena, 234
Eastwood, Clint, 233
Ebsen, Buddy, *126*
Edison, Thomas, *3*
Edwards, Darrell, 101*n*
Edwards, Eddie, 247
Edwards, Skip, 273
Edwards, Stoney, 27, 153
Emerson, Lee, 207
Emery, Ralph, 92, 96, 131, *131*
Emmons, Buddy, 173, 200, 205, 211, 218, 225, 243, 247
Eng, Steve, 299
England Dan, 239
Eshlimar, Billie Jean Jones (Williams), 84, 86, 101
Evans, Dale, 82, 88
Everly, Don, 47, 221
Everly, Ike, 3, 105
Everly, Margaret, 105
Everly, Phil, 50
Everly Brothers, 62, 96, 100, 104–105, *105*, 105–107, 117–118, 120, *120*, 234, 244, 251, 282
Exile, 241
Ezra Buzzington's Rube Band, 75

Fargo, Donna, 79, 157, 171, *171*, 172–173, 177, 196
Farr, Hugh, 49
Farr, Karl, 49
Feliciano, José, 165

Felts, Narvel, 50, 251
Fender, Freddy, 48, 186, *187*, 188–189, 282
Fender, Leo, 136, 225, 289
Ferguson, Bob, 157
First Edition, The, 148
Flatt, Lester, 60, 110, *110*, 168, 175, 191, 211, 299
Flatt and Scruggs, 91, 98–99, 124, *126*, 126, *126*, 131, 142–143, 150, 217
Fleming, Kye, 220
Flores, Rosie, 264
Flying Burrito Brothers, 72, 159, 180, 187
Foggy Mountain Boys, 110, *110*
Foley, Fern, 141
Foley, Ray, 63
Foley, Red, 6, 31, 33, 38, *38*, 45, 51, 53–54, 58, 64–65, 68, 71, 76, *80*, 81, 93–94, 96, 99, 127, 153–154, 283
Fonda, Jane, 164
Ford, Tennessee Ernie, 48, 83, 96–97, 124, 130, 134, 138, 184, 203, 290, 293
Ford, Whitey, 5, 68, 256
Forester Sisters, 138, 254
Fort Worth Doughboys, 40
Fortune, Jimmy, 98, 135, *219*, 230
Foster, Fred, 150
Foster, Radney, 112, 289
Fox, Curly, 45, 125
Fox, Noel, 175
Fox, Texas Ruby, 125
Francis, Archie, 164, 189, 195, 200, 205, 211, 218, 229, 238, 247, 260
Francis, Cleve, 153
Francis, Connie, 118
Frank, Joe, 55
Franklin, Paul, 288
Franks, Tillman, 118
Frazier, Dallas, 51, 146
Frickie, Janie, 76, 198, 209, 229, 237–238, 256
Friedman, Kinky, 72
Friend, Cliff, 65
Fries, Bill, 254
Fritz, Donnie, 170
Frizzell, David, 222, 224, 229
Frizzell, William Orville "Lefty," 24, 69, 82, *82*, 83–84, 87, 106, 130, *130*, 138, 179, 190, 221, 283
Fruit Jar Drinkers, 20, 231, 239

Gallen, Sandy, 164
Garcia, Jerry, 185
Gardner, Brother Dave, 118
Garland, Hank, 117–118
Garland, Judy, 256

Lynn, Mooney, 116
Lynn, Shelby, 281

McAlpin, Vernice "Vic," 219
McAuliffe, Leon, 7, 44, 267
McCall, Bill, 119–120
McCall, C. W., 186, 194, 254
McCartney, Linda, *181*
McCartney, Paul, *181*, 185
McClinton, Obie Burnett "O.B.," 64, 153, 261
McCoy, Charlie, 69, 170, *170*, 172, 178, 225
McDaniel, Mel, 70, 245
McDonald, Enos William "Skeets," 87, 87*n*
McDowell, Ronnie, 198–199, 267
McEnery, Red River Dave, 96
McEntire, Pake, 255
McEntire, Reba, 94, 147, 195, 197, 205, 234, 242,
    246–247, 250, 253–255, *255*, 257–258, 260,
    264, 271, 275, 279–281, 283, 286, 288–289,
    291, 294–296
McEntire, Suzie, 255
McFadden, Jack, 136, 143
McGee, Fibber, 33
McGee, Kirk, 5, 20, 24, 38, 45, 239
McGee, Molly, 33
McGee, Sam, 5, 20, 24, 38, 45, 191, 239
Mack, Warner, 50
McMichen, Clayton, 5, 9, 11, 23, 45, 49
McMichen, Pappy, 208
Macon, David Harrison "Uncle Dave," 4, 11, *14*, 15,
    17, *17*, 18–20, 22, 25, 29, 45, 47, 64, 68, 87,
    191, 211*n*, 231, 239, 267
Macon, Dorris, 231
McReynolds, Jesse, 131
McReynolds, Jim, 131
McWilliams, Elsie, 248
Maddox, Rose, 23
Maddox Brothers and Rose, 77, 77
Maher, Brent, 242
Mainer, J. E., 5, 30, 34, 42, *42*
Mainer, Wade, 30, 42, *42*, 50
Mainer's Mountaineers, 47, 273
Mandell, Steve, 178
Mandrell, Barbara, 76, 96, 127, 168, 173, 203,
    205, *205*, 210–211, 218, 220, *220*, 222–224,
    228–229, 237, 254
Mandrell, Irlene, 220
Mandrell, Louise, 220
Maness, J. D., 164, 168, 184, 195, 218, 229, 238,
    254, 260, 266, 273, 282, 296
Manners, Zeke, 31, 73
Manuel, Dean, 131
Manz, George, 200

Maphis, Joe, 256
Maphis, Rose Lee, 256
Mardin, Arif, 272
Mark O'Connor & The New Nashville Cats, 285,
    288
Marshall Tucker Band, 208, 221
Martin, Dean, 141
Martin, Grady, 118
Martin, Jimmy, 77, 131
Martin, Lecil Travis (Boxcar Willie), 40
Marvin, Frankie, 43
Massey, Louise, 69
Mattea, Kathy, 112, *230*, 239, 244, 261, 264, 266,
    272, 277, *278*, 279, 281, 283, *283*, 286, 299
Mayberry, Corky, 163
Maynard, Ken, 5, 40, 44
Meyers, Augie, 186
Michael, Danny, 195
Midler, Bette, 272
Midnight Riders, 211
Miller, Bob, 13, 42–43, 57, 158
Miller, Jody, 69, 136
Miller, Lost John, 38, *38*
Miller, Mark, 108, 240
Miller, Ned, 127, 251
Miller, Roger, 47, 112, 125, 130, 133, *133*,
    135–136, 140, 151, 165, 260, 297
Mills Brothers, 45
Milsap, Ronnie, 73, 165, 182–183, 193–195, 196,
    198, 200, 203–205, *207*, 210, 216, 222–224,
    229, 246, 251, 252–253, 259–260, 269, 280
Milton Brown and his Musical Brownies, 41
Mitchell, Guy, 138
Mix, Tom, 212
Mize, Billy, 136, 141, 146, 151
Moman, Chips, 188, 253
Monroe, Bill, 3, 6, 25, 29, *37*, 37–38, 51, 59–60,
    68, 93, 99, 110, 121, 124, 168, 243, 265, 273
Monroe, Birch, 60
Monroe, Charlie, 5, 29, *37*, 59–60
Monroe Brothers, 29
Montana, Patsy, *7*, 7, 39, *39*, 46–47
Montana Cowgirls, 39
Montgomery, Melba, 138, 182, 261
Mountain Smoke, 241
Moody, Clyde, 273
Mooney, Ralph, 143
Moore, Bob, 117–118
Moore, Melba, 50
Moore, Thurston, 173
Moore, Winston Lee, 87*n*
More, Frankie, 46
Morgan, Dennis, 220

Morgan, George, 20, 79, 112, 132, 182, 184, 190
Morgan, Loretta Lynn (Lorrie), 112, 184, 268, *268*, 273, 281, 286, 291, 294
Morris, Bob, 136, 141, 143
Morris, Chuck, 258
Morris, Gary, 76, 244, 272, 294
Morris, Zeke, 42, *42*
Morrison, Bob, 210
Mosby, Johnny, 151
Mosby, Jonie, 151
Moser, Scott "Cactus," 258
Mother Maybelle and the Carter Sisters, 71, 76, 99
Mullican, Aubrey "Moon," 6, 81
Murphey, Michael Martin, 73, 175, 179, 188, 229
Murray, Anne, 73, 161–162, *162*, 177, 182–183, 204, 217, 222–223, 228, 234, 237, 241–242, 246–247, 258, 286
Musical Brownies, 42

Nash Ramblers, The, 285, 292
Nashville Brass, The, 156–157, 163, 167, 172, 178, 181
Nashville Now Band, 247, 254, 260, 266, 273
Nassour, Ellis, 221
Nat King Cole Trio, 63
Neal, Bob, 238
Nelson, Gene, 266
Nelson, Ken, *128*, 136, 143
Nelson, Nikki, 258
Nelson, Paul, 266
Nelson, Rick, 64, 143, 147, 212, 248, 253
Nelson, Terry, 159
Nelson, Willie, 44, 85, 123, *123*, 131, 133, 170, 181, 184, 186, 188, 190, 194–197, 202, *202*, 203–204, 210–211, 216–218, 221, 223, 225–226, 228–229, 234, 236–237, 240–242, 244–249, *249*, 252, 254, 258, 271, 279, 286, 288, 293–294
New, Joyce, 158
New, Linda, 158
New Christy Minstrels, 148
Newman, Jimmy C., 23, 77, 99, 103
New Riders of the Purple Sage, 185
New South, The, 237, 268
Newton, Juice, 87, 223–224, 228
Newton-John, Olivia, 13, 76, 177, *177*, 178, 181, 183, 188, 194, 199, 204, 210
New Tradition, 268
Nitty Gritty Dirt Band, 154, 169, 174, *174*, 177, 179, 232, 272–273
Nixon, Richard M., 158, 184
Nolan, Bob, 46, 49, 168, 221
Norma Jean, 50, 137–138, 140, 147

Norris, Fate, 23
Nutt, Grady, 233

Oak Ridge Boys, 46, 76, 163, 193–194, *193*, 200, 205, 222–225, 228, 234, *234*, 236, 242, 253, 261
O'Connor, Mark, 254, 266, 273, 282, 288, 296
O'Daniel, W. Lee, 41
O'Day, Molly, 18, 84
O'Dell, Kenny, 178
Oermann, Robert K., 17
O'Hara, Jamie, 253
Orbison, Roy, 47, 62, 131, 140, 148, 218, 253, 264–265, 267, 271, 273
Original Playboys Band, 205
Original Texas Playboys, The, 200
Orr, Mark, 297
Osmond Family, 179
Osborn, Joe, 225, 238, 243, 247
Osborne, Bobby Van, 40
Osborne, Sonny, 49
Osborne Brothers, 131, 167
Oslin, K. T., 70, 230, 256–257, *257*, 257n, 259–260, 264–266, 271, 278, 286–287
Osmond, Marie, 179, 245, 253
Overstreet, Paul, 246, 253–254, 260, 285
Overstreet, Tommy, 48
Owen, "Fuzzy," 141
Owen, Randy, 79
Owens, Alvis Edgar "Buck," 27, 111, *111*, 115, 120, 126, 130, 135–136, 138, 140, 141, 142, *142*, 145–146, 150, 151, 165, 185, 264 250, *250*, 266
Owens, Bonnie, 42, 111, 136, 141, 146
Owens, Buck, 111, 136, 141–142, *142*, 144, 146, 151, 185–186
Owens, Randy, 232, *232*
Owens, Tex, 45–46
Owens, Texas Ruby, 127

Page, Patti, 62, 211
Palomino Riders, 184, 189, 218
Parker, Billy, 200, 205, 243
Parker, Col. Tom, 55, 64, 98, 103, 118, 201
Parker, Linda, 46
Parnell, Leroy, 103
Parris, Fred, 247
Parsons, Gram, 180, 187, 247
Parton, Dolly, 73, 106, 140, 143, 147–148, 151, 159, 163–164, *164*, 167, *181*, 182, 185, 188, 190, 194, 198–201, 203–204, 210–211, 216, 218, 223–224, 230, *230*, 231, 234, 236–238, 242–243, 245, 252, 254–255, 258–259, *259*, 260, 266, 271, 286, 294, 297

Parton, Stella, 79
Paul, Les, 194
Paycheck, Johnny, 69, 141, 203–204, 248, 271, 289
Payne, Leon, 7, 77
Pearl, Minnie, 6, 56, 66–67, *67*, 68, 76, 84, 112, 121, 132–134, 143, 164, 254, 289
Pederson, Herb, 241
Peer, Ralph, 9–10, 14–15, 18, 21–22, *22*, 23, 43, 117, 247
Pierce, Webb, 23, 77, 85, 87, *87*, 88–89, 91, 93, 97, 101, 121, 137, 192, 261, 283, 289
Penny, Hank, 297
Peppiatt, Joe, 157
Perkins, Carl, 93, 101, 117, 231, 253–254
Perkins, George, 42
Perkins, Luther, 98, 165
Perryman, Lloyd, 49
Peters, Ben, 172
Phelps, Doug, 297
Phelps, Ricky Lee, 297
Phillips, Sam, 82, 103, 117, 253
Phillips, Stu, 44, 134, 148
Phillips, Todd, 237
Pickard Family, 34, 35, *35*
Pie Plant Pete, 45
Pillow, Ray, 48, 121
Pinkard, Sandy, 224
Pirates of the Mississippi, 281
Poco, 169, 185
Pointer Sisters, The, 183
Polito, Joe, 150
Poole, Charlie, 5, 20, 22, 40
Poole, Cheryl, 151
Possum Holler Band, 195
Poulton, Curt, 40
Powers, Fiddlin', 18, 21*n*
Prairie Ramblers, 39
Presley, Elvis, 46, 77, 90, 93–94, *94*, 95, 97–99, 101, 101*n*, 102–103, 108, 117, 120, 124, 127, 138, 140, 141, *141*, 147, 150, 156–157, 162, 167, 170, 172, 175, 177, 179, 182, 185, 188, 190, 197–199, 201, 204, 212, 225–226, 231, 234, 236–238, 245, 252–253, 262, 264–265, 267, 280, 286, 294
Presley, Vernon, 212
Preston, Frances, 122
Price, Kenny, 261
Price, Ray, 23, 85, 89, 93, 98, 101, 106, *107*, 110, 113, 132–133, 138, 163, 165–167, 228, 236
Pride, Charlie, 25, 128, 153, *153*, 154, 161–162, 165–167, 171–172, 177, 188, 222, 228, 248
Prine, John, 54, 105, 158, 169, 244, 285
Pruett, Jeanne, 176, 179

Pruett, Jimmy, 205
Puckett, Riley, 4, 11, 18–19, 21, 21*n*, 22, 60
Pure Prairie League, 241
Putnam, Curly, 211, 218, 224

Quaid, Dennis, 239

Rabbitt, Eddie, 72, 165, 182, 189, 193, 200, 208, 217, 223, 248
Rabbitt, Timothy, 248
Radio Dot, 76
Rager, Mose, 3, 254
Rainwater, Cedric (Howard Watts), 60
Randolph, Boots, 146, 157
Rausch, Leon, 23
Raven, Eddie, 72, 231
Raye, Collin, 112
Rebel Playboys, 205
Reckless Heart, 232
Rector, John, 21, *21*
Red Headed Briar Hopper, 45
Red Rose Express, 195
Reed, Harold, *135*
Reed, Jerry, 148, 163, 165, 167, 169, 228, 292
Reeves, Del, 135, 297
Reeves, Jim, 19, 77–78, 89–90, *90*, 93, 98, 104, 109–110, 112, 115, 130–131, 135, 137, 140, 150, 158, 203, 212
Reid, Don, 73, *135*
Reid, Mike, 237, 247
Reinhart, D'jango, 202
Reneau, Blind George, 19
Reno, Don, 244
Restless Heart, 84, 96, 245, 250, 264–265, 272, 279
Reynolds, Allen, 175
Reynolds, Burt, 164, 169, 231
Rhodes, Michael, 273
Rhodes, Red, 136, 146, 151, 157, 178
Rice, Tony, 237
Rich, Charlie, 138, 175–178, 182–183, 186, 189, 198, 252
Rich, Don, 111, 142, 183, 185
Richie, Lionel, *232*
Ricky Skaggs Band, 229, 237, 242–243, 247, 254
Riders in the Sky, 266
Riders of the Purple Sage, 206
Riley, Jeannie C., 73, 148–149, *149*, 150–151
Rinehart, Cowboy Slim, 35
Ritter, Tex, 6, 31, 40, 44–45, 47, 57, 64, 71, 73, 91, 134, 136–138, 148, 164–165, 175, 184
Robbins, Hargus "Pig," 195, 199, 211, 218, 225, 229, 243

Williams, Audrey, 18, 89, 159, 191, 213
Williams, Bill, 106
Williams, Doc, 32, 169
Williams, Don, 50, 169, 175, 179, 196, 204–205, 209, 216–217, 224, 280–281
Williams, Hank, 3, 18, 43, 57–58, 60, 62, 64–65, *65*, 68, 77, 79, 81–82, 84, 86, *86*, 88–89, *89*, 90–91, 93, 101, 113, 121, 124, 132, *132*, 152, 157, 159, 178, 190–191, 213, 219, 233, 243, 248, 272–273, 283
Williams, Hank, Jr., 79, 128, 148, 151, 159, 189, 191, 213, 222, 224, 228, 237, 242–243, 246–247, 250, 252, 254, 257, 259–260, 262, *262*, 265–267, 271–273, 280–281, 288
Williams, Leona, 71, 111, 206
Williams, Lilly, 65
Williams, Tex, 7, 64, 74, 74*n*, 151, 168
Williamson, Carrie, 14
Willing, Foy, 206
Wills, Bob, 6, 34, *38*, 40–41, *41*, 44, 47, 50, 56–58, 64, 68–69, 71, 73, 147, 157, 183, 196, 244, 267
Wills, Johnnie Lee, 244
Wilson, Larry Jon, 200
Wilson, Norro, 183
Wise, Chubby, 60
Wiseman, Lulu Belle, 6, 33, *33*, 44, 64, 190, 225

Wiseman, Mac, 77
Wiseman, Scotty, 33, *33*, 44, 64, 225
Wolf, Glenn, 296
Wolfman Jack, 35
Wood, Del, 91
Wooley, Sheb, 15, 127, 137, 151
Wooten, Red, 146, 151, 229
Worth, Marion, 128
Wright, Bobby, 88
Wright, Johnny, *37*, 88, 135, 158
Wright, Louise, *37*
Wright, Michelle, 121, 296
Wynette, Tammy, 70, 127, 134, 144–145, *145*, 149–150, 155, 157, 159, 161, 176, 179, 182, 189, 198, 206, *206*, 219, 256, 271

Yancy, Arch, 225
Yanofsky, Zal, 170
Yearwood, Trisha, 131, 283–284, *285*, 286, 288, 294
Yoakam, Dwight, 101, 103, 111, 250, *250*, 254, 259, 264, 271, 286
Young, Faron, 42, 77, 85, *85*, 87, 97, 106, 110–111, 120, 123, 133
Young, Reggie, 238
Young, Steve, 70, 200

Z. Z. Top, 270

SONG TITLE INDEX

Loose Talk, 97
Lord, Mr. Ford, 169
Lost In The Fifties (In The Still Of The Night), 245, 246, 247
Louisiana Man, 147
Louisiana Saturday Night, 245
Louisiana Woman, Mississippi Man, 176, 180
Love, Love, Love, 97
Love at the Five and Dime, 1, 239, 244
Love Can Build A Bridge, 285
Love Hurts, 261
Love In The First Degree, 222
Love In The Hot Afternoon, 231
Love Is Like A Butterfly, 164
Love Is On A Roll, 169, 244
Love On Arrival, 278
Lover Please, 188
Love's Gonna Live Here, 126, 142
Lovesick Blues, 65, 79
Love Without End, Amen, 278
Lovin' What Your Lovin' Does To Me, 180
Low and Lonely, 70
Lucille, 198, 199, 200, 201, 207, 233
Luckenbach, Texas (Back To The Basics of Love), 198, 249
Lucky Old Sun, 152
Lulu Wall, 38
Lyin' Eyes, 187
Lynda, 257

Mabellene, 102
MacArthur Park, 156
Maiden's Prayer, 50
Make No Mistake, She's Mine, 259
Make The World Go Away, 135
Mama Bake a Pie, 158
Mama He's Crazy, 235, 241, 242
Mama Sang a Song, 112, 123
Mamas Don't Let Your Babies Grow Up To Be Cowboys, 203, 204, 219, 249
Mama Told Me Not To Come, 185
Mama Tried, 149
Man In Black, 158
Maple on the Hill, 47
Matchbox, 185
May The Bird Of Paradise Fly Up Your Nose, 135
Me & Bobbie McGee, 166
Meet In The Middle, 284
Meet Me In Montana, 245
Me & Jerry, 163
Mexicali Rose, 47, 51
Mexican Joe, 89, 90
Middle Age Crazy, 211, 212, 226

Mind Your Own Business, 65, 250
Minute Men Are Turning In Their Graves, The, 158
Miss Emily's Picture, 203
Miss Molly, 71
Mr. Bojangles, 174
Mr. Moon, 84
Misty, 188
Mohair Sam, 175
Mommy For A Day, 138
Moonlight and Skies, 40, 42
More And More, 93
Most Beautiful Girl, The, 176, 177
Mother the Queen of My Heart, 42
Mountain of Love, 127, 228
Move It On Over, 65
Muleskinner Blues, 164
Mule Train, 83
My Bucket's Got A Hole In It, 65
My Carolina Sunshine Girl, 27
My Clinch Mountain Home, 27
My Elusive Dreams, 145, 175
My Hang Up Is You, 166, 171
My Heart, 216
My Heart Skips A Beat, 130
My Heroes Have Always Been Cowboys, 216
My Home's In Alabama, 232
My Life's Been a Pleasure, 69
My Little Buckaroo, 51
My Mary, 42
My Old Pal, 23, 248
My Son, 158
My Special Angel, 104
Mystery Train, 97
My Way, 204
My Woman, My Woman, My Wife, 163

Nadine, 155
National Barn Dance, 39
Naw, I Don't Wanta Be Rich, 38
Nearer The Cross, 124
Near You, 198
Never Been So Loved (In All My Life), 222
Never Been To Spain, 185
Never No Mo' Blues, 248
New Salty Dog, 40
New San Antonio Rose, 51, 64
New Spanish Two-Step, 50, 73
Next To You, Next To Me, 278
Night They Drove Old Dixie Down, The, 169
Night Train To Memphis, 70, 152
1982, 274
9 To 5, 216, 222, 224, 238
Nobody, 227, 228

Under Your Spell Again, 111
Uneasy Rider, 208
Unwound, 222

Valley Road, The, 272
Very Special Love Song, A, 175, 182
Victim of Life's Circumstances, 241, 243
Viet Nam Blues, The, 158

Wabash Cannonball, 1, 50, 138
Waiting For A Train, 23
Waitin' In Your Welfare Line, 140, 142, 267
Wake Up Irene, 93
Wake Up Little Susie, 104, 105, 261
Walkin' After Midnight, 106, 119
Walking The Floor Over You, 54
Walk Right Back, 162
Wasted Days and Wasted Nights, 187, 188
Waterloo, 107, 110
Way Down, 199
Way On Down, 201
Way Out There, 49
Ways To Love A Man, The, 155
Wear My Ring Around Your Neck, 237
Wedding Bells, 65, 79
Wednesday Night Waltz, 23
We Might As Well Forget It, 71
We're Gonna Hold On, 176
We've Got Tonight, 234
What Am I Gonna Do About You, 257
What God Can Do, 273
What Is Life Without Love?, 74
What Is Life Without You, 78
What Made Milwaukee Famous (Has Made A Loser
    Out of Me), 152
What's He Doing In My World?, 135
What's Your Mama's Name, 176
What We're Fighting For, 158
What Would You Give In Exchange for Your Soul?,
    47
Wheel Hoss, 242
When I Call Your Name, 279, 281, 282, 288
When It's Springtime In Alaska (It's 40 Down
    Below), 101, 110
When It's Springtime in the Rockies, 50
When My Blue Moon Turns To Gold, 68
When The Bloom Is On The Sage, 212
When The Morning Comes, 185
When The Work's All Done This Fall, 20
When Two Worlds Collide, 133
When Will I Be Loved, 105, 187
(When You Feel Like You're In Love) Don't Just
    Stand There, 87

When You Gonna Bring Our Soldiers Home?, 159
When You're Hot, You're Hot, 165, 167, 169
When You Say Nothing At All, 264, 268
Where Does The Good Times Go, 144
Where The Soul Never Dies, 194
Where've You Been, 239, 261, 272, 277, 279, 281,
    283
Whippin' That Old T.B., 43
Whiskey, If You Were A Woman, 257, 258
Whiskey Ain't Workin, The, 291, 292
White Cross on Okinawa, 57
White Lightning, 110
White Sport Coat (And A Pink Carnation), 102, 104,
    115
Whoever's In New England, 250, 253
Whole Lotta Shakin' Goin' On, 104, 243
Who's Lonely Now, 258
Why, Baby, Why, 98, 101, 101n
Why Don't We Get Drunk And Screw, 179
Why Don't You Love Me (Like You Used To Do), 81
Why Me, 176, 177
Why Not Me, 138, 240, 242, 246
Wichita Lineman, 149, 150, 151, 156
Wide Open Road, 95
Widow Maker, 131
Wild and Blue, 228, 233
Wild-Eyed Dreamer, 251
Wildfire, 188
Wild Side of Life, 88
Wild Week-End, 112
Willow In The Wind, 283
Wind Beneath My Wings, 238, 242, 272
Window Up Above, The, 115
Wine Me Up, 85
Wings of a Dove, 115
Wish I Didn't Have To Miss You, 140
Woke Up In Love, 241
Wolverton Mountain, 120, 123
Woman In Love, A, 269
Woman (Sensuous Woman), 171
Wondering, 87, 289
Wonder Of You, The, 162
Won't You Ride In My Little Red Wagon, 297
Working Man's Prayer, A, 148
World Of Our Own, A, 149
Worried Man Blues, 38
Worried Mind, 64
Wound Time Can't Erase, A, 123
Wreck of the Old Southern 97, The, 12, 13, 16, 18,
    19
Wreck On The Highway, 30, 69
Wurlitzer Prize (I Don't Want To Get Over You),
    The, 198